JavaServer Pages™ For Dummies®

Frequently Used Standard JSP Tags

To access a JavaBean from a JSP page:

```
<jsp:useBean id="{beanName}" class="{fully.qualified.ClassName}"
scope="{beanScope}"/>
```

To set the value of a JavaBean property:

```
<jsp:setProperty name="{idOfBean}" property="{propertyName}"
{value="{literalValue}" | param="{parameterName}"}/>
```

To get the value of a JavaBean property:

```
<jsp:getProperty name="{idOfBean}" property="{propertyName}"/>
```

To include a page with dynamic content:

```
<jsp:include page="{relativeURL}" flush="true"/>
```

To forward to another JSP page:

```
<jsp:forward page="{relativeURL}"/>
```

To pass a parameter to an include or forward page, or an applet:

```
<jsp:param name="{paramName}" value="{paramValue}">
```

To include an applet or bean browser plug-in object:

```
<jsp:plugin type="{bean | applet}" code="{fully.qualified.ClassName}"
codebase="{relativeURLToCodeBase}"/>
```

Definitions of Scope

`page`: local to the given JSP page

`request`: available for the duration of a specific user request

`session`: visible to all requests from a given user

`application`: visible to all users of the JSP application

For Dummies: Bestselling Book Series for Beginners

BESTSELLING BOOK SERIES

JavaServer Pages™ For Dummies®

Cheat Sheet

Common Tasks for JSP Implicit Objects

To get the path to the top-level directory of a JSP application:

```
<%String path = request.getContextPath(); %>
```

To get a parameter from a user request:

```
<%String value = request.getParameter("parameterName"); %>
```

To set a request attribute (Note: The value must be a Java object):

```
<%request.setAttribute("name", value); %>
```

To get an attribute from the request object:

```
<%Object value = request.getAttribute("attributeName"); %>
```

To get an attribute from the session object:

```
<%Object value = session.getAttribute("attributeName"); %>
```

To set a session attribute (Note: The value must be a Java object):

```
<%session.setAttribute("name", value); %>
```

To get application-context parameter names:

```
<%Enumeration names = application.getInitParameterNames();%>
```

To get an application-context parameter value:

```
<%String value = application.getInitParameter("name")%>
```

Preventing JSP Page Caching

To prevent JSP page caching:

```
<%
  if(request.getProtocol().equals("HTTP/1.1")){
    response.setHeader ("cache-control", "no-cache");
  }
  else{
    response.setHeader ("pragma","no-cache");
  }
  response.setHeader ("expires","0");
%>
```

Cheat Sheet $2.95 value. Item 1544-6.
For more information about Hungry Minds, call 1-800-762-2974.

For Dummies: Bestselling Book Series for Beginners

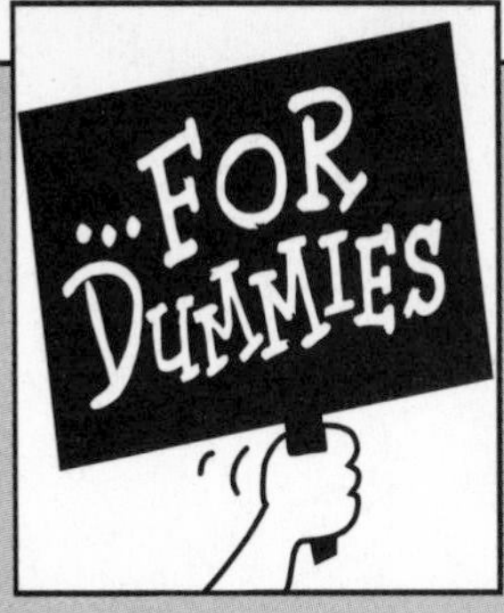

TM

References for the Rest of Us!®

BESTSELLING BOOK SERIES

Are you intimidated and confused by computers? Do you find that traditional manuals are overloaded with technical details you'll never use? Do your friends and family always call you to fix simple problems on their PCs? Then the For Dummies® computer book series from Hungry Minds, Inc. is for you.

For Dummies books are written for those frustrated computer users who know they aren't really dumb but find that PC hardware, software, and indeed the unique vocabulary of computing make them feel helpless. For Dummies books use a lighthearted approach, a down-to-earth style, and even cartoons and humorous icons to dispel computer novices' fears and build their confidence. Lighthearted but not lightweight, these books are a perfect survival guide for anyone forced to use a computer.

"I like my copy so much I told friends; now they bought copies."

— Irene C., Orwell, Ohio

"Quick, concise, nontechnical, and humorous."

— Jay A., Elburn, Illinois

"Thanks, I needed this book. Now I can sleep at night."

— Robin F., British Columbia, Canada

Already, millions of satisfied readers agree. They have made For Dummies books the #1 introductory level computer book series and have written asking for more. So, if you're looking for the most fun and easy way to learn about computers, look to For Dummies books to give you a helping hand.

1/01

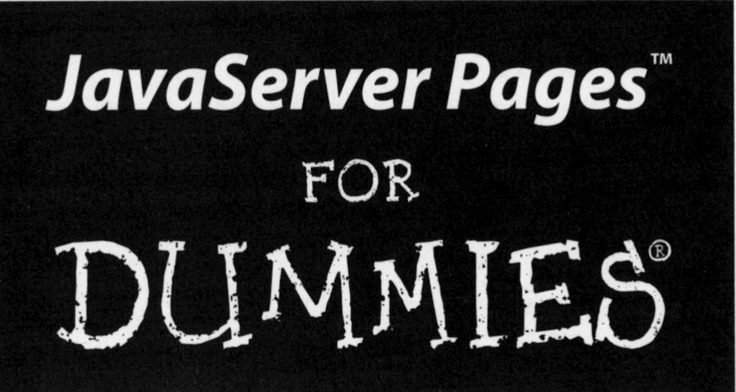

by Mac Rinehart

Best-Selling Books • Digital Downloads • e-Books • Answer Networks • e-Newsletters • Branded Web Sites • e-Learning

New York, NY ◆ Cleveland, OH ◆ Indianapolis, IN

JavaServer Pages™ For Dummies®

Published by
Hungry Minds, Inc.
909 Third Avenue
New York, NY 10022
www.hungryminds.com
www.dummies.com

Library of Congress Control Number: 2001092939

ISBN: 0-7645-1544-6

Printed in the United States of America

10 9 8 7 6 5 4 3 2 1

1B/QW/RS/QR/IN

Distributed in the United States by Hungry Minds, Inc.

Distributed by CDG Books Canada Inc. for Canada; by Transworld Publishers Limited in the United Kingdom; by IDG Norge Books for Norway; by IDG Sweden Books for Sweden; by IDG Books Australia Publishing Corporation Pty. Ltd. for Australia and New Zealand; by TransQuest Publishers Pte Ltd. for Singapore, Malaysia, Thailand, Indonesia, and Hong Kong; by Gotop Information Inc. for Taiwan; by ICG Muse, Inc. for Japan; by Intersoft for South Africa; by Eyrolles for France; by International Thomson Publishing for Germany, Austria and Switzerland; by Distribuidora Cuspide for Argentina; by LR International for Brazil; by Galileo Libros for Chile; by Ediciones ZETA S.C.R. Ltda. for Peru; by WS Computer Publishing Corporation, Inc., for the Philippines; by Contemporanea de Ediciones for Venezuela; by Express Computer Distributors for the Caribbean and West Indies; by Micronesia Media Distributor, Inc. for Micronesia; by Chips Computadoras S.A. de C.V. for Mexico; by Editorial Norma de Panama S.A. for Panama; by American Bookshops for Finland.

For general information on Hungry Minds' products and services please contact our Customer Care Department within the U.S. at 800-762-2974, outside the U.S. at 317-572-3993 or fax 317-572-4002.

For sales inquiries and reseller information, including discounts, premium and bulk quantity sales, and foreign-language translations, please contact our Customer Care Department at 800-434-3422, fax 317-572-4002, or write to Hungry Minds, Inc., Attn: Customer Care Department, 10475 Crosspoint Boulevard, Indianapolis, IN 46256.

For information on licensing foreign or domestic rights, please contact our Sub-Rights Customer Care Department at 212-884-5000.

For information on using Hungry Minds' products and services in the classroom or for ordering examination copies, please contact our Educational Sales Department at 800-434-2086 or fax 317-572-4005.

For press review copies, author interviews, or other publicity information, please contact our Public Relations Department at 317-572-3168 or fax 317-572-4168.

For authorization to photocopy items for corporate, personal, or educational use, please contact Copyright Clearance Center, 222 Rosewood Drive, Danvers, MA 01923, or fax 978-750-4470.

About the Author

Mac Rinehart is the president of Sextant Technology Consulting, a business dedicated to providing high-quality consulting services for the planning and implementing of Web-based applications and dynamic Web sites for businesses of all sizes. You can contact Sextant Technology Consulting on the Internet at `www.sextanttech.com`.

The author and his wife reside in the beautiful city of Portland, Oregon. When not programming or writing, both enjoy fine coffee, fine food, and the arts.

Dedication

This book is dedicated to my wife, Kristin Schuchman. She is an inspiration to me, and she has been incredibly patient with my busy schedule during the writing of this book. Thank you, Kristin. I love you always.

Author's Acknowledgments

Thank you to Steven Hayes, acquisitions editor; Linda Morris, project editor; and Teresa Artman, copy editor; all of whom deserve credit for creation of this book. A special thanks also goes to Ray Carnes, fellow author, my technical editor and advocate — you made this project possible. Additional thanks goes to the staff of Hungry Minds for everything they have done to make this book successful.

I'd like to thank my wife for her patience, support, and for the energy she devoted to our daily affairs (and the planning of our wedding) while I was busy writing. I'm in your debt.

My peers at Medical Management International deserve acknowledgment for creating a team that supported professionalism and for the great friendships I had there. In particular, thanks to Alejandro, Vadim, Huseyin, Chris, Jeff, Rob, Ron, Ken the mad scientist, Debra, and Nancy; they're the best team I've had the pleasure of working with.

Thanks to Mike Thorne and Doug Gould, who gave this starving student his first programming job . . . I'm holding you both personally responsible for the 30 pounds I've gained since then! And thanks to Jerry Nelson, who introduced me to the wonderful language of Java.

I'd like to thank my family and close friends who have created an atmosphere of support and creativity without which I would never have undertaken this book. Brian and Letha, thank you for the service of your dining room table as a writing hideout.

Finally, to the barristas at Stumptown Coffeehouse: Thank you for the copious amount of coffee that kept me working when nothing else could.

Publisher's Acknowledgments

We're proud of this book; please send us your comments through our Hungry Minds Online Registration Form located at www.dummies.com.

Some of the people who helped bring this book to market include the following:

Acquisitions, Editorial, and Media Development

Project Editor: Linda Morris

Senior Acquisitions Editor: Steven H. Hayes

Copy Editor: Teresa Artman

Technical Editor: Raymond Carnes

Editorial Manager: Constance Carlisle

Permissions Editor: Laura Moss

Media Development Specialist: Megan Decraene

Media Development Manager: Laura VanWinkle

Media Development Supervisor: Richard Graves

Editorial Assistant: Amanda Foxworth, Jean Rogers

Production

Project Coordinator: Ryan Steffen

Layout and Graphics: Joyce Haughey, Jackie Nicholas, Barry Offringa, Jill Piscitelli, Jacque Schneider, Betty Schulte, Brian Torwelle, Jeremey Unger

Proofreaders: Laura Albert, David Faust, TECHBOOKS Production Services

Indexer: TECHBOOKS Production Services

General and Administrative

Hungry Minds Technology Publishing Group: Richard Swadley, Senior Vice President and Publisher; Mary Bednarek, Vice President and Publisher, Networking; Joseph Wikert, Vice President and Publisher, Web Development Group; Mary C. Corder, Editorial Director, Dummies Technology; Andy Cummings, Publishing Director, Dummies Technology; Barry Pruett, Publishing Director, Visual/Graphic Design

Hungry Minds Manufacturing: Ivor Parker, Vice President, Manufacturing

Hungry Minds Marketing: John Helmus, Assistant Vice President, Director of Marketing

Hungry Minds Production for Branded Press: Debbie Stailey, Production Director

Hungry Minds Sales: Michael Violano, Vice President, International Sales and Sub Rights

Contents at a Glance

Cartoons at a Glance

By Rich Tennant

The 5th Wave By Rich Tennant
Visual Web Development Team

"Give him air! Give him air! He'll be okay. He's just been exposed to some raw HTML code. It must have accidently flashed across his screen from the server."

page 311

The 5th Wave By Rich Tennant

"What I'm looking for are dynamic Web applications and content, not Web innuendoes and intent."

page 345

The 5th Wave By Rich Tennant
Apparently this is a clarification of their last memo in which they asked everyone in Web design to use more Java.

page 7

The 5th Wave By Rich Tennant
Re'al Pro'gram·mers

Real Programmers know a lot about Java, but never know how to use the coffee machine.

page 57

The 5th Wave By Rich Tennant
SCREEEEEK...

"Is this really the best use of a Web-based shopping cart application? A bad wheel on the shopping cart icon that squeaks, wobbles, and pulls to the left?"

page 151

The 5th Wave By Rich Tennant

"Sometimes I feel behind the times. I asked my 11-year old to build a database for my business's Web site, and he said he would, only after he finishes the one he's building for his baseball card collection."

page 255

The 5th Wave By Rich Tennant
Progenitors of the Java Programming Language
Lava
Developed in Hawaii, objects would suddenly erupt into a hot flowing stream of information.
Guava
Objects "grew" on computer's tree structure which users could convert to a data jam to be spread across the Web.
Jabba The Hut
Named after the developer, objects tended to get lost in cyber-space.
Flava
Objects were referred to as "beans", but would repeat themselves when overused.

page 209

Cartoon Information:

Fax: 978-546-7747

E-Mail: richtennant@the5thwave.com

World Wide Web: www.the5thwave.com

Table of Contents

Introduction

Welcome to *JavaServer Pages For Dummies*! I wrote this for Web developers and Java coders who need an easily understood reference on JavaServer Pages (JSP) technology. You don't even have to be a Java expert to read this book.

If you're venturing into the JSP from a Web content designer's perspective, this book offers you the information you need to know to construct JavaServer Pages quickly.

If you're venturing into the JSP world from a Java developer's perspective, this book provides you with a reference on implementing more advanced features of JSP programming, including JavaBeans and custom tags.

No matter what your background or skill level, I show you how to implement some really cool JSPs!

What's in This Book

I divided this book into seven parts, organizing the parts by related groups of information and by audience. If you're a Web designer, you'll probably be more interested in Parts I and II. Web designers should also take a look at Chapter 12 and Chapter 14, which respectively cover the use of custom tags and deploying JSP applications. Java developers may find what they're looking for in the rest of the book. The Part of Tens has something for everyone.

If you don't like to read a book from cover to cover, this one's for you! Each chapter in the book focuses on a single topic, and you aren't required to read one chapter to understand the content of another. So jump in wherever you will! Here is an overview of the parts.

Part I: Laying the Foundation

In this part, I cover the basics, including some background information on JSP technology, how to set up your computer, and fundamental JSP language features of interest to Java developers and Web designers.

Part II: JSP for Web Designers

This part dives into the world of the Web designer. Here you can get information on JSP tags of particular interest to Web designers. You'll also find information on using JavaScript for form validation, and implementing some cool features on a Web browser.

Part III: Backstage with JSP

JavaServer Page technology provides Java developers an Application Programming Interface (API) for extending JSP page capabilities. This section provides information for interacting with the JSP environment, and developing JavaBeans (reusable components of Java code) to implement cool application features.

Part IV: Implementing a Database

JSP applications become powerful tools by collecting and storing data, and retrieving data to customize an end user's experience. This section provides the information that you need to connect to a database with Java, and to interact with the database through Java Database Connectivity (JDBC), a Java technology for interacting with databases.

Part V: Breaking the Envelope: JSP Advanced Features

Need help with JSP custom tags? Looking for information on cookies (not the kind of cookies you eat)? Do you want to deploy your JSP code with a WAR file? Would you like to know what the heck I'm talking about? Put on your flight vest and climb into the cockpit, you're about to break through the JSP sound barrier; in this section, you'll discover the power that JSP technology has to offer.

Part VI: The Part of Tens

This part is like the mystery grab bag of goodies. And I've put my favorite morsels of information in here for you. In these pages, you'll find URLs and reviews of my favorite Internet resources for JSP and Java information. You'll also discover ways to implement some really cool JSP application features. Finally, you'll find my top recommended strategies for developing better JSPs.

Part VII: Appendixes

Look to the Appendixes for great references on all kinds of nuts-and-bolts tools and help. Here I give you loads of information on how to install Java software development kits and the Tomcat JSP container.

The companion CD

I give you lots of sample code on the CD that comes with this book. This will save you the trouble of typing in all that code and prevent those pesky typos. But wait, that's not all! You also get five bonus chapters on the CD, including a sample JSP project and a chapter on developing JSP custom tags. Look here, too, for an introduction to Structured Query Language (SQL) syntax, and a primer on the Java language.

System Requirements

JavaServer Page technology is a platform-independent Web technology for generating dynamic Web page content. In order to take advantage of this technology, you need to install a couple of applications. Most of this software is included on the CD that accompanies this book, and the rest is available for free on the Web. Appendix B has a complete listing of all the software that comes on the companion CD. Appendix A includes guidance on locating software you need off the Internet, as well as installation instructions on required software you'll get from the Internet or the CD. The basic requirements are

- **A computer:** JSP programs can run on any Java-compliant operating system. Unfortunately, this book does not come with a computer . . . you'll have to supply your own. (I wanted to do this for you, but the publishers said it wouldn't fit on the CD.) If you have a current Windows, Unix, Linux, or Apple computer system, you should be okay on this front.
- **A JSP container:** A JSP container is a program for hosting JSPs. The CD with this book includes Tomcat, which is an open-source JSP container. The many different vendors of JSP containers are all required to provide the same support for JSP features. If you prefer, you can use a different vendor's solution, but I recommend using Tomcat because it's free, it works well, and it's a public domain software development project.
- **A browser:** JSP programs typically generate HTML output. You need a browser to test your JSP programs and ensure the output is correct. Because JSPs run on a server and send only the output to the browser, you don't need a particular variety of browser to create JSP programs. I do recommend that you have access to all the browsers that you want

your users to be able to use — you want to test your JSPs on each one. The two most important browsers to have right now are Internet Explorer, Version 5.5 and Netscape Navigator, Version 6.0.

The software on the accompanying CD is formatted for computers running the Microsoft Windows operating system. Because most of the programs are written in Java, they can run on Linux, Unix, and Mac operating systems, too. I provide you with links where you can get software in different formats if you're not using Windows. You can find the links in Appendix A, which describes the installation and setup process for all the software you need.

Conventions Used in This Book

People tell me that conventions are important, but all too often they seem to ignore their own advice. Because I am an admitted conventions freak, here are the fundamentals for this book.

Making sense of fonts and symbols

`All of the code in this book appears in this font.`

Sometimes it's necessary to provide a key for how to write the syntax of a particular statement. In syntax keys, optional elements will be delimited with square braces (`[ ]`). If you need to substitute your own variable for a portion of the syntax in a statement, I delimit the variable with angle brackets (`< >`). Repeatable elements in a syntax key are followed by an ellipsis (`. . .`). If you need to choose from multiple options, I surround the options list with curly braces (`{ }`) and divide each option with a single pipe character (`|`). All keywords will appear in the `code` monofont, as I indicate above.

Sometimes I like to play the role of Subliminal Man, telling you what to write and where to write it. To do so, I've come up with a very discreet way to influence your behavior without your realizing it. When I use a regular font, I send you a subliminal message indicating **in bold font** what you should write. The converse is true, also: **When I'm writing in bold font and I want you to write something, I identify the text that you need to write by printing it** in regular font.

Please follow along with the instructions below:

1. On a sheet of paper, write: **I've always wanted to be a space cadet.**
2. **Now, on the same sheet of paper, write:** my favorite hobby is cow tipping.

Great. If you find yourself in possession of a piece of paper that has some nonsense in your handwriting about wanting to be a space cadet, and valuing a good cow-tipping experience, don't think anything of it. Realize that everything is right on the world, and you're getting along just great.

Finally, I sometimes provide you with some direction on steps you should take when interacting with menus in applications and your computer's desktop. For example, when I tell you to open a file in a program, I write *Choose File⇨Open*. That means you should click on the program's file menu and then click on the Open command in the file menu. Another common direction is *Choose Start⇨Run*. In this case, Start refers to the windows Start menu, and Run is the command you should choose from the Start menu.

Discovering the icons of our time

This book is loaded with margin icons, which help you identify the key points for any particular topic. I use these margin icons to help you; take advantage of them.

I'm just full of advice and ideas on how to work with JSPs. And even though my word is not gospel, I like to offer you my insights periodically. When I have an idea to make your life easier and help you code faster and cleaner, I use this Tip icon.

These technical references can get a little heady at times. And when they do, it's kind of hard to sort out the wheat from the chaff — trying discerning important information from all the background noise. Although I try to keep the topics light and focused, there are times where things get complex. When I use the Remember icon, I'm emphasizing an important point. It's my way of identifying the kernel of truth for you.

Don't you sometimes hear yourself singin', "Gosh, it would be awful pleas'n, to reason out the reason, for things I can't explain. Then perhaps I'll deserve ya, and be even worthy of ya, if I only had a brain!" Well, the stuff you'll find under the Technical Stuff icon is there because I'm tryin' to please ya. But if you're not interested in technical mumbo jumbo, you can ignore them.

A lot of the material in this book is also on the CD. Look for this icon to guide you to the nuggets I place there. On the CD, you can find source code from all the examples, programs, and resources to help you get started with JavaServer Pages. Check out the bonus chapters on the CD, too. I use this icon to let you know when you can get something from the CD.

Take heed when you see this icon. A smart person learns from her mistakes, a wise person learns from the mistakes of others. I've discovered a lot of potential pitfalls by falling into them. I use the Warning icon to alert you to the danger.

I use this icon to point the way to another resource, usually another book or an article on the Web, that contains useful information that just happens to be outside the scope of this book. (Hey, I tried, but I can only do so much in a 400-page book.)

Sun Microsystems recently released a new version of the JSP specification: JSP 1.2. This book is primarily focused on developing JSP 1.2 applications. But because you'll find many JSP 1.1 applications already out there in the world, I don't want to leave you high and dry if you're working on one. I use the Version 1.1 icon to identify when I'm addressing JSP features specific to a JSP 1.1 application.

Foolish Assumptions

If you're considering purchasing *JavaServer Pages For Dummies*, you're probably either a Web designer or a Java programmer about to venture into the wonderful world of JSP technology. I've structured this book to provide you with the information you need in either case so you don't have to wade through extra details to get information. I do, however, have to make a few assumptions, to maximize the value of the book.

First off, this book assumes that you're familiar with HyperText Markup Language (HTML). I explain the key points in HTML code examples, but if you're not familiar with HTML, you'll need an additional resource. I recommend *HTML 4 For Dummies,* 3rd Edition, by Ed Tittel, Natanya Pitts, and Chelsea Valentine (published by Hungry Minds, Inc.).

If you're a Java programmer, you'll need to be familiar with the Java programming language. This book will provide information on all the Java APIs central to developing JSP content. For further help, take a look at *Java 2 For Dummies*, by Barry Burd, published by Hungry Minds, Inc.

Where to Go

If you're like me, you won't read a reference book from cover to cover. That's why I wrote this book to allow you to jump in wherever you want, without having to have read previous material. If your primary interest is Web content design, you'll probably find what you are looking for in the first two parts of the book. Developer topics are addressed in the remaining parts. So pick your poison, and enjoy!

Part I

Laying the Foundation

The 5th Wave
By Rich Tennant
©RICHTENNANT
Apparently this is a clarification of their last memo in which they asked everyone in Web design to use more Java.

In this part . . .

This part is designed to get you off to on the right foot with JavaServer Pages (JSP) technology. In Chapter 1, you see what JSP is and how it relates to other technologies. Chapter 2 launches you directly into the creation of your first JSP. This first part provides a great introduction into the technologies that you'll be working with as you proceed through the rest of the book.

Chapter 1

JavaServer Pages: The Lowdown

In This Chapter

- JavaServer Page (JSP) Technology: A brief history
- What you can do with JSP
- JSP technology's place in the Web-based application
- How JSP stacks up to related technologies
- What you need to write JSPs

You've probably heard the buzz about JSP technology: It's one of the hottest Web technologies on the market and an important part of Java's suite of technologies for enterprise applications. As you examine JSP technology further, you find it's easier to figure out the purpose of a new technology if you understand why it came to be and how it relates to other technologies. That's what this chapter is all about.

In the following pages, I give you the 30,000-foot overview of JSP technology. If you want to know a little history behind JSP, what the technology has to offer, how it relates to other Web technologies, and what you need to get started, look no further. If you want to jump right in to the programming business, you can skip this chapter.

JSP Technology: A Brief History

I'm no historian, but I do like to know a little about the chain of events leading to the introduction of a new technology. The history of a technology has a lot to do with what motivates its creation. History also helps me understand how to use a new technology to its fullest potential. Although I'm not seeking the Nobel Prize in History, I hope to throw a little light on why JSP technology is important, and what you have to gain from using it. Of course, if you like what I say, feel free to nominate me for the Nobel Prize; I won't turn it down if someone gives it to me.

Static everywhere: The early days of the Internet

In the early days the Internet was mostly a bunch of plain old boring text. In fact, in the beginning the Internet was just a place to put information for other people to find, kind of like a big electronic library. All this stuff on the Internet is called *content* — and in the beginning, it was all *static* content (content that doesn't change much). This premise was fine in the early days of the Internet, but a few visionaries had other plans for this huge resource.

Knock, knock: We have a visitor

As more and more people started storing their stuff on the Internet, some people began to think of the Internet as a huge marketplace. Making the transition from viewing the Internet as a document library to seeing the Internet as a marketplace required the creators of Web sites to make a major change to the way content was managed. Providers of Internet content had to make their content interactive.

A Web revolution was underway, and with it came the invention of the HyperText Markup Language (HTML) form: a document that people could fill out in order to request something specific from a content provider.

The nice thing about the introduction of forms on the Web was that people could request things that they wanted. But although the creation of HTML forms was a helpful initial step, some people weren't satisfied. A form couldn't tell you anything about who the customer was, what demographic the customer belonged to, or how to recognize that customer the next time he or she returned to your Web site.

Who's there?: A special customer

The architects of the Web economy weren't satisfied with simply having a huge pool of customers. They wanted to personalize their Web sites so that consumers would come back again and again. They wanted to know who their consumers were and what they liked. They needed new tools to make content dynamic and personalized to the Web consumer.

Dynamic (changing) server-side content was created to allow Web content providers to customize their Web sites for particular users. Generating dynamic server-side content simply means personalizing a Web page to the user who requests it. The page is *dynamic* because the information sent to the Web browser changes depending on who requested it. *Server-side* refers to the dynamic process, located on the Web server, that generates the content.

JSP is one of the technologies used to generate Web pages dynamically on a Web server. Like related technologies, using JSP also enables you to collect information about the users of your Web site, as well as helping you maintain information so that you can refer to it when those users come back. The best part about this technology is you get to decide what kind of information to save; you're only limited by your own creativity.

Unlocking the Potential of JSP

JSP technology is not just one of many competing technologies for creating dynamic Web sites; it is, in my humble opinion, one of the greatest. If I didn't believe it, my name wouldn't be on the cover of this book. Of course, I don't expect you to take my word for it without question, so here's why I think JSP is so great.

When people first started working with generating dynamic content from a Web server, the job was primarily left to a technology expert who really had to be a smarty. The early programs that generated dynamic content, such as servlets, mixed all the programming logic and the content together in one big pot, becoming a very complex mess. With no way to separate the two, anyone wanting to modify content had to know all the ins and outs of programming and also have a good eye for graphic design.

Complexity in a program is a bad thing, particularly in the fast-changing landscape of the World Wide Web. As you work on JSPs — or any programming effort — keep this number in mind: On average, 80 percent of the effort and cost of a software product is devoted to maintenance. Keeping code simple and adaptable is important because the biggest opportunity for saving money on software development is reducing maintenance expenses.

The creators of JSP technology recognized excessive complexity as a major shortcoming of existing Web technologies. They realized that people and businesses that put information on the Web need to modify the appearance of their Web content without having to change the complex programs used to generate the dynamic content. They also realized that when the programming logic has to change, the change should not affect how the page appears.

This is my sandbox; that's your sandbox

To facilitate easy updating and keep the content and programming logic separate, the innovators of JSP technology identified two distinct roles in developing dynamic server-side content: the Web designer and the programmer.

Bean me up, Scotty

JSP technology isn't great for Web designers alone. The creators of JSP technology understand that to make JSP an effective tool for programmers, JSP needs to be able to implement complex business processes simply. Therefore, JSP technology incorporates the Java's existing JavaBean specification.

JavaBeans, or beans for short, were originally envisioned to be small reusable programs for modeling graphic user interface (GUI) controls. These controls traditionally include things such as the Open, Save, and Print buttons available on the standard toolbars of most programs today. With JSP technology, instead of making visual elements with JavaBeans, programmers make small, reusable, non-visual programs for generating specific JSP content.

JavaBeans are often referred to as a *component-based* technology. Beans can be plugged into any program that needs them, just like adding a new component to your stereo system.

A *Web designer* is someone who crosses the boundaries of graphic artist and programmer, making creative and visually appealing Web pages. Web designers fill a critical role in converting a marketing vision into reality, specializing more in the browser-based Internet-scripting languages such as HTML and JavaScript.

Because most Web designers are already familiar with Web-scripting languages, the portion of JSP technology intended for Web designers is modeled after existing scripting languages. That's good news: JSP scripting is easy to learn if you already have some exposure to Web scripting languages.

The *pure programmer* has the technical know-how to work with complex languages, interact with databases, and write software to support complex business rules.

Distinguishing between these roles is a boon for programmers and Web designers alike because you don't have to be a superhero to write JSP code. If you're a Web designer, instead of working 24 hours a day trying to keep up with all the cool things programmers can do, you can specialize and focus your energy on a specific topic. Specializing leaves time for other important activities, like sleeping, eating, breathing, and occasional recreation! (I believe in leading a balanced life.)

Write once, run anywhere

I would be remiss to not mention the ubiquitous mantra of all Java technologies: *Write once, run anywhere*. JSP technology fits the bill perfectly. JSPs are based on the Java technology, which means that they can run on any Java-compliant computer. Also, no matter what kind of computer you use when you write JSPs, you can switch platforms and operating systems without having to change anything in the JSP or the Java classes supporting the JSP. If only all technologies were so nice!

Although you don't have to change anything if you move a JSP from one JSP container to another, like most things in life, there's actually a little more to it. If you write your JSPs to conform to the generic JSP specification, you shouldn't have any problem moving them to different JSP containers. (For more on JSP containers, skip down to the upcoming section "The JSP container.") But if you implement some of the custom solutions by third-party vendors in your JSPs, those pages will be tied to the vendor's JSP container. In this book, I stick with solutions conforming to the JSP specification.

The JSP specification is a technical document that describes how JavaServer Page technology is supposed to be implemented. JSP technology can be implemented by a variety of third-party vendors, who also have the option to add extensions to the language. Vendors are not even required to use Java for JSP technology implementations! The JSP specification is a very clear, concise, and well-written document. You can download the JSP specification from the Web page `java.sun.com/products/jsp/download.html`.

Hosting JSPs

JSPs don't run on their own. Just like you need to have a Web browser to run HTML pages, you need a special program on your Web server to run JSPs. This program is called a JSP container. Because of the JSP container, you don't need an advanced knowledge of how the Internet works. The JSP container coordinates all the interaction between users on the Internet and your JSPs.

A *JSP container* is actually just a Web server that includes support for JSPs. A *Web server* is the program that responds to users' requests for Web pages over the Internet. The JSP container portion of a Web server is like the special playground for JSPs.

There are several JSP containers on the market, provided by third-party software vendors. You can find a complete listing of available JSP containers at `java.sun.com/products/jsp/industry.html`. To help you get started, I include the Tomcat JSP container on the CD that comes with this book. Tomcat is the reference implementation of a JSP container, which means other vendors should refer to it as the official example of how to implement standard JSP container features.

Creating Web Applications with JSPs

JSP technology is part of the Java 2 Enterprise Edition (J2EE) specification. JSP technology is one part of a suite of Java technologies for developing Web-based, enterprise applications. Not only can you use JSP technology to create cool, dynamic content for Web sites, you can also use it to write sophisticated applications that run over the Internet or in a private business network. JSPs can also create dynamic eXtensible Markup Language (XML) pages. In all cases, JSP is just one element in a suite of tools. While you can create Web applications with JSPs alone, more sophisticated applications tend to use JSPs for the user interface alone.

Dynamic presentation is everything

JSP technology is primarily intended as a tool for creating Web pages — its most important role is to present dynamic Web content. You can think of a JSP as a document template. The Web page itself (HTML code) is the template, and JSP language elements insert dynamic content into the page. The product is a standard HTML page, which is sent to the user's Web browser.

Many of the JSP language elements are modeled after HTML or XML elements, thus Web designers don't have to learn a whole new language to create powerful, dynamic Web pages. Because JSPs are basically like any other Web page, with the exception of having a `.jsp` extension on the file, you can also include browser-based scripting languages such as JavaScript and VBScript in your JSP.

Although JSPs are specialized to manage the presentation process, they work well with other Java technologies intended for developing more complex application logic. The Java technologies frequently combined with JSPs include JavaBeans, servlets, and Enterprise JavaBeans.

Directing Internet traffic with JSPs

JSPs can also evaluate user requests, thus controlling the flow of a Web site or application from one page to the next. When the Web site does this, it's making conditional decisions based on user input.

With standard HTML pages, decisions about how to navigate from one Web page to another are made in the browser alone. When users request a page, that's the page that they get. But with JSPs, you can evaluate a user request on the Web server and decide to redirect that user to a different page if the situation warrants. A typical scenario where you might use this behavior is if a user attempts to access a secure page without logging in to your site. If a request for the secure page is not authorized, you can redirect the user to a log-in page.

Controlling the flow of a Web-based application or a Web site with JSP technology works fine for simple Web sites and for prototypes. When you get into more complex Web sites or applications, integrating JSP technology with another technology called servlets is a good idea. This integration is the JSP Model 2 Architecture. Read more about servlets in the next section of this chapter. For more about the JSP Model 2 Architecture, check out Chapter 15.

Relationship of JSPs to Servlets

JSP technology is closely related to servlet technology. *Servlets* are also Web-server-based programs used to generate dynamic Web page content. In fact, servlets were created before JSP technology, and for a while they performed the role that JSPs now fulfill.

The servlet scoop

Servlets are Java programs for handling Web-based requests for information and generating content that is sent back to the person who requested it. Servlets can generate a variety of content types including HTML pages, XML data, and portable document file (PDF) files. Servlets are very similar to JSPs with the exception that they mix Java code and HTML code all together in a way that is difficult to maintain. Servlets are also highly scalable: That is, increasing the number of users on your Website only has a marginal impact on response time of servlets.

Servlets are so scalable because they implement a feature called multithreading. *Multithreading* enables you to deploy just one servlet, and that one servlet can respond to many user requests at the same time. Multithreading is a benefit because it cuts down on the amount of work that a Web server has to do to respond to multiple requests from different users.

Servlets still perform a valuable role in the Web application, but the creators of JSP technology recognized that servlets were too complex for Web designers to work with easily. JSP technology was thus created as a response to the complexity of servlets.

JSP magic

Every JSP gets turned into a servlet by the JSP container, which is the program for running JSPs. Consequently, you don't have to know how to create servlets to benefit from the power that they provide. You can simply write JSPs, and the JSP container will turn them into servlets for you.

And as if JSP technology isn't cool enough, the JSP container also automatically reloads updated JSPs without having to be restarted. If you modify a JSP and want to update it online, you can deploy it directly to the JSP container without shutting down your Web site! The next time someone requests the updated page, the JSP container knows that a new version is available and automatically reloads the page.

To servlet or to JSP: That is the question

Because JSPs and servlets are so closely related, choosing between them comes down to deciding which is more appropriate for your needs. Generally speaking, if your primary purpose is to write Web pages devoted to presenting content, using JSP technology is the best choice. With JSPs, you get all the benefits of servlets and you don't have to be an expert programmer.

But if you need to write more complex programs in which you make complicated decisions on how to respond to user requests, using servlets or a combination of JSPs and servlets is a better idea. To discover more about how to make this decision — and to read ways to use JSPs and servlets together — take a look at Chapter 15.

JSP and Web Scripting Languages

Several scripting languages are available to make Web pages more interesting; two common languages are JavaScript and VBScript. These languages enable you to write code for a Web browser, which makes them client-side programs. They also enable you to perform some limited operations in the Web server, but they are not robust server-side technologies such as JSP.

JSP is often used in partnership with scripting languages. JSPs run on the Web server only and send only the content generated by the pages to a Web browser. If you want the Web page to be interactive on the Web browser, without talking to the Web server, you need to use a scripting language such as JavaScript or VBScript.

The good news is that writing script programs that run on a browser is pretty straightforward in most cases. You don't have to be a guru of all things technological just to work with JSPs. To discover more about JavaScript, thumb through Chapters 5 and 6. There you'll find plenty to get you up to speed for most of the things you'll want to do.

JavaServer Pages versus Active Server Pages

Microsoft's competing technology to JSP is Active Server Pages (ASP). ASP technology is similar to JSP technology in that it also enables you to generate dynamic Web pages.

What's an ASP page?

An *ASP page* is a Web page with embedded code for generating custom content based on a user's request. In that respect, it's very similar to a JSP. ASP is a technology developed and owned by Microsoft. The code that you embed into an ASP page can be VBScript, and you can make use of Visual Basic and Visual C++ programs from ASP pages. Just like JSPs, ASP pages run inside a Web server. In the case of ASP, the server of choice is generally Internet Information Server, provided by Microsoft.

If you're interested in finding out more about ASP pages, take a look at *Active Server Pages For Dummies,* 2nd Edition, by Bill Hatfield, published by Hungry Minds, Inc.

Why choose JSP?

What are the compelling reasons to choose JSP over ASP? I have to admit that I'm biased toward JSP. (Because I think JSP is the way to go, I'm writing a book about JSP instead of ASP.) However, no one ever does something just because someone tells you to, so here are my reasons for using JSP:

- **JSP technology doesn't bind you to a particular computing platform.**

  The Java language is the same, no matter what operating system or computer hardware you choose. Thus, you can run JSPs on something small to start with and later expand the hardware and operating system as your needs change.

- **JSP enables the use of custom tags.**

  Although JSP technology provides basic tags for incorporating dynamic content into your Web page, the creators of JSP technology also recognize that the basic tags aren't enough for more complex tasks. Consequently, the creators of JSP technology have included a custom tags feature for creating custom dynamic content. JSP custom tags allow JSP technology to evolve as the needs of Web developers change. You can even create you own custom tags if you want!

- **JSPs run in a JSP container.**

  Any software vendor can make a JSP container, which means you have a lot of flexibility and a lot more economic freedom when it comes to choosing a JSP container for your JSP application.

  You can use the JSP container Tomcat at no charge. (And free is a very good price!) If you really want to spend money, however, JSP containers are sold by a variety of vendors, which means you have the power to choose which one you want to use. With choice comes competition, and competition means lower prices.

  A copy of Tomcat version 4.0 is included on the CD that accompanies this book. Read more on Tomcat installation and configuration in Appendix A.

- **If you support open-source and community-source initiatives, JSP technology is the way to go.**

  JSP technology is licensed on Sun Microsystems' Community Source Licensing program. You can also get any of the software you need to run JSPs in open-source and community-source formats. Open- and community-source licensing programs are a great way to promote competition in the software marketplace, keeping the cost of software at a reasonable level and ensuring that vendors continue to advance technology while offering high quality products.

What You Need to Get Started

Although JSP programming is not difficult, you will need to do a little bit of preparation. Don't sweat this initial step: All the information you need to get started is documented right here in the book. And all the software you need to get started is available on the CD at the back of this book.

The JSP container

A *JSP container* is a program very similar to a Web Server but specialized to run JSPs. Actually, many Web server vendors have built a JSP container right into their Web servers, so you don't have to get an extra piece of software to run a Web site with JSPs.

The examples I give you in this book are deployed to the Tomcat JSP container, made by the Apache Software Foundation. Tomcat is termed the reference implementation of JSP containers because it has been picked by the people at Sun Microsystems to serve as the industry standard example of what a JSP container should do.

Tomcat is distributed under open-source licensing principles. Tomcat can host static Web pages, JSPs, and servlets — you don't have to install any other programs if you're looking for a simple solution to get started.

Tomcat is available on the Internet (`jakarta.apache.org`), but you can also get a copy of Tomcat from the CD at the back of this book. Also see information on installing and configuring Tomcat in Appendix A.

Tomcat is part of a subproject — the Jakarta-Tomcat project — of the Apache Software Foundation. Because of the way Tomcat is developed, new editions are released every night! Jakarta also has weekly builds, beta builds, and production builds of the Tomcat software package. The copy of Tomcat included on this book's CD is the latest production version available when this book went to press, but visit the Jakarta-Tomcat Web site to check for more recent editions.

Although you can use Tomcat as a Web server for your JSP application, you may want to consider integrating Tomcat with the Apache Web Server, also provided by the Apache Software Foundation. Integrating the two provides your Web site with more robust security than Tomcat offers on its own. I think this is important enough that I recommend it without qualification if you intend to serve JSPs over the Internet. If you're just developing and testing JSPs on your local computer, you can use Tomcat on its own.

One browser or two?

One of the tricky parts about developing software for the Internet is getting it to work on different versions of Web browsers. All browsers behave differently, and different versions of the same browser also behave differently. Of the several different kinds of Web browsers on the market today, the two most popular are Netscape Navigator (AOL) and Internet Explorer (Microsoft).

If you can, pick a single browser and make sure all your users are on it. Using a single browser works best when you're serving content to users in a controlled environment, such as a corporate intranet. If you're serving content to an Internet audience, this approach is obviously not realistic. In most cases, sites on the Internet support the latest release and the previous major release of both Netscape Navigator and Internet Explorer. Following this practice means testing everything you write on four different browsers, which is quite a bit of work.

Versions of Web browsers are available for download on the Internet if you don't have them already. To download Internet Explorer, go to `www.microsoft.com/windows/ie`. For Netscape, try `netscape.com/browsers/index.html`.

Dreamweaver UltraDev Version 4 by Macromedia includes a special auditing tool that you can use to determine whether your Web pages are not compliant with various browser brands and versions. A trial version of UltraDev is provided on the CD at the back of the book. To use this feature, open your Web page with UltraDev and then choose File⇨Check Target Browsers to start the tool. The tool provides a detailed report of any changes required to make your HTML page compliant with the selected target browsers.

Java editor or Integrated Development Environment (IDE)

If you're a Java developer, you'll want to have an editor for writing the code for JSPs. *Java editors* are programs that help you write and compile Java code. Most of these tools make your job easier by providing features such as automatic code formatting; syntax highlighting, to make code easier to read; and code completion, which helps reduce typographical errors by allowing you to complete code phrases from a menu rather than typing the whole thing yourself. *IDEs* are tools that enhance editors by providing project management features and wizards that help you create code faster.

Of the several Java editors on the market, I have a couple that I prefer and recommend:

- **Together Solo 5.0 by TogetherSoft:** This is my favorite Java IDE. This product integrates a modeling language called Unified Modeling Language with a Java and C++ editor.

UML allows you to design your software using graphical diagrams. Together Solo then converts your diagrams into Java or C++ code. Finally, you use the editor to finish development of the software. Because the editor and the modeling tool are integrated, as you make changes in the software with the editor, the UML model is automatically updated, making your software design a "living" document. You can discover more about Together Solo at the TogetherSoft Web site: `www.togethersoft.com`.

- **JBuilder 5.0 from Borland-Inprise Corporation:** JBuilder is a more traditional Java IDE, not offering modeling features of Together Solo. Prior to the last release of Together Solo, JBuilder did have a better Java editor. (Friends tell me this may no longer be the case, but that doesn't detract from the quality of JBuilder in my opinion). Finally, I really like JBuilder's customer service, and that's an important criterion in my book. You can find more on JBuilder at the Inprise Web site: `www.inprise.com`.

Software vendors may tell you that if you use their editor, then you should also use their Web server. Inprise, for example, develops both a Java editor and a Web server that runs JSP. Inprise also promotes its Application Servers, which are high-end Web servers that offer a lot more services than a simple JSP application needs. As long as you develop standard JSPs, which are the only thing I cover in this book, you don't need to buy your Web server from the same vendor as your Java development tool.

A Web page editor

You can write a Web page with Notepad if you want. The decision is, however, whether you really want to. Several Web page editors are available on the market with nice features for coding HTML, JavaScript, and JSP content. These features include color-coded syntax, automatic error detection, code formatting, and the ability to preview your pages as you write them.

Two very popular Web page authoring tools are HomeSite 4.5 and Dreamweaver UltraDev 4.0, both by Macromedia (`www.macromedia.com`). The companion CD for this book has a trial version of both tools. You can use either to create JSPs, and the choice really comes down to which you prefer.

Although Java editors and Web page editors are not required and can be expensive, my advice is to consider the purchase as an investment. Although I consider myself to be a pretty accurate coder, these tools have literally saved me hundreds of hours in development time over the duration of my career as a software developer. Time is money, and you'll find that these tools pay for themselves quickly.

Chapter 2

Writing Your First JavaServer Page

In This Chapter

- Designing JavaServer Pages (JSPs)
- Establishing a project directory structure
- Starting off with a static HTML prototype
- Deploying your JSP pages
- Making your page dynamic with JSP technology
- Creating Java classes
- Making your JSP monkey-proof with testing

The best way to discover how to do something is to get started doing it. In this chapter, you launch right into the creation of your first JavaServer Page (JSP). For your first attempt, I show you how to create a JSP from the Web designer's point of view. But even though I approach JSP from this perspective on this first pass, Java developers new to JSP should be interested in this chapter, too. Web designers are the consumers of the Java developer's work, so it's a good idea to understand how to prepare content that meets the needs of the Web designers.

Here I cover everything you need to know to get a rough introduction to JSP development. I start with design principles, work my way through developing the HyperText Markup Language (HTML) code, embedding JSP tags, and launch! You don't need to know Java, and I have you covered even if you're light on HTML experience.

In this chapter, I walk you through deploying a JSP to the Tomcat JSP container. Tomcat is a special kind of Web server program used to present JSP pages. It can also present static page content, including HTML and eXtensible Markup Language (XML) pages. Web servers that can present JSP content are called *JSP containers*. Several brands of JSP containers are available on the market. If you have a different JSP container, such as iPlanet or WebSphere, you need to follow the deployment directions for those containers. If you want to use Tomcat but have not yet installed it on your computer, refer to Appendix B for help with the installation process.

Dos and Don'ts of Designing JavaServer Pages

Designing your JSP application is one of the most important factors to minimizing development costs. JSP technology was created with the intent of dividing responsibilities of Web content development and application logic development. This division makes JSP development less expensive by encouraging Java developers to produce code that can be reused in a variety of applications, and by giving Web designers easy access to the power of that Java code without having to know how to program in the Java language.

Quality design ensures that your application will achieve these goals. Another perhaps even more important benefit to quality design is that while your peers are hacking code all through the night, you'll be sleeping with ease.

Here are a few basic considerations to help you build quality, reusable JSPs that I cover in greater detail over the following pages:

- Keep HTML and Web scripting code out of Java classes.
- Keep the Java code out of your JSP.
- Consider using custom tags whenever you are tempted to go against one of the tips above.

Although developing JSPs doesn't necessarily require two distinct people — a designer and a developer — remember that JSP development process employs two distinct roles. When you're working on your own, separating the responsibilities of graphic user interface (GUI) designer and application developer will help keep your JSPs clean.

Keep HTML code out of Java classes

The information in this section is directed primarily at Java developers. Prior to the creation of JSP technology, Java Web technologies encouraged the creation of Java classes that contain a lot of HTML code. In response to shortcomings with this approach (such as the complexity of the classes and maintenance nightmares that resulted), JSP technology was introduced. A primary objective of JSP code is to provide a technology that can keep the graphical elements of a Web page (such as HTML elements) separate from the Java code that generated the Web page. A secondary objective was to restore the sanity of overworked programmers like you and me.

One of the major benefits of JSP is that it enables Web designers to modify the appearance of a Web page without having to know Java. This benefit is achieved by ensuring that Java developers don't have to mix HTML code into their Java programs. If you put the HTML code in a Java class file, you lose this benefit.

Keep Java code out of your JSPs

My next tip is also primarily directed to Java developers: Don't introduce Java code into your JavaServer Pages. With JSP technology, you can write Java code in special tags (scriptlet tags) in a JSP. This feature may be beneficial for some rapid prototyping situations, but in the long run, it requires a lot more work and makes JSPs more difficult to maintain — after you embed Java code in a JSP, you can't reuse that Java code in any other page.

JSPs are the domains of Web designers. If you're a Web designer and you have to wade through a lot of Java code to figure out how to modify the look and feel of a Web page, the job will be a lot harder and your Web page is much more likely to get broken. Trust me, I've been there!

Know when and how to break the rules

I know what you're thinking: First I tell you to keep the HTML code out of your Java classes, and then I tell you to keep your Java code out of the JSP. And now, in almost the same breath, I'm telling you to be subversive and go against my own advice (JSP radical that I am). You're wondering when I'm going to get my story straight.

Sometimes the logic behind generating dynamic Web content is too complex to perform without some Java interaction. For example, if you have to build an HTML table for an invoice detail with a dynamic number of rows, constructing that table without using Java to control the table construction process can be pretty difficult.

Fortunately, the engineers at JavaSoft created custom tags that are intended for generating this dynamic Web content. Putting HTML in a custom tag is okay; that's what they were created for! I devote Chapter 12 exclusively to using custom tags in a JSP application. In addition, you can discover the art of creating your own custom tag in Bonus Chapter 4 on the CD.

Mixing Java and HTML code at some point is inevitable. In fact, many people cite this issue as a problem of JSP technology. Throughout this book, I identify other opportunities and techniques to help keep your JSPs free of excessive caffeine. (I mean, Java code.)

If you find yourself in a position in which you have to decide between writing Java code in a Web page or HTML code in a Java class, consider the following:

- If the Web designers of your team have to modify the look and feel of this Web page on a regular basis, maintaining that look is easier if the HTML code is in the JSP rather than in a Java class.
- If the HTML code doesn't change very much — and particularly if the same content is presented in multiple locations on your Web site — writing it in a Java class promotes reuse of code and helps cut down on errors.
- If you do end up writing Java in a JSP file, keep it simple, and keep it separate from the HTML source. You can find more information on this subject in Chapter 4.

Positive notes on design

In the earlier sections of this chapter, I explore the pitfalls to avoid when writing JSPs. But what about the things you should do? Here are my tips for creating great JSPs:

- **Start with a prototype of your JSP by writing a Web page using plain HTML.**

  Don't worry about building dynamic content until you have the page laid out and looking good.

  If you're writing this page for a customer, make sure that he likes the prototype and agrees that the page has all the content needed before moving forward.

- **Java developers should start working with JSPs when customers have accepted the HTML prototype.**

  Web designers and Java developers should work closely together to decide on the best solution for presenting dynamic content, and also to come up with standards for how to implement dynamic content. Teamwork rules!

- **When the Java developer finishes each piece of code that generates your page content, integrate that code into the prototype one piece at a time.**

- **Test each piece before doing the next. Working with the integration process in small steps is best because if something goes wrong, you'll have a better idea of where it happened, and how to fix it.**

  Java developers shouldn't worry about getting the perfect object-oriented design for their code on the first pass. Designing for reuse requires a lot of effort if you're not clear how a feature will be reused. While your application grows, you'll see opportunities when a feature can be written once and used in multiple places. When you see those opportunities, start thinking about how to design for them.

What to do, what to do. . . .

For your first JSP, I've created a sample JSP riddle page. This makes a good example because it exercises the following important features of JSP development:

- **The JSP contains content that changes depending on when you ask for it.** That makes the page content dynamic, which is what JSP is all about.
- **The JSP is broken into two parts: a question and an answer.** Because you have to check the answer after the user has responded to the question, the example shows how to display different kinds of content based on user input.
- **In this example, you put several features of JSP technology into use so that you can see how they work together.**

To do this example, you must

- **Provide some Java code that supplies a random riddle question, and four possible answers, one of which is correct.**

  All the code in this book, including JSPs and sample Java code, is available on the companion CD. If you prefer to copy and paste the code I have provided, you can find it there.

- **Embed the riddle code into a JSP, and then serve the riddle and the possible answers to a user.**

  The user should be able to submit an answer and see whether it is correct. The server should respond to a client's guess by notifying whether the client got the correct answer and presenting another riddle question.

- **Develop the entire solution with one JSP!**

  Well, if you get technical, there are a few *JavaBeans*, which are little Java programs that do some of the work for the JSP. But you don't have to be a Java programmer to finish the solution because I provide all the Java code for you.

Getting all this behavior into a single JSP may seem tricky, particularly if you haven't coded Web pages with dynamic content. As you proceed through the chapter, I'll break the task down into manageable pieces.

Creating a Project Folder Structure

With every type of software development, you can usually find a logical way to organize the work in your project to make it easier to understand and deploy. Writing Web programs with JSP is no different. To organize JSP projects, you want to create some special directories on your computer just for the JSP project. It's important for the project folder structure to replicate the deployment folder structure exactly. Doing so simplifies the deployment process. Here I guide you through the process with the JSP example. Follow these steps:

1. **Launch Windows Explorer.**
2. **Create a root folder for all your projects by placing your mouse pointer in the right pane of the Windows Explorer window, right-clicking, and choosing New⇨Folder from the pop-up menu.**

   A folder labeled `New Folder` appears.
3. **Rename the folder to something meaningful.**

   Right-click the folder to select it, and then click Rename from the pop-up menu that appears.

   Your cursor is now active in the folder's name field. Type the new name in this field. My root folder is `C:\projects`.

   Java programs expect to have directories named in all lowercase characters, with no spaces in the folder names. This is part of the Java package naming convention. Get in the habit of naming your directories that way so that the JSP container will be able to navigate to the JSP and Java classes you're about to create.
4. **Within the `projects` folder, create a subfolder for the riddle program you're about to start.**

   I name my project folder `riddler`.
5. **Under the `riddler` folder, create two additional folders: `dynamic` and `WEB-INF`.**

   The first folder holds the JSPs and the second holds Java classes. The second folder *must* be named `WEB-INF` because the JSP container will look for that particular folder to get information about your JSP program.

I like to keep all the JSPs that I create under the same folder tree, named something like `dynamic`, to indicate that they're dynamically generated pages instead of static HTML pages. The exact name of the folder is not important, but experts generally agree that it's not a good idea to reveal the kind of technology you use when defining your project folder structure. Thus, creating a `jsp` folder for JSP pages is discouraged because it doesn't add anything to the Web experience of a typical user, and it reveals your implementation strategy to potential hackers who could use the information against you.

6. **In the `WEB-INF` folder, create an additional folder named `classes`.**

   This folder stores the Java programs used by the `riddler` program.

Getting Started with HTML Content

Most JSPs are just regular old Web pages with some code on the Web server to help make them dynamic. The place to start writing a JSP is to create a prototype of what the client should see. For the first JSP, I want to have some HTML code that asks the riddle question, and then some more HTML code that presents the possible answers. I need a form control (such as radio buttons) for the users to select which answer they believe is correct, and then a button to submit the page back to the server. Designing a prototype of this page is a good place to start.

In this book, I cover a lot of topics, but space doesn't permit much background on HTML other than in the code examples. For a more complete reference on HTML, get a copy of *HTML 4 For Dummies,* 3rd Edition, by Ed Tittel, Natanya Pitts, and Chelsea Valentine, published by Hungry Minds, Inc.

Creating this Web page or any JSP file doesn't require a fancy program editor. You can write a JSP file with a text editor such as Notepad, if you want. Working with a program editor can make things easier, though. ***Note:*** I wrote most of the examples in this book assuming that you're working with Notepad. There are a couple of places where I include a screen shot of Dreamweaver UltraDev, Version 4, just to give you an idea of what's possible.

If you'd like to try using an editor, take a look at this book's companion CD. I include a trial edition of Macromedia Dreamweaver UltraDev 4 for your convenience.

To create a JSP, follow these basic steps:

1. **Choose Start⇨Programs⇨Accessories⇨Notepad to launch the Notepad editor.**
2. **When the Notepad editor appears, type in code in the window.**

Later in this chapter in Listing 2-1, I give you the code for the `riddle` JavaServer page so that you can try it out for yourself.

3. **When you're finished editing your JSP, save your file by choosing File⇨Save As.**

   Be sure to save your `jsp` pages in the `dynamic` folder of your riddler project. For more information on folder structures, see the previous section "Creating a Project Folder Structure."

4. **Make sure to give your file name a `.jsp` extension; the JSP engine cannot run JSP unless they have a `.jsp` extension.**

A lot of text editors add special characters that you can't see, such as special formatting characters, to documents. These Casper-like characters can cause your program to crash. If you use a text editor other than Notepad, make sure to save your file in a plain text format.

When you save a file in Notepad by choosing File⇨Save, Notepad adds a `.txt` extension to the file by default. This is a problem because JSP containers require JSP pages to have a `.jsp` extension. To work around this issue, choose File⇨Save As and provide your JSP with a `.jsp` extension. If you already have files with this problem, open Windows Explorer, navigate to the folder where you saved your document, and rename the file, removing the `.txt` extension. You may get a warning message from the Windows operating system, but ignore it (like you probably do for 90 percent of the Windows warning messages that you see).

After you open Notepad, write the HTML code for the riddle application. You can follow the code I provide in Listing 2-1. The HTML code in a JSP is called *template data* because it does contribute to the dynamic behavior of the JSP. Any content of a JSP that isn't a language element of JSP is called template data.

You can find all the source code in this book on its companion CD. Writing this code yourself will help if you're just learning HTML, but if you don't want to write it out, just go to the CD and copy it. (If anyone questions this practice, just say that you're making a backup.) All the source code on the CD is organized in folders corresponding to the chapter the code appears in. This code is located in the Chapter 2 folder.

Listing 2-1: The HTML Code for the Random Riddle Prototype

```
<HTML>
<HEAD>
<TITLE> The JSP Random Riddle Application (from JSP For
          Dummies)</TITLE>
</HEAD>
```

```
<BODY>
<FORM NAME="RiddleForm" METHOD="post"
          ACTION="http://localhost:8080/dynamic/riddler.jsp"
          >
<CENTER><H1>CONGRATULATIONS! YOU GOT IT RIGHT!</H1></CENTER>
<CENTER><H1>SORRY. THAT'S THE WRONG ANSWER.</H1></CENTER>
<P>
Here's the solution: Indiana and Oklahoma

<CENTER><H1>Riddle Me This!</H1></CENTER>
<INPUT TYPE="hidden" NAME="riddleName" VALUE="capitalRiddle">
<P>
What are the only two states that have their state name in
          the name of their capital?
<P>
<INPUT TYPE="radio" NAME="answer" VALUE="A">Oregon and
          Washington
<BR>
<INPUT TYPE="radio" NAME="answer" VALUE="B">Texas and Utah
<BR>
<INPUT TYPE="radio" NAME="answer" VALUE="C">Indiana and
          Oklahoma
<BR>
<INPUT TYPE="radio" NAME="answer" VALUE="D">New Jersey and
          Oklahoma
<P>
Make your best guess and then click here for the solution:
<INPUT TYPE="submit" NAME="riddleSolution" VALUE="Click to
          check your answer">
</FORM>
</BODY>
</HTML>
```

After you finish creating this file, save it, making sure to place a `.jsp` extension at the end of the file name. Take a moment to review a few important elements of the code in Listing 2-1. Note that

- **Most of the page is nested inside a `<FORM>` tag.**

  This is necessary because a Web page will send only user input entered inside a `<FORM>` tag back to the server. Notice the value of the `ACTION` attribute for the `<FORM>` tag is `"http://localhost:8080/dynamic/riddler.jsp"`. This value is the Universal Resource Locator (URL) to the `riddler.jsp` page on my computer. (A *URL* is a unique address that tells computers where to find a file on the Internet.) When I deploy this page to the Web server, I need to change that path to a Web address such as `"http://www.mywebsite.com:8080/dynamic/riddler.jsp"`.

  For your project, you need to put your computer name in place of the `localhost` in my URL. If you plan on deploying this page to a Web site, you'll need to change the URL to point to the location on the Web site where you deploy your JSP. The term `localhost` simply tells the computer to look for the Web page on locally, instead of on the Internet.

1. To get the name of your computer, choose Start⇨Settings⇨Control Panel.
2. Double-click the Network icon in the Control Panel window.
3. Select the Identification tab of the Network window that appears.

   Find your computer name in the Computer Name text field.

- **The hidden field under the form tag is called `riddleName`.**

  This field is used to store the identity of the riddle posed to the user so that the server knows how to find the correct answer when this page is sent back to the server.

- **The four radio button fields all have the same name ("`answer`") and a different value ("`A`", "`B`", "`C`", and "`D`")**

  The browser will only allow the user to select one of those buttons because the names are all the same. Also, the browser will send at most one of those values back to the server, depending on which value the user selects.

- **The button on the end is a SUBMIT button.**

  Clicking the Submit button causes the page to be sent back to the server, sending the page back to the URL specified in the action attribute of the `<FORM>` tag.

In this prototype, the answer to the riddle is displayed with the riddle. When you add the JSP code, this won't happen anymore.

Before adding any of the dynamic content that gives JSP its name, test your prototype for HTML errors. But before you do, add the code in Listing 2-2 to the top of your JSP page, before the first HTML tag:

Listing 2-2: HTTP Header Instructions

```
<%
  if(request.getProtocol().equals("HTTP/1.1")){
    response.setHeader ("cache-control", "no-cache");
  }
  response.setHeader ("pragma","no-cache");
  response.setHeader ("expires","0");
%>
```

The code in this listing is actually your first server-side code. It tells the server and the browser whether this page should be cached, and how long it should be cached before it's considered out of date. Because JSPs present dynamic content to a client, disabling caching on servers and the client is a good idea. When the browser requests the page more than once, it gets recreated each time with up-to-date content.

In Listing 2-2, the `setHeader` statements control the caching behavior of the server and the client. The first two `setHeader` statements tell the proxy server not to cache this page. The last statement tells your browser that this page expires as soon as it's received, which prevents the browser from caching the page.

A *proxy server* is a server between the Web browser and the site that the browser connects to. If the proxy server has a cached page that the browser requests, it returns the cached page instead of going all the way to the source site. This caching makes Internet communication more efficient, except for when the content is dynamic and has to be rebuilt each time. The proxy server only has the static content generated from the server and doesn't have the ability to generate dynamic content.

Deploying JSPs

After you create your JSP, you've reached a milestone: It's time to deploy your page to Tomcat and test it. (Don't worry; no animals will be harmed during this procedure.) The first time that you set up Tomcat for a new project always involves a little work, but it's not that difficult. The basic steps are creating a folder structure, updating Tomcat's configuration files, and testing to verify the solution works. In the following sections, I cover all these issues.

Directory assistance please

If you follow the instructions (of course you did, right?) in the earlier section "Creating a Project Folder Structure," you create the folder structure exactly as the Tomcat JSP container expects. The task of deploying your JSP project is as simple as copying the directories from your project area to the deployment area for Tomcat. I cover those steps here.

To create a folder structure for your Tomcat application, follow these steps:

1. **Create a new folder under the `webapps` folder and name it after your project.**

   In this case, name it `riddler`. (Frank Gorshin would be proud.)

2. **Create a folder under `riddler` named `dynamic` to store your `jsp` files.**
3. **Create a folder named `WEB-INF` to store your Java source files.**

   You'll make use of this folder later.

4. **Create two folders under your `WEB-INF` file: `classes` and `lib`.**

All the folders under the WEB-INF directory are for Java class files and libraries. All the other folders are for Web content: images, static HTML pages, JSPs, and other downloadable Web content.

Configuring the Tomcat environment

After you create a directory structure for your Tomcat application, the next step to deployment is to create the configuration files for Tomcat. Tomcat configuration files are created using XML. If you haven't used XML before, don't worry — it's very simple.

An *XML file* is a file that contains data stored in tags similar to HTML tags. The definition of the tag structure for an XML file is stored in a corresponding Document Type Definition (DTD) file. The XML file contains a link to the DTD. When a program reads the XML file, it follows the link to the DTD file to get information about the file format. The good news is all the DTD configuration files for JSP containers are already created and accessible by your computer over the Internet. All you have to do to create the XML file is follow the directions I provide here.

For a complete reference on XML, take a look at *XML For Dummies,* 2nd Edition, by Ed Tittel and Frank Boumphrey, published by Hungry Minds, Inc.

For every JSP application that you create, you have to create one program configuration file and modify the configuration file for Tomcat so it knows where to find your project. The program configuration file is named web.xml, and your JSP container uses it to discover what kind of content you have in your JSP program and where to find that content. The web.xml file is stored in the WEB-INF directory for your project. You can create a web.xml file using the following steps:

1. **Open Notepad.**
2. **Type the contents of Listing 2-3 in your document (or copy them from the CD-ROM that accompanies this book).**
3. **Choose File⇨Save As and save your document as** web.xml **in the** WEB-INF **directory in the project folder you just created.**

Listing 2-3: web.xml Program Configuration File for Tomcat

```
<?xml version="1.0" encoding="ISO-8859-1"?>

<!DOCTYPE web-app PUBLIC "-//Sun Microsystems, Inc.//DTD Web
Application 2.3//EN" "http://java.sun.com/dtd/web-
          app_2_3.dtd">

<web-app>
</web-app>
```

The web.xml file from 30,000 feet

You don't really need to know much about XML to create the configuration files for Tomcat, but it's nice to have a couple of principles in order to understand the code above. The first line in Listing 3-3 tells what version of XML is used in this document. The second tag, `<!DOCTYPE>`, specifies what kind of XML document this is (in this case, a Web application) and where to find the `dtd` document. (No, you don't find `<!DOCTYPE>` tags pinned on white physician coats: Dr. Jones, ENT.) The DTD acronym stands for Document Type Definition, and `dtd` documents contain the definition of how XML files are structured. The `dtd` document is used to verify the content of this XML file is correctly formatted. Sun has the `dtd` file for the `web.xml` file on its Web site. In this example, the `<web-app>` tag doesn't contain anything. I cover the content of `web.xml` files in detail in Chapter 14.

After your project configuration file is in place, you need to add a reference to your `riddler` application in the Tomcat configuration file. This file is called `server.xml`. All the necessary steps to modify the `server.xml` file are listed below:

1. **Open Windows Explorer and navigate to the directory you installed Tomcat in.**
2. **In the `conf` directory, located in the root Tomcat directory, find the `server.xml` file, and open this file with Notepad.**
3. **To get to the portion of this file you need to modify, choose View➪Search from the Notepad menu and search for the text `<context path`.**

   You should see a tag that looks like the code in Listing 2-4.

Listing 2-4: Context Tag for the Tomcat Sample Application

```
<Context path="/examples"
     docBase="webapps/examples"
     crossContext="false"
     debug="0"
     reloadable="true" >
</Context>
```

The tag in Listing 2-4 is Tomcat's entry for example applications provided with the Tomcat install. You'll be creating an entry in this file very similar to the one in Listing 2-4 for your Web application. After the closing tag of the context information for the Tomcat examples application, create another context tag with the information in Listing 2-5 and save the file.

Listing 2-5: Context Tag for the riddler Application

```
<Context path="/riddler"
    docBase="webapps/riddler"
    defaultSessionTimeOut="30"
    crossContext="false"
    debug="0"
    reloadable="true">
</Context>
```

After you have this information saved in the `server.xml` file, restart Tomcat. Run `shutdown.bat`, and then run `startup.bat` in the `bin` directory under the Tomcat root directory. Here are the steps:

1. **In Windows Explorer, choose the `bin` directory from the root Tomcat directory.**

   In the `bin` directory, you'll find several different versions of the `startup` and `shutdown` files for Tomcat.

2. **If you're running Windows, you'll want to use the `startup.bat` and `shutdown.bat` files.**

   I recommend making shortcuts to these files on your computer desktop because you'll be running them often.

3. **To run the `shutdown.bat` and `startup.bat`, double-click each icon. Run `shutdown.bat` first.**

For Windows computers, to make shortcuts to the `startup.bat` and `shutdown.bat` programs on your computer's desktop, follow the directions below.

1. **Resize Windows Explorer so that you can see part of the desktop of your computer.**

2. **From Windows Explorer, navigate to the `bin` directory as indicated in the previous set of instructions.**

3. **Select the `startup.bat` icon. Hover the mouse over this icon and then right-click. Hold the mouse button down and drag the mouse across the screen until it's over a visible portion of your desktop. Release the mouse button.**

4. **From the menu that appears, click the Create Shortcut(s) Here option.**

   This creates a shortcut to `startup.bat` on your desktop. Repeat Steps 2–4 for the `shutdown.bat` file.

Testing 1, 2, 3 . . .

Configuring Tomcat may seem like a lot of work, but after you get used to it, it's pretty easy. The last step to testing the `riddler.jsp` page is to copy it to the `riddler/jsp` directory in Tomcat and run it. Testing is as easy as 1, 2, 3! Just follow these steps:

1. **Copy your JSP file to the `riddler/jsp` directory.**
2. **Launch your Web browser.**
3. **Type the following path:** http://<*server_name*>:8080/riddler/jsp/riddler.jsp **into your address bar, where `<server_name>` is replaced by the name of the computer that's running Tomcat.**

That's it! You should see a Web page similar to the page in Figure 2-1. By the way, this is just the prototype, not the finished product. JSPs are easy, but not that easy.

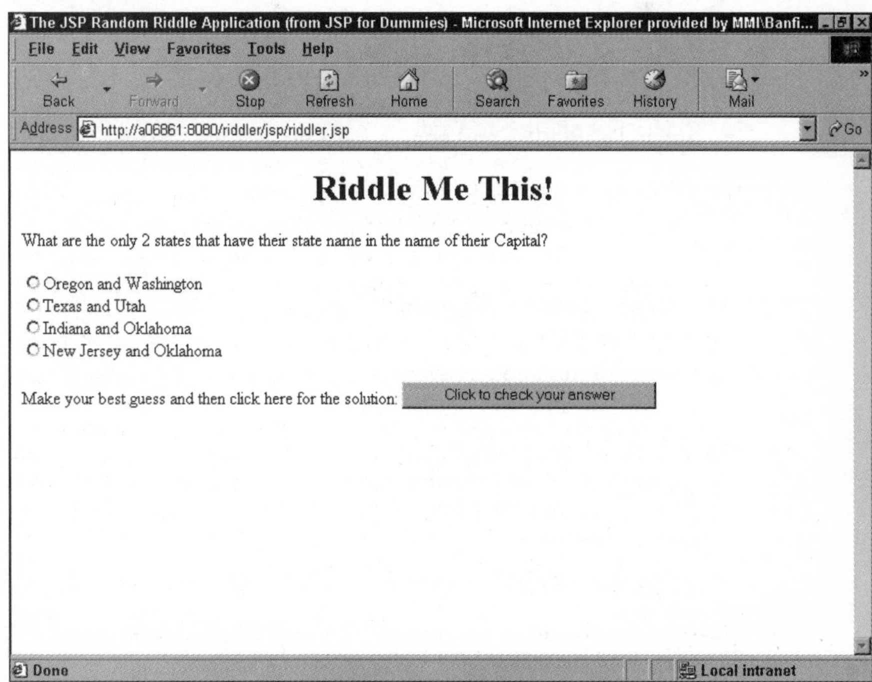

Figure 2-1: The riddler Web page.

If you have problems getting the riddler page displayed, skip to the section "Troubleshooting Your JSP Application" at the end of this chapter.

Going Dynamic

After you have a working prototype of your page, you must add the logic to your JSP to make it dynamic. One of the ways to do that is to use JavaBeans. JavaBeans are small, reusable Java programs that are embedded in JSP code using special tags. Good news for Web designers — you don't have to know beans — or Java, either — to use JavaBeans. JSP technology provides you with a way to use, set, and get JavaBean properties without writing Java code. The JavaBean is accessed with JSP tags, which are very similar to basic HTML tags.

I go into greater depth about the standard JSP tags and how they work in Chapter 3 and Chapter 4. For now, I'm not going to worry about all that background; I'm going to dig right in to embedding some dynamic server-side content.

Call me crazy, but I feel this would be a pretty boring Web page with only one riddle, so I plan to make all the riddle content dynamic. When working from a prototype, you can usually determine what parts need to be made dynamic by thinking about the audience you're presenting the Web page to.

Do you want to personalize some information based on who requests it? Do you want to have some content change randomly to keep your page new and interesting? These two opportunities are excellent clues for deciding when and where to insert dynamic content on a Web page. At any place in the JSP where you want content to change, you need to embed some JSP tags to make that part dynamic. Reviewing the prototype, the following elements are candidates for dynamic content:

- **The `riddleName` hidden field.** This field tells you which riddle the user is responding to. Thus, it needs to change every time a new riddle is displayed.
- **The riddle question.** Changing the question adds interest to your page and keeps users coming back for more. (Who wants to see the same riddle over and over?)
- **The riddle answers.** You can't change the question and not change the possible answers.
- **The riddle solution.** Again, the solution has to be for the riddle the user is responding to. (It would be rather embarrassing to show the same answer to every riddle in your riddle page!)

If you don't know Java, ask a Java programmer (nicely — remember, collaboration is the key) to write a JavaBean to provide the dynamic content for the page. Just for you, I created a JavaBean for this solution.

In order to make use of a JavaBean, you'll need to know some basic information about how to access information inside that bean. Each piece of information in a JavaBean is referred to as a *property*. In order to access these properties, you have to know their names. You also have to know the name for the bean. It's the responsibility of the Java developer (in this case, me) to publish the names of the JavaBeans and their properties. The following list tells you everything you need to know to work with the JavaBean I created for your riddler JSP.

- **The JavaBean is called `riddles.Riddler`.** In this name, `riddles` refers to the Java package that the Riddler bean is stored in. *Package* is Java lingo for a folder in your computer that contains Java programs. To make use of a JavaBean in your JSP page, you need to know the package it resides in. I address this subject in greater detail in Chapter 3.
- **The JavaBean has five properties for displaying a riddle and the possible answers:** `question`; `answerOne`; `answerTwo`; `answerThree`; and `answerFour`. The `question` property displays the current riddle. All the answer properties are for displaying the possible answers to the riddle.
- **The JavaBean has one property — `correctAnswer` — for getting the correct answer.**
- **The JavaBean has a method — `isCorrectOption()` — that reads the value of the option the user selects, and returns a true or false depending upon whether the selected option is correct.**
- **The JavaBean has one property — `riddleIndex` — to get the index for the current riddle.** The JavaBean has a list of riddles; the `riddleIndex` property tells the bean which riddle and possible answers to display on the JSP.

  Each time that a user requests the riddler JSP, the index in the JavaBean needs to be reset so that you can get a different riddle. In addition, to find the solution to a previously displayed riddle, you need to set the `riddleIndex` property to the value of the last riddle. To accomplish these two goals, I provided two methods that initialize the Riddler bean to the values that you need. The first, called `setRandomRiddleIndex()`, initializes the Riddler bean by selecting a random riddle for display in your JSP. The second, called `setRiddleIndex(int index)`, allows you to select a particular riddle based on the index value that you provide.

In the next section, "Tag, you're it. . . .," you see how to make use of the properties in this JavaBean and turn your static prototype Web page into a full-featured dynamic JSP.

Tag, you're it. . . .

JSPs are nothing more than Web pages with some special HTML-like elements used for inserting dynamic content. These special elements are called *tags,* and there are different kinds of JSP tags for performing different tasks. To turn your prototype JSP into a functioning dynamic Web page, you'll need to know a couple of these tags. The three tags you need to implement the riddler JSP are the `<jsp:useBean>`, `<jsp:getProperty>`, and `<jsp:setProperty>` tags. I provide a brief overview of their usage in this chapter. I provide more detail about these tags in Chapter 3.

One of the cool things about JSP tags is that the JSP container replaces the tag with the content you request. That means that the JSP tags are automatically removed before the page is sent to the user. If, for example, you want the content of an HTML element to be dynamic, you can place a JSP tag inside the `value` attribute for that HTML element, and the content you request will be automatically substituted for the JSP tag.

The JSP useBean tag

When you make use of a JavaBean in a JSP, you need to declare your intent to use the bean. Declaring the bean tells the JSP engine that it needs to get a copy of this JavaBean and make it ready for use. The `<jsp:useBean>` tag is the JSP tag that declares a bean. The syntax for the `<jsp:useBean>` tag is

```
<jsp:useBean id="<bean_name>" class="<bean_class>"
          scope="<bean_scope>"/>
```

The `<jsp:useBean>` tag has three attributes: `id`, `class`, and `scope`. I cover these attributes in greater detail in Chapter 3. For now, it's important to know the following:

- **`id`:** The `id` attribute is the name that you assign to the bean and that you use to make subsequent references to the bean with other JSP tags.
- **`class`:** The `class` attribute is the class name of the JavaBean. It needs to be a fully qualified class name, which means you provide the name of the JavaBean with package hierarchy in which it exists. (In the previous section "Going Dynamic," I discuss that the fully qualified name for the `riddler.jsp` page is `riddles.Riddler`. Type **`riddles.Riddler`** in the class attribute for the `<jsp:useBean>` tag.)
- **`scope`:** The `scope` attribute tells the JSP engine how long to maintain a copy of this bean for you. I cover all the possible scopes in detail for you in Chapter 3. For now, use a scope called `request`, which means that the bean will be available until you send the page back to the user who requests it.

The JSP getProperty tag

When you want to display the content of a JavaBean property in a JSP, you do so with the `<jsp:getProperty>` tag. The syntax for this tag follows:

```
<jsp:getProperty name="<bean_name>"
          property="<property_name>"/>
```

The `<jsp:getProperty>` tag has two attributes: `name` and `property`. These attributes tell the JSP engine which bean to request the property from, and which property to request from that bean.

- **`name`:** The `name` attribute refers to the `id` that you supply to the bean in the `<jsp:useBean>` tag described above. For example, if you give the bean the `id` of *riddles*, you type **`riddles`** in for the `name` attribute.
- **`property`:** The `property` attribute refers to the name of the property that you want to get out of the JavaBean. For example, you need to get the `riddleIndex` in the JSP, so you type **`riddleIndex`** in to get the value of that property.

I provide more information on the `<jsp:getProperty>` tag in Chapter 3.

The JSP setProperty Tag

When you need to set the value of a property in a JavaBean, you use the `<jsp:setProperty>` tag. One reason for using the `<jsp:setProperty>` tag is to supply a value to the JavaBean so that it can do some special calculation for you. The syntax of the `<jsp:setProperty>` tag follows:

```
<jsp:setProperty name="<bean_name>"
          property="<property_name>"
          value="<property_value>"/>
```

The `set` property tag has three attributes: `name`, `property`, and `value`.

- **`name`:** The first attribute is `name`, which is replaced with the `id` that you assign to the JavaBean in the `<jsp:useBean>` tag identified above.
- **`property`:** The second attribute is `property`. This attribute identifies which property in the specified bean that you want to set.
- **`value`:** The third attribute is the `value`, which identifies the value that you want to set the property to.

When you use a JavaBean in your JSP, you must put the `<jsp:useBean>` tag first before you make any other references to that tag. After the `<jsp:useBean>` tag, you also have to perform any initialization steps specified by the bean developer before you can make use of the bean.

Handling how to provide the correct response to a user's guess requires a different kind of solution than the bean approach. I discuss responding to the user's guess in the next section, "Controlling output with JSP scriptlets." Here I focus on embedding the JavaBean in your JSP (planting beans, as it were). To do so, perform the following steps:

1. **Close to the top of your JSP, type the `<jsp:useBean>` tag `<jsp:useBean id="riddler" class="riddles.Riddler" scope="request"/>`.**

   This code notifies the JSP that it's going to make use of a JavaBean named Riddler, which is located in a package called `riddles`. In this tag, the `id` attribute is the name that you use when referring to the JavaBean. The class is the name of the class for that JavaBean. The scope says how long the JavaBean is visible for. I cover scope in greater detail in Chapter 3.

   In Java lingo, a directory that contains Java files is referred to as a *package*. When I use the term *package*, I'm referring to a specific directory with Java classes in it.

2. **Immediately after the `<jsp:useBean>` tag, you need to initialize the bean's `riddleIndex` property by creating a scriptlet with the following code: `<%riddler.setRandomRiddleIndex();%>`.**

   This scriptlet tells the JavaBean to randomly pick a new riddle to display on the page.

3. **In each location where you want to present dynamic content, create a `<jsp:getProperty>` tag that gets the value of the property you want to display.**

   In Listing 2-6, I show examples of where to place the `<jsp:getProperty>` tags so that you can see how they are used in context. Note in the listing that I place some `<jsp:getProperty>` tags inside the value attributes for HTML elements. When the JSP is run, the `<jsp:getProperty>` tag is replaced with the content of that property, so only the value that you want is sent to the user's browser.

When finished, your JSP should look something like the page in Listing 2-6.

Be sure to save your updated JSP file and replace the prototype in your `riddler\jsp` directory with this new copy.

Listing 2-6: riddler.jsp with JSP Tags

```
<%
  if(request.getProtocol().equals("HTTP/1.1")){
    response.setHeader ("cache-control", "no-cache");
  }
```

```
  response.setHeader ("pragma","no-cache");
  response.setHeader ("expires","0");
%>
<jsp:useBean id="riddler" class="riddles.Riddler"
           scope="request"/>
<%riddler.setRandomRiddleIndex();%>
<HTML>
<HEAD>
<TITLE> The JSP Random Riddle Application (from JSP For
           Dummies)</TITLE>
</HEAD>
<BODY>
<FORM NAME="RiddleForm" METHOD="post" ACTION=
           "http://localhost:8080/dynamic/riddler.jsp">
<CENTER><H1>CONGRATULATIONS! YOU GOT IT RIGHT!</H1></CENTER>
<CENTER><H1>SORRY. THAT'S THE WRONG ANSWER.</H1></CENTER>
<P>
Here's the solution: <jsp:getProperty name="riddler"
           property="correctAnswer"/>
<CENTER><H1>Riddle Me This!</H1></CENTER>
<INPUT TYPE="hidden" NAME="riddleIndex"
           VALUE="<jsp:getProperty name="riddler"
           property="riddleIndex"/>">
<P>
<jsp:getProperty name="riddler" property="question"/>
<P>
<INPUT TYPE="radio" NAME="answer"
           VALUE="One"><jsp:getProperty name="riddler"
           property="answerOne"/>
<BR>
<INPUT TYPE="radio" NAME="answer"
           VALUE="Two"><jsp:getProperty name="riddler"
           property="answerTwo"/>
<BR>
<INPUT TYPE="radio" NAME="answer"
           VALUE="Three"><jsp:getProperty name="riddler"
           property="answerThree"/>
<BR>
<INPUT TYPE="radio" NAME="answer"
           VALUE="Four"><jsp:getProperty name="riddler"
           property="answerFour"/>
<P>
Make your best guess and then click here for the solution:
<INPUT TYPE="submit" NAME="riddleSolution" VALUE="Click to
           check your answer">
</FORM>
</BODY>
</HTML>
```

Controlling output with JSP scriptlets

The final detail is to specify conditionally whether the answer provided by the user is correct or not. This requires the use of a JSP scriptlet, which is the way that JSP enables developers to embed Java in the JSP. JSP scriptlets are delimited by `<%` and `%>` tags. Each time you see the `<%` and `%>` tags in a JSP, you know that the code in between is a scriptlet.

Did I write *embed Java in the JSP*? Yep, and this is exactly the kind of situation that calls for careful consideration. In this page, I plan to use scriptlets to decide whether the user picked the correct answer and then display the appropriate message. I do that because some conditional decision-making is a little more complicated than a `<jsp:useBean>` tag can handle.

When you add the complexity of JSP scriptlets to a JSP, determining what steps are necessary to implement the behavior necessary for handling that complexity is a good idea. The issue that I'm handling with JSP scriptlets is controlling whether a riddle answer is visible — and, if it is visible, which answer is visible. Your JSP needs to perform a couple of basic steps to handle this problem.

1. **The JSP needs to determine whether the user needs to have a solution for a riddle displayed.**

   This is fairly simple. When users make a request for your JSP, they could be coming to the page for the first time, or they could be submitting the page to get a solution. If they're submitting the riddle page for a solution, all the elements in the HTML page will be sent back to the server. Thus, if those elements are sent back to the server, you know that they must have submitted your page. Otherwise, they will be visiting for the first time.

   The scriptlet that I wrote uses this fact to determine whether an answer should be provided. If this is the first visit, the elements of the `riddler.jsp` page are not submitted, and you won't provide a riddle solution in the response. Otherwise, you will provide a riddle solution . . . but which one will it be?

2. **The JSP needs to determine which solution to display to the user.**

   If you find that a riddle solution is necessary, the next step is to determine which riddle solution to display. This is a simple problem. Review the `riddler.jsp` code, and you'll see that I include a hidden field that contains the name of the riddle presented to a user. When the user sends the response back, that field is available to read. Thus, each time you need to know which answer to show, you show the answer for the riddle with the same name as name in the hidden field.

The code in Listing 2-7 is an excerpt from the `riddler.jsp` file that shows how to accomplish the two steps above. For now, don't worry about the details; consider this code as a gift from your friendly developer (that's me). For more information on JSP scriptlets, read through Chapter 4. Some of the code in Listing 2-7 makes use of JSP implicit objects, such as the request object. You can find more information on that topic in Chapter 7.

Listing 2-7: The Scriptlet Code for riddler.jsp

```
...
<FORM NAME="RiddleForm" METHOD="post" ACTION="submitURL">
<%
if(request.getParameter("riddleIndex") != null){

            riddler.setRiddleIndex(request.getParameter("riddl
            eIndex"));
if(riddler.isCorrectOption(request.getParameter("answer")){
%>
<CENTER><H1>CONGRATULATIONS! YOU GOT IT RIGHT!</H1></CENTER>
<%
       }
       else{
%>
<CENTER><H1>SORRY. THAT'S THE WRONG ANSWER.</H1></CENTER>
<%
       }
%>
<P>
Here's the solution: <jsp:getProperty name="riddler"
            property="correctAnswer"/>
<%
    }
%>
```

Note that I have pure HTML code in between my scriptlet tags. When the JSP executes, it will print only the HTML in between the true conditions in the Java code. Thus, if this is not the first request, none of the HTML code from Listing 2-7 is displayed.

Building Java Classes

After you embed the JSP tags in your JSP, you're almost finished. The only step that remains is to build the Java class files that are used by your JSP application. The classes for this example are located on the CD-ROM at the back of this book. If you don't have access to the CD, I supply the code for creating the class in this section. If you have the CD, follow these steps:

1. **Go to the Chapter 2 folder on the CD.**
2. **Copy the `riddler` folder and its contents to the `WEB-INF\classes` folder in your riddler project.**

Java is a case-sensitive language. If you aren't copying the code from the CD, be sure to type the folder and file names exactly as they appear or you'll have errors when you try to run the `riddler` program.

If you don't have the CD, or would like to create the classes on your own, follow these steps:

1. **Create a folder under the `WEB-INF\classes` directory for your project. For this example, call it `riddler`.**
2. **Launch Notepad.**
3. **Create three separate files with the content shown in Listings 2-8, 2-9, and 2-10.**
4. **Save these files as `RiddlerInterface.java`, `Riddler.java`, and `RiddleQuestion.java`, respectively, in the `riddler` folder.**

Be sure that you create a separate file for each class, and be sure to give each file the same name as the class and add a `.java` extension.

Over the next several pages, I list all the code that's necessary to complete the Java classes for this project. I've already written the code for you, so you don't have to be a Java wizard to finish your first solution. In addition, I've

Class action primer

If you're not familiar with Java, you're probably wondering what I mean by all this Java class stuff. The Java language is an object-oriented language, which means that programs written in Java are intended to be broken into little pieces of related code called *objects*. For example, when you think of an object, there are concrete items (like an apple) or abstract items (like a fruit).

If you write a program in Java containing a representation of an apple and a representation of a fruit, you create two separate files: one with code for the apple, and one with code for the fruit. When you compile these files — turning them into the code that a computer can read — you turn them into *class files*. You create two classes: one of the type apple, and another of the type fruit.

Conceptually, a class is like a category of some kind of object. The class file tells your computer how to create an instance of the type of object it represents. So when your computer needs to create an apple, it looks at the apple class for the code to create an apple object.

This explanation is a little simplistic, but good enough if you aren't going to be working with Java a lot. Just remember that many people use the word *class* as a substitute for a file that contains Java code.

tested everything to make sure that it works. In fact, if you don't want to transcribe this code, you can just skip down to the next section, "Compiling Java code."

Here's what these do. Listing 2-8 contains a Java program called an interface. An *interface* is a program that defines a set of methods that other Java programs can implement, but it doesn't tell exactly how they should be implemented. The other two classes *implement* this interface, meaning that all the methods defined in the interface are included in the other two classes.

You may hear people say that class A communicates to class B through class B's interface. Class A is accessing the methods in class B, which are defined in an interface implemented by class B. To put it simply, an interface is a medium for classes to talk to each other, but doesn't tell them what to say.

The code in Listing 2-9 is for a class called `Riddler`. Basically, this class contains a bunch of riddles. It implements the `RiddlerInterface`, which gives your JSPs a standard way to talk to the class. Your JSP interacts directly with the `Riddler` class. The JSP can ask the `Riddler` class for a riddle, in which case the `Riddler` class just gets a random riddle. Or your JSP can ask the `Riddler` class for a specific riddle, and the `Riddler` class gets that specific riddle.

After the `Riddler` class gets a riddle, the JSP asks the `Riddler` class for specific information about the riddle. It asks for the question, then the possible answers; and after a user attempts to answer the riddle, the JSP checks to see what the actual answer is.

The code in Listing 2-10 is for a class called `Riddle`. The `Riddle` class just contains all the information associated with a particular riddle. Basically, the information about a riddle belongs to that riddle. So when the JSP asks the `Riddler` for a riddle question, the `Riddler` class turns around and asks the `Riddle` class what its question is. The `Riddle` class tells the `Riddler`, and the `Riddler` tells your JSP. The `RiddlerInterface` ensures that both the `Riddler` class and the `Riddle` class have the same methods so that they can maintain a chain of communication with each other to get all the information that the JSP requests. Thus a new caste of riddle bureaucrats is born, plotting to take over your computer with their twisted, wily doubletalk.

Listing 2-8: RiddlerInterface.java

```
package riddles;

public interface RiddleInterface {

  String getQuestion();
  String getAnswerTwo();
  String getAnswerThree();
```

(continued)

Listing 2-8 *(continued)*

```
  String getAnswerFour();
  String getAnswerOne();
  String getCorrectAnswer();
  boolean isCorrectOption( String answer );
}
```

Listing 2-9: Riddler.java

```
package riddles;

import java.util.*;

public class Riddler implements RiddleInterface {
  private Vector riddles;
  private int riddleIndex;
  private String correctOption;

  public Riddler() {
    String question = "What are the only 2 states that have
          their state name in the name of their Capital? ";
    String answer1 = "Oregon and Washington";
    String answer2 = "Texas and Utah";
    String answer3 = "Indiana and Oklahoma";
    String answer4 = "New Jersey and Oklahoma";
    String correctAnswer = "Indiana and Oklahoma";
    String correctOption = "three";
    riddles.add( new RiddleQuestion( question,
      answer1,
      answer2,
      answer3,
      answer4,
      correctAnswer ) );

    question = "What is the next letter in the series: 'B, C,
          D, E, G,...'? Why?";
    answer1 = "I";
    answer2 = "J";
    answer3 = "X";
    answer4 = "P";
    correctAnswer = "The next letter would be P. They all
          rhyme.";
    String correctOption = "four";
    riddles.add( new RiddleQuestion( question,
      answer1,
      answer2,
      answer3,
      answer4,
      correctAnswer ) );

    question = "What are the next two letters in this series:
          A E F H I K L M ?";
```

```
answer1 = "O and Z";
answer2 = "N and T";
answer3 = "S and R";
answer4 = "V and X";
correctAnswer = "N and T are next. Why? These are of the
       alphabet that do not curve.";
String correctOption = "two";
riddles.add( new RiddleQuestion( question,
  answer1,
  answer2,
  answer3,
  answer4,
  correctAnswer ) );

question = "If you wrote all the numbers from 300 to 400
       on a piece of paper, how many times would you have
       written the number 3?";
answer1 = "85";
answer2 = "110";
answer3 = "135";
answer4 = "120";
correctAnswer = "120";
String correctOption = "four";
riddles.add( new RiddleQuestion( question,
  answer1,
  answer2,
  answer3,
  answer4,
  correctAnswer ) );

question = "What are the next two letters in the
       following series and why? W A T N T L I T F S _
       _";
answer1 = "A and W";
answer2 = "M and T";
answer3 = "J and V";
answer4 = "R and U";
correctAnswer = "A and W (and why) - The pattern is the
       first letter of every word in the sentence.";
String correctOption = "one";
riddles.add( new RiddleQuestion( question,
  answer1,
  answer2,
  answer3,
  answer4,
  correctAnswer ) );

question = "These words belong to the same logical
       family:<BR>UNDECEIVABLE<BR>SIMULTANEOUS<BR>ALIMENT
       ATION<BR>CAUTIOUSNESS<BR>GLADIATORIAL<BR>FORAMINIF
       ERA<BR>Which of these words belongs too? Why?";
answer1 = "PHILANTHROPY";
```

(continued)

Listing 2-9 *(continued)*

```
    answer2 = "SEISMOLOGIST";
    answer3 = "ONOMATOPOEIA";
    answer4 = "REAPPEARANCE";
    correctAnswer = "REAPPEARANCE (All have 6 vowels and 6
           consonants.)";
    String correctOption = "four";
    riddles.add( new RiddleQuestion( question,
      answer1,
      answer2,
      answer3,
      answer4,
      correctAnswer ) );

    question = "Which of the following words don't belong in
           the group and why?<BR>CORSET, COSTER, SECTOR,
           ESCORT, COURTS";
    answer1 = "COURTS";
    answer2 = "COSTER";
    answer3 = "SECTOR";
    answer4 = "CORSET";
    correctAnswer = "COURTS. The remaining words are anagrams
           of each other.";
    String correctOption = "one";
    riddles.add( new RiddleQuestion( question,
      answer1,
      answer2,
      answer3,
      answer4,
      correctAnswer ) );

    question = "What animal can you spell using the letters:
           W-E-A-L-U?";
    answer1 = "ELEPHANT";
    answer2 = "ZEBRA";
    answer3 = "TIGER";
    answer4 = "CAMEL";
    correctAnswer = "Camel: Turn the W over to make an M, and
           turn the U sideways to make a C.";
    String correctOption = "four";
    riddles.add( new RiddleQuestion( question,
      answer1,
      answer2,
      answer3,
      answer4,
      correctAnswer ) );

  }

  public String getQuestion() {
    if( riddles.get( riddleIndex ) != null ) {
      return ( ( RiddleQuestion )riddles.get( riddleIndex )
           ).getQuestion();
```

```
    }
    else {
      return "riddleIndex has not been initialized";
    }
  }

  public String getAnswerTwo() {
    if( riddles.get( riddleIndex ) != null ) {
      return ( ( RiddleQuestion )riddles.get( riddleIndex )
          ).getAnswerTwo();
    }
    else {
      return "riddleIndex has not been initialized";
    }
  }

  public void setRandomRiddleIndex() {
    Random randInt = new Random();
    if( riddles.size() > 0 ) {
      riddleIndex = randInt.nextInt( riddles.size() );
    }
  }

  public String getAnswerThree() {
    if( riddles.get( riddleIndex ) != null ) {
      return ( ( RiddleQuestion )riddles.get( riddleIndex )
          ).getAnswerThree();
    }
    else {
      return "riddleIndex has not been initialized";
    }
  }

  public String getAnswerFour() {
    if( riddles.get( riddleIndex ) != null ) {
      return ( ( RiddleQuestion )riddles.get( riddleIndex )
          ).getAnswerFour();
    }
    else {
      return "riddleIndex has not been initialized";
    }
  }

  public String getAnswerOne() {
    if( riddles.get( riddleIndex ) != null ) {
      return ( ( RiddleQuestion )riddles.get( riddleIndex )
          ).getAnswerOne();
    }
    else {
      return "riddleIndex has not been initialized";
    }
```

(continued)

Listing 2-9 ***(continued)***

```
  }

  public String getCorrectAnswer() {
    if( riddles.get( riddleIndex ) != null ) {
      return ( ( RiddleQuestion )riddles.get( riddleIndex )
           ).getCorrectAnswer();
    }
    else {
      return "riddleIndex has not been initialized";
    }
  }

  public void setRiddleIndex( int index ) {
    riddleIndex = index;
  }

  public int getRiddleIndex() {
    return riddleIndex;
  }

  public boolean isCorrectOption( String answer ) {
    return
         ((RiddleQuestion)riddles.get(riddleIndex)).isCorre
         ctOption(answer);
  }
}
```

Listing 2-10: RiddleQuestion.java

```
package riddles;

public class RiddleQuestion implements RiddleInterface{
  private String answerOne;
  private String answerTwo;
  private String answerThree;
  private String answerFour;
  private String correctAnswer;
  private String question;
  private String correctOption;

  public RiddleQuestion() {}

  public RiddleQuestion(
    String question,
    String answer1,
    String answer2,
    String answer3,
    String answer4,
    String correctAnswer,
```

```
    String correctOption ) {

    this.question = question;
    this.answerOne = answer1;
    this.answerTwo = answer2;
    this.answerThree = answer3;
    this.answerFour = answer4;
    this.correctAnswer = correctAnswer;
    this.correctOption = correctOption;
  }

  public String getQuestion() {
    return question;
  }

  public String getAnswerTwo() {
    return answerTwo;
  }

  public String getAnswerThree() {
     return answerThree;
  }

  public String getAnswerFour() {
    return answerFour;
  }

  public String getAnswerOne() {
     return answerOne;
  }

  public String getCorrectAnswer() {
    return correctAnswer;
  }

  public boolean isCorrectOption( String answer ) {
    if( this.correctOption.equalsIgnoreCase( answer ) ) {
      return true;
    }
    return false;
  }
}
```

Compiling Java code

If you're creating the Java classes on your own, you need to compile them before they can be deployed. When you compile Java code, it gets converted from the Java language to a new format called Java Byte Code. This Java Byte Code gets stored in a new file with the same name as the file that you compile but with a `.class` extension. The Java Byte Code is the code that your computer reads when you run Java programs. If you have a Java code editor such as JBuilder, follow the instructions with the editor. If you use the Java SDK to compile your code, follow these directions:

1. **Open the command prompt window (DOS) by choosing Start⇨Run, typing** CMD.EXE**, and pressing Enter.**
2. **At the command prompt, type** javac <path_to_java_files>*.java **(for example:** `javac c:\riddler\*.java`**), and press Enter.**

If you don't have any compilation errors, you should get the command prompt again with no messages; otherwise, you'll have to correct the errors identified by the compiler.

On this book's companion CD, I provide the compiled class files for you. I recommend that you use these class files — which have already been thoroughly tested — if you're not familiar with Java.

If you'd like to go through the process of writing the code yourself and compiling the classes, be prepared to get errors. Even I get compiler errors on occasion. (I know you're shocked, but I cannot tell a lie.) It's difficult to understand what the compiler says when a mistake is made. My advice is to be sure to check for typographical errors first, and then make sure that you have proper punctuation in your statements. Usually that solves the problems.

Deploying the Java Code

You're almost finished! The only step remaining in creating your first dynamic JSP is to deploy the Java class files. After you compile the `.java` classes, you'll find a `.class` file with the same name as each `.java` file in the `riddler` directory. These files are the compiled Java code. Tomcat needs the `.class` files to generate dynamic content in your JSP.

Deploying these files is the same as deploying the files from the CD at the back of this book. Simply copy the `riddler` directory with your `.class` files from its present location into the `WEB-INF\classes` folder for your JSP program directory. Next, restart Tomcat. (Although you don't have to restart Tomcat if you are deploying new JSP files — or replacing old ones — you do have to restart Tomcat each time you deploy or change any of the content in the `WEB-INF` directory.) Running the full-featured JSP is the same as running the prototype — just type the URL to your `riddler.jsp` file in the browser.

The `riddle` directory is a Java package that contains the classes you create. When you deploy the Java classes, copy the `riddle` directory with all its contents into the `WEB-INF\classes` folder for your Tomcat deployment directory.

Troubleshooting Your JSP Application

In a perfect world, code works perfectly! In my world, things are imperfect. That's why I compiled this (long) list of troubleshooting tips to help address any problems that you might have with my examples. Even if you don't have trouble in your code, take a look at these troubleshooting strategies and file them away for future reference. Even the most infallible superheroes trip up every now and then.

Problem: When I run the JSP prototype or final solution, some of the page shows up in the browser but then it stops abruptly without loading completely.

Solution: This happens because the Web server sends part of the JSP to your computer and then encounters an error and stops. You're probably missing a close tag (>) after the last piece of text displayed in your HTML page. This close tag could either be a JSP or a HTML tag. Paragraph tags don't have to be closed (`<P>`), but other elements do.

Problem: I get a `Page Cannot Be Displayed` message when I type in the URL specified for the prototype or the final JSP solution.

Solution: First verify that Tomcat is started. If it is started, then verify that you typed the correct URL into your browser. Also verify that all the information in your context tag of your `server.xml` file is entered correctly, and verify that the content of the `web.xml` file is correct. The solution will most likely be found in one of these places.

Problem: I'm using Internet Explorer, and I get an `Error 404` message when I attempt to run the JSP.

Solution: `Error 404` is the catchall, friendly-but-nebulous error message for Internet Explorer. In other words, `Error 404` doesn't really tell you what's going on. When you're working with JSP programming, you'll want to get the exact error message. To do this, in Explorer, choose Tools⇨Internet Options. Click the Advanced tab, and clear (deselect) the `Show friendly HTTP error messages` check box. Click the Apply button and the close the options window. Try to run the JSP again, and this time you should get a more precise error message.

Problem: When I compile my Java code, I get the message `Public class <class_name> must be defined in a file called <class_name>.java.`

Solution: Verify that the name of your class and that the name of the file you stored your class in are the same name. They must also have their letters written in the same case.

Problem: When I compile my Java code, I get the message `Missing or Incorrect Package Statement`.

Solution: The `riddler` classes are in the package `riddler`. Make sure that all your classes have a statement on the first line that reads `package riddler`. Also verify that the files are stored in a directory named `riddler`. Remember that the case of the letters is important.

Problem: When I try to run the final solution for the `riddler` application, I get a stack trace with this message: `Cannot create bean of class riddles.Riddler`.

Solution: This message is displayed when your JavaBean code does not conform to the JavaBean specification. Check the following possible causes:

- The JavaBean class must have a constructor that takes no arguments.
- The non-primitive member variables of a JavaBean class must be initialized upon declaration.

For more detail on JavaBeans and the rules for creating them, see Chapter 8.

Part II
JSP for Web Designers

The 5th Wave
By Rich Tennant
Re·al Pro·gram·mers
Real Programmers know a lot about Java, but never know how to use the coffee machine.

In this part . . .

JavaServer Pages (JSP) technology envisions a sharing of development responsibility between Web designers and Java programmers. The content developers work primarily on the user interface of the JSP program while Java developers focus on creating software components that Web designers can incorporate into JSPs.

This part focuses on features of JSP technology and JavaScript that Web designers can use to build great user interfaces. But there's something for everyone, particularly in Chapters 3 and 4. In Chapter 3, you discover the complete scope of JSP standard tags. Chapter 4 dives into JSP scripting elements, which are used to integrate Java code into a JSP page.

Chapters 5 and 6 are devoted to illuminating JavaScript, which Web developers will find incredibly useful for performing user input validation. Chapter 5 provides an overview of JavaScript syntax, and Chapter 6 explores several useful validation rules that you can incorporate directly into your JSP application. If you're not working with JSP user interfaces, you can skip these chapters.

Chapter 3

Activating JSP Pages with Action Tags

In This Chapter

- Discovering the power of JSP actions
- Working with JavaBeans
- Nesting JSP pages inside JSP pages
- Forwarding action from one JSP page to another
- Working with browser plug-ins

JavaServer Pages (JSPs) are basically Web pages with some special JSP elements that interact with your Web server to supply dynamic content. There are different kinds of JSP elements, depending on what you need to do. This chapter covers a group of JSP elements called actions tags. *Action tags* are XML-like elements that tell your Web server to do something special.

Sometimes when people are talking about action tags, they shorten the term to *actions*. You'll also hear people refer to action tags simply as *tags*. To add to the techno-jargon jumble, when super-geeks talk about action tags in general and not a specific tag, they call them *action tags*. To limit the confusion, I refer to all of them as action tags unless I refer to a specific kind of tag. When I refer to a specific tag, I call it by its given name, such as `<jsp:useBean>` tag, which is one kind of action tag.

This chapter focuses on a particular group of action tags called standard actions. *Standard actions* are action tags defined by the JSP specification and available to all JSP programmers. Here's a preview of the eight standard action tags and what they do:

- The `<jsp:useBean>` tag allows you to embed *JavaBeans*, which are small Java programs, in your JSP pages.
- The `<jsp:setProperty>` tag allows you to assign a value to a JavaBean property. A *JavaBean property* is basically a variable in a JavaBean that holds some information.

- The `<jsp:getProperty>` tag allows you to get a value from a JavaBean property. You use this tag to get dynamic data from the JavaBean and place it in the JSP.
- The `<jsp:include>` tag allows you to include the content of another JSP in the current page.
- The `<jsp:forward>` tag allows you to direct a user from one JSP to another on your Web server. This is often referred to as a *redirect* because you force the user along a different path than the one they originally requested.
- The `<jsp:plugin>` tag allows you to embed an applet or a visual JavaBean into your JSP and send it to the user's browser. *Applets* and *visual JavaBeans* are little Java programs run by a host program called a plug-in, which is located in the user's browser.
- The `<jsp:param>` tag is nested inside `<jsp:include>`, `<jsp:forward>`, or `<jsp:plugin>` tags, and is used to send parameter values to the included JSP or plug-in program.
- The `<jsp:params>` tag is nested inside the `<jsp:plugin>` tag and contains all the `<jsp:param>` tags for the plug-in program. The `<jsp:params>` tag is only used with `<jsp:plugin>` tags.

Another group of action tags is custom tags. *Custom tags* are JSP action tags defined by third-party vendors as extensions to the standard action tags. Chapter 12 is entirely devoted to custom tags. In that chapter, you discover the process for including custom tags in your JSP applications. I also illustrate the process of creating your own custom tags.

This chapter is primarily directed toward Web designers because it deals with the creating of JSPs and not the development of Java programs. However, I recommend that Java developers review the material because it will help you get familiar with the needs of your Web designer brethren.

Although you can definitely accomplish a lot with action tags, they aren't the be-all and end-all of JSP programming. There are other JSP elements that you'll often need to use in addition to action tags in order to get the job done. I provide a little background on these other elements as necessary, just to maintain the continuity of the chapter.

Generating Dynamic Content with Bean Tags

One of the most common uses of action tags is interacting with JavaBeans in your JSP page. That's reflected by the fact that JavaBeans have three standard action tags all to themselves. These three tags are generically referred to as *bean tags*. The three action tags for working with JavaBeans are the `<jsp:useBean>` tag, the `<jsp:setProperty>` tag, and the `<jsp:getProperty>` tag.

JavaBeans come up over and over in JSP application development, and are critical to making a JSP application. You might be wondering what makes them so great. JavaBeans are often called *components* because they plug into a program just like stereo components plug into a stereo system. Writing programs with JavaBeans makes those programs easy to reuse — you can plug the same JavaBean programs into any JSP or Java program. And when the JavaBean changes, you just update it once and all the programs that use it are automatically updated. The bottom line is that slackers like myself love JavaBeans because they correlate to less work and more play!

To drive the relevance of the bean tags home, I'll be illustrating the use of each tag by creating a sample login page for a JSP application. This example is incrementally assembled as the chapter progresses, illustrating the use of each tag along the way. In the end, you end up with a JSP that illustrates the use of the standard JSP actions and the use of a JavaBean to support the pages behavior.

JSPs are used to present information, and JavaBeans are used to generate dynamic information. Thus, the JavaBean does all the work and the JSP reaps all the benefits. For some reason, this relationship seems vaguely Dilbertesque. Nonetheless, it is one fundamental principle behind quality JSP programs.

To help keep the focus on the action tags, I provide all the JavaBean code necessary to complete the example on this book's companion CD. The JavaBean used for this example is `LoginBean`. You'll also need another Java class called `LoginException`. You can find both under the `Chapter 3` folder on the CD.

Understanding JavaDoc documentation

In order to make use of a component like the `LoginBean`, you must first know how to reference and interact with it. To make it easier to understand how a Java program, or class, is used, JavaSoft created the JavaDoc specification. *JavaDoc* is a standard HTML documentation format generated automatically from special comments written by Java developers inside the programs that they code. If you have a Java developer supplying you with JavaBeans, he or she should also supply you with a JavaDoc that describes how to use the beans in a JSP.

In Figure 3-1, you can see a view of the JavaDoc for the `LoginBean` I created. For more information, you can browse the JavaDoc and the source code for this bean on the CD that accompanies this book.

JavaDoc Web pages typically contain the fully qualified name of a class, a field summary section (shown in Figure 3-1), and a method summary (not visible in Figure 3-1). The *fully qualified name* of a Java class is the name including the names of the packages in which the class is contained. A *package* is a folder that contains a related set of Java classes, and it can contain other Java packages.

When typing the fully qualified name of a class, you type each package that contains the bean, separated by a period (.), and the class name last. In the JavaDoc illustrated in Figure 3-1, the package name that contains this bean is `security`, displayed in bold directly above the name of the bean. The fully qualified name for this bean is `security.LoginBean`.

The field summary identifies and describes the fields in a Java class. The method summary identifies and describes the methods in a Java class. Each of the methods and fields has a hyperlink to a more detailed explanation, respectively located in the method detail and field detail sections later on the same page.

All Classes

Packages
security

security
Classes
LoginBean
LoginException

security
Class LoginBean

public class **LoginBean**

The LoginBean is an example JavaBean created to illustrate the use of JavaDoc for communicating the function of Java Classes. This class is used for verifying a login to a secure website. This bean is only an example, and does not perform any real validation.

Author:
Mac Rinehart
Version: 1.0
Since: June 23, 2001

Field Summary	
private String	**errorMessage** The property that holds the number of retry attempts.
private String	**password** The property that holds the password.
private int	**retryCount** The property that holds the password.
private String	**userName**

Figure 3-1: JavaDoc example for the LoginBean.

Java developers should be using JavaDoc documentation to explain the purpose of the fields and methods in the classes they write. Any special considerations or rules for using the fields and methods of a Java class should be clearly explained in the JavaDoc. The JavaDoc that explains the `LoginBean` is located on the CD that comes with this book. You can browse it to learn more about interacting with the `LoginBean` class.

Declaring a JavaBean

For each JSP page in which you intend to use a JavaBean, you must declare the use of that bean. Declaring a bean is accomplished by means of a standard JSP action tag called the `<jsp:useBean>` tag. A typical `<jsp:useBean>` tag is written with the following syntax:

```
<jsp:useBean id="nameYouAssign" scope="{page | request |
           session | application}"
           class="{fully.qualified.ClassName}"/>
```

The `<jsp:useBean>` tag above is called an empty tag because it does not have a body. (How sad.) The `<jsp:useBean>` tags can have a body, however, in which case the declaration would look something like this:

```
<jsp:useBean id="nameYouAssign" scope="{page | request |
           session | application}"
           class="{fully.qualified.ClassName}">
   < some code for the body of the bean here>
</jsp:useBean>
```

Making use of the `LoginBean` class illustrated in Figure 3-1, I use the following code to make a simple declaration of the JavaBean:

```
<jsp:useBean id="login" class="security.LoginBean"
           scope="page"/>
```

JSP tags are case-sensitive, so you have to write them exactly as they appear in the examples.

Listing 3-1 displays the code for a log-in JSP page that makes use of this empty bean declaration in the line in bold. As you can see, the style of the `<jsp:useBean>` tag is very similar to the standard HTML content of the JSP page.

Listing 3-1: A JSP That Declares the LoginBean

```
<html>
<head>
<title>Login Page</title>
<meta http-equiv="Content-Type" content="text/html;
            charset=iso-8859-1">
</head>
<jsp:useBean class="security.LoginBean" id="login"
            scope="page"/>
<body bgcolor="#FFFFFF" text="#000000">
<form name="loginPage" method="post"
            action="//localhost:8080/login/jsp/login.jsp">
  <div align="center">
    <h1>Welcome to the Secure Website! </h1>
  </div>
  <p>Please enter your username:
    <input type="text" name="userName" size="10"
            maxlength="10">
    <br>
    Please enter your password:
    <input type="password" name="password" size="10"
            maxlength="10">
    <input type="hidden" name="retryCount" value="0">
  </p>
  <p>
    <input type="submit" name="Submit" value="Submit">
    <br>
  </p>
  <jsp:include page="/jsp/copyright.jsp" flush="true"/>
</form>
</body>
</html>
```

JSP useBean attributes

The `<jsp:useBean>` tag, and all other action tags, contains information stored in fields called attributes. *Attributes* are used to define features of the requested JavaBean to the JSP container. Every `<jsp:useBean>` tag must have two attributes: `id` and `scope`. In addition, a `<jsp:useBean>` tag can have three optional attributes: `class`, `type`, and `beanName`. The attributes of a `<jsp:useBean>` tag can appear in any order, but you cannot use them all at the same time. Table 3-1 contains a list of the `<jsp:useBean>` parameters and the rules for their use.

Table 3-1 useBean Attributes

Attribute Name	*Attribute Usage*
id	This required attribute describes the name you give to a bean. The id must be unique to a particular JSP page, meaning you cannot have two <jsp:useBean> tags with the same id in a given JSP page. The id for a bean is case-sensitive, must begin with a letter, and can only contain letters and underscore (_) characters.
scope	This attribute defines the range in which a bean is visible. When the JSP container executes a <jsp:useBean> statement, it first searches for a bean of the given id and scope. If it finds one, it uses that bean; otherwise, it creates a new instance of the bean specified in the class or type attribute. If only the id and scope are included in the <jsp:useBean tag>, a bean matching the id and scope must already be defined.
class	This attribute defines the fully qualified class name of the bean you wish to use. If a bean with the same id and scope as the bean you request is identified by the container, this attribute is ignored. Otherwise, this attribute is used to create a new instance of the bean you request. The class and type attributes can be used interchangeably, but class is the preferred of the two.
type	This attribute defines the type of variable used to contain the bean you create. Generally, it's not a good idea to use this attribute because it can override some features of a JSP container that optimize the performance of your JSP pages.
beanName	This attribute can be used to dynamically specify the bean you wish to use based on user input. If you use this attribute, you are required to use the type attribute and cannot use the class attribute.

Because of confusion regarding the purpose and rules on use of the id attribute JSP 1.1, the new release significantly redefines and tightens control on this attribute. As of the JSP 1.2 specification, the following rules apply:

- Although the <jsp:useBean> tag is the only standard tag using an id attribute, you can use custom tags that also have an id attribute. The role of the id attribute in all uses is to define the name of a variable to be created by the tag.

- In the JSP 1.2 specification, an `id` must be unique across a JSP page, regardless of the type of tag (standard or custom) in which it is used. You cannot have a `<jsp:useBean>` tag with an `id` of "Bob" and then create another `<jsp:useBean>` tag or another custom tag that also has the `id` of "Bob". Every JSP page has a Bob quota — only one Bob allowed per page, please.

Although the `class` attribute is optional, as long as you don't use the `type` or `beanName` attributes, I recommend always including the `class` attribute in your `<jsp:useBean>` tags. The JSP container needs to know the class to create a new instance of a JavaBean for you. If you have to create a new instance of a JavaBean and you only define the `id` and `scope` attributes of the `<jsp:useBean>` tag, your JSP page will bomb the first time that someone requests it. Nothing worse than a `<jsp:useBean>` bomb . . . the smell alone will knock you down at 50 paces.

JSP scope primer

The `scope` attribute of the `<jsp:useBean>` tag is one of those places where it's difficult to write about action tags without taking a short detour. Basically, the `scope` determines which JSPs have access to the bean that you declare in the `<jsp:useBean>` tag. There are four different scopes, which provide a continuum of scope choices, from very narrow scopes to very broad scopes. The four scopes are

- **`page`:** The `page` scope is the narrowest of scopes. `page` scope beans are like temp workers — they do all the work and are the first to get axed when a job is done (sad, but true). Beans of this scope can only be used by the page in which they're declared.
- **`request`:** This scope means that the bean exists from the time that it's declared until the time that a JSP is sent back to the user. Beans in the `request` scope are visible to all JSP pages that process a particular user request, and are not visible to any other request.
- **`session`:** The `session` is both a scope and a Java object. JavaBeans of the `session` scope are stored in the `session` object. Each user has its own `session` object, and that object is available for the user as long as the user is actively using your Web site. `session` scope JavaBeans are typically used to store global information about a particular user, such as their identity and preferences. JavaBeans remain in the `session` until the `session` expires, or until you delete them from the `session`. You discover more on the `session` object in Chapter 8.
- **`application`:** `application` scope beans are visible to all users of your Web site. From the time that you declare an `application` scope bean, all users of your Web site will have access to that bean and its contents. Because `application` beans are so accessible, they are typically used for very limited circumstances. One typical example is a hit counter to show how many times your Web site has been visited. (Some beans are just more gregarious than others.)

Using class and type attributes together

In Table 3-1, I mention that `class` and `type` attributes are interchangeable. If you are a novice with Java, take my advice — don't use them together. In fact, unless you consider yourself to be a power programmer, my advice is to avoid using the `type` attribute altogether.

If you have extra beans floating around, the result is a bunch of beans full of sound and fury and signifying nothing. You won't know which beans are required and which beans are along for the ride. You'll end up with a case of bloated bean management. That means you'll have to spend more money on your Web server or do a bean downsizing. And demoting or axing beans could cause your JSP application to toss its beans. A Technicolor bean burp is not pretty. I could go on, but I think you get the picture. Just take my advice: Assign your beans to the narrowest scope possible.

Figure 3-2 below illustrates how beans of different scopes can be used by various JSPs in a JSP application. Note that `page` scope beans are only used by one JSP each. On the other end of the spectrum, `application` scope beans can be used by JSPs of different users.

When assigning beans to `session` or `application` scope, the oft-dreaded issue of synchronization arises. *Synchronization* describes the process of coordinating access of a single object between two or more users in the same time span. Without going into too much detail, having one user read the content of an object (such as a hit counter on a Web site) while another user is updating that content can cause the content to be inconsistent or incorrect, and may result in other problems you can't easily predict. Java has a mechanism — synchronization — for handling this issue. If you think that a bean needs to be stored in `session` or `request`, the person who creates the bean should know that the bean needs to have its methods synchronized. Your resident Java programmer should handle the task of synchronization for you (hint, hint).

Parameterized bean declaration

Listing 3-1 declares a bean, but it doesn't get you very far with a log-in page. Verifying logins requires the bean to verify the username and password of the user. Listing 3-1 doesn't include any code to initialize these values. JSP provides two techniques for initializing JavaBean values, by using a `<jsp:setProperty>` tag, as I describe in the section "Setting JavaBean properties" later in this chapter, and using a parameterized bean declaration. A parameterized bean declaration occurs when you nest `<jsp:setProperty>` tags inside a `<jsp:useBean>` tag.

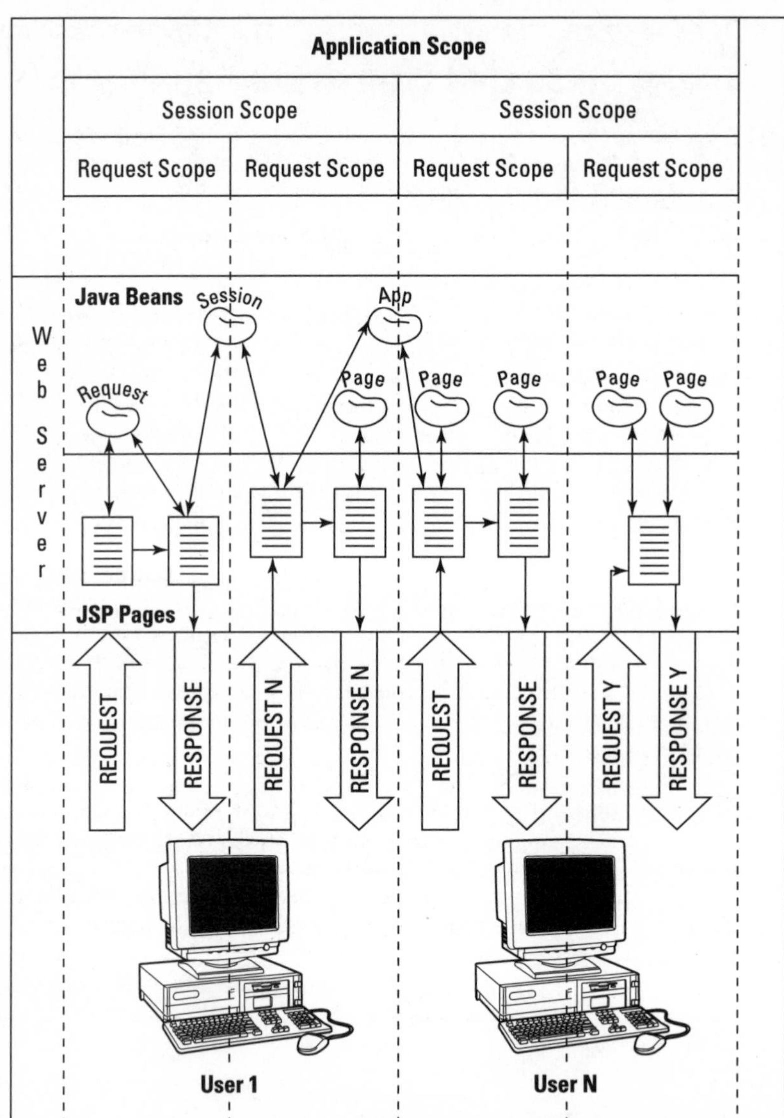

Figure 3-2: Seeing different scopes in action.

In the case of the `LoginBean`, for the bean to do its job of verifying the user's identity, it needs to know the username, password, and how many times the user has tried to log in. (For security reasons, you may want to limit users to two or three unsuccessful logins to prevent password guessing attempts.) The `LoginBean` will decide whether the user gets access to a secure Web site, or whether the user has to try to log in again. Thus, the example provides a good case for using a parameterized bean declaration. The code below illustrates the parameterized declaration of a bean.

```
<jsp:useBean id="beanId" class="fully.qualified.ClassName"
          scope="beanScope">
    <jsp:setProperty name="beanId" property="propertyName"
          param="propertyValue">
    [<jsp:setProperty name="beanId" property="propertyName2"
          param="propertyValue2"> . . .]
</jsp:useBean>
```

In the example above, notice that the bean declaration now has an opening tag, the first line, and a closing tag, which is the final line of the example. All lines between are the body of the bean declaration. If you've got sharp eyes, you probably noticed a very subtle difference between the first line in a `<jsp:useBean>` tag with a body and the empty `<jsp:useBean>` tag. The empty `<jsp:useBean>` tag ends with a `/>` symbol, and the first line of the `<jsp:useBean>` tag with a body ends with a `>` symbol. This distinction applies to all JSP action tags; if the tag has a body, the first line of the tag ends with a `>` symbol, but if the tag does not have a body, the first line ends with `/>` symbol.

I describe in detail the `<jsp:setProperty>` tags inside the body in the upcoming section "Setting JavaBean properties." Setting properties of a bean inside the `<jsp:useBean>` tag has two consequences. First, when a non-empty bean tag creates the bean, the properties of the bean will be initialized before the page is granted access to the bean. This is a clean approach for any bean that requires certain properties to be defined before action can be taken based on the bean content.

There's a gotcha that will occasionally getcha when you use a parameterized `<jsp:useBean>` tag. If the JSP container finds a bean with the `scope` and `id` of the `<jsp:useBean>` tag, the body of the `<jsp:useBean tag>` is ignored. That means the `<jsp:setProperty>` tags in the body won't get executed. This is one more good reason to declare beans in as narrow a scope as possible. If you have to set the properties of the bean to the values you specify in the `<jsp:setProperty>` tags even when you're not reusing an existing bean, you shouldn't place the `<jsp:setProperty>` tags in the body of the `<jsp:useBean>` tag.

Getting JavaBean properties

In the real world, we may think of an object, such as a chair, as being defined by its properties. Examples of the properties of a chair may be the number of legs it has, the style of the legs, the height of the chair back, type of covering, and a variety of other features of the chair. When you observe a chair, you are observing its *properties*.

Likewise, a JavaBean has properties. JavaBean properties are the observable parts of the JavaBean — they're the features that other programs like JSP pages can look at. To observe these properties, you have to get them from the JavaBean using special JavaBean methods called *getter methods*. The JSP specification allows your JSP page to get a property just by knowing the property name. The JSP action tag for getting a property is called `<jsp:getProperty>`, and the syntax is illustrated below:

```
<jsp:getProperty name="{idOfBean}"
          property="{beanPropertyName}"/>
```

To use the `<jsp:getProperty>` tag, you must first declare the bean with the `<jsp:useBean>` tag. When you declare the bean with the `<jsp:useBean>` tag, you assign the bean an `id`. This becomes the name of the bean. After you declare the bean with the `<jsp:useBean>` tag, the `id` that you assign to the bean is used to reference that bean in the remainder of your JSP.

In the previous section "Parameterized bean declaration," I illustrate the `<jsp:useBean>` tag with a JavaBean called `LoginBean` that is used to verify the username of a user for a secure Web site. Imagine that there is another position in the same log-in JSP where I want to write a piece of dynamic information to the HTML document that is sent to the user's browser. This dynamic information is the *retry count*, which shows the number of log-in attempts that the user has made. I write this information onto the JSP with the `<jsp:getProperty>` tag, as illustrated in Listing 3-2 in the bold text.

Listing 3-2: A JSP Page with a <jsp:getProperty> Tag

```
<html>
<head>
<title>Login Page</title>
<meta http-equiv="Content-Type" content="text/html;
          charset=iso-8859-1">
</head>
<jsp:useBean class="security.LoginBean" id="login"
          scope="page"/>
<body bgcolor="#FFFFFF" text="#000000">
<form name="loginPage" method="post"
          action="//localhost:8080/login/jsp/login.jsp">
  <div align="center">
    <h1>Welcome to the Secure Website! </h1>
  </div>
  <p>Please enter your username:
    <input type="text" name="userName" size="10"
          maxlength="10">
    <br>
    Please enter your password:
    <input type="password" name="password" size="10"
          maxlength="10">
```

```
    <input type="hidden" name="retryCount"
           value="<jsp:getProperty name="login"
           property="retryCount"/>">
  </p>
  <p>
    <input type="submit" name="Submit" value="Submit">
    <br>
  </p>
  <jsp:include page="/jsp/copyright.jsp" flush="true"/>
</form>
</body>
</html>
```

Note that the `<jsp:getProperty>` tag is surrounded by the quotes of the value attribute for the `<INPUT>` element named `retryCount`. When the JSP container runs this JSP, the value of the `retryCount` property in the `LoginBean` will replace the `<jsp:getProperty>` tag. This implies an important feature of the JSP `<jsp:getProperty>` tag: All properties of a bean will be converted to a `String` representation when they are placed in a JSP page. This conversion is necessary because an HTML browser is not aware of type with respect to the content of HTML elements.

Because the output of a `<jsp:getProperty>` tag must be converted to a `String`, any JavaBean property with a getter method must support the ability to be coerced into the `string` by the JSP container. When an object is *coerced*, it is converted from one type to another. For Java, all primitive datatypes (types such as `int`, `float`, `char`, and `byte`) are coerced into `Strings` using the Java language objects for those types. For any other Java object other than a `String` object, you have to coerce the object to a `String` yourself, using the Java cast operator.

Setting JavaBean properties

Oftentimes, your JSPs' JavaBeans need to respond to user input. The `<jsp:setProperty>` tag allows you to accept user input from an HTML document and use that content to initialize properties of a JavaBean. Almost all JavaBeans need to have some properties set before they can be used.

You can choose from two forms of `<jsp:setProperty>` action: one that accepts input from a user's request, and another that allows you to set the value of a property manually. See the syntax for the `<jsp:setProperty>` tag illustrated below:

```
<jsp:setProperty name="{beanId}" property="{propertyName}"
           [value="{literalValue}" |
           param="{parameterName}"]/>
```

Table 3-2 describes the attributes of the `<jsp:setProperty>` tag, and their use.

Table 3-2 Attributes of the <jsp:setProperty> Tag

Attribute Name	*Description*
`name`	This required attribute identifies which JavaBean the property belongs to.
`property`	This attribute identifies the property inside the bean that you wish to set. You can obtain this name from the JavaDoc for the JavaBean you are working with.
`value`	This optional attribute identifies the value that you assign to the bean. It cannot be used if the `param` attribute is used.
`param`	This attribute identifies the name of the parameter submitted by the user that you wish to assign to this property. A parameter submitted by the user will have the same name as the HTML form element that contained the user input. This value is optional, and cannot be used if the `value` attribute is used.

Both the `param` and `value` attributes are optional, which may seem counter-intuitive considering that the goal of the `<jsp:setProperty>` method is to assign some value to a property of a bean. You may think that to set a property, you have to identify or provide some value to the `<jsp:setProperty>` action. This is not the case. If both `param` and `value` are not used, the JSP container will attempt to find a parameter supplied by the user with the same name as the `property` attribute. If such a parameter is found, it will be used to set the property in question. Although this is a nice convenience, always state the source of a value for a property that you wish to set.

Benefiting automatic type conversion

To make the job of assigning values of a `<jsp:setProperty>` tag easier for you, the JSP container automatically performs type conversion on the values you supply. Here's a primer on the behavior to expect from automatic type conversion:

- Any value assigned to a JavaBean property using the `param` attribute of the `<jsp:setProperty>` tag will benefit from automatic type conversion.
- Any literal value assigned to a JavaBean property using the `value` attribute of the `<jsp:setProperty>` tag will benefit from automatic type conversion.

Use of the * wildcard

As a convenience for JSP coders, the JSP specification provides a wildcard asterisk (*) character for you to use when you want to set all the properties of a JavaBean to corresponding parameters submitted in the user request. The code to implement this technique is

```
<jsp:setProperty
   name="beanName"
   property="*"/>
```

Although this may seem like a nice feature on the surface, I never use it for a couple of reasons:

- Using the * wildcard makes maintenance of a JSP more difficult. Months later when you return to the JSP to make a change, you will no longer be familiar with how that page works, and there will be no explicit code that shows the relationship between the JSP and the bean it uses.
- If you use the * wildcard in your JSPs, you make it easier for hackers to assign arbitrary and possibly malicious values to the properties in your bean. Remember that for the * wildcard to work, the HTML elements in your form must have the same name as the properties in the JavaBean. That means hackers can discover the property names of your JavaBean by viewing the source of the HTML form in their browser. Then they create their own HTML form that assigns different values than the ones you intend. And wouldn't it be great for a hacker to buy a new car from your site for no money down and no payments, ever? Well, you'd think so if you were the hacker.

To prevent this kind of security issue from coming up, my advice is to never use the * wildcard operator, to always use either the `param` or the `value` attribute of the `<jsp:setProperty>` tag, and to give different names to HTML elements and their corresponding properties in a bean.

Assigning runtime expressions to a JavaBean

You can use the `<jsp:setProperty>` tag to assign a runtime expression to JavaBean properties. A *runtime expression* is a segment of code that generates a value as the JSP page is processing a user request. To set a property to a runtime expression, you must use the value attribute of the `<jsp:setProperty>` tag, as in the following example:

```
<jsp:setProperty name="myBean" property="sessionId"
         value="<%=session.getId()%>">
```

The bold text in the previous code sample is a runtime expression, also known as an *expression* in JSP-centric lingo. To discover more on the topic of expressions and scripting JSP pages, take a look at Chapter 4.

If you use a runtime expression in a `<jsp:setProperty>` tag, the JSP container will not attempt to convert the type to that of the JavaBean property. That means the result of the runtime expression must be assignable to the JavaBean property in question.

Demonstrating the <jsp:setProperty> tag

Returning to the `login.jsp` code sample started in the section "Declaring a JavaBean," the purpose of this JSP is to verify a username and password before granting access to a secured Web site. The JavaBean declared with the `<jsp:useBean>` tag will determine whether the username and password are correct. But to do that, it needs to get access to the username and password supplied by the user. In Listing 3-3, the `<jsp:setProperty>` tag is used to assign the username and password values supplied by the user to their respective JavaBean properties in the `LoginBean`.

Listing 3-3: Using the <jsp:setProperty> Tag to Initialize JavaBean Properties

```
<html>
<head>
<title>Login Page</title>
<meta http-equiv="Content-Type" content="text/html;
          charset=iso-8859-1">
</head>
<jsp:useBean class="security.LoginBean" id="login"
          scope="page">
  <jsp:setProperty name="login" property="retryCount"
          param="retryCount"/>
  <jsp:setProperty name="login" property="userName"
          param="username"/>
  <jsp:setProperty name="login" property="password"
          param="password"/>
</jsp:useBean>
<body bgcolor="#FFFFFF" text="#000000">
<form name="loginPage" method="post"
          action="//localhost:8080/login/jsp/login.jsp">
  <div align="center">
    <h1>Welcome to the Secure Website! </h1>
  </div>
  <p>Please enter your username:
    <input type="text" name="userName" size="10"
          maxlength="10">
    <br>
    Please enter your password:
    <input type="password" name="password" size="10"
          maxlength="10">
    <input type="hidden" name="retryCount"
          value="<jsp:getProperty name="login"
          property="retryCount"/>">
  </p>
  <p>
    <input type="submit" name="Submit" value="Submit">
    <br>
  </p>
```

```
</form>
</body>
</html>
```

Notice that the code in Listing 3-3 shows the <jsp:setProperty> tags in the body of the <jsp:useBean> tag, making this a parameterized bean declaration. Parameterized bean declarations are appropriate when a JavaBean must have its properties set before it can be used. <jsp:setProperty> tags can be used in the body of a <jsp:useBean> tag, or after the <jsp:useBean> tag, but not before.

Nesting JSP pages with the include Tag

In virtually every Web site that you encounter, some features (such as navigation menus, a company logo, and copyright statements) are duplicated on virtually every page. If you're like me, you'll want to do as little work as possible to implement and maintain such features. The idea is to write these solutions once, and then use them over and over again (and no, I'm not suggesting just copying and pasting them repeatedly).

At your disposal are three techniques for accomplishing this goal, depending on how complex the task is: the include directive, the <jsp:include> tag, and creating a custom tag. In this section, I focus on the <jsp:include> tag. You can discover more about include directives in Chapter 4. Custom tags are covered in detail in Chapter 12.

The <jsp:include> tag is used to include dynamic or static content in the JSP page on which it's located. Using this action, you can include the content of a file (such as a plain text document), or you can include the content of another JSP page. A good example of a case where you might want to use a <jsp:include> tag is if you need to dynamically load an advertising banner onto your JSP page. The <jsp:include> tag can be used to dynamically pop different advertisements into the banner as the page is constructed for a user.

When you use the <jsp:include> tag to nest template content inside your current JSP page, the final page sent to a user's browser is the combination of the two pages. You must be sure that the finished page is syntactically valid. For example, if you were to include an entire HTML document inside the <BODY> tags of another HTML document, the resulting Web page would crash. The final output of a JSP must be a properly formed document, or your users will have problems.

Using the <jsp:include> tag is fairly straightforward but requires some special attention to detail in order to ensure that it works properly. The <jsp:include> tag, like the <jsp:useBean> tag, may or may not have a body. The basic syntax with an empty body is

```
<jsp:include page="{relativeURL}" flush="true"/>
```

The include tag has two attributes: the page attribute and the flush attribute. The *relative URL* (Uniform Resource Locator) in the <jsp:include> tag is replaced with a relative path and filename for a file located in the JSP application that you create. The flush attribute tells the JSP container that you want the included JSP page to be output before control is returned to the including JSP page.

For guidance on defining the relative URL in the <jsp:include> directive, refer to the upcoming sidebar "A relatively simple relative URL explanation."

The <jsp:include> tag can also be written with a body that contains parameters to send to the included page. The syntax looks like this:

```
<jsp:include page="{relativePageURL}" flush="true">
  <jsp:param name="{paramName}" value="{paramValue}"/>
  [<jsp:param name="{paramName2}" value="{paramValue2}"/> . .
           .]
</jsp:include>
```

Read more about the param tag illustrated in the code sample above in the next section "Passing Parameters with the param Tag."

Listing 3-4 shows a code sample illustrating the use of the <jsp:include> tag to display a standard copyright clause in the log-in page from the previous examples in this chapter.

Listing 3-4: Example of a <jsp:include> Tag

```
<html>
<head>
<title>Login Page</title>
<meta http-equiv="Content-Type" content="text/html;
           charset=iso-8859-1">
</head>
<jsp:useBean class="security.LoginBean" id="login"
           scope="page">
  <jsp:setProperty name="login" property="retryCount"
           param="retryCount"/>
  <jsp:setProperty name="login" property="userName"
           param="username"/>
  <jsp:setProperty name="login" property="password"
           param="password"/>
</jsp:useBean>
<body bgcolor="#FFFFFF" text="#000000">
<form name="loginPage" method="post"
           action="//localhost:8080/login/jsp/login.jsp">
  <div align="center">
    <h1>Welcome to the Secure Website! </h1>
```

```
  </div>
  <p>Please enter your username:
    <input type="text" name="userName" size="10"
           maxlength="10">
    <br>
    Please enter your password:
    <input type="password" name="password" size="10"
           maxlength="10">
    <input type="hidden" name="retryCount"
           value="<jsp:getProperty name="login"
           property="retryCount"/>">
  </p>
  <p>
    <input type="submit" name="Submit" value="Submit">
    <br>
  </p>
  <jsp:include page="/jsp/copyright.jsp" flush="true"/>
</form>
</body>
</html>
```

The `<jsp:include>` tag is located on the line in bold (the last line before the `<FORM>` element is closed), meaning that the content of the `copyright.jsp` page will be displayed at the bottom of the `login.jsp` page. Figure 3-3 shows the finished `login.jsp` page with the copyright information provided by the `copyright.jsp` page.

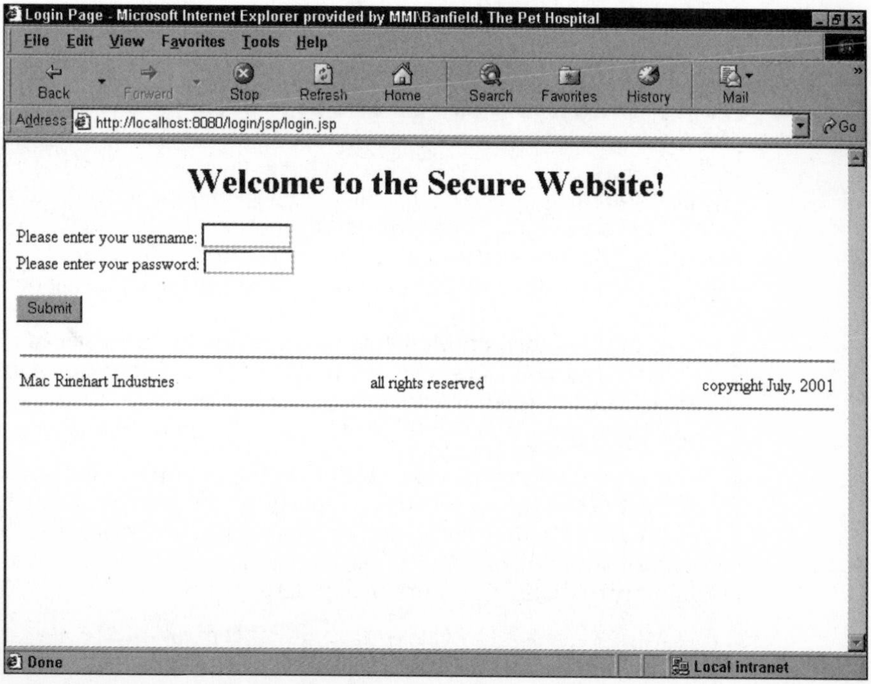

Figure 3-3: Output from login.jsp page.

For the JSP 1.1 specification, the `<jsp:include>` tag's `flush` attribute must always be set to `true`. Failure to do so causes the JSP container to lose the content of the included JSP before it is sent to the user.

In JSP 1.2 applications, you are free to set `flush` to `true` or `false`. In JSP 1.2 applications, the value of `flush` defaults to `false`. If `flush` is set to `true`, all the JSP content processed up to the `<jsp:include>` tag will be sent to the user immediately. If `flush` is set to `false`, then all the content of the including page and the included page will be buffered according to buffering rules identified in Chapter 4.

You cannot use the `<jsp:forward>` tag in a JSP page after using a `<jsp:include>` tag when the `flush` attribute is set to `true`. In addition, after you cause a portion of a JSP page to be flushed with the `<jsp:include>` tag, you can no longer take advantage of the JSP container's built in error handling features. Flushing a JSP page causes data to be sent to a user across the Internet. The bottom line is, after the JSP container starts sending content back to a Web page, there are no take-backs.

When a response from a JSP page is prepared, a JSP page typically has access to a section of the response called the header. The *header* contains information about how the response is formatted and also allows the JSP programmer to add cookies to a response for delivery to the user. This is the typical case, but JSP pages that get included in another JSP page don't have a header. Consequently, you cannot perform operations on a response header from a JSP page included in another JSP page.

Passing Parameters with the param Tag

In the case of `<jsp:include>`, `<jsp:forward>`, and `<jsp:plugin>` tags, you can pass parameters to the *target* file, JSP page or plug-in application. By *target*, I mean that if you include one JSP within another, the included JSP is the target of the `include` action. Passing a parameter with the JSP `<jsp:include>`, `<jsp:forward>`, or `<jsp:plugin>` tags can serve the following benefits:

- **Parameters can communicate information to the target of a `<jsp:include>`, `<jsp:forward>`, or `<jsp:plugin>` tag.** If, for example, you have information with a `page` scope that you need to pass to an included page, you would need to pass that information as a parameter.
- **Parameters can be used to initialize information required for the target of the action to work properly.** As an example, if you have a `<jsp:plugin>` tag for an applet plug-in, the applet may require certain information to perform its task. You can use the `<jsp:param>` tag to supply that information to the applet.

Using the <jsp:param> tag is a little different than previous action tags that I illustrated in this chapter because it must be included in the body of a <jsp:include>, <jsp:forward>, or <jsp:plugin> tag. You can include as many parameters as you want inside the body of one of these tags. Illustrating the param action with the include action, the param tag syntax follows:

```
<jsp:include page="{relativePageURL}" flush="true">
  <jsp:param name="{paramName}" value="{paramValue}"/>
  [<jsp:param name="{paramName2}" value="{paramValue2}"/> . .
          .]
</jsp:include>
```

The value that you pass with a <jsp:param> tag is treated just like a parameter received from a user. That means that the JSP that is the target of a <jsp:include> or <jsp:forward> tag will access values passed by the <jsp:param> tag the same way that it accesses values passed by a user request. There are a couple special considerations, though:

- **First, when you use the <jsp:param> tag nested in a <jsp:include> tag, the value of the <jsp:param> tag is only visible in the included JSP.** After the included page is finished processing, the value of the <jsp:param> tag is destroyed.
- **Second, if a user submits a value with the same name as the value of a <jsp:param> tag, the value of the <jsp:param> tag takes precedence over the value submitted by the user.** For example, if a user submits a page with the parameter username="Mac" and you add a parameter with the action tag <jsp:param name="username" value="Mud"/>, the target of the <jsp:param> tag will have a parameter username="Mud", "Mac".

To illustrate the use of the <jsp:param> tag, consider the example of including copyright information into a JSP, as shown earlier in Listing 3-4. Imagine that instead of including a static copyright statement, I want to include a copyright statement in which the date and the copyright owner can be modified via parameters. This allows me to update the copyright information as the page changes.

To accomplish this goal, I must perform two tasks:

- Update the copyright page to accept the parameter and include it into the page output
- Include the <jsp:param> tag in my previous example to pass the parameter to the copyright page

I implement the solution for using a parameter first because the `copyright.jsp` page may be included in several different Web pages, and how the `copyright.jsp` page uses the parameter will determine the name that each page using it must pass as a parameter. I use two pieces of dynamic information and call them `copyrightDate` and `copyrightOwner`. Listing 3-5 shows the code to make use of a `param` with an expression tag including the implicit `request` object.

Don't worry about how the expression tag or the implicit object work right now. You can read more about expression tags in Chapter 4, and I cover implicit objects in detail in Chapter 7.

Listing 3-5: Accessing a Parameter with an Expression Tag

```
<table width="100%">
  <tr>
    <td colspan="3"><hr></td>
  </tr>
  <tr>
    <td width="33%">
      <%=request.getParameter("copyrightOwner")%>
    </td>
    <td width="34%"><div align="center">all rights
           reserved</div></td>
    <td width="33%">
      <div align="right">
        <%=request.getParameter("copyrightDate")%>
      </div>
    </td>
  </tr>
  <tr>
    <td colspan="3"><hr></td>
  </tr>
</table>
```

Having created the `copyright.jsp` page to accept `copyrightOwner` and `copyrightDate` parameters, the next order of business is to supply the values for these parameters to the JSP using the `<jsp:param>` tag. Listing 3-6 contains the updated code for the `login.jsp` page, which passes the `copyrightOwner` and `copyrightDate` parameters to the `copyright.jsp` page. Look for the bold code at the bottom of the listing to see the `<jsp:param>` tag in action.

Listing 3-6: Passing Parameters with the param Tag

```
<html>
<head>
<title>Login Page</title>
<meta http-equiv="Content-Type" content="text/html;
           charset=iso-8859-1">
```

```
</head>
<jsp:useBean class="security.LoginBean" id="login"
         scope="page">
  <jsp:setProperty name="login" property="retryCount"
         param="retryCount"/>
  <jsp:setProperty name="login" property="userName"
         param="username"/>
  <jsp:setProperty name="login" property="password"
         param="password"/>
</jsp:useBean>
<body bgcolor="#FFFFFF" text="#000000">
<form name="loginPage" method="post"
         action="//localhost:8080/login/jsp/login.jsp">
  <div align="center">
    <h1>Welcome to the Secure Website! </h1>
  </div>
  <p>Please enter your username:
    <input type="text" name="userName" size="10"
         maxlength="10">
    <br>
    Please enter your password:
    <input type="password" name="password" size="10"
         maxlength="10">
    <input type="hidden" name="retryCount"
         value="<jsp:getProperty name="login"
         property="retryCount"/>">
  </p>
  <p>
    <input type="submit" name="Submit" value="Submit">
    <br>
  </p>
  <jsp:include page="/jsp/copyright.jsp" flush="true">
    <jsp:param name="copyrightOwner" value="Mac Rinehart
         Industries"/>
    <jsp:param name="copyrightDate" value="July, 2001"/>
  </jsp:include>
</form>
</body>
</html>
```

Directing Flow with the forward Tag

Managing the flow of a Web site from one page to another is straightforward with a static Web site. You can allow users to choose their own adventure by navigating through hyperlinks; or, if you use forms, you can specify a URL to direct the user to the `action` attribute of the HTML `<FORM>` tag. With dynamic Web sites, you can direct the flow of a user across a Web site based on dynamic criteria that you specify. JSP implements this capability with the `<jsp:forward>` tag. The `<jsp:forward>` action allows you to direct a user to a new page from inside the JSP container.

A relatively simple relative URL explanation

Universal Resource Locator (URL) is basically a special name for a unique path to some document. The term *relative URL* refers to the path to a given document, relative to some other path. If you have a document located at `C:\firstDirectory\secondDirectory\myDocument.doc`, the path `\secondDirectory\myDocument.doc` is the URL relative to the path `C:\firstDirectory`. The rules for relative URLs that I describe in this sidebar apply to all cases in JSP applications where a relative URL is used, regardless of what type of JSP element uses the URL.

Your JSP container stores the URLs to the root level of every JSP application that you create. Consequently, you can access JSP pages simply by specifying the relative URL to each document in a project, and the Web server will figure out exactly where that page is located.

The two acceptable URL forms are an application-relative URL and a page-relative URL. Application-relative URLs are relative to the top-level directory of the JSP application, and are characterized by an initial forward slash character (/) in the URL string. An example of an application relative URL is `/jsp/myNextPage.jsp`. The JSP container combines this URL with the path to the top-level directory of your JSP application to make a complete URL to the given JSP page.

Page-relative URLs are characterized by the absence of a forward slash in the first character of the URL text. An example of a page-relative URL is `nextLevel/myTargetPage.jsp`. If you use a page-relative URL, the JSP container combines the path to the source page with the relative path of the page you wish to forward to, forming a complete URL to the target page. For example, if the source page URL is `C:/tomcat/webapps/myApplication/jsp/mySourcePage.jsp` and I provide a page-relative URL of `nextLevel/myTargetPage.jsp`, the JSP container will join the two to form a complete URL of `C:/tomcat/webapps/myApplication/jsp/nextLevel/myTargetPage.jsp`.

As an example, consider the log-in page I use as an example throughout this chapter. If a user's login is successful, the user should proceed to the site requested. However, if the user's login is invalid, you want to force a return to the log-in page. When you use a `<jsp:forward>` tag, you cause the JSP container to *redirect* a user to a JSP page other than the one they originally requested. With regard to the log-in page, the ability to redirect a user to a new JSP page inside the JSP container means that you don't have to expose any page except the `login.jsp` page to the user until login is successful.

If the login is successful, the `login.jsp` page should redirect a user to a secure page in your Web site. But if the login is not successful, the user will never get access to more than the `login.jsp` page because the `action` attribute of the JSP that you send to the user will never be more than the URL to the log-in page.

When you redirect a user request using the <jsp:forward> tag, the application permanently transfers control from the source page to the target page. Any page scope beans in the source page are released by the JSP container and are not available to the next JSP page. Finally, any output created by the original JSP will be cleared before the <jsp:forward> action happens, thus any output of the source page will not be sent to the user.

For JSP 1.1 applications, if you use a <jsp:include> tag in a JSP, you can no longer use a <jsp:forward> tag in that same page. The <jsp:include> action sends the included content directly to the user . . . and there are no take-backs after something is sent to the user. In JSP 1.2 applications, you cannot use the <jsp:forward> tag if you first use a <jsp:include> tag with the flush attribute set to true. JSP addresses this need with the <jsp:forward> tag, which is used to permanently transfer the control user's request from one page to another page on the same server. The JSP <jsp:forward> tag can be written in a basic form, which does not include parameters, or a more complex form that does include parameters. The basic syntax for the <jsp:forward> tag is

```
<jsp:forward page="relativelocalURL"/>
```

The <jsp:forward> tag can also include parameters, in which case it is written with a body, containing <jsp:param> tags, as I describe in the previous section. The syntax of the <jsp:forward> tag with parameters is:

```
<jsp:forward page="{relativeLocalURL}">
  <jsp:param name="parameterName" value="parameterValue"/>
  [<jsp:param name="parameterName2" value="parameterValue2"/>
          . . .]
</jsp:forward>
```

Returning to the login.jsp page I use as an example throughout this chapter, the <jsp:forward> action provides you with the final puzzle piece you need to complete this page. The goal of the login.jsp page is to verify the username and password of a user, and to redirect that user to a secure Web site page if a valid username and password is supplied. So far, the JSP I have created will infinitely loop on the JSP login page because it has no <jsp:forward> action. To complete the logic, I use a <jsp:forward> action that gets executed only if the username and password supplied by the user are valid. The final login.jsp page that implements this solution is displayed in Listing 3-7.

Listing 3-7: Login Page Example

```
<html>
<head>
<title>Login Page</title>
<meta http-equiv="Content-Type" content="text/html;
          charset=iso-8859-1">
```

(continued)

Listing 3-7 ***(continued)***

```
</head>
<jsp:useBean class="security.LoginBean" id="login"
          scope="page">
  <jsp:setProperty name="login" property="retryCount"
          param="retryCount"/>
  <jsp:setProperty name="login" property="userName"
          param="username"/>
  <jsp:setProperty name="login" property="password"
          param="password"/>
</jsp:useBean>
<body bgcolor="#FFFFFF" text="#000000">
<form name="loginPage" method="post"
          action="//localhost:8080/login/jsp/login.jsp">
  <div align="center">
    <h1>Welcome to the Secure Website! </h1>
  </div>
  <%
    if(login.isValid()){
  %>
      <jsp:forward page="welcome.jsp"/>
  <%
    }
    else{
  %>
      <jsp:getProperty name="login" property="errorMessage"/>
  <%
    }
  %>
  <p>Please enter your username:
    <input type="text" name="userName" size="10"
          maxlength="10">
    <br>
    Please enter your password:
    <input type="password" name="password" size="10"
          maxlength="10">
    <input type="hidden" name="retryCount"
          value="<jsp:getProperty name="login"
          property="retryCount"/>">
  </p>
  <p>
    <input type="submit" name="Submit" value="Submit">
    <br>
  </p>
  <jsp:include page="/jsp/copyright.jsp" flush="true">
    <jsp:param name="copyrightOwner" value="Mac Rinehart
          Industries"/>
    <jsp:param name="copyrightDate" value="July, 2001"/>
  </jsp:include>
</form>
</body>
</html>
```

Take a moment to review Listing 3-7. In addition to the JSP action tags I add to this page throughout the chapter, this page now includes another feature of the JSP technology: scriptlets. *Scriptlets* are special JSP elements that mark off an area of the JSP page to include native Java code. Each scriptlet is delimited by <% and %> tags, and all together they form a complete statement in the Java language. Inside the scriptlets, I wrote an if-else statement in Java. The statement tells the JSP container: If the login is valid, run the `<jsp:forward>` action; otherwise, execute the `<jsp:getProperty>` action to display an error message. I describe scriptlets in detail in Chapter 4.

Also note the action attribute of the HTML `<FORM>` tag in the bold line of the `login.jsp` page. This action tag specifies the `login.jsp` page as the place to submit the content of a client request. All the content of the JSP is being sent back to itself. The only way to leave this page is by executing the JSP `<jsp:forward>` tag, and the only way to execute the `<jsp:forward>` tag is to provide a valid username and password to the `login` JavaBean. Because the `<jsp:forward>` tag occurs on the Web server, using this solution prevents unauthorized users from getting access to a secure part of your Web site by looking at the source of your HTML page.

Using the JSP plugin Tag for Browser Plug-ins

A *browser plug-in* is a program that soups up your Web browser with added functionality by plugging in to a standard interface with the browser and providing a container for specialized applications to run in. As an example, Java has a browser plug-in that allows Web browsers to run applets and JavaBeans inside the browser. This plug-in adds value because it guarantees that the operating environment of the browser will support the services required by the applet. Without the plug-in, the applets may or may not work, depending on what features you implement and whether the Web browser supports those features or not.

Many Java programmers, myself included, avoid the use of applets like the plague because browsers have historically been very inconsistent in their support of applets. There are a lot of other ways to implement the features that you might normally try to accomplish using an applet, and some of those alternative ways are both more stable and faster.

Consider using Flash, by Macromedia, which is a great way to add visual gusto and sophisticated application features to a Web browser. I've used Flash to create some really great Web browser features and have yet to be disappointed. You don't need to use a `<jsp:plugin>` tag to add Flash programs to your JSP. To discover more on Flash, look up *Flash 5 For Dummies,* by Gurdy Leete and Ellen Finkelstein (Hungry Minds, Inc.).

Typically, plug-ins are implemented using one of two HTML tags, either `<OBJECT>` or `<EMBED>`, depending on what kind of browser makes the request. If you're writing a crossplatform Web application that uses applets or JavaBeans on the browser, you have to handle the logic of determining what kind of browser makes the request, and delivering either the `<EMBED>` tag content or the `<OBJECT>` tag content.

When the JSP technology was defined, the people at JavaSoft decided that knowing which kind of element to use and how to use it was more trouble that it's worth, so they created a solution that simplifies your life called the `<jsp:plugin>` tag. The `<jsp:plugin>` tag gives Web designers one standard syntax for specifying what plug-in needs to be provided to the client. The JSP container is then responsible for determining what kind of browser a particular request originates from, and to generate the proper HTML code to handle the plug-in for that browser.

According to the JSP specification, the `<jsp:plugin>` tag is required only to support applet and JavaBean plug-ins.

The JSP plugin tag syntax

The `<jsp:plugin>` tag is the most complex of all the standard action tags. The good news with both of these sections is that most of the attributes of `<jsp:plugin>` tags are taken directly from the HTML specification. If you've used `<OBJECT>` or `<EMBED>` tags before in HTML, most of this section will be review. If not, you're in the right place. I go over the required attributes first, and then I address optional attributes and review the body of the `<jsp:plugin>` tag.

JSP plugin required attributes

In its simplest form, the `<jsp:plugin>` tag has three required attributes: `type`, `code`, and `codebase`. The syntax looks like this:

```
<jsp:plugin type="{bean | applet}"
          code="{fully.qualified.NameOfBeanOrApplet}"
          codebase="{URLtoCodeBase}"/>
```

In the `type` attribute, you specify whether the object you identified in the code attribute is a JavaBean (using the keyword `bean`) or an applet. In the `code` attribute, you identify the fully qualified name of the object that you intend to embed in the JSP page. (The fully qualified name includes the entire package structure and the class name of the JavaBean or applet.) The `codebase` attribute represents the URL to the folder containing the root package of the JavaBean or applet.

Both the code and codebase attributes of the plug-in action are defined in the HTML specification and are not native to JSP technology. The code identifies the name of the applet to load, and codebase defines the URL for the browser to find the source of the code. Here's a sample usage of the JSP <jsp:plugin> tag:

```
<jsp:plugin type="applet" code="greetings.HelloWorld.class"
          codebase="//localhost:8080/applets"/>
```

From this example, the JSP container will make either an <OBJECT> or <EMBED> tag containing the information needed for the requested Web browser to load an applet called HelloWorld.class located in the objects subdirectory of your JSP application.

JSP plugin optional attributes

In addition to the three required attributes, the <jsp:plug-in> action tag has a multitude of optional elements, many of which are defined in the HTML specification, and some of which are unique to JSP technology. Table 3-3 contains a summary of all the optional attributes of the plug-in action tag and their usage.

Table 3-3 JSP plugin Tag Optional Attributes

Attribute Syntax	*Description*
align="{alignment}"	align is defined in the HTML specification and indicates that the alignment of the object inside the space allocated for the plug-in on the HTML page. There are several legal values that vary depending on which browser you use.
archive="{supportingFileURLs}"	archive is an attribute of the <OBJECT> element in HTML. You can use the archive attribute to identify a space delimited list of URLs pointing to supporting files required by the class loaded in the <OBJECT> element.
height="{height}"	height is an HTML attribute that identifies the vertical space allocated to the browser plug-in, either as a number of pixels or a percentage of the screen height on the requesting computer.

(continued)

Table 3-3 *(continued)*

Attribute Syntax	***Description***
`hspace="{margin}"`	The `hspace` attribute specifies the margin width on the left and right sides of the plug-in. This attribute is defined by the HTML specification.
`jreversion="{versionNumber}"`	The `jreversion` attribute identifies the version of the Java Runtime Environment required for the applet or JavaBean to run. This attribute is part of the JSP specification, and the default value is `1.1`.
`name="{elementName}"`	The `name` attribute is the name assigned to the `<OBJECT>` or `<EMBED>` element in the Web page, as defined by the HTML specification.
`vspace="{margin}"`	The `vspace` attribute specifies the margin width on the top and bottom sides of the plug-in. This attribute is defined in the HTML specification.
`title="{documentTitle}"`	The `title` attribute supposedly refers to the `<TITLE>` HTML element, allowing you to define the document title. Beware when using this attribute because only one `<TITLE>` element is allowed per HTML document — if you already defined it elsewhere, you will have problems.
`width="{elementWidth}"`	The `width` attribute is defined by the HTML specification and identifies the amount of horizontal space allocated to the `<OBJECT>` or `<EMBED>` tag as a percentage of the screen width, or a number of pixels.

Attribute Syntax	Description
nspluginurl="{URLtoJavaPlugin}"	The nspluginurl is defined by the JSP specification and is the URL to a location where Netscape Navigator can download the Java plug-in to run the specified object. This attribute has a default value specified by the JSP container implementation, thus the default value depends on which JSP container you choose.
iepluginurl="{URLtoJavaPlugin}"	The iepluginurl is defined by the JSP specification and is the URL to a location where Internet Explorer can download the Java plug-in to run the specified object. This attribute has a default value specified by the JSP container implementation; the default value depends on which JSP container you choose.

In JSP 1.1 applications, when you specify the height and width of a <jsp:plugin> tag, you must hardcode the values. In other words, you can't have height and width attributes that get set dynamically when the JSP page is processed.

JSP 1.2 applications support the use of runtime expressions to set the values height and width attributes in a <jsp:plugin> tag. That means you can set height and width properties dynamically by using a scriptlet or expression tag. Using scriptlet and expression tags is covered in Chapter 4.

JSP plugin body elements

The <jsp:plugin> tag has two possible body elements: the <jsp:params> tag and the <jsp:fallback> tag. The <jsp:params> element can contain one to many <jsp:param> tags that specify the parameters provided to the applet or JavaBean identified in the class attribute of the <jsp:plugin> tag. The <jsp:fallback> tag identifies alternative content to display in the browser if the Java plug-in fails to load. The syntax for these two elements follows:

```
<jsp:plugin type="{bean | applet}"
          code="{fully.qualified.NameOfBeanOrApplet}"
          codebase="{RelativeURLtoRootOfDirectoryOfCode}"
          [{optional attributes}]>
```

```
   <jsp:params>
     <jsp:param name="parameterName" value="parameterValue"/>
     [<jsp:param name="parameterName" value="parameterValue"/>
          . . .]
   </jsp:params>
   <jsp:fallback> arbitrary_text </jsp:fallback>
</jsp:plugin>
```

The <jsp:fallback> and <jsp:params> tags are only used in the body of a <jsp:plugin> tag. Only one <jsp:fallback> tag is allowed per JSP <jsp:plugin> tag.

The fact that there's a <jsp:fallback> tag for the <jsp:plugin> should give you an idea about the confidence level of applet plug-ins in the Java development community. Basically, it's a big red flag that says, "Let the buyer beware" to me.

A plug-in example

To round out the examples for this chapter, I finish off the login example by providing our user with a welcome page after a successful login. This welcome page gives me a nice opportunity to illustrate the use of the <jsp:plugin> action, and I have created the HelloWorld applet to give our user a custom greeting. The code in Listing 3-8 illustrates the creation of my HelloWorld applet.

Listing 3-8: Code for the HelloWorld Applet

```
package client;

import java.applet.Applet;
import java.awt.Graphics;

public class HelloWorld extends Applet {
    private int xOrigin;
    private int yOrigin;
    private int width;
    private int height;
    private String message;

    public HelloWorld() { super(); }

    public void init() {
        try{
            xOrigin =
           Integer.parseInt(getParameter("xOrigin"));
            yOrigin =
           Integer.parseInt(getParameter("yOrigin"));
```

```
            width = Integer.parseInt(getParameter("width"));
            height =
           Integer.parseInt(getParameter("height"));
            message = getParameter("message");
        }
        catch(NumberFormatException e){
            xOrigin = 0;
            yOrigin = 0;
            width = 100;
            height = 100;
            message = "invalid parameter format for applet
           dimentions.";
        }
    }

    public void start() {
        repaint();
    }

    public void stop() { }

    public void destroy() { }

    public void paint( Graphics g ) {
        g.drawRect(xOrigin, yOrigin, height, width);
        g.drawString( message, yOrigin + 5, width - 5);
    }
}
```

In the applet example from Listing 3-8, you see five parameters to be set by the JSP `<jsp:plugin>` tag:

- **`xOrigin`:** The `xOrigin` attribute defines the x-coordinate for the upper-right corner of the applet container on your Web page. This value must be a whole number.
- **`yOrigin`:** The `yOrigin` attribute defines the y-coordinate for the upper-right corner of the applet container. This value must be a whole number.
- **`width`:** The `width` attribute defines the width of the applet container. This value defines the number of pixels of width allocated to your applet container on the Web page and must be a whole number.
- **`height`:** The `height` attribute defines the height of the applet container. This value defines the number of pixels of height allocated to your applet container on the Web page and must be a whole number.
- **`message`:** The `message` attribute defines the message to print to the user inside the applet. For the purposes of this example, the message must fit in the width defined by the `width` attribute.

I set these parameters with the <jsp:param> tag portion of the <jsp:plugin> tag. I set the parameters defining the size and position of the applet using static values, but the message is dynamically assigned based on the value supplied as the username from the JSP login page. That is possible because the JSP login page forwards the user's request to the welcome page, meaning that the data supplied by the user in the log-in page is still available in the request object. The result is a welcome message that presents a personalized greeting to each user who logs into a Web site using the log-in example developed in this chapter. See how I craft this in Listing 3-9.

Listing 3-9: The Source Code for the JSP Welcome Page

```
<html>
<head>
<title>Welcome Page</title>
<meta http-equiv="Content-Type" content="text/html;
          charset=iso-8859-1">
</head>

<body bgcolor="#FFFFFF" text="#000000">
<jsp:plugin type="applet" code="client.HelloWorld"
          codebase="//localhost:8080/applets">
  <jsp:params>
    <jsp:param name="xOrigin" value="0"/>
    <jsp:param name="yOrigin" value="0"/>
    <jsp:param name="width" value="100"/>
    <jsp:param name="height" value="100"/>
    <jsp:param name="message" value="Welcome
          <%request.getParameter("userName")%> !"/>
  </jsp:params>
  <jsp:fallback> Unable to load Applet </jsp:fallback>
</jsp:plugin>
</body>
</html>
```

JSP standard actions are relatively straightforward and powerful features of the JSP language. They provide a clean system for integrating dynamic application content into a Web page without adding a great deal of complexity to the Web page itself. They promote reuse of standard HTML content by providing a means for including that content on multiple pages.

Perhaps most importantly, they provide a clean separation between Web page content and the internal mechanics of the Java classes that generate dynamic content. The separation of Java code and JSP pages is important because it allows Java developers to maintain JavaBeans and other application resources without affecting the JSP pages created by Web designers. Likewise, Web designers can reuse the JavaBeans created by Java developers without being concerned about the internal mechanics of the JavaBean.

Chapter 4

Scripting and Directing JavaServer Pages

In This Chapter

- Using directives
- Scripting in Java
- Commenting your code
- Declaring scripting variables
- Expressing yourself with expression tags
- Scripting with scriptlets

In an ideal world, you could implement JavaServer Pages (JSPs) by using only the action tags that I cover in Chapter 3 because action tags are based on an easy-to-learn eXtensible Markup Language (XML) syntax. Unfortunately, the standard JSP actions don't do everything you need in a JSP.

Perhaps you need to make some conditional decision that affects the flow of your JSP application. Or you need to generate a HyperText Markup Language (HTML) table without knowing exactly how many rows of data the table will contain. Maybe you need to interact with the JSP container to provide some special instructions on how to process the page. For all these tasks, you may find that JSP action tags don't adequately address your needs.

This chapter picks up the reins where JSP actions leave off. JSP technology has two additional kinds of elements: JSP directives and JSP scripting elements. JSP *directives* enable you to send directions to the JSP container about how to configure the JSP environment and handle special operating concerns, such as how to respond to errors. JSP *scripting elements* enable you to employ the full power of the Java language as a scripting language for your JSP. In this chapter, you discover the role that JSP directives and scripting elements play in the creation of JSPs.

Sending Directives to the JSP Container

The three fundamental types of JSP elements are actions, directives, and scripting elements. *Directives* are used to interact with the JSP container, either to configure the environment, to extend the functionality of the JSP syntax, or to include static (nonchanging) content in a JSP. All JSP directives are delimited by directive tags. The beginning directive tag is `<%@` and the ending tag is `%>`.

Configuring a JSP

A JSP commonly needs access to special resources beyond those offered to the page by default. The JSP specification anticipates this need by providing the JSP page directive, with which you instruct the JSP container to provide your JSP with the resources that it needs — to an extent.

All JSP page directives are either optional or set to a default predefined value so you may not have to specify page directives unless you need access to some resource that's not provided to the JSP by default. The page directive syntax is illustrated below:

```
<%@ page {attribute}="{value}"%>
```

When specifying page directive attributes, you can include several attributes in the same page directive or you can divide attributes into different page directives. You can also specify page attributes at any point in the body of a JSP. However, you cannot have the same attribute in more than one page directive for a given JSP. As an example, the following code snippet is legal (it works properly) in a single JSP:

```
<%@ page import="java.util.*"%>
<%@ page isThreadSafe="true"%>
```

However, the code snippet in the next example is not legal in a single JSP because both page directives have the an `import` attribute:

```
<%@ page isThreadSafe="true"%>
<%@ page isThreadSafe="false"%>
```

An exception to the aforementioned rule is that it's okay to specify multiple page directives with import attributes. This is done mainly because import statements could get pretty long if you had to write them all on a single line. Besides, what's a rule without an exception?

See a complete listing of the page directive attributes in Table 4-1.

Table 4-1	Page Directive Attributes
Attribute	***Description***
`info`	Stores a string description of the page
`language`	Identifies the scripting language
`import`	Imports Java classes for use in your JSP
`session`	Indicates whether this JSP participates in session management
`buffer`	Indicates minimum level of buffering for page output
`autoFlush`	Indicates whether the JSP container can automatically flush the buffer
`isThreadSafe`	Indicates whether the JSP can support multiple threads
`isErrorPage`	Indicates whether this page handles errors
`errorPage`	Identifies the error page for this JSP.
`contentType`	This attribute defines the MIME type and optionally the character encoding for a JSP page. In JSP 1.2 application, you can define the character encoding with the `pageEncoding` attribute.
`pageEncoding`	This attribute is added in JSP 1.2 to allow you to specify the character encoding of a JSP page. By default the character encoding is ISO-8859-1, which is appropriate for most Western uses.

I recommend that you place page directives at the top of a JSP where they can be easily spotted by anyone who works with that page in the future. Creating a separate page directive for each attribute that you define is easier to read than specifying multiple attributes in the same directive.

Specifying page information

You can place a little information in a JSP that can be queried by other JSPs or by the JSP container to find out what the JSP does. Accomplish this goal with the `info` attribute of the JSP page directive. Here's an example of storing some information about a JSP:

```
<%@ page info="This is some information about this JSP
          page."%>
```

I haven't encountered any great reasons for using the `info` attribute of a JSP yet, although depending on what brand of JSP container you choose, the JSP container may be able display the `info` attribute of a JSP to the person who administers your JSP container. This might be important if you need to convey any important information on the JSP to the administrator of your JSP container.

Specifying your scripting language

The JSP specification, although explicit about many features of JSP technology, doesn't require that JSP technology be implemented in a particular language. In fact, it's possible for other technology companies to provide a JSP implementation based on a language completely different from Java, provided that they supply the same set of functionality required by the JSP specification.

Hypothetically, because another software vendor could choose to implement JSP technology with a different scripting language, the JSP has an attribute that enables you to specify which scripting language you want to use. The default value for this attribute is `Java`; thus, you don't have to include a page attribute specifying the language unless you explicitly want to use a different language. The syntax for the language attribute is

```
<%@ page language="Java"%>
```

Of course, because you won't find any scripting for JSPs other than Java at this time, the `language` attribute of the page directive currently has less practical application than the `info` attribute.

Importing Java classes

Although you may not ever use the `info` or `language` attributes of a JSP, if you do any scripting with Java in a JSP, you'll almost always use the `import` attribute of the JSP. In Java, if you need to use a Java class inside your JSP, you have to import the class into the page. You can import a single Java class or use an asterisk (*) wildcard character to import all the Java class files of a package.

A *package* in Java is represented as a folder and contains a set of logically related class files. The package is used to provide a logical grouping of classes based on their roles. Packages can contain Java classes or other packages that define more specialized roles. For example, the `javax.servlet` package contains classes used in the servlet Application Programming Interface (API). JSP technology defines classes that get converted by a JSP container into servlets. Thus, the classes of the JSP API are located in the `javax.servlet.jsp` package.

Here's an example of the `import` attribute of the page directive in use:

```
<%@ page import="java.util.*"%>
```

This example imports all the class files located in the `java.util` package, which defines utility classes for working with sets of data. In the next example, two different classes are imported. When importing more than one class, as in the following example, separate each class with a comma character (`,`).

```
<%@ page import="java.util.Vector,java.util.Iterator"%>
```

Each page automatically imports `java.lang.*`, `javax.servlet.*`, `javax.servlet.jsp.*`, and `javax.servlet.http.*`. Therefore, if you intend to use any classes located in those packages, you don't need to import them.

Enabling session management

HyperText Transport Protocol (HTTP) is the medium through which you send information back and forth across the Internet. An `HttpSession` is a Java class that stores information about a particular user while that user interacts with your JSP application. The `HttpSession` class allows you to maintain information about a user across multiple JSPs. Without it, you would have to treat each request sent to you from the Internet as a separate user, whether they originated from the same person or not. In order to access `HttpSession` classes, JSPs provide an object called `session`, which contains the `HttpSession` information for a user.

The `session` object is one of a group of objects provided by a JSP container that are generically called implicit objects. *Implicit objects* are objects that you have access to automatically because they're supplied by the JSP container for you. For more on the `session` object and other implicit objects, see Chapter 7.

By default, a JSP automatically participates in session management, meaning that it can read data from and write data to an `HTTPSession`. You can toggle this feature on and off by using the `session` attribute of the page directive. The syntax is

```
<%@ page session="{false | true}"%>
```

Buffering page output

Buffering is a process in which your computer optimizes input and output of data by writing a specified amount of data to a *buffer*, which is a temporary storage area in memory. When the buffer gets full, your JSP can send all the content of the buffer to the output, enabling you to control the size and number of messages that you send to a user's Web browser.

By default, JSPs have a buffer of 8K for outputting JSP content. A buffer at least 8K in size is created to temporarily store the output of your JSP before sending the output to the client. If you desire, you can control the size of the buffer or turn the buffer off by using the `buffer` attribute of the page directive. The `buffer` attribute accepts either a value of `"none"` to indicate that no buffering is allowed or some whole number followed by `"k"` to indicate the minimum number of kilobytes that the buffer can hold before the content of the buffer is sent to the user's browser. In the first sample below, the buffer is disabled for a JSP. In the second example, the buffer is set to a minimum size of 16K.

```
<%@ page buffer="none"%>
<%@ page buffer="16k"%>
```

Controlling buffer flushing

When the content of a buffer is sent to a user's browser, it is flushed. (Restrain yourself from the obvious analogy.) By default, JSPs flush the buffer automatically. However, you can assume more manual control of the buffer by turning off the automatic flushing feature. The syntax for the `autoFlush` attribute is

```
<%@ page autoFlush="{true | false}"%>
```

The default setting is `true`, which means that `autoFlush` is enabled, and any plumbing emergencies are averted.

If you turn off the `autoFlush` feature of a JSP, you must manually flush the buffer before the size limit of the `buffer` attribute is exceeded. Failure to do so results in a runtime error in your JSP. If you set the buffer attribute to `"none"`, you can't set `autoFlush` to `false`. My advice: Don't play with `autoFlush` and buffer attributes unless you're directly descended from a Greek god. (In case you're wondering, that rules me out — my lightning bolt privileges were just suspended.)

Controlling multithreading behavior in JSPs

One of the more complex topics of JSP programming is multithreading. *Multithreading* is a mechanism whereby the same program can be run multiple different times simultaneously. In a multithreading program, you find only one instance of the program in memory, and a new thread of execution is created for each user of the program.

You can see how multithreading programs increase performance: They allow multiple users to work with the same program at the same time. The alternative is to require all users to wait until the current user of the program is finished with it. (Yawn.) JSPs support multithreading by default; thus, multiple users can run the same JSP at the same time. The syntax for controlling whether multithreading is supported by a JSP is

```
<%@ page isThreadSafe="{true | false}"%>
```

If a JSP is thread-safe (that is, if it supports multithreading), the `isThreadSafe` attribute is set to `true`. By default, the `isThreadSafe` attribute of the page directive is set to `true`.

The tricky part of multithreading programs is that they typically have some resources that are private to each thread as well as some that are shared and visible to all the threads. In the case of shared resources, if two different threads attempt to read or write information to a single shared resource, a conflict can occur, resulting in some unpredictable behavior. Unpredictable behavior may be anything from the information in the shared resource being incorrect to the JSP container locking up and being unable to respond to additional user requests.

When multithreading is supported, make sure that access to any shared resource of a JSP is synchronized — that the resource is only accessible to one thread at a time. This task is generally referred to as *concurrency management.*

Although managing shared resources in a multithreading environment is more complex than it is with single threaded programs, the benefits far outweigh the risks. I recommend leaving multithreading at its default setting unless you have a special reason to turn it off. Throughout the book, as I address topics that may affect thread management, I tell you what special considerations you need to make to implement proper concurrency management.

Handling Java Exceptions

Because JSPs are basically HTML templates and the intent of the JSP designers was to keep exception handling as simple as possible, JSPs have some special features for exception handling. An *exception* is a Java-centric term for an application error. Unlike normal Java classes, JSPs have the ability to specify a default error-handler page to capture any unhandled Java exceptions and perform some appropriate action. This default error handler is referred to as the *JSP error page*.

The typical behavior for Java exception handing is to place Java statements that can throw exceptions in a `try-catch` block of code, as in the following example:

```
try{
    Connection conn = DriverManager.getConnection();
}
catch(SQLException e){
  // Handle exception
}
```

In the previous example, the statement in the `try` block attempts to make a connection to a database, and the `catch` block handles the exception if one occurs. With JSPs, you don't have to use `try-catch` blocks to handle exceptions as long as you specify an error-handler page using the `errorPage` directive.

Every JSP can have a page directive that points it to a default error page. In addition, every JSP is identified as an error page or not. By default, a JSP is not an error page. Also by default, no error page is specified for a JSP. To specify whether a JSP is an error page, use the following syntax:

```
<%@ page isErrorPage="{ true | false }"%>
```

To indicate the error page for a JSP, use the following syntax:

```
<%@ page errorPage="{errorPageURL}"%>
```

In this case, the errorPageURL is replaced with the relative path to a JSP error page. A JSP error page must have the isErrorPage attribute of the page directive explicitly set to true. When creating a JSP error page, the error page itself can be a JSP page, or you can make it a static HTML page.

If you don't specify an error page for your JSP and an error occurs, the JSP container will catch the error and spit a stack trace out to your user's browser. You don't want this outcome: It's like the blue screen of death on a Windows operating system. It tells you what the application was doing when the crash occurred. (A stack trace can also be described as the proverbial Technicolor burp.)

A JSP error page can be a valuable debugging tool while you are developing your JSP application, but unless you actually handle your errors in the error page and give some reasonable output to users, ensuring that you don't have to depend on an error page is best. The code in Listing 4-1 contains an error page implementation used to show the current content of all the variables in a JSP when an error occurs.

Listing 4-1: A JSP Error Page for Debugging Purposes

```
<@ page isErrorPage="true"@>
<html>
<head>
<title>Error Page</title>
<meta http-equiv="Content-Type" content="text/html;
          charset=iso-8859-1">
</head>

<body bgcolor="#FFFFFF" text="#000000">
<%-- The exception.getMessage() statement returns the name of
          the error --%>
The error is: <%=exception.getMessage()%>
<P>
<%-- The exception.printStackTrace() statement returns the
          stack, which is all the classes in the execution
          path. --%>
The stack trace is: <%=exception.printStackTrace()%>
<hr>
<P>
Here are the attributes of the application:
<%-- The following for loop presents all the attributes
          stored in the implicit application object. --%>
<%
  for(int index = 0; index <
          application.getAttributeNames().length; index++){
%>
    <BR><%=application.getAttributeNames()[index]%>:
          <%=application.getAttributeValue(
          application.getAttributeNames()[index])%>
```

```
<%
  }
%>
<hr>
<P>
Here are the attributes of the session:
<%-- The following for loop presents all the attributes
           stored in the implicit session object. --%>
<%
  for(int index = 0; index <
           session.getAttributeNames().length; index++){
%>
    <BR><%=session.getAttributeNames()[index]%>:
      <%=session.getAttributeValue(
           session.getAttributeNames()[index])%>
<%
  }
%>
<hr>
<P>
Here are the attributes of the request:
<%-- The following for loop presents all the attributes
           stored in the implicit request object. --%>
<%
  for(int index = 0; index <
           request.getAttributeNames().length; index++){
%>
    <BR><%=request.getAttributeNames()[index]%>:
      <%=request.getAttributeValue(
           request.getAttributeNames()[index])%>
<%
  }
%>
<hr>
<P>
Here are the parameters of the request:
<%-- This block shows all the request parameters sent by the
     user. There are two loops because request attributes can
     have more than one value per name. The out loop steps
     through all the parameters and the inner loop steps
     through all the values for each parameter. --%>
<%
  for(int index = 0; index <
           request.getParameterNames().length; index++){
    for(int loop = 0; loop <
           request.getParameterValues(request.
getParameterNames()[index]); loop++){
%>
      <BR><%=request.getParameterNames()[index]%>
           [<%=Integer.toString(index)%>]:
```

(continued)

Listing 4-1 *(continued)*

```
<%=request.getparameterValues(
          request.getAttributeNames()[index])[loop]%>
<%
    }
  }
%>
<%-- The implicit page attributes cannot be displayed because
          as soon as
the page that throws an error is out of scope, the attributes
          are
     no longer available --%>

</body>
</html>
```

Defining the content type of a JSP

Every JSP page is identified by two attributes that tell JSP containers how to read the characters on the document and how to transport them back to the user's Web browser. These attributes are the content type and the character encoding. The *content type* of a JSP page identifies the "format" of the document. Some common content types are "text/html", "text/xml" and "pdf".

These content types tell a computer how to read a document from a computer's perspective (that is, bits and bytes). The character encoding of a JSP page identifies the language of the characters on the page from a human's perspective. Character encoding schemes are based on the symbols (or letters) that people use to communicate with each other. For example, most Western languages are based on Latin characters, whereas many other different languages around the world don't have Latin characters at all.

You can use the `contentType` attribute of a page directive to define both the content type and the character encoding of a JSP document. The syntax is illustrated below:

```
<%@ page contentType="text/html;ISO-8859-1"%>
```

Note that the content type appears before the semicolon and the character encoding appears after. The code example illustrates the default content type and character encoding for a JSP page. You do not have to use the `contentType` attribute if you are creating JSP pages with the default values.

Using the `contentType` attribute, you can specify the content type of a JSP page and not specify the character encoding. The syntax is simply `contentType="text/html"`, or whatever content type you prefer. In fact, the JSP 1.2 specification introduces the `pageEncoding` attribute discussed next. When working with JSP 1.2 applications, it's probably better to set the character encoding with the `pageEncoding` attribute.

Defining the character encoding of a JSP

In the Java world, all text is represented internally based on the character-encoding scheme, Unicode 2.0. Although all Java programs, including those written with JSP technology, must support Unicode 2.0, they may also support different character-encoding schemes. The `pageEncoding` of a document refers to the character-encoding scheme used to write that document.

The `pageEncoding` attribute was introduced in the JSP 1.2 specification. Prior to that specification, you must use the `contentType` attribute discussed previously to implement character encoding schemes other than the default scheme.

Because JSPs may support different character-encoding schemes, you implement the `pageEncoding` page attribute to specify which character-encoding scheme you wish to use. The syntax for the `pageEncoding` page directive attribute is

```
<%@ page pageEncoding="ISO-8859-1"%>
```

The sample `pageEncoding` page directive above uses the Latin-1 character-encoding scheme, which is the default encoding scheme for JSPs. All JSP containers must support Unicode and Latin-1 character-encoding schemes. Beyond that, the creator of the JSP container is free to implement any kind of encoding scheme desired — as long as it is supported by the JSP container.

When you specify the character encoding of a JSP, the character encoding that you specify becomes the content type assumed for all character content of the page, whether it's content printed from Java code or template data such as the HTML elements and HTML content in the JSP.

Because the `pageEncoding` attribute determines how the JSP container interprets character symbols on a JSP, it must appear as close to the top of the page as possible. The JSP specification requires that all characters prior to a `pageEncoding` attribute stand for themselves, which means they cannot be part of a special character-encoding system. Failure to observe this rule could cause your JSP file to change encoding schemes in the middle of page processing, which could lead to some unpredictable and perhaps unpleasant behavior, not unlike a toddler in the cookie aisle of your local supermarket.

Embedding static documents in JSPs

Sometimes you may need to include static content from an external file in your JSP. In Chapter 3, I illustrate the use of the `<jsp:include>` tag to include either static or dynamic content from another document into a JSP.

JSP technology provides another mechanism — the include directive — for accomplishing a similar end. The syntax for the include directive is

```
<%@ include file="{relativeFileURL}"%>
```

Note that the URL pointing to the location of the file attribute can be relative to the current JSP file in which the include directive is used, or relative to the root of the JSP application. If you want the URL to be relative to the root of the application, the URL must start with a / character. For URLs relative to the JSP file, the URL cannot start with a / character. For more on how applications are structured, refer to Chapter 14.

The include *directive* is different from the include *action* for the following reasons:

- The include directive can only be used to place static content inside a JSP. You can't use it to include dynamic content, such as output from another JSP.
- Although the <jsp:include> tag gets processed when a user requests content from a JSP (request-time processing), the include directive is only processed when the JSP is converted into a Java class. This conversion — *translation* — only happens once in the life of a JSP before anyone uses the JSP.

Because the include directive is processed at translation time, the content of a static file can be embedded directly into the JSP when it's translated — the process of embedding the file only happens once. JSP containers are not required to update the content of an included file in a JSP page after translation. So if you use the include directive, and the file you include changes at a later date, the JSP page is not guaranteed to be updated.

Extending JSP actions with custom tags

In Chapter 3, I cover the usage of standard JSP actions, which are XML-based tags used to perform a set of standard JSP tasks. And although JSP standard actions are powerful, they apply to a relatively small set of tasks.

When the creators of JSP technology recognized that mere mortals (people like you and me) might want more JSP action tags that the specification defines, they created a mechanism to define our own custom actions. All custom actions must be included in *custom tag libraries*, which are basically XML-based descriptions of the syntax for a custom tag. Support for custom tags is a very nice feature of the JSP technology. If you find yourself performing a lot of scripting to implement your JSPs, you'll probably benefit from using custom tags.

In Chapter 12, I cover the nitty-gritty details of using JSP custom tag libraries. If you want to dive in to creating custom tags, refer to Bonus Chapter 4 on the CD. Here, however, I identify the `taglib` directive. Use this directive to get access to the content of a custom tag library. If you plan to use custom tags in your JSPs, you must identify the libraries that you use in each page with the `taglib` directive. Here is the syntax:

```
<%@ taglib uri="{tagLibraryURI}" prefix="{tagPrefix}"%>
```

In this syntax, the `uri` attribute (which stands for *U*niversal *R*esource *I*dentifier, a more generalized term for a URL), refers to either a directory relative to the JSP application root or to some Internet address where the description of the tag library can be found. The prefix identifies the term place before the colon in the action tag to indicate that an action from this particular `taglib` is being used.

As an example, the people involved with the Jakarta-Tomcat project have created a custom tag library called Struts. If you want to use the Struts custom tag library in your JSP, first download the source for the `struts` library and then place one or more of the following `taglib` directives somewhere in your page:

```
<@ taglib uri="/WEB-INF/struts-bean.tld" prefix="bean" %>
<@ taglib uri="/WEB-INF/struts-form.tld" prefix="form" %>
<@ taglib uri="/WEB-INF/struts-logic.tld" prefix="logic" %>
<@ taglib uri="/WEB-INF/struts-template.tld"
           prefix="template" %>
```

After these `taglib` directives are executed, you can refer to the custom actions in these libraries using the prefix for each library, plus the identifier of the action you wish to perform. One example using the `struts-template` library is `<template:get name='header'%>`. Using custom tags such as the `<template:get>` tag is syntactically similar to using the standard JSP action tags identified in Chapter 3.

The `struts-template` library example is specific to the use of Tomcat for a JSP container. Different JSP containers may have additional rules for integrating custom tag libraries into your JSP application. To learn more about Struts or using it in your JSPs, check out the Struts official Web site at `http://jakarta.apache.org/struts`.

The JSP specification reserves certain `taglib` prefixes as reserved words that can only be used to identify standard tags provided by JavaSoft or Sun Microsystems. The reserved `taglib` prefixes are `jsp:`, `jspx:`, `java:`, `javax:`, `servlet:`, `sun:`, and `sunw:`. Beyond these reserved prefixes, you can pick any prefix that you desire to identify the content of a particular tag library. (Try to keep it clean, though.)

Scripting in Java

In this chapter, I cover a lot of topics that illustrate the use of Java as a scripting language in JSPs. Most of these examples are pretty simple, and if you have some exposure to JavaScript, you should be able to follow them easily enough. If you find yourself getting lost, read Bonus Chapter 2 on the CD for an overview of some Java fundamentals.

Bonus Chapter 2 is intended as a resource to help you understand the examples in this book; a complete reference of the Java language is beyond the scope of the book.

If you're just getting started with the Java language, check out the *Java 2 Bible,* by Aaron Walsh, Justin Couch, and Daniel H. Steinberg, published by Hungry Minds, Inc.

The JSP specification doesn't require Java to be the only scripting language for JSP scripting. It does, however, require that any language used for JSP scripting is able to provide the same syntactical elements required by the JSP specification. It also requires support for some functionality that is native to Java, such as exception handling. Consequently, you can probably assume that Java will be the only scripting language implemented for JSP scripting. I make that assumption in this book for simplicity's sake.

Commenting Your Code

Commenting is one of the most important tasks of programming. Commenting is crucial because the comments communicate your intentions to other developers who work with your code, and perhaps even to yourself. We're all guilty, myself included, of not providing enough comments to clearly describe what we're doing. Commenting the code is pretty difficult if you're not sure how, so read on for the skinny.

JSP technology supports two mechanisms for commenting code:

- **Where is it?!:** The `"hidden"` comment. (About now you're asking yourself, "Why go through the effort of creating a comment no one can read?" Hold your horses — I'm getting to that.) *Hidden comments* are comments that are removed by the JSP container before the output of your page is sent to a user. If you have anything to say behind a user's back, put it in a hidden comment.

- **Stylin':** HTML style comments. *HTML style comments*, like all HTML content, are ignored by the JSP container, which means that they get sent to the user's browser. You can write any kind of comments here when it doesn't matter who reads the comment. Place your code copyright comments in HTML style comments.

If you want to write hidden comments (not visible in the HTML output of a page), you can use the alternative mechanism for commenting JSPs — the JSP comment. JSP comments are delimited by `<%--` and `--%>` tags, and you can write anything in the body of the comment except a closing comment tag (`--%>`). The following code snippet is an example of a JSP style comment:

```
<%-- this is a JSP comment --%>
```

If you're already familiar with Web page development, the HTML style comment is nothing new. Set off by `<!--` and `-->` tags, it's characterized by the fact that it's visible in the source of the HTML code sent to a user's browser. You can write anything that you want in the body of an HTML comment except for the closing tag `-->`, which is reserved. The following code snippet is an example of an HTML style comment.

```
<!-- this is an HTML comment -->
```

Declaring Scripting Variables

Java is a strongly typed language, meaning that you have to declare the type of data you want to store in a variable before you use the variable. When you declare a variable, the Java Virtual Machine (JVM) — the container that runs all Java programs — creates a placeholder for the identifier that you specify, which is then used to refer to the variable you create. A declaration scripting element is a block of Java code in a JSP delimited by `<%!` and `%>` tags. The syntax for the declaration(s) scripting element is illustrated below:

```
<%! {declaration(s)} %>
```

The declaration syntax can be used to declare scripting variables or it can be used to declare a method. You can also include multiple declarations in a single declaration scripting element. Here are two examples:

```
<%! int rowCount = 0; %>
<%! public String talkBack(String talk){ return talk; }%>
```

In the first example, the rowCount of type int variable is declared and initialized to a value of 0. In the second example, the talkBack method is declared. The talkBack method takes a String with some text and returns the same String back. In both cases, the variable or the method can be reference from any declaration, expression, or scriptlet tag in the JSP.

You can place multiple declarations inside a single set of declaration tags.

Being able to declare methods inside a JSP is pretty cool. But if you want to reuse the same method in other JSPs, take cool up another notch and declare the method in a JavaBean class. JavaBeans are not bound to a particular page, and the same JavaBean can be used in multiple JSPs at the same time. Finally, if you ever need to change the method you create, all you have to do is modify one JavaBean instead of hunting down and updating all the JSPs in which you declared the method.

With declaration tags, you can create certain variables and methods in a JSP that are static. They are class scope, and all the instances of the JSP work with the same values. If you use the static modifier in a variable or method declaration for a JSP and your JSP supports multithreading, you must synchronize access to that variable or method. Otherwise, more than one thread can manipulate the variable or method, resulting in inconsistent behavior in your JSP application.

Expressing Yourself with Expression Tags

JSP expression tags are used to convert the output of a JSP expression into a String and print that String out to the user. In plain English, an expression can be equated to either a sentence fragment or a sentence. The expression in Java can stand on its own and generates a single value as output. The syntax of an expression tag is

```
<%= {expression} %>
```

An example of an expression is

```
<%= (new java.util.Date()).toLocaleString()%>
```

This expression creates a Date object in Java, which stores the current system data and time and then prints that date and time out as a String. Because the content is already a String, the content of the expression is written directly to output, which is subsequently sent to the user. If the type of an expression is not a String, the JSP container attempts to convert the content to a String before sending the output to a user. If the JSP output cannot be converted to a String, the JSP container raises an error.

Use an expression tag to insert dynamic content into the appropriate position in a JSP. Suppose that you want to create a personalized greeting for a user of your Web site. Presuming that you have the user's name stored as an attribute in the implicit `request` object, print that name in the greeting with some code like this:

```
<P> Hello, <%=(String)request.getAttribute("userName")%>!
```

If you execute a program and supply the name `Mac Rinehart` in the `request` attribute for `userName`, the output on an HTML page would be `Hello, Mac Rinehart!`

In the previous example, notice the lack of a semicolon to terminate the expression. In expressions, semicolons are not used to terminate statements. The JSP container creates a statement out of the expression your supply and provides its own statement terminator.

Breaking It Down with Scriptlets

JSP scriptlet tags are very similar to expression tags. And if you've written ASP pages, you'll be very comfortable with the scriptlet tag because the syntax for scriptlet tags is identical to the syntax of a script in Active Server Pages (ASP). The basic syntax is

```
<% {statement fragment | one or more statements} %>
```

Note a few differences between scriptlets and expressions:

- Scriptlets don't always generate output on a JSP, but expressions always do.
- A scriptlet does not have to be a complete and valid statement as long as a sequence of scriptlets forms a complete and valid statement. In contrast, an expression tag must contain a complete, valid statement.
- Statements in a scriptlet must be terminated with an appropriate statement terminator: semicolons (;) for simple statements and a curly brace ({) for compound statements. JSP expressions can't be compound statements and can't have a statement terminator.

To drive these points home, a few examples of scriptlets are in order. In the first example, an if-else structure is used to determine which part of the template data in a JSP is displayed:

```
<% if(retryCount > 1){%>
  You've tried this more than once.
<%}else{%>
  This is your first attempt.
<%}%>
```

In this example, note that all the scriptlets taken together form a complete compound statement in Java. Because this scriptlet forms a complete statement, it is legal. Now for the interesting part. If the condition in the `if` clause of the scriptlet evaluates to `true`, this JSP will print `You've tried this more than once`. Otherwise, the page will print `This is your first attempt`. In this example, the scriptlet is used to control the output of the page; depending on the way the condition evaluates in the `if` statement, different content from the JSP template data is printed.

In the next example, the scriptlet is used to perform a set of Java operations that don't generate any output:

```
<%
  DataWriter write = Database.getDataWriter("customer");
  write.setAttribute("firstName", "Mac");
  write.setAttribute("lastName", "Rinehart");
  write.setAttribute("ssn", "999-99-9999");
  write.setAttribute("creditRating", "iron pyrite");
  Write.insertData();
%>
```

In this example, I use the hypothetical class `DataWriter` to write some information about myself into a customer record, which is then inserted into the database. The example does not generate any output, and it contains multiple statements. Because all the statements are fully formed and properly terminated with semicolons, this scriptlet block should execute without any trouble.

Although you can use scriptlets throughout a JSP, my recommendation is to keep the tasks you perform with a scriptlet very simple. Experience has shown me that scriptlets make a JSP more difficult to maintain and more error prone. Excessive use of scriptlets is also a good clue that the design of your application needs reworked. (As an example, the JSP error page in Listing 4-1 illustrates the excessive use of scriptlets.)

A better approach to coding JSPs is to use the standard action tags that I discuss in Chapter 3 and to extend those tags with a third-party tag library such as Struts. If you do find yourself in a pinch and need a script to implement some feature, be sure to keep it simple. For more information on using custom tag libraries, check out Chapter 12.

Chapter 5

JavaScript Fundamentals

In This Chapter

- Getting the jist of JavaScript
- Declaring JavaScript variables and datatypes
- Figuring out JavaScript control structures and operators
- Using JavaScript arrays
- Writing JavaScript functions
- Creating objects and multidimensional arrays in JavaScript

The primary mission of this book is to provide you with an accessible reference to the JavaServer Pages (JSP) technology, but JSP applications that don't take advantage of browser scripting languages such as JavaScript are missing out on a powerful and flexible tool for enhancing the user experience.

Today's Internet users are much more sophisticated than they were just a year or two ago. To make a good impression, businesses have to deliver Web content that's not only personalized but also interactive. That means implementing client-side scripting languages and dynamic HyperText Markup Language (HTML) to present personalized and interactive content. These issues should be of particular concern to Web designers because they affect the look and feel of a Web site and the quality of a user's experience, and because they contribute as much to the aesthetic quality of a Web site as they do to the function of the site.

JavaScript is one of the most-established scripting languages for this task, and I certainly couldn't profess to be interested in the Web designer's experience if I didn't devote some significant space to JavaScript.

In this chapter and Chapter 6, I provide you with as much of an overview of JavaScript as I can within the scope of this book. This chapter is devoted to the basics of the JavaScript language: I strive to provide thorough coverage, but I can't cover everything in only two chapters. This chapter will get you a significant foothold on the topic of JavaScript if you're using it for the first time.

If you already feel comfortable with JavaScript fundamentals, you should probably skip ahead to Chapter 6. In Chapter 6, I digress from the reference mold for a while and provide you with some tips and tricks that I've picked up over the years that you can use to make some pretty nifty Web pages!

This book is full of recommendations on other resources that cover what I can't within the scope of this book. But if you are only able to heed one or two of those recommendations, look no further than two books by Danny Goodman: *JavaScript Bible,* 4th Edition (Hungry Minds, Inc.) and *Dynamic HTML: the Complete Reference*. In my opinion, Danny is the best author on the topic of HTML and Web scripting writing today. These two books are absolute must-haves for anyone who is serious about developing Web content.

What Is JavaScript?

JavaScript is a scripting language created to run inside Web browsers. JavaScript is used to create interactive Web sites and to validate user input on an HTML form. If you browse popular Web sites, you've probably seen sites with interactive menus and buttons that change colors when you roll over them with your mouse pointer. These features are implemented using JavaScript.

JavaScript is written to work closely with the HTML content on a Web page by interacting with the attributes of HTML elements — either by reading the values of those attributes or setting them when certain events happen in a Web browser. Any kind of action that you might take with a Web browser usually has an event associated with it. For example, when the `<BODY>` element of an HTML document finishes loading, a load event is created. When you click a button, a click event is created.

By using JavaScript, you can write functions that are executed when these events happen. JavaScript functions can do simple tasks such as making sure that data entered into a text field is the correct format. Or, JavaScript functions can perform very sophisticated tasks, such as moving `<OPTION>` elements from one `<SELECT>` element to another.

Although you can perform very sophisticated tasks with JavaScript, keep in mind that JavaScript is a scripting language, which means that it's not particularly fast. In addition, all the JavaScript code on a page has to be downloaded to a browser, meaning that Web pages with lots of JavaScript code may take longer to download.

The <SCRIPT> element

Web browsers don't automatically know when you are writing JavaScript; you have to tell them. To do so, HTML includes a special element called the <SCRIPT> element. When you get started writing JavaScript, the first task is to create a <SCRIPT> element and place your JavaScript code inside that element. When you create a <SCRIPT> element, you need to specify which scripting language you are using, such as in the following example:

```
<SCRIPT LANGUAGE="JavaScript">
  // all the code between the script tags is JavaScript
</SCRIPT>
```

Declaring JavaScript

The <SCRIPT> element can be placed just about anywhere in an HTML page, as long as it's between the <HTML> and </HTML> tags. When you send an HTML page to a Web browser with <SCRIPT> elements, the browser reads those script elements in the order that they appear in the HTML file. Inside a <SCRIPT> element, you can declare JavaScript variables and functions and you can execute JavaScript code.

Don't nest other HTML elements inside a <SCRIPT> element. Doing so will result in browser errors.

Executing JavaScript

Any JavaScript statement inside a <SCRIPT> that's not part of a declaration gets executed as soon as the browser reads the statement. If you want to execute code inside the script tag, you must obey a couple of rules:

- You must declare JavaScript functions before you execute them. If you attempt to execute a function before you declare the function, the browser won't know what to do and will throw a scripting error.
- If you reference other HTML elements in a <SCRIPT>, those elements must be completely loaded by the browser. The browser must have read the whole HTML element (including the opening tag and the closing tag for that element) before you try to use the element in a JavaScript function.

Try to avoid executing JavaScript statements inside <SCRIPT> tags and instead only write declarations inside the tags. Keep in mind that all JavaScript statements can be executed as needed when events are created in an HTML page. Virtually all HTML elements have special event handlers built into them that you can use to execute JavaScript functions. All you have to do is decide which element handles the events that you need to respond to, and then place a call to your JavaScript function inside the event handler for that HTML element.

The following code snippet illustrates usage of the `<BODY>` `onLoad` event handler to perform initialization of JavaScript variables.

```
<HTML>
<SCRIPT LANGUAGE="JavaScript">
  function initializeScript(){
    // do some initialization here
  }
<SCRIPT>
<HEAD>
</HEAD>
<BODY onLoad="initializeScript()">
</BODY>
</HTML>
```

Commenting in JavaScript

JavaScript uses *C-style* comments, which should be familiar to you if you've used programming languages such as Java, C, or C++. Multiline comments are indicated by `/*` and `*/` delimiters at the beginning and end of the comment, and single-line comments begin with a `//` delimiter. Everything following a `//` delimiter is part of the comment until the end of that line. Here are some JavaScript comment examples.

```
<SCRIPT LANGUAGE="JavaScript">
  /* This is a
     multi-line comment.
  */
  function initializeScript(){
    // this is a single line comment
  }
<SCRIPT>
```

JavaScript Variables

JavaScript variables are very simple and flexible. JavaScript, unlike Java, is not a strongly typed language. You don't have to declare the datatype of a variable when you create it. The datatype of a variable is automatically changed to support any kind of value that you choose to write into it. The following statement declares a JavaScript variable:

```
var giantSpeak = "Fee, Fi, Fo, Fum, I smell the breath of an
        Englishman."
```

Variable datatypes

JavaScript automatically defines the datatype of a variable based on what type of data that you place in the variable. The following list of types identifies the types of data that JavaScript stores in variables.

- After you create a variable and before you assign a value to it, the variable type is `undefined`. Variables of type `undefined` cause JavaScript errors if you try to use them in a JavaScript expression, with the following exception. JavaScript has a built-in function called `undefined()` that accepts a variable, which returns a Boolean `true` or `false`, depending on whether the variable is defined or not.
- Variables are of type `String` when you store any value that is delimited either by single quotes or double quotes.
- Any numeric value assigned to a variable that is not delimited by quotes is a `Number` type.
- If you store the Boolean values `true` or `false` to a variable (not delimited by single or double quotes), the type of the variable is `Boolean`.
- Finally, you can store null to a variable, which means the variable has no value.

If you first assign a value of one type to a variable and then replace that value with another value of a different type, the variable type automatically changes to the value of the second type.

Variable scope

JavaScript variables have three scopes: page (global to the HTML page); function (local to a JavaScript function); and statement (limited to the duration of a JavaScript statement). Global variables in JavaScript can be referenced anywhere in the HTML document in which they are declared. The following code snippet illustrates variables of all three scopes in bold type:

```
<SCRIPT LANGUAGE="JavaScript">
  var global = "I am a global variable"

  function varExample( varExampleParameter){
    // function parameters are local to the function

    var local = "I am local to the varExample function"
```

```
    if(true){
      var statementScope = "only visible inside curly braces"
    }
  }
</SCRIPT>
```

Casting, conversion, and coercion

Casting, *conversion*, and *coercion* are all terms referring to the task of changing the type of variable from one type to another. The rules for changing the datatype of a variable are very simple in JavaScript:

- When you append any value to a String (using the + operator), the result of the operation is a string. For example, the operation `"same" + 4` yields the value `same4`.
- Any math operation involving numeric datatypes yields the type value resulting from the operation. Two whole number integers may become a floating-point value when one divides the other. That differs from strongly typed languages such as Java, where the result of integer math is always an integer.
- A JavaScript variable always assumes the datatype of the last value assigned to it.

JavaScript provides a special operator called `typeof`, which you can use to determine the type of a value before you perform an operation. If you need to determine the type of a value, place the `typeof` operator before the variable. JavaScript evaluates the variable and outputs a String corresponding to the type of the variable. The following code snippet illustrates the use of the `typeof` operator.

```
var myNumber = 1
var myString = "testing"
var isNumeric = (typeof myNumber == "number")
// value of isNumeric: true
var outputType = typeof myString
// value of outputType: String
```

Operator, Can You Help Me?

JavaScript operators are very similar to those found in Java. Table 5-1 provides a listing of JavaScript operators in their order of precedence. JavaScript operators are evaluated from the highest order of precedence to the lowest. Operators of the same precedence are evaluated from left to right.

Table 5-1 JavaScript Operators in Order of Precedence

Operators	*Description*
`(, )`	Scope operators are evaluated from the innermost parentheses in an expression to the outermost.
`!, -, ++, --, typeof`	Boolean `not`, `negation` (when applied to the front of a value or variable), `increment`, `decrement`, and `typeof` operators are all in the same order of precedence.
`*, /, %`	Multiply, divide and modulo operators.
`+, -`	Addition and subtraction.
`==, !=`	Equal and not equal.
`&&`	Logical and.
`||`	Logical or.
`=, +=, -=, *=, /=, %=`	Assignment operators. When an assignment operator is attached to a math operator, the math operator evaluates the variable to the left of the operator and the result of the expression on the right of the operator, and the result is assigned to the variable on the left.

JavaScript Conditional and Loop Statements

Conditional and loop statements are the basic control structures of JavaScript. They enable you to perform stepwise and conditional operations. These operations control the order in which other statements are processed in your JavaScript functions. The two conditional statements are the `if` statement and the `case` statement. JavaScript provides three loop statements: `while`, `do-while`, and `for`.

if statements

JavaScript `if` statements evaluate a logical expression and perform the statements inside the `if` statement when that logical expression evaluates to a Boolean `true`. The following example illustrates the syntax of the `if` statement.

```
if(logicalExpression == true){
  // excecute statements inside the curly braces
  // this is the body of the if statement
}
```

One of the most frequent coding errors I encountered in JavaScript is confusing the logical equals (==) operator with the assignment operator (=). If you use an assignment operator inside the logical expression of a JavaScript `if` statement, the value following the assignment operator is assigned to the value proceeding the assignment operator, and the statements inside the body of the `if` statement are executed every time.

Multiple if conditions

If you need to make chains of `if` statements, you can do so by creating `if-else` statements. In addition, you can nest `if` statements inside other `if` statements. The following example illustrates the use of `if-else` statements and nested statements.

```
if(condition){
  // do this part if condition is true
  if(secondCondition){
    //this is a nested if statement.
  }
}
else{
  // do this part if condition is false
}
```

switch statements

`switch` statements in JavaScript evaluate an expression and perform the set of operations associated with a case if the variable equals the value of the case. `switch` statements in JavaScript can evaluate any type of expression, whereas Java switch statements can only evaluate integral expressions. The following code illustrates the syntax of a `switch` statement:

```
switch(expression){
  case label1:
    //statements if expression == label1
    [break] /* optional syntax causes execution to continue
           on the next line
               after the switch statement.*/
  case label2:
    // statements if expression == label2
    [break]
  case labelN:
```

```
    // statements to execute if expression == labelN
    [break]
  [default:]
    /* statements in the default case execute if none of the
          prevous cases is
       executed. The default case is optional. */
}
```

Note that each case clause has a label, which is the value the expression of the switch statement is compared with. If the label and the expression are equal, the case is executed. Unless you specify a break statement inside a case, when the browser is finished executing the case statement, it will continue to evaluate each of the following case statements. If you want some default operation to be performed in the event that none of the other cases is executed, you can provide a `default:` label in your case statement. The `default:` label is optional.

while loop

You should use `while` loops when you have a repetitive task that must be performed an undetermined number of times or may not need to be performed at all. `while` loops evaluate a condition and execute the statements in the body of the loop if the condition evaluates to a Boolean `true`. Inside the body of a `while` loop, some operation should occur that changes the result of the condition when the loop no longer needs to execute. The following example illustrates the syntax of a `while` loop.

```
while(whileExpression == true){
  // execute statements inside while loop
  if(exitCondition == true){
    // be sure to provide a way to exit the while loop
    whileExpression == false;
  }
}
```

If you don't provide a way to break the `while` loop, it's called an *infinite loop*. Infinite loops cause a Web browser to execute the same set of instructions over and over until the Web browser runs out of memory and crashes. Because it's generally a good idea to avoid situations that cause a Web browser to crash, I recommend not creating infinite loops.

do-while loop

If you have a repetitive set of operations that need to be executed at least once and may execute an unknown number of times, use a `do-while` loop.

The do-while loop executes once and then evaluates an expression and continues to execute as long as the expression evaluates to a Boolean true. The following example illustrates the syntax of a do-while loop.

```
do{
  // execute these statements at least once
  if(exitCondition == true){
    doWhileCodition = false
  }
}while(doWhileCondition == true)
```

Provide a mechanism inside each loop to exit the loop when your repetitive task is completed.

for loops

If you need to execute a set of repetitive tasks a predetermined number of times, you should use a for loop. The following statement illustrates the syntax of a for loop:

```
for(var loopIndex = minValue; loopIndex < maxValue;
           loopIndex++){
  // execute these statements
}
```

In the for loop the first line contains three statements:

1. The first statement defines a loop control variable that is used to track the number of times the loop has executed. The loop control variable is initialized to the minimum value of the loop. The loop control variable can be referenced anywhere inside the body of the for loop but cannot be used after the loop finishes executing.
2. The second statement is a logical expression that's evaluated before the body of the for loop is executed. The logical expression is evaluated once for each iteration of the for loop. When the logical expression evaluates to false, the for loop is terminated and the program continues to execute on the next line after the for loop statement.
3. The third statement is used to increment the value of the loop control variable. The third statement is executed once for each iteration of the for loop after the last statement in the body of the loop is evaluated.

JavaScript Arrays

Arrays are used to store ordered sets of data. In plain speak, a *set* is a logically related group of items. When you have an ordered set of data, the set of related items is stored in specific order. JavaScript makes working with arrays flexible and easy. Peer past your Opti-Grabs at the following code example that illustrates the declaration of an array that contains three elements.

```
// an array declaration
var allINeed = new Array(3) // declare an array with three
          elements

allINeed[0] = "this lamp"
allINeed[1] = "this phone"
allINeed[2] = "this thermos bottle"
```

The order of elements in an array is determined by an array index. The array index is referenced inside the square brackets following the variable named of the array, as illustrated in the previous example.

Because JavaScript is not strongly typed, any Jerk can store pretty much any type of value that he needs inside a JavaScript array. JavaScript also enables you to store different types of data in different indexes of an array. This is certainly atypical of programming languages, and it can lead to some pretty confusing code. I recommend that all the values that you store in an array are of the same type.

Size doesn't matter

JavaScript doesn't constrain the size of an array to the size that you specify when you declare it. That means that you can dynamically increase the number of elements in an array simply by assigning values to new index positions in the array. In the previous section, I declare a new array with a length of 3, but I could add more elements at any time as illustrated in the following example.

```
// an array declaration
var allINeed = new Array(3) // declare and array with three
          elements
allINeed[0] = "this lamp"
allINeed[1] = "this phone"
allINeed[2] = "this thermos bottle"
allINeed[3] = "this blankie"
allINeed[4] = "coffee"
```

Given that size doesn't matter, you may wonder why you specify the size of an array. The problem with dynamically increasing the size of an array is that it requires the browser to find more memory for the array each time you add a new element. If you specify the size of an array in advance, the memory for that array is allocated all at once, making the operation more efficient.

Accessing array values

In JavaScript programs, you will probably find yourself in the position of having to perform some kind of operation on each element of an array. Because you can determine the size of an array in advance, you can use a `for` loop to step through each index of any array and perform an operation on each element in the array.

Every JavaScript array has a length attribute that you can use to determine the number of items stored in the array. In the following code example, I initialize the values of an array using a `for` loop and referencing the length of the array.

```
var myArray = new Array(5)
for( var index = 0; index < myArray.length; index++){
  /* note I use the loop control variable to identify which
             index of the array I
     am initializing. */
  myArray[index] = "defaultValue"
}
```

JavaScript Functions

JavaScript functions are the units of code that you write to perform tasks on a Web page. A JavaScript function must be written inside `<HTML>` script tags. The basic syntax for creating a JavaScript function is illustrated in the following example.

```
function myFunction(param1, param2, paramN){
  // declare function scope variables
  // execute some statements
  [return returnValue] // optionally return some value
}
```

Declaring functions

Each JavaScript function is identified by the keyword `function`, followed by the name of the function. In the previous example, the name of the function is `myFunction`. The entire function, from the function keyword to the closing curly brace of the function's body, is the function declaration.

If you want your JavaScript function to accept parameters, you declare the parameters in the first line of the function. The parameters are defined as a comma-delimited list inside the parenthesis on the first line, as illustrated in the previous code example.

In JavaScript, you can add an optional return statement to a function to return a single value from the function.

Using JavaScript functions

The first line of the JavaScript function is called its *signature*. If you want to execute a JavaScript function, you write the name of the function and pass the same number of parameters that the function defines in its signature. If the function returns a value, you can assign that value to a variable. The following code example illustrates calling a JavaScript function.

```
var param1 = "first parameter"
var param2 = "second parameter"
var param3 = "third parameter"
var functionResult = myFunction(param1, param2, param3);
```

Passing parameters by reference or value

Passing a variable by value means that a copy of the value stored in the variable is passed to the function. When variables are passed by reference, a reference to the same variable is passed. The difference between these two techniques is evident when you modify the content of a parameter in a function.

If the parameter is passed by value, modifying the value inside a function doesn't change the value of the variable outside the function. But if you modify a variable that was passed by reference, changing the value of that variable inside a function will cause it to be changed outside the function. The parameter inside the function and the variable outside the function reference the same value.

In many programming languages, you can specify whether you want to pass variables by value or by reference. In JavaScript, the rules for passing variables are predefined and can't be changed. These rules apply not only when a variable is passed to a function but also when a variable is involved in an assignment or comparison operation.

The rules for passing variables in JavaScript are outlined in the following bullets.

- If you pass a variable that is a number or a Boolean datatype, the variable is always passed by value. Likewise, if you assign a variable of type `Boolean` or number to another variable, a copy of the value is created and placed in the target variable. Consequently, if you change the value of the target variable, the original variable will not be affected.

- If you are passing an object, array, or function, the variable is always passed by reference. Likewise, assignments that assign a function, object, or array to a variable are assigned by reference, which means that the target variable references the same object, function, or array as the original variable after the assignment is complete. Consequently, changes to either variable will affect the other.
- Strings are special. When they are passed to functions, they are passed by reference; but when they are compared, they are compared by value. If you pass a string to a function and then change it inside the function, the original variable also changes. However, when you compare two strings, the values of the strings are compared.

If you want to pass an array to a function and you don't want changes inside the function to impact the contents of the array outside the function, you need to pass a copy of the array to the function. Fortunately JavaScript allows you to create explicit copies of arrays, using the `Array.slice()` function, as illustrated in the following example:

```
var myArray = new Array()
var result = myFunction( myArray.slice(0))
```

The `Array.slice()` function creates a copy of the specified section of an array, as indicated by a `startIndex` parameter and an optional `endIndex` parameter. In the previous example, I specify a `startIndex` of 0 and no end index. The result is a copy of the array that begins on the 0 index of the array and contains all the elements of the array following the 0 index.

JavaScript Built-in Functions

In addition to the functions you write, all JavaScript programs have access to several built-in functions. Built-in functions can be used anywhere in your JavaScript functions and perform several useful tasks.

The eval() function

Given the name of the object, you can use the `eval()` function to get an object reference to an object. This function plays a critical role in making dynamic HTML possible because you can use this function to get references to HTML elements in a Web page — now you can read and modify their properties in JavaScript. To get a reference to an object on your HTML page, you need to supply the fully qualified name or `id` of the object as a string. The following code illustrates the use of the `eval()` function.

```
<HTML>
  <HEAD>
  </HEAD>
  <SCRIPT LANGUAGE="JavaScript">
    function goDynamic(){
      // first I get an object reference to the example HTML
          element
      var obj = eval("document.all.example")
      // next I check to make sure my object reference is not
          undefined
      if( obj != undefined ){
        // change the value of the example text field from
          JavaScript
        obj.value = "Now you're writing Dynamic HTML!"
      }
    }
  <SCRIPT>
  <BODY onLoad="goDynamic()">
    <FORM>
      <INPUT TYPE="text" NAME="dynamicExample" ID="example">
    </FORM>
  </BODY>
</HTML>
```

Functions for numbers

Because JavaScript doesn't have strongly typed variables and all the values of HTML elements are strings, JavaScript provides several functions for converting string data to a numeric format and for determining whether the value of a string is numeric or not.

The isNaN() function

The `isNaN()` function is shorthand for *is not a number*. The `isNaN()` function accepts a String parameter containing the value to be tested. If the String supplied cannot be converted to a number, the function returns `true`. Otherwise, the function returns `false`. You can use this function to determine whether a user has entered the correct kind of data in a text field. The following code sample illustrates the use of the `isNaN()` function.

```
function checkType( param){
  if( isNaN(param)){
    alert("this parameter is not a number")
  }
  else{
    alert("this parameter is a number")
  }
}
```

The parseFloat() and parseInt() functions

The `parseFloat()` and `parseInt()` functions are respectively used to convert String values to a decimal number or an integer number. Both functions take a String parameter and attempt to convert the String to a number. In addition, the `parseInt()` function can accept a radix, which identifies the number system, such as base 10 or binary, to convert the String to. If you want your numbers converted to a base 10 number using `parseInt()`, you should specify a radix of 10. The following code sample illustrates the use of the `parseInt()` and `parseFloat()` functions.

```
var intValue = parseInt("120", 10)
// intValue = 120
var floatValue = parseFloat("2.005")
// floatValue = 2.005
var funkyExample = parseFloat("5.02 is the value of this
          String")
// funkyExample = 5.02
var funkyExample2 = parseFloat("the value of this String is
          5.02")
// funkyExample2 = Number.NaN
```

Both `parseInt()` and `parseFloat()` functions can convert Strings that start with a numeric digit to a number. Basically, they convert the numeric portion of the String, and ignore the remaining characters, as in the `funkyExample` above. In order to take advantage of this feature, the String parameter must begin with a number. If the first character of the String is not a number, the result of the function will be the constant value `Number.NaN`, which is the way that JavaScript tells you the value supplied is not a number.

String functions

JavaScript provides two string functions for converting variables to a string datatype. The `String()` function creates a string based on the contents of the value supplied as a parameter. The value supplied can be a literal value or an object reference. The `String()` function converts the supplied value into a string object and returns a reference to the object.

When you assign a literal string value to a variable, such as the case `var example = "some text"`, the literal text is actually stored as an array of characters by your Web browser and is not the same as a string object. When you create a string object, you get several convenient methods with the object for working with string values. Hence, it's a good idea to create string objects out of literal strings.

The second function is the toString() method. The toString() method is a method of every JavaScript object. When you call the toString() method of an object, your Web browser will return a string corresponding with the object you call the toString() method on. The return value may be a string representing the value of the object or it may be a string form of the object name.

Objects in JavaScript

JavaScript enables you to create objects to represent complex entities. Objects can contain attributes and methods. Defining an object in JavaScript is identical to creating a function. Here's an example:

```
function myObject(param1, param2, paramN){
  this.attrib1 = param1
  this.attrib2 = param2
  this.attrib3 = paramN

  this.sumAttributes = function(){return attrib1 + attrib2 +
          attrib3 }
}
```

In the previous example, the key difference between a function and an object in JavaScript is the presence of the this operator. The object in the previous example uses the this operator to assign parameters to corresponding attributes of the function.

In addition to assigning parameters to attributes of this object, the previous example illustrates the creation of an object method. The name of the object method is defined as an attribute of the object; in this case, it's called sumAttributes. The method is identified by the function keyword and does not take any parameters. In this case, the method has a return statement that returns the sum of the three attributes defined in the object.

Note that support for nested methods inside JavaScript objects depends on the kind and version of browser you are using. Some browsers don't support nested methods in JavaScript objects at all.

To make use of a JavaScript object, you have to create an instance of that object. You create an instance of an object by using the new operator and writing the signature of the object (its name and parameters). When creating a new object, you have to store the instance of the object in a variable in order to reference it later. The following code sample illustrates the creation of an instance of a JavaScript object, which is stored into a variable.

```
var obj = new myObject(param1, param2, param3)
var attribSum = obj.sumAttributes()
```

Multidimensional Arrays

When you employ JavaScript's object technology and array technology, you can create object arrays that act like multidimensional arrays. The following code sample creates a multidimensional array and uses it to store information about invoice line items.

```
// this is the object declaration for an invoiceItem
function invoiceItem(description, itemNo, quantity,
          unitPrice, taxRate){
  this.description = description
  this.itemNo = itemNo
  this.quantity = quantity
  this.unitPrice = unitPrice
  this.taxRate = taxRate
  this.extendedPrice = function(){return unitPrice * quantity
          + (unitPrice * quantity * taxRate)} // extended
          price is calculated
}

// this array contains invoice objects
var invoice = new Array()
invoice[0] = new invoiceItem("shirt", 345, 1, 25.00, .08)
invoice[1] = new invoiceItem("pants", 739, 2, 35.00, .08)

for(var index = 0; index < invoice.length; index++){
  /* to reference the attributes of the object, refer to the
          array[index] and the
     attribute name */
  alert( invoice[index].description + ' ' +
          invoice[index].itemNo + '. . .')
}
```

Cataloging Functions in a JavaScript File

Two common tasks you perform when writing JavaScript programs are implementing Dynamic HTML functionality (such as menus in a Web site) and form validation. As you develop JavaScript functions to perform these tasks, you'll find that some operations are the same in virtually every HTML page you write. Rewriting these functions over and over doesn't make sense.

To promote reuse of JavaScript functions, you can store them in a separate file, called a *JavaScript file,* and include that file in every HTML Web page that needs to use the functions. JavaScript files have a `.js` file extension. With `.js` files, you can catalog related sets of functions that you use in many Web pages. When you write a JavaScript file, you don't enclose JavaScript functions in `<SCRIPT>` tags.

To include a JavaScript file in a Web page, you make a reference to the URL of the source file using the src attribute of the <SCRIPT> element. When you use a <SCRIPT> element to include an external JavaScript file, you must leave the body of the <SCRIPT> tag empty. After you include a JavaScript file in your HTML Web page, you can call any of the functions in that file and create any objects of that file as if those functions and objects were defined on the Web page. The following code sample illustrates including the contents of a JavaScript file called formcheck.js.

```
<!-- THE BODY OF THE SCRIPT TAG MUST BE EMPTY!!! -->
<SCRIPT LANGUAGE="JavaScript"
            SRC="http://www.somesite.com/formcheck.js">
</SCRIPT>
```

In this case, the src attribute of the <SCRIPT> tag is a URL to a file on a Web site. You can also specify a URL that is relative to the directory containing the HTML file that you deploy to a Web browser. Remember that the output of a JSP file is HTML, so it's valid to use a URL relative to the JSP file that you use to create an HTML file.

Chapter 6

Performing Form Validation with JavaScript

In This Chapter

- Getting the basics of JavaScript form validation
- Checking out some typical validation scripts
- Implementing event handlers for validation rule violations
- Mastering techniques for alerting users of violated rules

Validation rules are the preventative maintenance of JSP programming. They ensure that the information supplied by users is properly formatted and consistent with the needs of your JSP application. Without validation rules, users can easily cause your JSP application to crash. Then they'll get mad, send you angry e-mails, and leave you wondering what happened.

Perhaps the most common reason for a JSP application to fail is the lack of sufficient validation rules. This is such an important topic that software testers have a special type of testing for form validation called the *Monkey Test*. Basically, the testers act like a monkey on a computer, typing whatever they want wherever they want and submitting partially completed forms. If your JSP program crashes, you lose. (But really, who wins in this scenario? Your application may crash, but at least you haven't spent hours pounding on a keyboard, eating bananas, and grooming your friends.)

With JavaScript validation rules, you can show those monkeys that you're smarter than they are. This chapter introduces the topic of JavaScript validation rules, providing several examples of the types of validation rules that you may need to implement in your JSP application.

Why Should I Use JavaScript for Form Validation?

One of the biggest challenges of working with JSP applications is ensuring that users enter the correct kind of data in fields of a Web page. All HTML data is submitted to the Web server as a string of text. Although JSP applications do automatically attempt to convert all HTML data to the type that your JSP application requires, if a user enters an invalid type of information into an HTML form field, that conversion fails and your JSP application crashes.

Because of the potential for users entering incorrect data, the need for implementing validation rules is indisputable. However, you can implement validation rules in JSP applications on the Web server and you can also implement validation rules in HTML forms using JavaScript. Thus, the question arises: Which approach is the best?

I prefer implementing JavaScript validation rules because they execute before an HTML form is submitted. A user gets immediate feedback if a rule is violated instead of waiting for the HTML form to be submitted by the browser, evaluated by the Web server, and then returned to the browser for correction.

Users don't like to wait for feedback, and transmission of information across the Web is still the slowest part of a typical user's Web experience. Implementing validation rules in JavaScript prevents the user from submitting information only to find that it's incorrectly entered.

Keep in mind that JavaScript validation rules aren't good for all kinds of validation. When users enter a credit card number into an HTML form, for example, you can use JavaScript to verify that the credit card number is in the correct format, but you can't verify that the credit card is valid until you attempt to process the credit card transaction. Thus, some validation rules have to be implemented on a Web server.

Generally, JavaScript can be used to verify that the type and format of data supplied by a user is correct. When verifying the type of data a user provides, you should ensure that the user enters legal characters for the type and that values are in a legal range for the data type. When verifying format, you should apply any rules on the actual characters entered in an acceptable range. For example, all credit card numbers have check-digit numbers that are always the same for every card of that type. You can verify that the check-digit numbers are correct to help ensure that the user correctly entered his or her credit card number.

Implementing Typical Validation Scripts

When you write validation scripts using JavaScript, keep your scripts generic so that you can reuse them for other fields of the same kind. You can write generic scripts to verify the formats for dates, integers, floating-point numbers, and character fields. By default, these scripts should ensure that the values entered are legal (will work) for the language that you use on the Web server to process the data. For JSP applications, you should implement validation rules to apply to Java data types.

If you have more specific constraints on a particular field, you can write a specialized validation function that executes the generic type check function and then adds additional validation rules.

Consider the following example. If your users supply dates in a text field, you need to verify that the values they supply are valid dates. You can do that by writing a generic date validation function, such as the `isValidDate` function in the following pseudocode example. If one of your form fields needs to have a date in the future, you can specialize the generic function with an additional function that tests for a valid future date, as illustrated with the `isFutureDate` function in the following example.

```
<SCRIPT LANGUAGE="JavaScript">
  function checkFutureDate( date){
    validDate = isValidDate(date);
    if(validDate == true){
      validDate = // verify this is a future date
    }
    return validDate;
  }

  function isValidDate(date){
    if(dateIsValid){
      return true;
    }
    return false;
  }
</SCRIPT>
```

Although all dates supplied by users must be valid, they do not all have to be in the future. But since all future dates must also be valid dates, the `isFutureDate` uses the `isValidDate` function to ensure that the value supplied is a valid date, and then provides its own code to ensure that the date is in the future. This approach makes your code more reusable.

When you create validation scripts, write them in a separate `.js` (JavaScript) file and include that file in each HTML page. See Chapter 5 for coverage on the creation and use of `.js` files in HTML pages. By writing all your generic form validation rules in a single `.js` file, you can reuse those functions in multiple Web pages.

An ounce of prevention

Before you write JavaScript validation rules, first consider how you can prevent users from violating rules in the first place. A well-designed Web page constrains users' options on the kind of data that they can enter so that entering invalid data isn't an option. Preventing users from entering invalid data may not enhance a Web user's experience, but preventing users from having to deal with incorrectly entered data prevents them from being frustrated when they have to correct their mistakes. (Sneaking in the spinach, as it were.) Here are some tips on how to constrain user input to reduce errors.

- **Use radio button `<INPUT>` elements (implemented with the code `<INPUT type="radio">`).** If you need a user to pick one of a narrow range of values on an HTML form, use radio button `<INPUT>` elements. For example, if you need the user to specify the type of credit card for a payment, use a radio button list to provide the user with the credit card options. Using radio buttons constrains user choices to only valid options, and prevents them from selecting more than one option. That's exactly what you need when the user is only allowed to choose one option from a short list of choices.
- **Use check box `<INPUT>` elements (implemented with the code `<INPUT type="check">`).** Check box elements are excellent controls to use for implementing Boolean elements. Any kind of question or input that requires a user to respond with a yes, a no, a true, or a false response is traditionally implemented with a check box. Remember that when you use check box elements, you can have multiple boxes checked on a page, but each one represents a separate choice. Don't use a check box if you need to give users an alternative between yes and no; they could conceivably throw everything into confusion by choosing both boxes.
- **Use `<SELECT>` elements.** `<SELECT>` elements contain a list of `<OPTION>` elements, from which a user can pick one or more values. If you have less than four options to choose from and a user can only pick one of those options, using a radio button may be preferred. But if you have a lot of choices that a user can pick from the `<SELECT>` element is preferred. One typical implementation of a `<SELECT>` element is to provide a list of states for users to pick from when providing their mailing address.

  While a user typically should only pick one state from a list, you can set up `<SELECT>` elements that allow the user to choose multiple options from the list. You can present a user with multiple choices of the same type and allow the user to choose more than one. A typical example is providing users with a list of e-mail addresses and allowing them to send their e-mail to more than one address in the list.

- **Set a `maxlength` attribute on text `<INPUT>` elements.** Text input elements should only be used when a user is allowed to enter free-form data such a number, name, or street address. Because this data is free-form, all the validation rules in this book are directed toward ensuring text input is correct. One trick that you can use to help ensure text input doesn't violate a validation rule is to set the `maxlength` attributes of the text field in HTML.

  The `maxlength` attribute of a text `<INPUT>` element specifies the maximum number of characters that a user can enter into the text field. Use this attribute to prevent users from entering a value that's longer than the legal value for that field. As an example, the number of characters allowed in a name or street address is typically constrained by the width of the database field that stores that information. Implementing the `maxlength` constraint in the HTML field to the maximum number of characters allowed in the database prevents your program from crashing when your user tries to supply invalid data to be stored in your database.

Checking for valid dates

If your Web application caters to an international audience, validating the correct entry of a date field can be challenging. Depending on where your user resides, the date format could be different. U.S. folks typically use the numeric month/date/year (mm/dd/yyyy) format and those in other countries may use the numeric date/month/year (dd/mm/yyyy) style. Although you may want to implement validation that accepts dates in different formats, such solutions can get rather complex.

To keep things simple, I recommend that you specify the format you expect for a date field on the HTML form next to the field, and then verify that the date is entered in that format. Here are some things to verify when you check a date:

- **Set acceptable values:** Ensure that the values entered in mm/dd/yyyy positions are acceptable values. Some users may enter dates in a different order than you expect (dd/mm/yyyy order or yyyy/mm/dd order).
- **Set a four-digit year:** Ensure the user provides a four-digit year (2002 versus 02). Four-digit years prevent confusion regarding which century the user is entering.
- **Set boundaries on the range of acceptable dates:** Ensure the date supplied by the user is within a reasonable range for its purpose. For example, if a user is supposed to enter his birth date, make sure that it's in the past (or be prepared to call the Time Traveler's Hotline for verification) but not too far back (or expect to make calls to the Ponce de Leon Fountain of Youth Hotline).

- **Set leap-year safeguards:** Ensure that the date conforms to leap-year rules, or you'll have Sadie Hawkins on your back.

JavaScript date objects are loaded with all kinds of defects in older browsers, making date validation difficult and potentially flawed. The JavaScript function in Listing 6-1 illustrates code that ensures that all the aforementioned rules are validated, but it does not work for older browsers. Whether you choose to use this example or write your own date validation scripts, remember to test them on all the browsers that you intend to support. In your tests, ensure that date validation rules handle leap years and Y2K issues properly.

You can use a couple of different sources to discover more on date bugs in Web browsers. *The JavaScript Bible, 4th Edition*, by Danny Goodman and Brendan Eich (published by Hungry Minds, Inc.), has pages of material that provide a detailed explanation of all the defects you can encounter. Alternatively, you can use Dreamweaver UltraDev, version 4, to perform a check for you. Just write your validation script in the editor, and then choose File⇨Check Target Browsers. Using this tool, you can generate a report that documents all the places in the code where you may have problems.

Listing 6-1: A JavaScript Date Validation Script

```
function checkDate(textField){
  // First store the textField in a string so I can parse it.
  var stringValue = new String(textField.value)
  /* Regular expressions are an excellent way to ensure that
   * a field has a particular format. I use one here in this
   * example. The regular expression ensures the string
   * provided has values of 01 to 12 supplied for the month,
   * followed by a / character, followed by values 01 to 31
   * for the day, followed by a / character, followed by a
   * four-digit year accepting values 0000 to 9999 inclusive.
   */
  var regularExpr =
          /(\b[0][123456789]|\b[1][012])\/([0][123456789]|[1
          2]\d|[3][01])\/\d\d\d\d/
  if(stringValue.length == 10 &&
          regularExpr.test(stringValue)){
    /* Now we need to check the leapyear rules. I do this by
     * creating a date object. If the user provides an
     * invalid date string, the date object will
     * automatically roll the fields until a valid date is
     * reached (i.e. 02/29/2001 is rolled to 03/01/2001).
     * I verify the user string is correct by creating a date
     * based on the string, and then converting the date back
     * to a string. If the string supplied by the user and my
     * date string are identical, then the date is a real
```

```
     * date.
     */

     // Months in JavaScript are 0 based (0 - 11).
var month = stringValue.substr(0,2) - 1
     var day = stringValue.substr(3,2)
     var year = stringValue.substr(6, 4)
     // I create a new date object, and set all the fields.
     var dateValue = new Date() // current date and time
     dateValue.setFullYear( year)
     dateValue.setMonth(month)
     dateValue.setDate(day) // to address leap year, set day
          last
     // Now I convert the date back to a string.
     month = new String(dateValue.getMonth() + 1)
     //Next, ensure that the month is two digits
     if(month.length < 2){
       month = '0' + month
     }
     day = new String(dateValue.getDate())
     if(day.length < 2){
       day = '0' + day
     }
     var stringDate = new String(month + '/' + day + '/'+
          dateValue.getFullYear())
     /* If the user supplied a valid date, none of the fields
      * will change when the date is created, and the
      * following comparison will return true.
      */
     if(stringValue.indexOf( stringDate) != -1){
       // the user supplied a valid date
     }
     else{
       // the date is not valid
     }
  }
  else{
    // this is an invalid date.
  }
}
```

The code in Listing 6-1 uses a *regular expression* (see bold code) to help determine whether the user has entered a valid date. *Regular expressions* are objects that compare text to a pattern of characters. In JavaScript, a regular expression is started and terminated with a forward slash character (/). Everything between those characters is special code that tells JavaScript what kind of pattern to look for. In this example, my pattern requires the data entered by the user to be a date with a two-digit day followed by a forward slash (/), a two-digit month followed by a forward slash, and then a four-digit year.

Checking for valid text data

Checking for valid text can be simple or challenging, depending on the task. The simple part about verifying text is that all data entry in an HTML form gets sent to the browser as text. You don't need to do anything to ensure that a text string will actually be a `String` when it's handled by Java. However, pay attention to these other considerations for text values.

- **Text length:** Your application, particularly if it uses a database, may require that text data be less than a certain length.
- **Character limitations:** Your application may exclude some specific characters in text items. Likewise, you may have other constraints that limit what character the text can start with.

If you need to validate data entry to ensure that text is an appropriate length, specify the `maxlength` attribute on the text `<INPUT>` element in your form. If you need to ensure that text entered does not include certain characters, the challenge is more difficult.

Preventing users from entering certain characters in a text field requires a pattern-matching solution, and you can accomplish this with regular expressions. I could write an entire book on regular expressions alone. Instead of doing that, I recommend you that take a look at *JavaScript Bible*, 4th edition, by Danny Goodman and Brendan Eich (published by Hungry Minds, Inc.), for an excellent introduction to the subject.

Limiting text length is very simple, as I illustrate in the following code snippet.

```
<input type="text" name="date" maxlength="10">
```

Checking for valid numeric data

Ensuring that a user supplies valid numeric data is pretty simple. When you check for valid numeric data, be sure to check the following:

- Check the numbers to ascertain that they're valid for the number system that you intend users to use. (The standard numbering system is base 10, which contains the numeric characters 0–9.)
- If your solution cannot include decimal values, make sure that the number is a whole number.
- Make sure the supplied number is within a reasonable range of values for the expected purpose.

The easiest way to verify that numeric data supplied by a user is correct is to use JavaScript's built-in function `isNaN()`. This function returns `true` if the supplied value is not a number and `false` if it is a number.

But using the `isNaN()` function is sometimes not sufficient. If you need to verify that a user-supplied value is an *integral* number (no decimal value), you can do so with the *modus* operator (%). Using the *modus* operator causes the browser to return the remainder of the first value divided by the second value (for example, the expression `10 % 1 == 0` evaluates to `true`).

The modus operandus for any whole number modus 1 is to return 0. (If the browser does anything else, there's a problem.) But if the number has a decimal value, the number modus 1 will never return 0, no matter how insignificant that decimal value is. The code in Listing 6-2 illustrates two number functions that verify correct number formats.

Listing 6-2: Number Validation Scripts

```
function isBaseTenNumber(textField){
  if(isNaN(textField.value)){
    // not a number
  }
  else{
    // this is a number
  }
}

function isIntegralNumber(textField){
  if(isNaN(textField.value)){
    // not a number
  }
  else{
    if(textField.value % 1 != 0){
      // is not integral
    }
    else{
      // is integral
    }
  }
}
```

To ensure that numbers written in numeric systems other than base 10 are correct, you have to get a little more elaborate. The solution in Listing 6-3 relies on the behavior of the `parseInt()` function in JavaScript to determine whether a number is valid or not. Given a text String, the `parseInt()` function returns the value `Number.NaN` if the first character in the string is not a valid character for the specified numbering system. For each iteration of the code in Listing 6-3, the code checks to see whether the number starting from the index position and continuing to the end of the string is a valid number. Because the index position increments on every iteration, every character in the supplied text is checked to determine whether it's valid for the supplied numbering system. If any character in the text is incorrect, the function sets the `isValid` flag to `false`, indicating that the number is not valid.

Listing 6-3: Verifying Numbers Other Than Base 10

```
// radix parameter tells function what numbering system the
          original
// number is written in. 2 means binary, 10 is base 10, 8 is
          octal, etc
function isValidNumber(textField, radix){
  isValid = true
  sourceNumber = new String(textField.value)
  for(var index = 0; index < sourceNumber.length; index++){
    if(parseInt(sourceNumber.substr(index), radix) ==
          Number.NaN){
      isValid = false
      break
    }
  }
}
```

Validating a password entry or change

When users enter or change a password, you usually request that they enter it twice to ensure that the user input is correct. The challenge with this task is that you have to compare the values of two different fields. All the validation solutions I have reviewed so far in this chapter can be performed on a single field and triggered after that field is updated. Comparing two fields gets a little more complicated.

With password validation, you have to perform the validation after both fields are updated. Because you don't necessarily know in which order a user will supply passwords, password validation is usually performed when a form is submitted. That means you also have to dynamically look up the values for the two password fields in the form and then compare them with each other.

Of the several techniques available for making a reference to a particular element in an HTML form, the simplest one is to reference password fields by their fully qualified name. The code in Listing 6-4 illustrates the technique for referencing two password fields from the HTML form inside a JavaScript function. The bold text in Listing 6-4 identifies the fully qualified names of two password fields.

Listing 6-4: Validating a Password

```
<html>
<head>
<title>Untitled Document</title>
<meta http-equiv="Content-Type" content="text/html;
           charset=iso-8859-1">
</head>
<script language="JavaScript">
<!--
function checkPassword(){
  var newPassword = document.passwordForm.newPassword.value
  var confirmPassword =
           document.passwordForm.confirmPassword.value
  if(newPassword == confirmPassword){
    // password valid
    alert("valid")
  }
  else{
    // password invalid
    alert("invalid")
    return false;
  }
}
//-->
</script>
<body bgcolor="#FFFFFF" text="#000000">
<form name="passwordForm" method="post" action="">
  <table width="75%" border="1">
    <tr>
      <td colspan="2">
        <div align="center">Password Change Form</div>
      </td>
    </tr>
    <tr>
      <td>
        <div align="right">Old Password:</div>
      </td>
      <td>
        <div align="center">
          <input type="password" name="oldPassword" )>
        </div>
      </td>
    </tr>
    <tr>
      <td>
        <div align="right">New Password:</div>
      </td>
      <td>
        <div align="center">
          <input type="password" name="newPassword">
        </div>
```

(continued)

Listing 6-4 ***(continued)***

```
        </td>
      </tr>
      <tr>
        <td>
          <div align="right">Confirm New Password:</div>
        </td>
        <td>
          <div align="center">
            <input type="password" name="confirmPassword">
          </div>
        </td>
      </tr>
      <tr>
        <td colspan="2">
          <div align="center">
            <input type="submit" name="Submit" value="Change
              Password" onClick="checkPassword()">
          </div>
        </td>
      </tr>
    </table>
  </form>
</body>
</html>
```

Checking for valid credit card information

Although you can't actually confirm that a credit card number is valid unless you get it authorized by a bank, you can perform certain measures to make sure that a user has properly keyed in his or her credit card information. Given any brand of credit card, you can determine whether a user has entered in the correct credit card number by checking the following rules:

- **Valid prefix characters:** The *prefix characters* are the first numbers on the credit card number. Also referred to as *check-digit* numbers, each credit card company has its own rule for how many digits are included in the prefix, as well as what digits are allowed.
- **Number of digits:** Each credit card company has rules governing how many total digits are included in a credit card number. With some companies, the number of allowed digits depends on which prefix is used.
- **Check-sum calculations:** Most credit card companies follow a check-sum rule to determine whether the digits supplied by the user could represent a valid credit card number. This rule is designed to check for fat-finger mistakes, such as accidentally keying in the incorrect number. All the credit cards in Table 6-1 use a check-sum validation rule (the LUHN Formula). Read more on this in Table 6-1.

Table 6-1 displays validation rules that you should implement in JavaScript for credit card numbers depending on what type of credit card is being checked. These rules are valid as of the printing of this book but are subject to change. Similar rules apply to other credit cards. You should request documentation on how to validate credit card numbers from each credit card vendor that you plan to accept payment from.

Table 6-1 Credit Card Validation Rules

Rule	*Visa*	*Master Card*	*American Express*	*Discover*
Prefix	Any four-digit number	51, 52, 53, 54, or 55	34 or 37	6011
Number of digits	13 or 16	16	15	16
Check-sum calculation	LUHN Formula (include prefix)	LUHN Formula (include prefix)	LUHN Formula (exclude prefix)	LUHN Formula (exclude prefix)

The LUHN formula

The LUHN Formula is a rather complex mathematical algorithm that's applied to all the digits in a credit card number. I'm not sure what LUHN stands for, but it could be "Largely Unintelligible Hunk o' Numericism." The formula is implemented in the following steps:

1. Remove all non-numeric characters from the credit card number (that is, remove all dashes, spaces, or other separator characters supplied by the user).
2. If the check-sum rule for that vendor says *exclude prefix*, trim the prefix off the card number supplied. (Check out Table 6-1.)
3. Starting from the second-to-last digit and working toward the first digit, multiply every other digit by 2. Then add the digits of each product together so that if the product has more than one digit, add the first digit to the second digit. For example, if the second to last digit is 7, multiply 7 x 2 to get 14. Then add the first and second digits of 14 (1 + 4) to get 5.
4. Add the results of all the calculations in Step 3 together.
5. Starting from the last digit in the credit card and working toward the first digit, add every other digit together.
6. Add the results of the calculations from Steps 4 and 5 together.
7. The result from Step 6 modus 10 should equal 0. If it does, the number supplied is a valid credit card number. Otherwise, it is not.

Filing your taxes should be so easy.

On the companion CD at the back of this book, you can find an HTML file — `creditCard.html` — that performs credit card validation checks for Visa, MasterCard, and American Express credit cards. The `valid` function checks the prefix digits, number of digits supplied, and the result of the LUHN Formula for each type of card. Feel free to use it.

Using Element Event Handlers for Validation

When you perform validation of input on HTML forms, you perform an event-driven task. Form validation is event-driven because validation rules need to be triggered by events. *Events* are actions that occur on a Web page that may be of interest to the HTML elements in the Web page.

When you or the Web browser perform various actions, such as moving a mouse, using the keyboard, or loading a Web page, the Web browser creates a special object called an `event` that captures information about that activity. These event objects are then sent through the various objects in the Web page, and any object that has a registered interest in that type of activity is notified.

Event handlers 101

Every HTML element in a Web page is endowed with certain event handlers. *Event handlers* are special methods that are triggered when you or your Web browser perform various activities while working with a Web page. For example, the HTML `<BODY>` element has an `onLoad` event handler that is called when the `<BODY>` element is loaded by the Web browser. `<INPUT>` elements have an `onChange` event handler that is triggered when the value of an `<INPUT>` element is changed.

By default, the various HTML element event handlers don't perform any special tasks. But you can add functionality to an element's event handler by placing JavaScript code inside the event handler for a specific control. To do so, you include the event handler in the tag for that element and execute JavaScript code or call a JavaScript function inside the event handler. The following code illustrates an HTML `<BODY>` element with an `onLoad` event handler that calls a JavaScript function to initialize the contents of the Web page.

```
<BODY onLoad="initialize(this)">
```

When a Web browser executes the previous example, the browser executes the initialize JavaScript function and passes a reference to the body object for the given Web page to the function.

In the following example, two JavaScript statements are written directly into an event handler. If you write multiple statements or function calls in a JavaScript handler, you must separate them by a semicolon.

```
<BODY onLoad="initialize(this);alert('body is initialized')">
```

Form validation and event handling are related because the validation rules that you write in JavaScript have to be executed by event handlers. For each field that you need to perform validation on, you have to execute that validation rule with an event handler in the field. Generally, the two times to implement event handling for validation rules are when

- An event occurs in the HTML element that needs to be validated
- The <FORM> containing the HTML elements is submitted

Handling validation for <INPUT> elements

If you need to verify input on a specific field and that input is not dependent on the value associated with any other field, place the validation rules in an event handler for that particular element. Validation of individual fields is usually performed on <INPUT> elements because these are the only elements that actually accept free-form text.

The two best places for implementing an event handler for a specific input field are the onBlur event and the onChange event. The onBlur event handler is triggered when you leave an HTML field (such as an <INPUT> or <SELECT> element), either by tabbing to another field or selecting another field with a mouse. The onBlur event gets triggered every time that you leave a field.

The onChange event only gets triggered when you change the value of a field. Thus, if you change the content of a field and leave the field, the onChange handler is triggered. However, if you tab in and out of a field without changing the value, the onChange event is not triggered.

The following example illustrates two input fields in which validation rules are fired using the onBlur and onChange event handlers.

```
<input type="text" name="birthdate"
           onBlur="checkBirthdate(this)">
<input type="text" name="creditLimit"
           onChange="checkInteger(this)">
```

Typically, performing validation rules on `<INPUT>` elements is best triggered from the `onChange` event. You don't need to check a validation rule if the value has not changed and the validation rule has already been performed once. However, if the HTML element that you're validating has an invalid value by default (such as an empty field that you require a user to fill out), you may want to perform the validation for that field in an `onBlur` event handler to ensure that the user supplies a valid value.

You may want to use the `onBlur` event handler when you have a `<SELECT>` element that has the value `choose one` as the first option. You don't want to have the user submit the `choose one` value, so you can use the `onBlur` event to prevent the user from tabbing through the field without changing the value.

Handling validation on <FORM> submission

Generally, I recommend that you notify a user of a violation in a validation rule as soon as possible after the validation rule is finished. To do this, most of your validation rule handlers should be implemented in the HTML elements that need to be checked.

For these circumstances, however, I recommend deferring validation of HTML elements until a user attempts to submit the HTML form.

- When you have validation rules that depend on the values of multiple HTML elements, you shouldn't perform the validation until the HTML form containing those elements is submitted. You can't predict in what order users will supply those values, and you want to be sure that you give users a chance to enter all their information before performing the validation rule.
- When you have required fields in an HTML form, verify that the user has completed those fields when the form is submitted. Again, this rule is based on the assumption that you can't control the order that a user chooses to fill out fields. For example, a user may tab through some required fields without supplying information in order to get to other fields.

Performing validation routines on an HTML form when it's submitted is a little more complex than performing validations on a particular field as it's changed. Your JavaScript validation functions have to get a reference for each field that needs to be validated to get the value for that field and check it. Check out these tricks for getting a reference to an HTML field that you need to perform a validation rule against.

- **Be sure to assign a name to the `<FORM>` element in your Web page.** If you have a name assigned to a form, you can reference an HTML field by using its fully qualified name. The fully qualified name for an HTML field starts with the word `document` and is followed by the form name and the field element name, with each word separated by a period. For example, `document.myForm.myTextField` gets a reference to the `myTextField` element located in the `myForm` `<FORM>` in the current document.
- **Given the name of the `<FORM>`, you can search for an element in an HTML form.** HTML `<FORM>` elements contain a special array object called *elements* that holds references to each HTML element located in the form. You can find a specific HTML element by looping through the elements in the elements array and then comparing the name of each element with the name you're searching for.

Listing 6-5 illustrates using each of the aforementioned techniques to get references to HTML elements contained in a `<FORM>` and perform validation tasks on them.

Listing 6-5: Referencing Elements in an HTML Form from JavaScript

```
<html>
<head>
<title>Untitled Document</title>
<meta http-equiv="Content-Type" content="text/html;
          charset=iso-8859-1">
</head>
<script language="JavaScript">
<!--
  function validate(thisForm){
    /* The following example references the HTML element
          sampleDate
     * directly. The date is passed to a JavaScript
          checkDate()
     * validation function. The document prefix is not
          necessary
     * because we already have a reference to the form
          element.
     */
    checkDate(thisForm.sampleDate)

    /* The following example scrolls through the elements
          array for
     * this form. When the password fields are found, they
          are assigned
     * to JavaScript variables. These variables are then
          passed to a
     * verifyPassword() validation function.
     */
```

(continued)

Listing 6-5 *(continued)*

```
      var password1 = null
      var password2 = null
      for(var index = 0; index < thisForm.elements.length;
             index++){
        if(thisForm.elements[index].name == "newPassword"){
          // assign to reference to newPassword element to
             variable
          password1 = thisForm.elements[index]
        }
        if(thisForm.elements[index].name == "confirmPassword"){
          // assign to reference to confirmPassword element to
             variable
          password2 = thisForm.elements[index]
        }
      }
      // pass references to password fields to validation
             function
      verifyPassword(password1, password2)
    }
  //-->
  </script>
  <body bgcolor="#FFFFFF" text="#000000">
  <!-- The following form has an onSumbit event handler that
             passes a copy form to the validate function.
  -->
  <form name="sampleForm" method="post" action=""
             onSubmit="validate(this)">
    <p>date field
      <input type="text" name="sampleDate">
    </p>
    <p>Password field
      <input type="password" name="newPassword">
    </p>
    <p>Password confirmation field
      <input type"password" name="confirmPassword">
    </p>
    </form>
  </body>
  </html>
```

Notifying Users of Failed Validation

When validation rules fail, you need to notify users so that they can correct them. Actually, you don't have to tell them if you don't want to. I guess if a user enters an invalid credit card and you don't tell them to fix it, you just won't get paid. But that doesn't matter, because it's love that makes the world go 'round, not money.

Wait! Who wrote that? Money makes the world go 'round, not love. So telling that user to fix the credit card number is important after all. In the following sections, I review a few features in JavaScript and HTML that you can use to notify users of failed validation rules.

Using the alert box

The *alert box* is a custom message box that you can use in JavaScript to present a message in a special box that floats above the Web browser. After creating an alert box, the browser sets focus to the alert box, meaning the user must acknowledge the message in the box by clicking an OK button in the box. The user cannot interact with the browser until the alert box is acknowledged. An alert box is created with the following syntax:

```
alert("write a message to display")
```

The message inside an alert box can be a literal string or the contents of a variable. You can also combine variables and literal strings using the plus (+) operator, as in the following example. All variables passed to alert boxes are automatically converted to a text string.

```
fooValue = 12345
alert("the value of foo is " + fooValue)
// ouput: "The value of foo is 12345"
```

Setting focus to an invalid field

When you encounter a validation rule failure, one nifty trick that will make your user's life easier is to set the focus on the HTML form to the invalid field. This prevents the user from having to tab through all the elements in an HTML form to get to the field that needs corrected. To set focus to a field, obtain a reference to the field in question and execute its `focus()` method.

All `<INPUT>` elements have a `focus()` method, so you can perform this operation on any type of `<INPUT>` element that you want. The following code sample shows a validation function in JavaScript that uses the alert box and `focus()` method together to notify a user of invalid input and set focus to the field in question.

```
function isBaseTenNumber(textField){
  if(isNaN(textField.value){
    alert(textField.name + " must contain a number") //
           notify user
    textField.focus() // set focus to the field
```

```
    }
    else{
      // this is a number
    }
  }
```

Writing validation rules can be as simple or as complex as you want to make it. There's more than one way to peel an orange, which is the politically correct way to say that you can accomplish the same validation rule goals with a variety of different techniques. Just remember that some validation rules are really difficult to perform in a browser and are more easily left to your JSP application. You can discover more about implementing validation rules in JSP applications in Chapter 9.

Part III

Backstage with JSP

"Is this really the best use of a Web-based shopping cart application? A bad wheel on the shopping cart icon that squeaks, wobbles, and pulls to the left?"

In this part . . .

It takes two to tango. In this part, Java developers discover the important role that they play in the development of JavaServer Pages (JSP) applications. This part is devoted to the Java technologies that are integrated with JSPs to create full-featured Web applications.

Chapter 7 kicks off this exploration of Java technologies with JSP implicit objects, which are Java objects available in JSPs to support scripting. Although it requires some basic Java skills, Web designers should not neglect Chapter 7.

Chapters 8 and 9 are devoted to creating JavaBeans and implementing validation rules for user input in Java. *JavaBeans* are Java programs used to integrate databases, Java code, and JSPs. Java-based validation rules are an important feature of JSP applications to support user input validation on rules that cannot be implemented easily or reliably with JavaScript.

Chapter 7

The Implications of Implicit Objects

In This Chapter

- Discovering the hidden domain of implicit objects
- Using implicit objects for input and output
- Setting the stage with context objects
- Implicit actions to direct application behavior
- Implicit error handling

Before the creation of JavaServer Page (JSP) technology, Sun Microsystems had an established Application Programming Interface (API) called the Servlet API, available for developer dynamic Web pages. Although the Servlet API is powerful, it was considered a little too complex to satisfy the needs of most Web developers.

The JSP specification was built on top of the existing Servlet specification to implement an easy-to-use set of tools for generating dynamic Web content. Because the JSP API extends the Servlet API, its tools simplify the development of dynamic Web pages and also provide access to all the power of the Servlet specification.

When creating a JSP, you can use any of the Java classes in the Servlet API — and any class in the JSP API — without importing them. JSPs automatically import all the classes in both APIs to simplify the process of accessing those classes. In addition to automatically importing the Servlet and JSP APIs, a JSP container also automatically creates several Java objects based on the classes in these APIs and provides them to JSP programmers automatically.

The objects that the JSP container automatically creates for you are called *implicit objects* because they are always available for your use. Implicit objects simplify JSP development a great deal, providing you with some powerful resources for JSP development.

In this chapter, I review a lot of content requiring familiarity with the Java language. Some of this content requires you to be familiar with the implementation of type casting and exception handling. Reviewing the basic rules of the Java language is beyond the scope of this book. Appendix A provides a cursory overview of Java programming terms and concepts. The *Java 2 Bible* by Aaron Walsh, Justin Couch, and Daniel H. Steinberg (published by Hungry Minds, Inc.) is an excellent resource for tutorials and reference information on the Java language.

Implicit Object Types

Communication across the Internet uses various different communication mediums referred to as *communication protocols*. Two examples of communications protocols are File Transfer Protocol (FTP) and HyperText Transport Protocol (HTTP). Because the Servlet API had to provide the flexibility necessary to support different communications protocols, it's designed with a generic set of classes for use with any protocol and also supports specialization of those classes to handle particular communications protocols. In addition to the generic classes, the Servlet specification provides one standard extension for HTTP, which is the primary vehicle for sending HyperText Markup Language (HTML) content across the Internet.

Creating objects based on the type of communication protocol requires previous knowledge of what communication protocol that a user employs to send messages. Determining the communication protocol can add a lot of extra overhead to your program, but it's worth knowing — if you know the communication protocol, you can create objects that have specialized functions for the protocol in use.

The architects of the JSP specification are all for limiting complexity, and in this case they have done JSP developers another favor. Although an implicit object can be specialized based on the communication protocol, the JSP specification requires the implicit object to be the specialization for the protocol of the user's request. You get all the benefits of specialized implicit objects without having to do any extra work to determine what kind of protocol is in use.

Table 7-1 identifies all the implicit objects of the JSP framework and indicates when the object is specialized based on the communication protocol.

Table 7-1 JSP Implicit Objects

Variable Name	*Variable Type*	*Description*	*Scope*
`request`	`javax.servlet.ServletRequest` or subclass	Contains information from the user	request
`response`	`javax.servlet.ServletResponse` or subclass	Response to a user's request	page
`out`	`javax.servlet.jsp.JspWriter`	Supports buffering and output	page
`page`	`java.lang.Object`	Reference to this page	page
`session`	`javax.servlet.http.HttpSession`	Identifies a user across multiple request, only valid for HTTP protocol	session
`application`	`javax.servlet.ServletContext`	Supports communication with the JSP container	application
`pageContext`	`javax.servlet.jsp.PageContext`	Provides JSP page access to page attributes and Servlet API objects	page
`config`	`javax.servlet.ServletConfig`	Provides initialization information from the JSP container to the JSP page	page
`exception`	`java.lang.Throwable`	A wrapper class that contains any runtime error generated by a JSP page	page

Implicit Objects and Scope

In Chapter 3, I introduced the topic of scope in relation to assigning scope to a `<jsp:useBean>` tag. A JavaBean can be assigned one of four scopes:

- The `page` scope indicates the JavaBean is visible only in this JSP page. As soon as a JSP page is finished processing, a JavaBean in this scope is no longer available.

- The `request` scope indicates that the JavaBean is visible throughout a user request, regardless of how many pages are involved in the request. As soon as a user's request is handled and responded to, JavaBeans of this scope are no longer available. A request spans one or more JSP pages.
- The `session` scope means the JavaBean is visible for the duration of a user session. A *user session* is started when a user first requests a page from a Web application, and ends after the session has expired, which occurs at some point after the user's last requested page from the Web application. You can configure the timeout interval in your JSP container. Refer to the administrator's documentation for more information about configuring your JSP container. A session spans one or more requests from a single user's computer.
- The `application` scope means that all users of a JSP application have access to a JavaBean. The application scope does not expire, meaning that your Web application can sit around and not accept user requests for an indefinite amount of time, while maintaining application scope JavaBeans.

When you assign a scope to a JavaBean, the JSP container uses one of four implicit objects to manage that scope. The four implicit objects that manage JavaBean scope are the `page`, `request`, `session`, and `application`. Each of the aforementioned objects has the ability to hold references to other objects. A *reference* is nothing more than a placeholder that points to the object.

When you use the `<jsp:useBean>` tag to create a JavaBean, a reference to the JavaBean is stored in the implicit object that corresponds to the `scope` attribute of the `<jsp:useBean>` tag. This operation is accomplished with a method common to the `page`, `request`, `session`, and `application` objects: `setAttribute(String name, Object attribute)`.

Here's a look at what happens when you create a JavaBean with the `<jsp:useBean>` tag:

1. **The JSP container looks for a JavaBean of the given class (or type) and scope.**

   If the scope is page, the JSP container will look for the JavaBean in the page object; if the scope is request, the JSP container looks in the request object.
2. **If a JavaBean with the same class or type and name is found, that JavaBean is made available to the page.**
3. **If a JavaBean of the given name and type is not found, the JSP container creates a new JavaBean of that type.**

   Then a reference to the new JavaBean is stored in the implicit object that corresponds to JavaBean's assigned scope.

The *scope* of a JavaBean determines its lifespan in the JSP container. The `page`, `request`, `session`, and `application` implicit objects manage this lifespan. Basically, as long as each one of these objects is available in the JSP container, the JavaBeans referenced by them will also be available. As soon as the implicit object is destroyed, the JavaBeans attached to it are released, meaning that they are no longer in scope.

Categories of Implicit Objects

The nine implicit objects — implicit objects all correspond with objects available in the Servlet programming framework — can be broken into four basic categories:

- **Browser communication:** The first category handles communication with the Web browser. These objects are `request`, `response`, and `out`. When someone submits information to you from a Web page, that information gets written to the `request` object. Likewise, when you send information back to someone (such as another Web page), that information is written to the `response` object. The `out` object is another output object that ultimately writes information to the `response` object, which is sent back to the browser.
- **Servlet access:** The second category gives you access to the servlets that are generated from your JSPs. These implicit objects are the `page` object and the `config` object. The `page` object gives developers access to the servlet that is generated by the JSP. The `config` object allows developers to define custom configuration information.
- **Environment definition:** The third category of implicit objects comprises objects that allow you to define the environment in which a JSP page runs. These objects are context objects: `application`, `session`, and `pageContext`. The `application` object is a global object visible to all users. It stores information that you want all your users to have access to. The `session` object is global to a particular user — it's available as long as that user is accessing your Web site but isn't visible to any other user. You can store information in the `session` that needs to be available across multiple JSP pages but shouldn't be visible to other users. Finally, the `pageContext` object provides you with an alternate method for accessing all the other implicit objects.
- **Error handling:** The final category is handling errors. This sole object, `exception`, is created when an error occurs while the JSP is being processed. This object gives you access to what kind of error occurred, as well as the sequence of events that lead to the error.

Implicit Objects for Input and Output

JSP pages have three implicit objects for managing input and output: the `request`, `response`, and `out` objects. The `request` object containers all the input from the user and can also be used as a placeholder for storing variables that you create while handling a user request. The `response` and `out` objects are primarily employed by the JSP container to send the dynamic content that you generate in a JSP back to the user.

Accepting user input with the request object

The `request` object is the vehicle for transporting information from a user request through the JSP container. Any time that you need access to the data submitted by a user, the `request` is the place to find it. In addition, if you need to store an object reference you use to process a single user request, the `request` object is the place to store it.

The `request` object is constructed from a protocol specific subclass of the `javax.servlet.ServletRequest` class. If your user is communicating to you via the HTTP communication protocol, the `request` object will be constructed from the `javax.servlet.http.HttpServletRequest`. Table 7-2 identifies some commonly used methods of the `request` object.

Table 7-2 Commonly Used Request Methods

Method	*Java Class*	*Description*
`getParameter (String name)`	`javax.servlet. ServletRequest`	Returns the first value stored for a parameter with the specified name. Value returned from the method is a string.
`getParameter Names()`	`javax.servlet. ServletRequest`	Returns the names of all the parameters in the request. The return value is an array of string objects.
`getParameter Values (String name)`	`javax.servlet. ServletRequest`	Given a parameter name, returns all the values stored for that parameter name as an array of strings.
`getAttribute (String name)`	`javax.servlet. ServletRequest`	Given the name of an attribute, returns the value stored for the attribute. The return type is `java.lang.Object`.

Method	*Java Class*	*Description*
`getAttributeNames()`	`javax.servlet.ServletRequest`	Returns the names of all the attributes for the request as an array of string objects.
`setAttribute(String name, Object value)`	`javax.servlet.ServletRequest`	Allows you to store a value in the request with the specified name. The value cannot be a primitive datatype.
`getCookies()`	`javax.servlet.ServletRequest`	For HTTP requests only. This method gives you access to any cookies stored by the client. The return value is an array of `javax.servlet.http.Cookie` objects.

Responding to user input with the response object

The JSP container uses the `response` object to pass output from your JSP back to the user. In the case of JSP pages, the information passed to a user is initially written to the `out` object, which is used to buffer the output. When the `out` object's buffer is flushed, the output of the buffer goes to the `response` object. This process is mostly invisible to JSP authors, so you don't really have to worry about the internal mechanics of the process very much.

JSP pages give you access to most of the request attributes that you need to be concerned about through the page directive element, which I describe in detail in Chapter 4. But when dealing with HTTP responses, note the one very important task that the page directive does not support: controlling the lifespan of your response data on proxy servers and the user's Web browser.

Proxy servers are computers located on the user's private network that route Internet requests and buffer content sent to a user. Proxy servers buffer Web pages requested by a user so that the user can get a faster response time if the same page is requested within a given period of time. Likewise, Web browsers can store a Web page in a temporary directory on the user's computer so it can be rapidly accessed if the user returns to that page.

Although proxy servers and browser buffering are great for improving Web response time, they can be a problem when it comes to displaying dynamic content. Content from the proxy server and the Web browser represents the static output of the response object and can't be updated based on changes that occur after an initial request is processed.

Fortunately, the `request` object gives you access to the HTTP header object, which can be used to control the expiration of data sent by a JSP page. The HTTP header is used to store information about the content of an HTTP request or response. That information includes what kind of data is contained in the response, what character-encoding scheme is used, and special instructions on how the data contained in the response is supposed to be handled. You can manipulate the content of an HTTP header by using the `response.setHeader()` method. This method is only available for HTTP responses. Table 7-3 shows several usage examples of typical operations you may want to perform to set the header contents.

Table 7-3 Examples of the response.setHeader() Method

Usage Example	*Description*
`response.setHeader ("expires", "0")`	The `expires` attribute of the HTTP header controls the number of minutes that a response is valid for. If set at `0`, the content of the header will expire as soon as it is delivered, and the browser requeries your Web server if the user requests this page again.
`response.setHeader ("pragma","no-cache")`	Older proxy servers (conforming to the HTTP 1.0 protocol) use the `pragma` attribute of the HTTP header to determine whether a page should be cached. Proxy servers will cache the content of a response by default. To prevent this from happening, you can use this method to explicitly prevent caching for this page. You should include this method to support backward compatibility for proxy servers not using the current HTTP protocol.
`response.setHeader ("cache-control", "no-cache")`	The `cache-control` attribute of the HTTP header is the current method used to determine whether a page should be cached or not. Content of the JSP is cached by default; don't use this method unless you want to turn caching off. This method applies to HTTP/1.1 protocol, and may not be supported by all proxy servers.

Using the implicit out object

The implicit `out` object buffers the output of your JSP and writes output to the `response` object. You can control the buffering behavior of the `out` object with the `autoFlush` and `buffer` attributes of the page directive. I describe the page directive in detail in Chapter 4.

Every JSP page is composed of two kinds of content: JSP elements, which represent all the content defined by the JSP specification; and template data, which represents everything not defined by the JSP specification. Actions, directives, and scripting elements are JSP elements, whereas HTML content, JavaScript content, and any other content that you may send to a browser is template data. Because a JSP container doesn't understand the semantics of template data content, it treats the template data like a series of text strings. Before a JSP page is used for the first time, the JSP container converts the JSP page into a servlet. During the conversion process, the JSP container parses the template data content and places each line of template data in an `out.println()` statement using the implicit `out` object.

The implicit `out` object is an instance of the `javax.servlet.jsp.JspWriter` class. Under most circumstances, you shouldn't need to interact directly with the `out` object. The exception is if you choose to build a custom tag using the classes in the `javax.servlet.jsp.tagext` package. Find usage of the `out` object in Bonus Chapter 4.

Implicit Objects for Context

The context of a JSP page is the environment in which the JSP operates. The three layers of context implemented with implicit objects are the page, session, and application contexts.

- **Page context:** Includes contextual information pertaining to a specific JSP and provides access to all other contextual information.
- **Session context:** Contains information pertaining to HTTP sessions, which are used to track the entire duration of an encounter between a single user and the JSP application. All JSP pages accessed by a single user during an encounter are part of the same session.
- **Application context:** Contains information pertaining to the entire JSP application and all its users. All JSP pages running on a single JSP container share the same application context.

The objects used to track JSP contexts — `pageContext`, `session`, and `application` — are primarily used to store data for a JSP application, and correspond respectively with the `page`, `session`, and `application` scopes described in the earlier section "Implicit Object Scope."

The pageContext object

The `pageContext` object is an instance of the `javax.servlet.jsp.PageContext` class. The `PageContext` class is an abstract class subclassed by the JSP container to provide access container dependent functionality.

The pageContext object has several convenient methods intended to provide single point of access for data in all the different JSP contexts. Table 7-4 shows the convenience methods of the pageContext object and their descriptions.

Table 7-4 Methods of the pageContext Object

Method	*Description*
`getAttribute (String name)`	Returns the attribute by the specified name in the page scope, or null if the attribute is not found.
`getAttribute (String name, String scope)`	Returns an attribute of the specified name in the specified scope. Scope must be `page`, `request`, `session`, or `application`.
`findAttribute (String name)`	Searches for an attribute of the specified name in the `page`, `request`, `session`, or `application`, in that order, and returns the first attribute found, or null if no attribute by the given name is found.
`getNamesInScope (String scope)`	Returns the names of all the attributes in the specified scope. Scope must be `page`, `request`, `session`, or `application`.
`getAttributesScope (String name)`	Returns the name of the scope for the specified attribute, or null if the specified attribute is not found.
`removeAttribute (String name)`	Removes the specified attribute from the page object.
`removeAttribute (String name, String scope)`	Removes the specified attribute from the specified scope. If the scope is `session`, this operation triggers an `HttpSessionBindingEvent`.
`setAttribute (String name, Object value)`	Adds the specified attribute to the `pageContext` object identified by the specified name.
`setAttribute(String name, Object value, String scope)`	Adds the specified attribute to the specified scope with the specified name. If added to the session scope, this operation triggers an `HttpSessionBinding Event`.

Although I don't use the pageContext very often, in the later section "Getting attributes in any scope," I give an example of how to use the pageContext object in a way that I find very useful.

If you attempt to add an attribute with either of the `setAttribute()` methods in the `pageContext` object and an attribute of that name already exists in targeted context, the `setAttribute()` method removes the old attribute and then adds the new attribute.

Working with the session

The implicit `session` object is an instance of the `javax.servlet.http.HttpSession` class. A session spans the entire duration of a single user's encounter with a JSP application. The `session` object is most often used as a storage place for data that needs to be maintained across multiple JSP pages.

When using the `session`, you need to be concerned about how much data is stored in the `session`. Remember that a new session is created for each user accessing your Web site. Each of these users will have a personal copy of all the data that your JSP application writes to the `session`. Consequently, on a high volume Web site, even a very small amount of `session` data can translate into a huge drain on your Web server's memory.

Table 7-5 provides a listing of the commonly used methods of the `session` object.

Table 7-5 Commonly Used Methods of Session Objects

Method	*Description*
`getAttribute (String name)`	Returns the value of an attribute with the specified name, or null if an attribute by the specified name is not found.
`getAttribute Names()`	Returns the names of all the attributes in the session as an Enumeration object.
`setAttribute (String name, Object value)`	Adds the specified value to the session with the specified name. Fires an `HttpSessionBindingEvent`.
`removeAttribute (String name)`	Removes the specified value to the session with the specified name. Fires an `HttpSessionBindingEvent`.

In my time as a JSP programmer, I have seen too many examples where the `session` is used as a convenient dumping ground for data that does not deserve `session` scope. This is particularly a problem when different users access the same Web application from the same computer. The JSP container will only build one `session` per Web browser that encounters the computer. If you maintain a user's login authorization in the `session` and another user accesses your Web site from the same computer, the other user has access to all the information accessible by the first user.

If you attempt to add an attribute to the `session` with the `setAttribute()` method and an attribute of that name already exists in the `session`, the `setAttribute()` method removes the old attribute and then adds the new attribute.

The session event listeners

One very cool feature of `session` objects is their ability to send event messages when objects are bound to and unbound from the `session`. These events are broadcast using an object called the `HttpSessionBindingEvent`. This class contains two methods, `getName()` and `getSession()`, that respectively report the name of the attribute that was bound to the `session` and the session `id` the attribute was bound to.

An attribute is bound to the `session` when the `setAttribute()` method of the `session` is executed or the `pageContext.setAttribute()` method is executed with the `session` scope specified as a parameter. An attribute is unbound from the `session` when the `removeAttribute()` method of the `session` is executed, or the `pageContext.removeAttribute()` method is executed with `session` scope specified as a parameter.

Any class can catch its own `HttpSessionBindingEvent` by implementing the `HttpSessionBindingListener` interface. The `HttpSessionBindingListener` has two methods — `valueBound()` and `valueUnbound()` — each of which take the `HttpSessionBindingEvent` as a parameter. If a class implements the `HttpSessionBindingListener` each time that an object of that class is bound to or unbound from the `session`, the JSP container will send an `HttpSessionBindingEvent` to the appropriate method in that object.

You can use the `HttpSessionBindingListener` to perform special initialization and destruction instructions for an object that you store in the `session`. If, for example, you have an object that needs to write its internal state to a database when it's removed from the `session`, this object should implement the `HttpSessionBindingListener` and also provide a solution for persisting itself in the `valueUnbound()` method. If a user's session expires before your JSP application explicitly writes the state of the object to the database, the JSP container automatically removes all the attributes from the session. This causes your object's `valueUnbound()` method to be executed, and the state of the object will be written to the database. See an example of a JavaBean implementing the `HttpSessionBindingListener` in Chapter 8.

The application object

The `application` object represents the most global of all JSP context objects. The `application` object is an instance of `javax.servlet.ServletContext`.

Each JSP container has a single `ServletContext` object for each JVM that it runs on. If your JSP application runs on a single Web server, there is only one JVM, and consequently only one `ServletContext`. But if you have your JSP application set up as a distributed application, which is controlled by the way that a JSP application is deployed, you have multiple JVMs, and consequently multiple `ServletContext` objects.

The `application` object can be used to communicate with the JSP container and to maintain global information for all users of a JSP application. Table 7-6 has a listing of commonly used `application` object methods.

Table 7-6 Commonly Used Application Object Methods

Method	*Description*
`getAttribute (String name)`	Returns an attribute of the specified name from the `application`, or null if the attribute does not exist.
`setAttribute (String name, Object value)`	Adds an attribute with the specified value and name to the `application` object.
`removeAttribute (String name)`	Removes an attribute with the specified name from the `application` object.
`log(String message)`	Provides access to the JSP container's message log, which you can use to trace the execution of a JSP application.
`log(String message, Throwable error)`	Provides access to the JSP container's error log, which you can use to report errors.

If you attempt to add an attribute to the `application` object with the `setAttribute()` method, and an attribute of that name already exists in the `application` object, the `setAttribute()` method removes the old attribute and then adds the new attribute.

Application and session multithreading

When you store and access data in the `application` and `session` objects, you need to pay special attention to multithreading issues. The term *multithreading* describes a process whereby a single instance of a class is created, and then multiple users gain access to that class at the same time. Each process using the class is called a *thread*. A JSP is a multithreading class by default and allows each new user of the JSP to create a new thread for that page. That means multiple users can access a single JSP page concurrently, resulting in a dramatic improvement in performance.

When different threads of the same multithreading class share access to class attributes, the threads have to be synchronized to avoid concurrent access to the shared attributes. For example, if you have a JavaBean that tracks the number of users on your Web site, and you place that JavaBean in your JSP container's application object, two users may try to attempt to update the JavaBean attribute that tracks the number of users at exactly the same moment. It is also possible that one user may attempt to read the number of users while another attempts to write to that number at exactly the same time. If that happens, the counter itself may be corrupted, or be left in an inconsistent state.

Synchronization is a process that forces threads using a shared resource to stand in line, and access that resource one at a time. Because multiple JSP pages can potentially share attributes in `application` and `session` objects, synchronization of those objects is important.

Multithreading and synchronization can be very complex topics depending on what behavior you need to implement. Aside from this honorable mention, they are both beyond the scope of this book. Because of the complexity associated with concurrency management, I recommend avoiding use of the `application` object completely unless you are familiar with concurrency management.

Multithreading issues are less significant in `session` objects than they are in `application` objects. Only when you store a multithreaded object in the `session` do you run into multithreading issues in a `session`.

The multithreading behavior of a JSP page can be turned off with the `isThreadSafe` attribute of the page directive, which I cover in detail in Chapter 4. Turning multithreading off results in a substantial decline in the performance of a JSP, and it will not remove the requirement that you have to manage concurrent access to `application` and `session` objects.

Implicit objects and <jsp:setProperty> tags

Sometimes it's desirable to set JavaBean properties based on information you've stored in attributes of the `page`, `request`, `session`, or `application` implicit objects. You can accomplish this goal using value attribute of the `<jsp:setProperty>`. Because implicit objects are set when the application is in use, they are called request-time expressions. Here are some examples of using request-time expressions in the `<jsp:setProperty>` tag:

```
<jsp:setProperty name="foo" property="stuff"
  value="<%=(String)request.getAttribute("stuff")%>"/>
<jsp:setProperty name="foo" property="fighters" value=
  <%session.getAttribute("fighters")%>/>
```

In the first <jsp:setProperty> tag, the request-time attribute `stuff` is converted to a `String` and assigned to the JavaBean property. In the second example, the request-time attribute is not converted to a `String`. Note that if the attribute is converted to a `String`, you can place it inside double quotes. If you don't convert it to a `String`, you cannot place it in quotes.

While `param` attributes and `String` constant values can take advantage of the implicit type conversion rules of <jsp:setProperty> tags, request-time expressions cannot. If you assign an invalid type of object to a JavaBean property from a request-time expression, you get an error. In the previous two examples, the first example still applies normal implicit type conversion rules of <jsp:setProperty> tags, as defined in Chapter 3. The second example doesn't apply the conversion rules.

The Implicit Exception Object

To err is human, to exception handle is divine. One of my favorite features of the Java language is its built-in exception handling capability. I'm particularly impressed with how JSPs implement exception handling. Within a JSP, you can write scriptlets that perform exception handling for all exceptions that you wish to handle. But unlike most Java classes, when compiled, JSPs automatically throw any exception that isn't explicitly handled in the JSP.

If your JSP throws an unhandled exception, the JSP container catches the exception. At that point, the JSP container takes one of two actions:

- If your JSP specifies an error page using the `errorPage` attribute of the page directive, the JSP container automatically forwards the user request and exception to the error page.
- If no error page is specified, the JSP container prints the stack trace of your exception to a default page and sends the default page to the user's browser.

The implicit exception factors into JSP development if you have an exception forwarded to an error page. The `exception` object is an instance of `java.lang.Throwable`, the base interface for all runtime exceptions. The implicit `exception` object is only available in an error page. Error pages are identified by the `isErrorPage` attribute of the page directive being set to true with the directive `<%@ page isErrorPage="true"%>`.

In a sense, a JSP error page is the default catch block for any `exception` thrown by a JSP. Inside the error page, you can perform an appropriate action to recover from an error situation, or you can log information about the state of the JSP application at the time that the exception occurred. The two methods of the implicit `exception` that I use most frequently are the `exception.getMessage()` method and the `exception.printStackTrace()` method.

The first gives the text description of the error that occurred, and the second reports all the methods on the call stack when the exception occurred. See Chapter 4 for an example of a JSP error page used for logging the state of a JSP when an exception is thrown to the error page.

Implicit Objects for the Servlet

Each JSP page is ultimately translated into a servlet by the JSP container before a user accesses it for the first time. The servlet created by the translation process is referred to as the *JSP implementation class*. The actual translation of the JSP page is automatic and implemented by the JSP container. The implicit `page` object and `config` object give you access to methods called by the JSP container while the JSP implementation class is invoked (initialized) and destroyed.

The page object

The `page` object is a reference to the JSP implementation class, as the `type` object. If a user request is transmitted via HTTP, the actual interface the JSP implementation is based on is the `javax.servlet.jsp.HttpJspPage` interface. Otherwise, the class is based on the `javax.servlet.jsp.JspPage` interface.

In Java, the implicit `page` object is the equivalent of the keyword `this`. When you write declarations of attributes or methods, those declarations become a part of the JSP implementation class. Throughout the JSP, you can use scriptlets or expression tags to use those methods. When using those methods, they are accessed through the `page` object. The following example illustrates the use of the implicit `page` object to execute a method declared with a declaration tag.

```
<%!
  private Connection conn = null
  public void getDatabaseConnection(){
    // some code to get a database connection goes here
    return connection;
  }
%>

<%
  // this code illustrates use of the page object
  conn = page.getDatabaseConnection();
%>
```

In addition to providing your own custom methods for the JSP implementation class, you can also implement two methods of the `JspPage` or `HttpJspPage` interfaces that your implementation class is derived from. Those methods are `jspInit()` and `jspDestroy()`.

The `jspInit()` method is typically reserved for any initialization activities that you need to perform when a JSP page is loaded in to memory. It gets executed once when the JSP container loads a page into memory. The `jspDestroy()` method is reserved for activities that must occur before a JSP implementation class is released from memory. Because `jspInit()` and `jspDestroy()` are executed only once in the lifecycle of a JSP implementation class, they can't be used to initialize information based on specific user requests. The `jspInit()` and `jspDestroy()` methods are executed automatically by the JSP container and should not be executed in the body of a JSP page.

Every JSP container is required to provide default `jspInit()` and `jspDestroy()` methods unless you declare these methods in a JSP declaration scripting element. If you do declare these methods, they will override the default behavior specified by the JSP container, which may result in reduced performance.

If you need to use the same `jspInit()` and `jspDestroy()` methods in more than one JSP page, you're better off writing an implementation of `JspPage` or `HttpJspPage` and using the extends attribute of the page directive to ensure that your JSP pages are based on the class you write.

The config object

The implicit `config` object gains your JSP pages access to initialization parameters that you can specify when you deploy your JSP page. JSP initialization parameters are specified in a file called the *deployment descriptor*, which is an eXtensible Markup Language (XML) file that describes the contents of your JSP application. How to deploy JSP applications and how to define initialization parameters are covered in Chapter 14.

The implicit `config` object is an instance of the interface `javax.servlet.ServletConfig`. The `ServletConfig` interface has two methods identified in Table 7-7.

Table 7-7 Methods of ServletConfig

Method	*Description*
`getInitParameterNames()`	Gets the names of all the parameters defined in the JSP application's deployment descriptor file.
`getInitParameter(String name)`	Gets the value of an initialization parameter given the name of the parameter. The return type of this method is `java.lang.String`.

Translating Common Actions to Code

Before the JSP container first runs your JSP page, the page goes through a process called *translation*. In the translation process, all of the non-Java code in your JSP page is converted to Java. The file created by the translation process is a *servlet* and is called the JSP *implementation class*. All the JSP actions and directives are translated into native Java code, and all the JSP template data is enclosed in `out.println()` statements. The content of JSP expression tags is placed inside `out.println` statements, while the content of JSP scriptlets appears in the JSP implementation class exactly as it appeared in the JSP page.

Occasionally you may need to perform a task in a scriptlet that would normally be performed using a JSP action. For example, if you need to execute a method on a JavaBean that's not a property of that JavaBean, you won't be able to execute the method using a `<jsp:setProperty>` or `<jsp:getProperty>` tag. In those cases, you have to use a scriptlet to perform the task. To assist you in the task of working with scriptlets, the following sections identify how to implement common actions in Java code.

Executing a method on a JavaBean

The `<jsp:setProperty>` or `<jsp:getProperty>` tags are typically used to execute methods on a JavaBean. They work by identifying the name of the JavaBean and the property to work with. If you need to execute a method on a JavaBean declared with the `<jsp:useBean>` tag but the method is not a property, calling the method directly is no problem. Follow the next example that uses a property to compare the two techniques. In the following code snippet, I use the `<jsp:useBean>` and `<jsp:setProperty>` tags to include a JavaBean in a JSP page and set one of its properties:

```
<jsp:useBean id="myCustomer" class="mybeans.CustomerBean"
          scope="request"/>
<jsp:setProperty name="myCustomer" property="firstName"
          value="John"/>
<jsp:setProperty name="myCustomer" property="firstName"
          value="Doe"/>
```

To set the properties of the JavaBean without using the `<jsp:setProperty>` tag, I write a scriptlet with the following code:

```
<jsp:useBean id="myCustomer" class="mybeans.CustomerBean"
          scope="request"/>
<%
  myCustomer.setFirstName("John");
  myCustomer.setLastName("Doe");
%>
```

Although the JSP container generates some more sophisticated code to perform the same task, this illustrates that each `<jsp:setProperty>` tag is the equivalent of executing a method of the JavaBean in Java code. Carrying the example one step further, if I have some method in the JavaBean that isn't a property — and thus has to be called directly — I execute that method using a scriptlet. Say I execute a method called `persistCustomer()` that writes the content of the CustomerBean to a database. I can execute that method with the following scriptlet code:

```
<jsp:useBean id="myCustomer" class="mybeans.CustomerBean"
          scope="request"/>
<%
  myCustomer.persistCustomer();
%>
```

The `id` that you assign a JavaBean in the `<jsp:useBean>` tag is the same as the variable that you use to reference in a JSP scriptlet.

Getting a parameter from the request object

Sometimes you need to pass a request parameter to a function in a scriptlet. When this is the case, you cannot rely on the `<jsp:setProperty>` tag to do the job for you. In the event that you have to get a request parameter and you cannot use the `<jsp:setProperty>` tag, choose from one of the following three strategies:

- You can get request parameters that have a single value using the `request.getParameter()` method. More on this topic follows in the section "Getting a single request parameter."
- For request parameters that could have multiple values, you can use the `request.getParameterValues()` method to retrieve an array of parameter values. A deeper review of this topic follows in the section "Getting multivalued request parameters."
- You can get all the parameters from the request object using a combination of two methods. The `request.getParameterNames()` method returns an array of all parameter names in the request object. With the parameter names in hand, you can use `request.getParameterValues()` to retrieve all the values for each parameter. More is presented on this topic in the section "Getting all parameter values from a request."

Getting a single request parameter

If you need to get a specific request parameter, you know the name of the request parameter, and the request parameter only holds a single value, you can use the `request.getParameter()` method to retrieve the parameter. Using the `param` tag to pass a single value to a JavaBean with the `<jsp:setProperty>` tag can be translated directly to the `request.getParameter()` method call, as illustrated by the following example. In the first code snippet, I use the `<jsp:setProperty>` tag to set a JavaBean property based on a request parameter.

```
<jsp:useBean id="myCustomer" class="mybeans.CustomerBean"
          scope="request"/>
<jsp:setProperty name="myCustomer" property="firstName"
          param="firstName"/>
```

Notice the `param` attribute of the `<jsp:setProperty>` tag, which is the queue to the JSP container to get a parameter with the name `firstName` out of the request. The same task is accomplished with the following scriptlet code:

```
<jsp:useBean id="myCustomer" class="mybeans.CustomerBean"
          scope="request"/>
<%
  myCustomer.setFirstName(
          request.getParameter("firstName"));
%>
```

If there is more than one value stored in a request, the `request.getParameter()` method returns only the first value. Thus, if there is a possibility of the user adding more than one value to the parameter, you should not use the `request.getParameter()` method to retrieve the values. Instead, use the `request.getParameterValues()` method reviewed in the next section.

Getting multivalued request parameters

Getting the values of a request parameter with multiple values is a little trickier than getting a single parameter. The following code illustrates the storage of multiple values for the same property name into an array in a JSP page. In the sample, I take the content of a parameter called `allergies` that can have multiple values and store it into an array. (That explains all the sneezing: It's allergies, and all this time I just thought I had a bad code.)

```
<%
  public String allergy = new String[
          request.getParameterValues("allergies").length];
  allergy = request.getParameterValues("allergies");
%>
```

The first line of code in the previous example initialized a new `String` variable called `allergy` with an array length equal to the number of parameters in the request named `allergies`. In the second line of code, an array of parameters is returned from the `request` object, and stored in the `allergy` object. Note that the array returned from the `request.getParameterValues()` method is a `String` array.

If you know you have a multivalued parameter, and you only want to return the first value from that parameter, you can use the `request.getParameter()` method. If you want to return a single value and if the value you desire is not the first parameter, you can accomplish your goal using the `request.getParameterValues()` method, as illustrated in the following snippet:

```
public String thirdValue =
          request.getParameterValues("allergies")[3];
```

Getting all parameter values from a request

In the final example of getting parameter values from a request, I assume a situation in which you know neither the parameter names nor their values. This is a typical usage scenario of a default error page, in which you are not sure which request you're processing and you need to print the state of the request object to a JSP page. The following code snippet accomplishes that task using the `request.getParameterNames()` method and the `request.getParameterValues()` method:

```
<%
  for(int index = 0; index <
          request.getParameterNames().length; index++){
    for(int loop = 0;
        loop <
          request.getParameterValues(request.getParameter
          Names()[index]);
        loop++){

      out.print( "<BR>");
```

```
      out.print(request.getParameterNames()[index]);
      out.print("[").print(index).print("] : ")
      out.println( request.getparameterValues(
            request.getAttributeNames()[index])[loop]);
    }
  }
%>
```

In the previous example, the outer `for` loop steps through all the parameter names in the request, and the inner `for` loop steps through all the values for a given parameter name. The implicit `out` object is used to write the name and value of each parameter to response.

Getting attributes in any scope

The previous section illustrates use of the `getParameterNames()` and `getParameterValues()` methods of the request object to get all the values of all the parameters in a request. The code segment is provided as an example of a snippet that you may wish to include in a JSP error page. The following code provides corresponding support for getting all the attributes you have stored in the `page`, `request`, `session`, and `application` objects. In this example, I declare a generic method that uses the `pageContext` object to print the data.

```
<%@ page import="java.util.*"%>
<%!
  private Enumeration attributeNames = null;
  public void printDataByScope(String scope){
    out.println("printing attributes of the " + scope +
           "object:");
    attributeNames = pageContext.getNamesInScope(scope);
    while(attributeNames.hasMoreElements()){
      String name = (String)attributeNames.getNextElement();
      out.print("<BR>").print(name).print(": ");
      out.println(pageContext.getAttribute(name, scope));
    }
  }
%>
```

Having declared this method, I can now call it from a scriptlet inside the JSP error page to print the current values of all the attributes in the various contexts of this JSP page. This is illustrated with the following example.

```
<%
  page.printDataByScope("page");
  page.printDataByScope("request");
  if(page instanceof javax.servlet.jsp.HttpJspPage){
    page.printDataByScope("session");
  }
  page.printDataByScope("application");
%>
```

Chapter 8

Jazz It Up with JavaBeans

In This Chapter

- Figuring out the who, what, when, where, why, and how of JavaBeans
- Creating JavaBeans
- Explaining JavaBean properties
- Using session-aware JavaBeans
- Enhancing your JavaBean experience

Some poor programmers work hard all day long every day from sunup to sundown without a break. The rest of us — with a life — use JavaBeans to do our work. If you believe in working smarter and not harder, JavaBeans are for you. If you like the idea of writing a program once and then using it over and over, JavaBeans are for you. If you're a Java programmer with little exposure to the concept of component-based programming, this chapter is for you.

But if you believe that object reuse is for sissies, you won't like this chapter much or Java programming in general. But, hey — it's your call. My money is on taking full advantage of the Sun Microsystems JavaBean specification (an incredibly powerful and easy-to-use tool) to make your life easier — that is, assuming you have a life to start with.

In this chapter, you discover the process for creating JavaBeans and integrating them into your JSP application. You also discover a couple of techniques for creating JavaBeans that respond to JSP application events.

What Are JavaBeans?

JavaBeans are really nothing more that small programs written in Java to perform repetitive tasks. The idea of JavaBeans is that they perform some task common to many different applications, and that they are reused for the same task in each different application. For example, the behavior in a Save button can written using a JavaBean, and then that Save button JavaBean can be reused in several different applications that require Save buttons.

As you might gather from this Save button example, many JavaBeans have some visual element that is represented. The Save button has a position on the file menu, and thus is a visual element. But JavaBeans used by JSPs don't have visual elements. In JSP development, JavaBeans are used to supply reusable content to JSPs, effectively separating the look and feel of a JSP from the content displayed by the JSP. This is an important division because although content may be reused in a variety of contexts, the way that content is displayed may change from context to context.

For example, my business may have a variety of types of addresses that a user can supply, such as billing and shipping addresses. I can create a JavaBean with a property that contains the names of all the types of addresses that the business allows. But the JSP will determine how to present those addresses. In one JSP, I may want to display the types of addresses in an HTML `<SELECT>` element. In another, I may want to display each type of address in its own text field. Because the JavaBean only contains content — the types of addresses — I can use it for both tasks.

JSPs are primarily used to layout and control the visual display of dynamic content. If you write code for generating content into a JSP, that code becomes difficult to reuse and ultimately requires more development and maintenance effort on your JSP application. By generating content through JavaBeans, you can separate the display of content from the creation of content, which reduces development effort and maintenance costs.

Creating JavaBeans

To create a JavaBean, you must follow five simple rules:

- **That empty feeing:** Every JavaBean must have an empty constructor; thus, it follows that the JavaBean has to have a constructor that takes no parameters. Remember, a *constructor* is a special method in a class that has the same name as the class and is used to create instances of the class. The creation of an empty constructor allows the Java Runtime Environment (JRE) to create an instance of a JavaBean class at runtime.
- **Privacy is important:** Every JavaBean should have all member variables of the bean declared private. *Member variables* are the variables defined in a Java class that have a class scope. By making member variables private, you prevent external classes from changing variables directly. This allows the internal implementation of a member variable to change without affecting any class that uses that member variable.

- **First things first:** All properties of a JavaBean must be initialized when they are declared. All JavaBean properties must have default values defined when the code is written. If you deal with a primitive datatype such as an `int` or a `boolean` property, this is a rule of the Java language for all classes. But JavaBeans are special because the non-primitive properties must also be initialized.
- **Meet the basic qualifications:** To qualify a property, a member variable must have a getter method. By convention, the name of a getter method is the name of the JavaBean property that it applies to with `get` prefixed on the method name and a return value that is the same type as the property. For example, given the JavaBean property `foo`, a JavaBean must have a getter method called `getFoo()` that returns the type of the `foo` attribute.
- **Satisfying extended qualifications:** Any property of a JavaBean that you need to update must have a corresponding setter method. If you don't intend to supply values to a JavaBean property from outside the JavaBean — such as setting the value from a JSP — the property doesn't need to have a setter method. By convention, a setter method for a JavaBean property has the name of the property with `set` prefixed that accepts a value for the property as an argument. For example, given a property named `foo`, the setter method must be `setFoo(FooType foo)`.

If you haven't reviewed this list, it's time to do a reality check. As I mention before, JavaBeans are pretty easy to create, and you discover just how easy in the next few pages. However, they do require some understanding of Java programming fundamentals. If you're feeling a little lost when you read terms such as *constructors*, *parameters*, *variables*, and *primitive* versus *non-primitive types*, that's an indicator that you could benefit from a Java language refresher. I recommend taking a look at *Java 2 Bible*, by Aaron Walsh, Justin Couch, and Daniel H. Steinberg (Hungry Minds, Inc.).

For JavaBeans, the term *property* typically refers to a member variable, the member variable's getter method, and the member variable's setter method if one exists. Illustrating these rules, the following `Foo` class is a legal JavaBean.

```
public class Foo{
 private String fooName = new String(); // default value

 // the empty constructor
 public Foo(){
 }

 // Note the name and return value; this is a getter method.
public String getFooName(){
  return fooName;
 }

 // Note the parameter type and name; this is a setter
```

```
method.
 public String setFooName(String name){
  this.fooName = name;
 }
}
```

Creating an empty constructor

If you don't specify a constructor for a class in Java, the Java compiler will create a default constructor for you. If you do specify a *non-empty constructor* (a constructor that takes parameters), the compiler won't create an empty constructor.

One aspect of JavaBeans that distinguishes them from typical Java classes is they must have an empty constructor, which means that you have to include the empty constructor in the definition of the class. The code snippet below illustrates the creation of an empty constructor for a class called `Foo`.

```
public class Foo{
 // The empty constructor follows.
public Foo(){
 }
}
```

Although JavaBeans require an empty constructor, you can specify additional constructors that accept parameters. If a JavaBean requires that certain properties are initialized before the bean can be used, you may choose to implement a constructor that accepts the initial values for the JavaBean as parameters. The trade-off is that you can't use a non-empty constructor in a `<jsp:useBean>` tag. For JSPs, therefore, you have to create an instance of the JavaBean using a declaration tag or a scriptlet.

Initializing bean properties

Bean properties are `class` scope attributes of a Java bean that have corresponding getter methods. To qualify as properties, these attributes must be declared private and be initialized upon declaration. Initializing a property on declaration means that the property must have an initial value assigned to it. The example below illustrates the proper initialization of several bean properties:

```
public class Foo{
 // properly initialized properties
 private int fooCount = 0; // initialized primative attribute
          to 0

 // Initializing non-primitive attribute to an empty string.
```

```
private String fooName = new String();

 // The empty constructor follows.
public Foo(){
 }
}
```

Note that this rule varies from basic Java rules because a Java class that is not a bean must have all primitive variables initialized but does not require non-primitive variables to be initialized. (I guess you could say that for a bean to have class, it must tame its primitive variables lest it make a public foo' of itself.)

Figuring out getter and setter methods

All JavaBean properties are identified by a public getter method and optionally by a public setter method. The getter, setter, and attribute methods combined are referred to as a property of the JavaBean. By convention, getter and setter methods follow the naming convention of prefixing `get` and `set` to the property name to form the method name. Listing 8-1 illustrates the use of getter and setter methods in a hypothetical class called `Foo`.

Listing 8-1: Use of Getters and Setters in the Foo Class

```
public class Foo{
 // properly initialized properties
 private int rowCount = 0; // initialized primative attribute
          to 0

 // Initializing non-primitive attribute to an empty string.
private String name = new String();

 // a boolean property
 private boolean valid = false; initialized to state of false

 // The empty constructor follows.
public Foo(){
 }

 // Public getter for rowCount must have int return type.
public int getRowCount(){
  return this.rowCount;
 }

 // Public setter for rowCount must accept int parameter.
public setRowCount(int count){
  this.rowCount = count;
 }
```

(continued)

The origins of Foo

The Foo class has a long and illustrious history in the annals of programming jargon. Foo is like the John Doe of software development. Typically, any time that you see an example of how to implement some particular functionality in a technical reference, examples are provided using a Foo class. Originally coined in WWI, the term *Foo* is primarily western — and international audiences of Internet technology specifications understandably demanded an explanation of what Foo stands for. The result was a Foo specification, which is written with such deadpan gravity that is proves both informative and entertaining. You can find the Foo specification at ftp://ftp.isi.edu/in-notes/rfc3092.txt.

Listing 8-1 ***(continued)***

```
  // Public getter for name property must return a String.
  public String getName(){
   return this.name;
  }

  // Name setter is declared private to prevent external
           access.
  private setName(String name){
   this.name = name;
  }

  // Boolean properties allow a getter prefix of is for
           readability.
 public boolean isValid(){
   return valid;
  }
 }
```

In the previous code listing, I use the prefix is for the getter method of the boolean property valid. By convention, substitute is for get to improve readability when a getter method calls for boolean properties.

Variations on JavaBean Properties

In the earlier sections of this chapter, I illustrate the use of simple JavaBean properties — those properties containing a single value. JSPs support the setting and retrieval of simple properties with the <jsp:setProperty> and <jsp:getProperty> tags. Chapter 3 provides additional detail on JSP tags.

Complementing simple properties, JavaBeans can also have *indexed properties*, which are properties having multiple values. Finally, both simple and indexed properties can be bound and constrained. *Bound properties* are properties that cause certain events to happen when they are set. *Constrained properties* are properties that can only be set to a specific range of values.

Although you may find several good uses for these features when developing JavaBeans for JSPs, the JSP container is not required to implement the full JavaBean container. Thus, many JSP containers may not support all these features.

Indexed properties can hold multiple values, typically in the form of an array of values. Like simple properties, indexed properties are set with a setter method and the values are retrieved with a getter method.

Getting and setting indexed properties

The getter and setter methods of indexed properties are slightly different from getters and setters in simple properties. Because indexed properties have multiple values, they can accept lists of values in their getters and setters. Alternatively, they may accept a single value at a time and add that single value to the end of the index of properties. Listing 8-2 illustrates setting indexed properties in a hypothetical class called `Foo`. (C'mon, first-stringers — don your favorite jersey and suit up for a little fooBall.)

Listing 8-2: Options for Setting Indexed Properties

```
import java.util.*

public class Foo{
 private String[] fooBalls = {new String()}
 private ArrayList fooJersies = new ArrayList();
 // empty constructor
 public Foo(){}

 /* Arrays in Java are a fixed length. Because I don't know
          the size
  * of the balls array, I'll have to re-initialize the
          fooBalls
  * array at runtime to resize it.
  */
 public void setFooBalls(String balls[]){
  // This StringBuffer will hold the initialization values
  // for the fooBalls array.
StringBuffer sb = new Stringbuffer();

  // Here I step through all the values in the balls array
  // and add them to the StringBuffer.
```

(continued)

Listing 8-2 ***(continued)***

```
for( int index = 0; index < balls.length; index++){
   sb.append(balls[index]); // adding a value to the
           StringBuffer
   if(index < balls.length - 2){
    sb.append(','); // I add a comma between each value
   }
  }

  // After I have the StringBuffer built, I can reinitialize
           the
  // fooBalls array to the length of the balls array with the
           values
// from the StringBuffer.
  fooBalls[balls.length] = {sb.toString()}
 }

 // This method sets the value of fooJersies with a list of
// values. That's possible because the datatype of fooJersies
           is
 // based on a list.
 public void setFooJersies (List jerseys){
  // Note I add the values to fooJersies, instead of
           replacing them.
// Your class should add values, as that is the expected
  // behavior of a setter method.
  fooJersies.add(jerseys);
 }

 // This is an example of adding a single value to the
           fooJersies
 // property.
public void setFooJersies(String jersey){
  // adding jersey to the end of the fooJersies  property.
  fooJersies.add(jersey);
 }
}
```

Like with setting indexed properties, getters for indexed properties can return a single value at a time or all the values of the indexed property at once. When an indexed value returns all its values at once, the syntax is very similar to the getter for a simple property. When indexed properties return single values, you must provide a method for your property that says how many values the indexed property holds. Listing 8-3 shows examples of both alternatives. (Time for an out-of-bounds play.)

Listing 8-3: Options for Getting Indexed Properties

```
import java.util.*

public class Foo{
 private String[] fooBalls = {new String()}
 // empty constructor
 public Foo(){}

 // This getter returns the full list of properties.
 public String[] getFooBalls(){
  return fooBalls;
 }

 // If returning a single value from an indexed property, you
          have
 // to provide a way to get the number of values stored in
          the indexed
 // property.
 public int getFooBallCount(){
  return fooBalls.size;
 }

 // To return a single value from an indexed property, the
          index
 // position must be supplied as a parameter. If the index is
          invalid,
 // this method throws an ArrayIndexOutOfBounds exception,
          which is
 // defined in the java.lang package of the Java API.
 public String getFooBalls(int position) throws
          ArrayIndexOutOfBounds{
  if(position >= 0 && position < fooBalls.length){
   // The return statement inside the if statement will
          prevent the
   // rest of the method from being executed.
   return fooBalls[position];
  }
  // If the condition of the if statement evaluates to false,
  // the return statement doesn't execute, causing the
          exception
  // to be thrown.
  throw new ArrayIndexOutOfBounds();
 }
}
```

I recommend providing getter methods that return single and indexed values on indexed properties. This adds flexibility to your JavaBean and makes it easier to use in a variety of contexts.

Using indexed properties in JSPs

Although JSPs are capable of handling single value properties with the `<jsp:getProperty>` and `<jsp:setProperty>` tags, there is no native functionality for handling indexed properties in JSP pages. Depending on whether you're getting or setting indexed properties, you can use different techniques.

When setting indexed properties from a JSP, you will typically be setting the indexed properties from a list of values provided on an HTML form. Because you generally can't predict how many values are supplied, you have to use one of the following options:

- You can write a scriptlet in your JSP that receives the user request with the values that need to be passed to an indexed property. When using this technique, you have to pull the values passed by the user directly out of the request object.
- You can set the entire indexed property in a single method call if your indexed property accepts an array of values as a parameter. Both techniques are illustrated in the code snippet below.

```
<jsp:useBean id="fooStuff" class="Foo" scope="page"/>
<%
 // Use request.getParmeterValues(name) to return multiple
          values
 // of a single property submitted by the user. Returns a
          String
 // array. The size of the userInput array is set at runtime.
 String
          userInput[request.getParameterValues("fooBalls").l
          ength] =
  request.getParameterValues("fooJersies ");

 // Sets indexed property one value at a time.
 for(int index = 0; index < userInput.length; index++){
  fooStuff.setFooJersies (userInput[index]);
 }

 // Setting multiple values of an indexed property at once.

          fooStuff.setFooBalls(request.getParameterValues("f
          ooBalls"));
%>
```

To get values from indexed properties, you have three scenarios with which you may get the values of the property on your JSP:

- **Getter:** Create a getter method that formats and returns the entire set of property values to the HTML page as a single value. This strategy is the least preferred because it forces you to include HTML elements in the JavaBean, resulting in a less portable JavaBean as well as HTML output that's difficult to manipulate with Cascading Style Sheets (CSS).
- **Scriplet:** You can retrieve indexed properties from a JSP by writing a scriptlet that loops through all the properties of the index, returning them one at a time. This technique makes the JSP more difficult to maintain. Nevertheless, this method is preferred over creating a getter method because it preserves the portability of the JavaBean by allowing the JavaBean to implement standard getter and setter methods.
- **Custom tag:** You can create a custom tag that retrieves and formats the value of the property for you, which is the preferred solution. Custom tags are the best solution for two reasons. First, they preserve the portability of the JavaBean, meaning that you can reuse the same JavaBean in several different applications, even in applications that don't have a JSP user interface. Second, they keep Java code out of the JSP, making the page easier to maintain and less error-prone.

I provide complete coverage of using custom tag libraries in Chapter 12. Explore Bonus Chapter 4 on the CD for useful information on creating your own custom tags. The following code snippet illustrates using a scriptlet to get the values of an indexed property.

```
<jsp:useBean id="fooStuff" class="Foo" scope="page"/>
<%
 int fooSize = fooStuff.getFooBallCount();
 for(int index = 0; index < fooSize; index++){
  out.print("<BR>").print(fooStuff.getFooBalls(index));
 }
%>
```

Creating Session-Aware JavaBeans

Although I don't recommend overloading your session with JavaBeans, the session offers some nice features that you can use to enhance your JSP application's behavior. When you add an object to the session [using `session.setAttribute(name, object)`], or remove an object from the session [using `session.removeAttribute(name)`], the session fires a `HttpSessionBindingEvent`.

By listening for `HttpSessionBindingEvent` objects, your JavaBeans can implement behaviors when they're added to or removed from the session object. In effect, when you set up your JavaBeans to listen for `HttpSessionBindingEvent` objects, you're making your JavaBeans session-aware. That means the JavaBeans become aware of actions in the session that affect them.

You can use the HttpSessionBindingEvent to manage the lifecycle of a JavaBean. For example, you may have a JavaBean that knows how to initialize itself from a database when added to a session and save itself to a database when removed from the session. By implementing a listener for the HttpSessionBindingEvent, your JavaBean can implement behavior to initialize its state when it's bound to a session and save itself when it's removed from the session.

If you give a JavaBean session scope with the <jsp:useBean> tag, the session fires an HttpSessionBindingEvent. I cover the <jsp:useBean> tag in detail in Chapter 3.

Implementing support for session binding events is very simple. When you create a JavaBean (or any class for that matter) that needs to handle session-binding events, your JavaBean has to implement the HttpSessionBindingListener interface. The HttpSessionBindingListener interface has two methods:

- valueBound(HttpSessionBindingEvent event): The session object uses this method to notify an object that it is being bound to the session. If you want your object to perform some action when it's attached to the session, you can write the code to implement that action in this method.
- valueUnbound(HttpSessionBindingEvent event): The session object uses this method to notify an object that's being removed from the session. If you want your object to perform some action when it's removed from the session, you can write the code to implement that action in this method.

The code in Listing 8-4 provides a final solution for our Customer JavaBean from previous examples by implementing the HttpSessionBindingListener. In this example, the Customer bean uses the HttpSessionBindingListener to implement its own session manager.

If you haven't had the opportunity to use inner classes before, such as the session manager class in Listing 8-4, there's a great article on them available at the JavaRanch Web site (www.javaranch.com), entitled "Getting in Touch with your Inner Class." This provides an entertaining look at what inner classes do and the guidelines for using them.

Listing 8-4: Implementing the HttpSessionBindingListener Interface

```
import java.beans.*
import java.servlet.http.*;

public class Customer implements HttpSessionBindingListener{
 private String name = new String();
 private String sessionName = new String(); // name in the
```

```
session
private HttpSession session = null; // reference to the
          session
 private Timer timer = new Timer(30000); // creates a timer

 // This method gets called when this bean is attached to the
          session.
 public void valueBound( HttpSessionBindingEvent event){
  this.sessionName = event.getName();
  this.session = event.getSession();
  try{
   timer.start();
  }
  catch(IllegalThreadStateException e){
  }
 }

 // This is an inner class containing a timer.
 // The timer has to be on a separate thread so it doesn't
          interfere
 // with the execution of the Customer class.
 public Timer extends Thread{
  long timeout = 0; // duration until timeout occurs

  // constructor for the timer Thread
  public Timer(long timeoutMilliseconds){
   // sets the timeout duration
   this.timeOut = timeoutMilliseconds;
  }

  // This method causes the timer to sleep for the specified
  // timeout duration, and then fire the timer's unbind
          method.
// After that, the run method completes and the Thread stops
// executing.
  public void run(){
   try{
    sleep(this.timeout);
    unbind();
   }
   catch(InterruptedException e){
   }
  }

  // This method removes the Customer JavaBean from the
          session.
  private unbind(){
   session.removeAttribute(sessionName);
  }
 }
```

(continued)

Listing 8-4 ***(continued)***

```
 // This method gets called when this bean is removed from
          the session.
 public void valueUnbound( HttpSessionBindingEvent event){
   timer = null; // clears the reference to the timer,
          allowing Java garbage collector to reclaim the
          timer.
 }

 // First I create a VetoableChangeSupport class that manages
          the
// registration of listeners and distribution of change
          events.
 private VetoableChangeSupport distributor = new
          VetoableChangeSupport(this);

 public Customer(){}

 // Because the name property is Bound, I use the distributor
          to send
// notification of changes inside the setter method for the
          name
 // property.
 public void setName(String name){
  // Because this change can be vetoed, I'm putting a try-
          catch block
// into the method that handles the PropertyVetoException.
try{
   if(distributor.hasListeners("name")){
    PropertyChangeEvent event = null;
    if(name.length == 0){
     // If name has not been defined by the setter, it will
          be an
     // empty string, and I pass a null indicating that the
          oldValue
     // is unknown.
     event = PropertyChangeEvent( this, "name", null, name);
    }
    else{
     event = PropertyChangeEvent( this, "name", this.name,
          name);
    }
    // The following method call causes this event to be sent
          to
    // all the listeners registered for this property.
    distributor.fireVetoableChange(event);
   }
   // Finally I change the value of the name.
this.name = name
  }
  catch(PropertyVetoException e){
   // Here you can perform some sort of evaluation to notify
          the JSP
```

```
// page that the property change failed. Because the
// fireVetoableChange is the source of this exception, when
          the
   // exeception is thrown, the name change is skipped,
          meaning the
   // JavaBean is not updated.
  }
 }

 // This method supports classes that want to listen for the
          changes to
 // all bound properties in this class. It wraps a call to
          the
 // corresponding method in the VetoableChangeSupport class.
 public void addVetoableChangeListener(VetoableChangeListener
          listener){
  distributor.addVetoableChangeListener( listener);
 }

 // This method supports classes that want to listen for the
          changes
 // to a particular bound property in this class. This method
          wraps a
 // call to the corresponding method in the
          VetoableChangeSupport
 // class.
 public void addVetoableChangeListener(String propertyName,
          VetoableChangeListener listener){
  distributor.addVetoableChangeListener( propertyName,
          listener);
 }

 // This method supports classes that want to unsubscribe
          from all
 // property changes of all bound properties in this class.
          This
 // method wraps a call to the corresponding method in the
 // VetoableChangeSupport class.
 public void removeVetoableChangeListener(
          VetoableChangeListener listener){
  distributor.removeVetoableChangeListener(listener);
 }

 // This method supports classes that want to unsubscribe
          from all
 // property changes of a particular bound property in this
          class.
 // This method wraps a call to the corresponding method in
          the
 // VetoableChangeSupport class.
 public void removeVetoableChangeListener( String
          propertyName, VetoableChangeListener listener){
```

(continued)

Listing 8-4 *(continued)*

```
    distributor.removeVetoableChangeListener(propertyName,
            listener);
  }
}
```

Dividing Responsibility with JavaBeans

Remember that JavaBeans are intended to be reusable components of software, just like the components in a stereo system. If you purchase a component-based stereo system, you'll probably avoid purchasing a non-standard component because you'll be forced to conform the rest of your system to that non-standard component, which limits the choices of how you can change or enhance your stereo system in the future.

The same logic applies to designing JavaBeans. When you create a JavaBean, you want to limit the scope of each JavaBean class to a scope that makes sense. To help with determining an appropriate scope, think of some JavaBeans as data beans and other JavaBeans as service beans.

A *data bean* is a JavaBean that contains data pertaining to a particular entity, either in a database or in the real world. The Customer JavaBean I use as an example in this chapter is an example of a data bean. Because the Customer JavaBean represents a customer entity, I want to limit the contents of the Customer JavaBean to those methods and properties that are intrinsic to the actions and properties of a Customer.

Service beans, on the other hand, are JavaBeans that implement some service. The `PropertyChangeService` class is a perfect example of a service bean. This class performs the actions necessary to manage a particular kind of service: namely, notifying other objects when a change occurs on a JavaBean.

As you develop JavaBeans, try to write a one-sentence description about the responsibility for that JavaBean. Then limit the scope of the JavaBean to that task. If you cannot describe the responsibility of a JavaBean in one sentence, evaluate the responsibilities of the JavaBean and see whether you can create more than one JavaBean to handle the responsibilities. Doing so may improve the reusability of your code.

Implementing the Serializable Interface

The content in this chapter should cover most uses that you need to perform to develop great JSP applications. As an added suggestion, implement the `Serializable` interface on your JavaBeans if they are to be a part of a JSP application. The `Serializable` interface belongs to a category of interfaces called marker interfaces. *Marker interfaces* are declarative, meaning that they declare a class to be of a certain type. Marker interfaces do not contain any methods. Thus, implementing the `Serializable` interface does not require you to add any methods to a class, and only serves the purpose of telling other classes that your class is `Serializable`. The following snippet illustrates a class that implements the `Serializable` interface.

```
public class MyClass implements Serializable{
  //... no methods required.
}
```

When an class implements the `Serializable` interface, the Java Virtual Machine (JVM) can convert an object of this class to a set of data that can be written to a hard disk on your computer or sent across a network connection. If your JavaBeans implement the serializable interface, you're telling the JVM that the bean can be serialized. The JVM handles all the behavior associated with serializing a class, so you don't need to do anything else.

I recommend that you implement the `Serializable` interface on your JavaBeans because may JSP containers will attempt to serialize the state of a user's data if that user hasn't accessed your JSP application after a set amount of time. If your JavaBeans don't implement the `Serializable` interface, your JSP container won't be able to perform this behavior, and it also won't be able to serialize any object holding a reference to your JavaBean.

Serializing an object is not always a good idea. If your object depends on static information (class-level attributes), you may not want to make it serializable because static data does not get serialized with an object and may be lost.

If you do make your object serializable, be sure that all the attributes held by your object are also serializable. If your object contains references to other objects that are not serializable, the JVM will not be able to serialize your object.

Chapter 9

Implementing Validation Rules

In This Chapter

- Implementing validation rules in JavaBeans
- Handling validation failures
- Exception handling and logging application errors

Writing applications with errors is an unfortunate fact of life. I've never seen a perfect program, and even the most thoroughly tested programs have some bugs that users inevitably encounter. I recommend that you begin writing programs with the assumption that something will go wrong, remembering to write software that recovers from most predictable error conditions.

When writing JavaServer Pages (JSP) applications, write software that can recover from the following kinds of common error conditions:

- **Invalid data entry:** This is probably the number one cause of errors. Whether unintentional, accidental, or malicious, users invariably enter information incorrectly if given the opportunity. Your JSP application should be able to check every piece of data entered by a user and ensure that all are valid.
- **Service failures:** These are critical points where JSP applications can break. If your JSP application relies on access to a database and the database goes down, you may be out of business for a while. However, users will still try to access your Web site, so you need to anticipate those problems and provide some feedback to the user.

Deciding Where to Validate User Input

Every program should provide some code that determines whether user input is valid and prompts uses for corrections if the input is invalid. Such code is often referred to as *validation rules* because the rules for determining whether input is valid are written into the code. Implementing validation rules for user input can be accomplished on several levels in a JSP application.

- You can write validation rules in JavaScript and have those rules run on a Web browser. I devote Chapter 6 entirely to performing validation rules with JavaScript.
- You can implement validation rules in the JSP and JavaBeans.
- If your JSP application uses a database, you can also implement validation rules in the database itself. The SQL language has many features for implementing validation rules on data.

Database validation rules are beyond the scope of this book, but you can discover more on the topic by reading *SQL: The Complete Reference*, by James R. Groff and Paul N. Weinberg, published by McGraw-Hill Professional Publishing.

Deciding whether to implement validation rules for your JSP application with JavaScript, in the JSPs and JavaBeans, or in that database, is a challenge. Here is my view on the relative merits of each option:

- **On a Web browser:** Implementing validation rules in JavaScript to run in a Web browser would be the greatest solution if you could rely such validation rules consistently. JavaScript validation rules offer the benefit of immediate feedback to a user when data entry is incorrect. Feedback is important in Web applications because the delay between the submission of a Web page and the response from a server should be as brief as possible. The problem with this approach is that JavaScript has very different capabilities from browser to browser, depending on the version and type of browser. Users also have the ability to disable JavaScript in a browser, which some users may do because of perceived security risks associated with JavaScript running in the browser. When users choose to disable JavaScript in their browser, any validation rules that you place there will no longer function.
- **In the JSP itself:** Validation rules can be implemented in JSPs and JavaBeans running on the Web server. Implementing validation rules in the JSP application offers the benefit of predictability: You can predict that the behavior of different servers will be virtually identical because Java is a "write once, run anywhere" solution. The drawback is increased response time for a user when validation rules fail because the data has to be sent to the server to verify and sent back to the browser to check.

  At a minimum, JSP applications should implement validation rules for type checking. *Type checking* is a validation task to ensure that any piece of data submitted can be converted to the datatype expected by the JavaBean that uses it. In addition, some complex validation tasks are easier to perform on a Web server. For example, determining whether an e-mail address is correct or determining whether a credit card has sufficient funds for a purchase are two validation tasks that are easier to accomplish using the Java language than they are with JavaScript.

- **In a database:** Validation rules can be implemented in the database. By using Structured Query Language (SQL), you can define a variety of rules in relational databases that are verified before a piece of data gets inserted or updated in the database. These rules are ideal for verifying that data supplied by a user conforms to all the constraints required by your business. Some constraints that you can establish in a database include how many characters are allowed in a field or the range of values that a field can contain. Because the database is the last line of defense against invalid data, any constraint placed on data submitted by the user should be implemented and validated in the database, particularly if the data supplied by the user is mission-critical for the success of the business. *Mission-critical* data is any data that your business must have in order to perform routine tasks. For hospitals, that data includes patient medical records. For online stores, the data includes sales and shipping information.

Based on my experience, I think that maintaining validation rules in all three layers of a JSP application (the browser, JSPs and JavaBeans, and the database) is appropriate. I recommend that JavaScript validation rules be implemented that are based on the rules in the database. This gives a user instant feedback if any database rules are violated. In parallel, JSPs should perform type checking to ensure that data is a valid type and to check more complex validation rules, such as verifying e-mail addresses.

JSP-Based Validation Rules

Metaphorically speaking, the data submitted by a user of your JSP application goes on a great trek. The trek starts when the user submits an HTML page to your server. After that, all the data is converted into a series of parameters and sent across the Internet to your Web server. The *parameters* represent information supplied by a user. In the context of Internet applications, this information is always represented as `String` data.

Now the fun begins:

1. Your JSP maps the parameters to properties in the JavaBeans that you use in your JSP application. This is accomplished with `<jsp:setProperty>` tags, which I discuss in detail in Chapter 3.
2. As the JSP uses the `<jsp:setProperty>` tag, user input from the parameters is converted from a `String` to the type of the JavaBean property.
3. After the JavaBean properties are set, the JavaBean may perform interactions that forward that parameters supplied by the user to a database or cause the JSP application to prepare another Web page and send it back to the user.

In this trek, I have found two frequent points at which the JSP application will break:

- **Datatype-conversion errors:** JSPs often break when converting parameters from `String` type to the type expected by the JavaBean. Conversion errors occur because the type of information supplied by the user is not in the range of values allowed by the JavaBean type. For example, if your JavaBean expects an `int`, then the value supplied by the user must be a `String` representation of an `int`. That means that if you expect the user to supply the digit *1* and the user instead supplies the word *one*, the value cannot be converted by the JSP into an `int` and the application will crash. I address handling errors of this kind in the upcoming section "Implementing type checking in JSPs."
- **Violating property constraints:** The second most common point of breakage in a JSP application is violating constraints on JavaBeans. A *constraint* is a rule that controls the range of values allowed in a property. For example, if you have a property that is supposed to contain names of foods, then *carrots*, *peas*, and *corn* are values that conform to the constraint. But the value *radiator fluid* cannot be assigned to the property because it's not the name of a food — even though I hear it can taste pretty good. Constraints are typically more narrowly defined than the previously stated type rules. I address constraint-based validation rules in greater detail in the upcoming section "Implementing validation rules in JavaBeans."

Implementing type checking in JSPs

All values (supplied by a user or by you) that are passed to JavaBeans start out as `String` data. When you use `<jsp:setProperty>` tags to set the value of a JavaBean property with some data, the JSP container automatically attempts to convert the value that you provide from a string to the type expected by the JavaBean.

The `<jsp:setProperty>` tag only implements automatic type conversion for JavaBean properties with the following types: `boolean` or `Boolean`, `byte` or `Byte`, `char` or `Character`, `double` or `Double`, `int` or `Integer`, `float` or `Float`, and `long` or `Long`.

For automatic type conversion to work, the parameter supplied by the user must be appropriate for the type expected by the JavaBean. Thus, if the JavaBean expects an `int` value, the parameter supplied by the user must be convertible from a `String` to an `int`. If the type cannot be converted, the `<jsp:setProperty>` tag throws an exception.

One of the most common approaches to handling type conversion errors in a JSP is to send the same page back to the user with a message at the top requesting a correction of the invalid input. As with the previous example, if the user supplies *one* when an `int` is expected, you could send the page back with a message stating, "The value you have supplied in the field *X* is incorrect. Please provide a whole number value (such as 1, 2, or 3)."

You can accomplish this task with two approaches:

- **Scriptlet-based exception handling:** Whenever a type conversion error occurs, an exception is thrown by the `<jsp:setProperty>` tag. You can catch the exception by placing the `<jsp:setProperty>` tag in a `try-catch` block and respond by printing the error message directly on the JSP page and sending it back to the user. See the upcoming section "Using scriptlets to check for errors" for more information.
- **Custom tag-exception handling:** *Custom tags* are programs that you can write in Java to create your own JSP action tags. You could create a custom tag for catching exceptions, which gives the Web designers working on your JSP application a tag-based solution for handling exceptions. See the upcoming section "Using custom tags to check for errors" to discover more.

If you don't explicitly handle conversion errors, one of two things will happen. If you identify an error page for your JSP, the error gets forwarded to the error page. If you don't identify an error page, the JSP container sends a stack trace, which is the equivalent of a Windows-based blue screen of death, back to the user.

Using scriptlets to check for errors

One trick for handling conversion errors in JSP pages — or any kind of exception, for that matter — is to use scriptlets. With scriptlets, you can write a `try-catch` block around each property that you need to set in a JSP page. A *try-catch block* is a Java language construct used to handle Java exceptions. Attempt to set each property inside a `try` block. If the attempt to set the property fails, use the `catch` block to write an appropriate error message back to the JSP and then send the JSP back to the user.

In Listing 9-1, I implement a couple of exception handlers inside a JSP. These handlers use scriptlet-based `try-catch` blocks for handling invalid input by a user. The first `try-catch` block handles cases when the user provides a value that cannot be converted to a number. The second handles an exception when the JavaBean receiving the value rejects it for any reason.

Listing 9-1: Implementing Scriptlet-Based Validation Rules

```
<html>
<head>
<title>Foo Sample</title>
<meta http-equiv="Content-Type" content="text/html;
        charset=iso-8859-1">
```

(continued)

Listing 9-1 *(continued)*

```
<!--
  In this example I use the following style tag to make all
  HTML div elements red because these elements will hold
  error messages.
-->
<style type="text/css">
<!--
div {  color: #FF0000; text-decoration: underline}
-->
</style>
</head>
<%! boolean isValid = true; //declaring a page variable%>
<body bgcolor="#FFFFFF" text="#000000">
<jsp:useBean id="foo" class="dummy.Foo" scope="request"/>
<% try{ %>
  <jsp:setProperty name="foo" property="count"
           param="count"/>
<%} catch(NumberFormatException format){%>
    <!--This message gets printed if the count param is not a
           number-->
    <P><DIV> The value for count must be a whole
           number.</DIV>
<%  isValid = false; //since a param is bad, this page is not
           valid
  } catch(PropertyVetoException veto){%>
    <!--JavaBeans can also veto changes, I get a veto message
           here-->
    <P><DIV>
<% veto.getMessage();
   isValid = false;
  }
%></DIV>
  <input
    type="text"
    name="count"
    value="<%if(request.getParameter("count") !=
           null){request.getParameter("count");}%>">
  <!--
    The input element is initialized to a request parameter
    if it exists. If one of the excecptions above is thrown,
    the offending value will be present in the html element.
  -->
  <!--
    If the page is valid, process it, and forward, otherwise
    it is sent back to the user.
  -->
 <%if(isValid){
    foo.postData();
```

```
%>
  <jsp:forward page="nextPage.jsp">
<%}%>
</body>
</html>
```

In Listing 9-1, the JSP performs its normal behavior only if all the properties of the Foo JavaBean are successfully set. If any of the properties are rejected, the `isValid` attribute of the page is set to `false`. That prevents the page from performing its normal behavior. The result is that the page, including its error message and the data provided by the user, is sent back to the Web browser so that the user can correct the input.

Although this is perhaps the most direct method for implementing type checking in a JSP and providing appropriate error messages to a user, it's definitely not the most elegant approach. With this method, the JSP is cluttered with a lot of extra Java code and the page is more difficult to maintain, particularly if you're not a Java guru. In addition, the solution is not reusable, a problem that is solved by using custom tags.

Using custom tags to check for errors

When implementing error handling with JSPs, custom tags hold a lot of promise. The benefit of custom tags is that you can easily use them even if you're not a Java guru. All you have to do is include the custom tag library in your JSP and then use them as you would any standard JSP actions such as the `<jsp:useBean>` and `<jsp:forward>` tags. For general information about using custom tags, read Chapter 12. If you're interested in creating your own custom tags, check out Bonus Chapter 5.

To assist you with handling JSP errors, the Struts custom tag library contains a tag called `errors` that displays any errors in a JSP (if they exist). The Struts custom tag library is an open source tag library developed by participants in the Apache Software Foundation. The Struts tag library is provided on the companion CD, and you can find more information at its home page `http://jakarta.apache.org/struts/`.

Although I'm a big fan of custom tags in general and of the Struts tag library, I don't care for the `errors` custom tag provided by Struts. In my opinion, custom tags should replace scriptlets, and the `errors` custom tag does not satisfy that goal. Although you may find some benefit in the errors tag that I haven't seen, I think scriptlets are preferable to the `errors` custom tag.

Although I haven't seen any really good custom tag solutions that address exception handling without requiring scriptlets, I'm confident that a custom tag solution is feasible. Unfortunately, implementing the solution is no small task. The following list outlines which features I think that a custom tag exception handler should support.

- **No more scriptlets:** Custom tag exception handlers should be able to handle exceptions without requiring the JSP author to write scriptlets. Web designers should be able to use custom tags without having a deep knowledge of Java. If custom tags require scriptlets to work properly, they fail in this fundamental task.
- **Exception identification:** Custom tag exception handlers should allow the JSP author to specify the precise type of exception to handle and to ignore any exceptions that aren't specifically mentioned.
- **Exception refinement:** Within the scope of a custom tag exception handler, the user should be able to add and remove specific exceptions from the list of handled exceptions, also using custom tag elements.
- **Error message display:** JSP authors should be able to associate the type of exception handled with a specific error message and have that message displayed on the JSP if the exception handler is triggered.

Implementing validation rules in JavaBeans

You may notice that Listing 9-1 includes an exception handler that catches a `PropertyVetoException`. A `PropertyVetoException` is an exception throw by a JavaBean that implements constraints on the values accepted by its properties. Implementing JavaBean constraints can be accomplished with two approaches:

- **Internal constraint checking:** This is the simplest approach to implementing property constraints. In this approach, you check the value assigned to a property in its setter method. If the value violates a constraint, throw the `PropertyVetoException`. I refer to this as *internal constraint checking* because it's done inside the JavaBean. However, there's a caveat to this approach — it's not the preferred solution, which I identify below. But because very few programmers use either approach, if you just do this, you'll be ahead of the game. For details, see the upcoming section "Creating internal property constraints."
- **Bound property constraints:** These are constraints that are enforced by other JavaBeans. This is the solution preferred by the creators of the JavaBean specification. In this approach, you create a JavaBean. You then use classes supplied in the JavaBean Application Programming Interface (API) to bind the JavaBean to another JavaBean. This other JavaBean evaluates the change, and if the change is not acceptable, it throws a `PropertyVetoException`. This approach adds more complexity to the task of implementing property constraints and is definitely a power-user feature.

Implementing bound properties and bound property constraints is an advanced topic that is beyond the scope of this book. That should not deter you from investigating the subject further. The JavaBeans specification is a good resource for discovering more about bound and constrained JavaBean properties. Section 7.4 addresses bound and constrained properties. You can download a copy of the JavaBeans specification from Sun Microsystems by visiting the page:

```
http://java.sun.com/products/javabeans/docs/spec.html
```

Creating internal property constraints

Most JavaBean properties will be constrained in some way. Typically, the properties are constrained in the range of values that they allow. And also typically, you can determine in advance what values are allowed. When you need to implement some kind of constraint, the simplest strategy is to check the value to be assigned to a JavaBean property inside the setter method for the property. By doing so, you are implementing an internal property constraint.

Implementing internal property constraints is simple. Just follow these steps:

1. **In setter method for the property, indicate that the property throws a** `PropertyVetoException`.

   For example, with the property named `foo`, the setter method would be

   ```
   public setFoo(String foo) throws
           PropertyVetoException{...}.
   ```

2. **In the body of the setter method, write some code to determine whether the value supplied is valid.**

   See upcoming Listing 9-2 for an example.

3. **If the value is not valid, you need to construct a** `PropertyChangeEvent` **object.**

   The `PropertyChangeEvent` object contains information about the present value of the JavaBean property, the value supplied to the setter method, the name of the property, and the bean containing the property.

4. **Throw a** `PropertyVetoException`, **supplying an error message and the** `PropertyChangeEvent` **object as parameters.**

The code in Listing 9-2 provides an example of a JavaBean property that uses the `PropertyVetoException`. In this example, the JavaBean property expects a value representing a valid e-mail address. If the supplied e-mail address is not valid, the setter method throws a `PropertyVetoException`.

Listing 9-2: Example of an Internal Property Constraint

```
import javax.mail.*;
import javax.mail.internet.*;
import java.beans.*;

public class SendMail{
    /**
     * email address property for sender's email address
     */
    private InternetAddress sender;

    /**
     * empty constructor
     */
    public SendMail(){};

    /**
     * This is the setter for the sender property.
     */
    public setSender(String senderEmail) throws
            PropertyVetoException{
        // First I try to create the e-mail address.
        try{
            /* The following statement throws an
             * AddressException if the supplied value is not
             * a valid e-mail address
             */

            this.sender = new InternetAddress(senderEmail);
        catch(AddressException e){
            /* When the address is invalid, create a
             * PropertyChangeEvent. this event identifies the
             * JavaBean, the property name, the former value
             * of the property, and the invalid value.
             */

            PropertyChangeEvent event = new
           PropertyChangeEvent(
                this, "sender", this.sender, senderEmail);
            // Create an error message.
            String msg = "The sender email address is not
           valid";
            // throw the PropertyVetoException
            throw new PropertyVetoException( msg, event);
        }
    }

    /**
     * This is the getter for the sender property.
```

```
        */
        public String getSender(){
            return sender.getAddress();
        }
    }
```

If you consistently use PropertyVetoException objects to implement constraints on your JavaBean properties, you simplify the task of handling constraint violations in JSP pages. You can provide your Web designers with training on handling the PropertyVetoException, including a little sample code, without having to train them on the entire Java language. Listing 9-1 contains an example JSP that includes a scriptlet that handles a PropertyVetoException.

What to Do When All Else Fails

With JSP applications, as with all applications, you have some failures that a user can do nothing to resolve. If the database is down, your JSP application is going to crash, and a user can't do anything about that. If the application code itself has a flaw, the problem isn't correctable without programmer intervention.

When you can't recover from an application error, the primary mission of the application should be to log all the information available about the state of the application and to notify users that the application is inaccessible.

Taking exception to the rules

You'll want to keep a handle on a couple of important Java exceptions when you create JSPs. An *exception* is a Java class that contains information about an error condition. You use different kinds of exceptions to use in different contexts, and JSP programming has a couple of exceptions of its own. If you encounter an error condition that can't be handled immediately, then you should probably use one of the following exceptions:

- javax.servlet.jsp.JspException is a generic exception for JSPs that's familiar to the JSP container. Raising a JspException causes the JSP container to invoke its built-in error handling capabilities.
- javax.servlet.jsp.JspTagException is a generic exception for use when you encounter an exception situation inside a custom tag. Bonus Chapter 5 provides complete coverage of creating custom tags. If, inside a custom tag, you encounter an error condition that cannot be handled, then you should throw a javax.servlet.jsp.JspTagException.

In JSP 1.2, the JspException can be created with a root cause that identifies any underlying problem that resulted in the JspException. You can create an exception with a root cause when you create a JspException in response to another exception that you receive. To create a JspException with a root cause in JSP 1.2, use the following constructor:

```
JspException( java.lang.String message, java.lang.Throwable
             rootcause);
```

Using the good ol' JSP error page

The last line of defense for handling errors in a JSP application is the JSP error page. JSP error pages are identified by the isErrorPage attribute of the page directive. The basic syntax is

```
<%@ page isErrorPage="true"%>
```

In a system under development or in testing, the JSP error page is a good place to display the state of an application when it crashes. (For examples of JSP error pages that accomplish this goal, see Chapter 4 for a JSP error page solution built with scriptlets and see Chapter 12 for a JSP error page solution that's implemented with custom tags.)

After you create a JSP error page that satisfies your needs, you can have other JSPs pointed to that error page using the errorPage attribute of the page directive. The syntax is

```
<%@ page errorPage="relativeErrorPageURL"%>
```

When you create and use JSP error pages, remember that a JSP can either point to an error page by using the errorPage attribute or it can be an error page by setting the isErrorPage attribute to true. However, a JSP cannot be both an error page and point to an error page. Read through Chapter 4 for more complete coverage on the usage of both the errorPage and isErrorPage attributes of the page directive.

Logging errors

In a *production system* (an application available to your users), I recommend that you only display a brief non-technical error message when a JSP application fails. Then log the rest of the error information on the Web server. Logging error messages prevents your users from being overwhelmed by meaningless and potentially confidential or proprietary information.

In addition, you may choose to create error pages that e-mail error reports to your support team or send a pager message to an administrator about the problem. Read through Chapter 18 for help accomplishing that task.

The most direct method for logging messages is to write them to the log file for the Web server that you use. You can accomplish this task by using the logging capability built into the `application` object, which is a JSP implicit object. Table 9-1 identifies the two methods of the `application` object that you can use to implement standard logging functionality.

Table 9-1 Methods of the Application Object for Logging

Method	*Description*
`log(String message)`	By using this method, you can pass a message to the JSP application object. The Web server that you use for your JSP application writes this message to the server's log.
`log(String message, Throwable error)`	Use this method when you need to log an exception to accept both a message and an instance of the `Throwable` interface. All Java exceptions implement `Throwable`, meaning this method can log any Java exception.

The code in Listing 9-3 illustrates the use of the application logging capability to store data in a JSP application to the JSP container's log from a JSP error page.

Depending on what brand of JSP container you choose for your JSP application, the container's log may have a different name and be housed in a different location. To discover more information about viewing log messages for your JSP container, check your container's documentation.

Listing 9-3: Logging Error Information

```
<%@ page isErrorPage="true"%>
<%@ page import="java.util.*"%>
<html>
<head>
<title>Error Page</title>
<meta http-equiv="Content-Type" content="text/html;
        charset=iso-8859-1">
</head>

<body bgcolor="#FFFFFF" text="#000000">
<%-- The exception.getMessage() statement returns the name of
        the error
```

(continued)

Listing 9-3 *(continued)*

```
 --%>
<P>
An error has occurred that prevents us from servicing your
           request at this time.
<P>
The error is: <%=exception.getMessage()%>
<%
  application.log(exception.getMessage(), exception);
%>
<%-- The following for loop presents all the attributes
     stored in the implicit application object. --%>
<%
  StringBuffer sb = new StringBuffer();
  application.log("application objects follow:");
  Enumeration loop = application.getAttributeNames();
  while (loop.hasMoreElements()){
    sb = new StringBuffer();
    String name =  (String) loop.nextElement();
    sb.append(name).append(": ");
    sb.append(application.getAttribute( name).toString());
    application.log(sb.toString());
  }
%>
<%-- The following for loop presents all the attributes
     stored in the implicit session object. --%>
<%
  application.log("Here are the attributes of the session:
           ");
  loop = session.getAttributeNames();
  while (loop.hasMoreElements()){
    sb = new StringBuffer();
    String name =  (String) loop.nextElement();
    sb.append(name).append(": ");
    sb.append(session.getAttribute( name).toString());
    application.log(sb.toString());
  }
%>
<%-- The following for loop presents all the attributes
     stored in the implicit request object. --%>
<%
  application.log("Here are the attributes of the request:
           ");
  loop = request.getAttributeNames();
  while (loop.hasMoreElements()){
    sb = new StringBuffer();
    String name =  (String) loop.nextElement();
    sb.append(name).append(": ");
    sb.append(request.getAttribute( name).toString());
    application.log(sb.toString());
  }
```

```
%>
<%-- This block shows all the request parameters sent by the
     user. There are two loops because request attributes can
     have more than only value per name. The out loop steps
     through all the parameters and the inner loop steps
     through all the values for each parameter. --%>
<%
  application.log("Here are the parameters of the request:
          ");
  loop = request.getParameterNames();
  while (loop.hasMoreElements()){
    String name = (String) loop.nextElement();
    for(int index = 0;
        index < request.getParameterValues(name).length;
        index++){
      sb = new StringBuffer();
      sb.append(name).append(": ");
      sb.append(request.getParameterValues( name)[index]);
      application.log(sb.toString());
    }
  }
%>
<%-- The implit page attributes cannot be displayed because
     as soon as the page that throws an error that is out of
     scope, the attributes are no longer available. --%>

</body>
</html>
```

Part IV

Implementing a Database

The 5th Wave
By Rich Tennant
PROGENITORS OF THE JAVA PROGRAMMING LANGUAGE
Lava
Developed in Hawaii, objects would suddenly erupt into a hot flowing stream of information.
Guava
Objects "grew" on computer's tree structure which users could convert to a data jam to be spread across the Web.
Jabba "The Hut"
Named after the developer, objects tended to get lost in cyber-space.
Fava
Objects were referred to as "beans", but would repeat themselves when overused.

In this part . . .

Interacting with databases is a fact of life for most programs. But database interaction doesn't have to be difficult. In this part, you discover the features of Java Database Connectivity (JDBC) that make database interaction easy. In Chapter 10, you find all the reference information that you need to set up a database connection and perform all manner of SQL statements against a database from Java programs.

In Chapter 11, you see where databases fit into the overall picture of JavaServer Pages (JSP) applications and you also discover a couple of strategies for integrating JavaBeans and databases.

Chapter 10

Accessing a Database with JDBC

In This Chapter

- Creating a database
- Identifying connection properties
- Checking out Java Database Connectivity (JDBC)
- Connecting to a database
- Executing database queries
- Working with query results

Connecting your JavaServer Pages (JSP) application to a database is a great way to enhance the power and flexibility of your JSP applications. Databases enable you to store and retrieve demographics about the users of your Web site and the content on your Web site. Don't let the concept of databases intimidate you: Although databases may seem complex, the task of managing data about users and about your own JSP application would be infinitely more complex without the help of a database.

In this chapter, I provide an overview of the process for creating a database and for connecting to and getting information out of a database using Java. Java has a special Application Programming Interface (API) for databases called Java Database Connectivity (JDBC). If you're already familiar with JDBC, you may want to skip to Chapter 11, where I address using JDBC to extend the power of JSP applications.

In this chapter, you find a sample database created in a database engine called MySQL. A copy of MySQL for Windows computers can be installed from the CD in the back of this book. Check out the MySQL Web site at `www.mysql.com` for the latest version of MySQL, including installation files for different operating systems and the latest MySQL information. You can find directions for installing and configuring MySQL in Appendix A.

I also assume in this chapter that you have a basic understanding of the Structured Query Language (SQL) programming language, which is the language used to interact with databases. If you're not familiar with SQL, check out the brief primer on the basics located in the bonus chapter on the CD accompanying this book.

Creating a Database

The process of defining a new database is a vast topic, and several books have been written on the subject. The theory and principles that govern the creation of a database are outside the scope of this book, but I do need to have a sample database to work with for the purposes of this chapter.

If you'd like to discover more on the topic of creating databases, pick up a copy of *Database Development For Dummies*, by Allen G. Taylor, published by Hungry Minds, Inc.

On the companion CD with this book is a script file — `database.sql` — that includes all the statements you need to execute to create a database for use with this book. The most direct path to getting your new database set up is to run this script file for your database. The instructions are provided in Appendix A, along with the instructions for installing MySQL.

If you choose, you can create the database using a database engine other than MySQL. The instructions in Appendix A give you some guidance on the changes necessary to the `database.sql` script to accomplish the task.

If you choose to use a different database than MySQL, you need to find a JDBC driver for the database you choose. A JDBC driver is a special program supplied by database and third-party vendors that allows Java programs and databases to talk to each other. Each driver only applies to a specific database brand.

Some databases do not support pure JDBC drivers, in which case you may be able to find a JDBC-ODBC bridge driver for the database you intend to use. A JDBC-ODBC bridge driver accomplishes the same goal as a JDBC driver, but in a more labor-intensive (and consequently slower) way. ODBC stands for Open DataBase Connectivity, and is a technology specification sponsored by Microsoft to provide a standard way for programming languages to talk to a database. To discover whether the database tool you intend to use has JDBC drivers available, visit your database vendor's Web site and search for drivers using the terms *JDBC* or *JDBC-ODBC*.

Working with JDBC

The JDBC API is a set of classes defined in Java that you can use to interact with a database. These Java classes are backed by a set of interfaces located in the `java.sql` package that comes with the Standard Java Development Kit. To interact with a particular kind of database, all you have to do is use the interfaces in the `java.sql` package. But for a particular kind of interface to support this interaction, the database vendor or a third party must create a JDBC driver for the database.

The java.sql package provides a basic structure that all database vendors must follow when they create a JDBC driver. Inside the JDBC driver, the database vendor provides all the implementations to the interfaces specified in the java.sql package. This driver is then packaged in a Java ARchive file (JAR) and made available to database programmers like you and me.

To interact with the database, just provide the URL to the database driver and the name of the class that implements the driver to get an instance of the driver class. From that point on, any interaction is supported through the standard interfaces of the java.sql package.

Setting Up the JDBC Database Driver

To work with your database from Java, you need to have a JDBC driver for the database you choose. For the MySQL database I use in this book, I include a JDBC driver on the CD in the back of this book.

If you're working with a database other than the MySQL database that I provide with this book, you have to get a driver that works with your brand of database. Most database vendors should have a list of acceptable database drivers that work with their products. In addition, a complete list of JDBC drivers is maintained on the Internet by Sun Microsystems. The Internet address is http://industry.java.sun.com/products/jdbc/drivers.

Perform the following steps to deploy the MySQL JDBC driver to your computer. Note that these steps apply to those using the Tomcat JSP container, and they may be somewhat different if you use a different JSP container.

1. **In your computer's CD-ROM drive, insert the CD that comes with this book.**
2. **From the Start menu, choose Run and type** explorer **at the command prompt.**

   This launches Windows Explorer.
3. **Double-click the My Computer icon on the left side of Windows Explorer to display the drives on your computer.**

   You can navigate to a particular directory by double-clicking a drive and then the folders underneath that drive. Do so until you can see the lib directory for your Tomcat installation. On my own computer, the path is C:\tomcat\jakarta-tomcat-3.2.1\lib.
4. **Expand the CD-ROM drive on your computer using the same technique to find the file named** mm.mysql-2.0.4-src.jar.zip.

   That file contains both the JDBC driver, and the source code used to write the driver.

5. **Open the file** `mm.mysql-2.0.4-src.jar.zip` **with your archive file viewer.** Archive file views are programs such as WinZip or PKUnzip that allow you to view the contents of a ZIP file, and extract files from the contents of a ZIP file onto your computer. You can open a ZIP file automatically when you double click on the file with your mouse. Scan down the contents of the file, looking for a file called `mysql.jar`. That file is the actual JDBC driver for the MySQL database.
6. **Highlight the file named** `mysql.jar` **and choose extract.** Most archive file views have a button labeled `extract` that you click to extract a file. The actual steps required depend on which program you use.
7. **Choose to extract the file to the lib folder under the top-level folder of your Tomcat installation.** The archive view should prompt you to identify the location where you want to extract the mysql.jar file. The JSP container should come with release notes that advise you about where to place Java library files, including JDBC drivers. Follow those directions.

After you deploy the JDBC driver to Tomcat, you need to add the driver to the `CLASSPATH` on your computer. For Windows 95/98/Me computers, perform the following steps:

1. **Open the** `autoexec.bat` **file in a text editor.**

   In Windows Explorer, double-click the C drive and locate the `autoexec.bat` file on the right side of your screen. Right-click this file; from the pop-up menu that appears, choose Edit. This should open the `autoexec.bat` file in your computer's default text editor.

2. **Find the line that starts with** `SET CLASSPATH` **and add the path to the JDBC file to the end.**

   The `SET CLASSPATH` line may wrap across several lines, so make sure that your cursor is at the very end. The line should end with a semicolon (`;`) character. If it doesn't, add a semicolon. Then type the full path to the JDBC file that you installed in the previous set of instructions. On my own computer, the path is `C:\tomcat\jakarta-tomcat-4.0\lib\mysql.jar` (as shown in Figure 10-1).

3. **Save the changes and exit the editor.**

   You're finished setting up the JDBC driver, but you must reboot your computer for these changes to take effect.

If you're working with a Windows NT or 2000 computer, follow these steps to add the JDBC driver to your computer's `CLASSPATH`.

1. **From the Start menu, choose Settings⇨Control Panel.**
2. **In the Control Panel window, find the System icon and double-click it to display the System properties of your computer.**
3. **Choose the Environment tab in the System Properties window.**

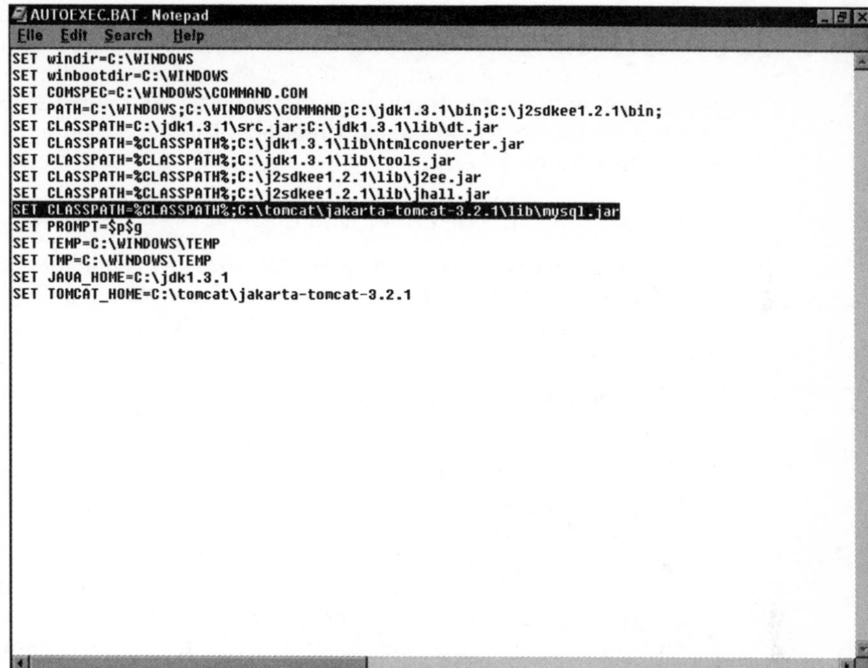

Figure 10-1: Autoexec.bat file with JDBC driver path highlighted.

On Windows 2000 computers, you need to choose the Advanced tab and click the Environment Variables.

In the Environment tab, you find two panes. The top one is labeled `System Variables`, and the bottom one is labeled `User Variables`. Choose the top pane and scroll through the properties until you highlight the `CLASSPATH` variable.

At the bottom of the Environment tab, you see two textboxes: `Variable` and `Value`. The `Variable` text box should read `CLASSPATH`. If it doesn't, make sure you have the `CLASSPATH` variable highlighted in the `System Variables` pane before continuing.

Select the `Value` textbox and press the End key (on your keyboard) to get to the end of the value. If the last character is not a semicolon (`;`), type a semicolon on the end. Then type the full path to the JDBC driver that you copied to your computer in the first set of instructions above. The path on my own computer is `C:\tomcat\jakarta-tomcat-4.0\lib\mysql.jar`.

4. **Click the Apply button and the OK button on the bottom of the System Properties window.**

   This completes setting up the JDBC driver on your computer, and you should be able to use it without restarting your computer.

Connecting to a Database in Java

After you set up the JDBC driver on your computer, you're ready to create a connection to the MySQL database. Creating a JDBC connection to a database involves the following steps:

1. **Register the database driver with the `java.sql.DriverManager` class.**

   The `DriverManager` class can hold references to several database drivers and coordinates the process of getting a connection to a database. For more information on this, flip ahead to the upcoming section "Registering the driver."

2. **Determine the URL of the database to which you need to connect.**

   All databases have a device called a *listener* that, umm, listens for and responds to contention requests from remote users. The listener, located on the computer you installed the database in, is found in a communication device called a *port.* Each computer has many ports, and a unique number identifies each port. To connect to the database, you use a URL that includes the URL to the computer and the port number assigned to the database listener. To find out the URL for your database, check out "Discovering your database URL" later in this chapter.

If you've already done some work with Tomcat, you've been using a port without even knowing it. The URL used to connect to the Tomcat examples area is `http:\\localhost:8080\examples.html`. The `8080` part of that URL is the port number that Tomcat uses to listen for requests for JSP pages over the Internet.

Don't drown in the details: I break each of these tasks down in the following sections so that you can see exactly what you need to do to make a connection to a database. Although the first attempt takes a little effort, you'll soon have the pieces in place.

Registering the driver

Registering a driver with the `DriverManager` class is pretty simple. To do so, you need the *fully qualified* Java class name for the JDBC driver you're using. The *fully qualified* name of a Java class is the name of a class including all the packages in which it is located. A *package* in Java is a folder that holds a related set of Java classes, and can contain other packages. Each package is equivalent to a folder on Windows. In the case of the MySQL JDBC driver I use with this book, the fully qualified name is `org.gjt.mm.mysql.Driver`. Notice that Java packages are separated by periods, rather than slashes. The code for registering a database driver is illustrated in the following example:

```
Class.forName("org.gjt.mm.mysql.Driver");
```

In this example, you're telling Java to find the `Class` object associated with the JDBC driver and load it into memory in your computer. Once you have executed this statement, a class called DriverManager finds the Driver class in memory and registers it for you. This may seem a little like Java magic, but just have faith and everything will work fine.

If you're using a JDBC driver other than the driver provided on the CD that comes with this book, check the documentation for the name of the driver class for your JDBC driver. The driver class for the JDBC driver that you use is the class that implements the `java.sql.Driver` interface.

Discovering your database URL

After you have a driver registered for your database, you need to get a connection to the database itself. In order to get a connection, you need to know the URL to the database. This information is supplied to the driver class so that it can find and attempt to connect to the database.

For JDBC, the URL comprises four different parts: the protocol; the database name; the address for the computer that the database is located on; and the port number that the database listener is listening on. The syntax looks something like this:

```
jdbc:{databasename}:{serverAddress}:{portNumber}
```

Table 10-1 breaks the preceding example apart, describing each piece.

Table 10-1 A Database URL for JDBC

URL Component	*Description*
`jdbc:`	The protocol that is used to connect to the database.
`databasename`	The name for the database. It is supplied with the database documentation. Supply the name of your database here.
`serverAddress`	The address to the computer that has your database loaded. Supply the URL to your database server here.
`portNumber`	The port number that your database listens on. Supply the port number that your database listens on here.

For the MySQL database, the database name used to connect to the database is `mysql`. That, incidentally, is the name of the utility provided with MySQL for writing SQL statements to be performed by the MySQL database. If you're using a database other than MySQL, you'll have to get the database name from the documentation. The easiest place for finding this information is probably the user documentation for the driver that you're using.

The next thing to find is the port number used by your MySQL database. The port number for the MySQL database is displayed in the MySQL administration console. To display it, follow these steps:

1. **Click the stop sign icon located in your task bar and choose Show Me from the pop-up menu.**

   This should display the WinMySQLadmin tool. The WinMySQLadmin tool is displayed in Figure 10-2.

2. **Click the my.ini Setup tab.**

   There you see a text area. Near the bottom is a line that starts with the text `#port=` followed by the port number assigned to MySQL. That's the port number that you need to use to connect to the MySQL database. The port number for the database on my computer is highlighted in Figure 10-2.

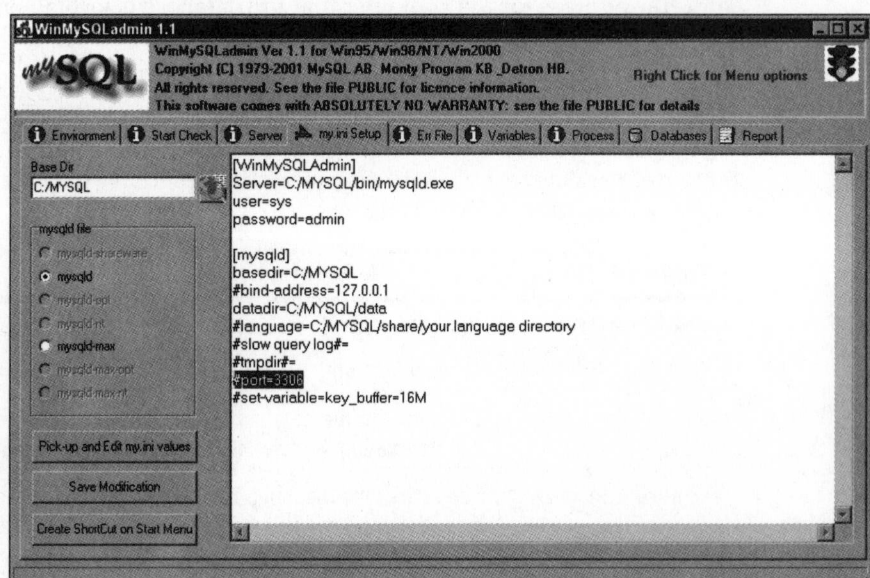

Figure 10-2: View of the MySQL admin tool.

If you're using a database other than MySQL, check your documentation to determine how to find the port number for your database.

Having completed the tasks identified above, you're ready to connect to the MySQL database. Because the MySQL database on my own computer listens on port 3306, I connect using the following URL:

```
jdbc:mysql://localhost:3306/dummy_sales
```

In the previous example, `jdbc:` identifies the connection protocol, `mysql:` is the name of the database, and `//localhost:3306/dummy_sales` is the address to the MySQL database identified in the earlier section "Creating a Database."

Notice that the URL connection syntax for connecting the MySQL database is a little different than that I describe in Table 10-1. For starters, the port number (in this case `3306`) is included in the database server address. Secondly, the database server address ends with a `/dummy_sales` directory. These differences are because of deviations that MySQL made from the Standard SQL implementation. In this case, the `dummy_sales` database is the name of the database that I create in the earlier section "Creating a Database." If you use a different driver, check the driver documentation to get the exact format of the expected URL.

Getting connected

After you have your driver installed and registered with the `DriverManager`, you need to get a database connection. A *database connection*, or connection for short, is like a channel through which your Java program and the database can communicate. In Java, the database connection is held by the Java class `java.sql.Connection`. The `DriverManager` returns this class after a connection is established with the database. You can then use the `Connection` class to interact with the database.

Getting the connection is pretty simple: Execute the `DriverManager.getConnection()` statement, passing in the URL, user name, and passwords as parameters. The following example shows the process of registering a driver and getting a connection together. The bold code is the statement that gets a connection to the database.

```
Connection conn = null;
try{
    // register the driver
    Class.forName("org.gjt.mm.mysql.Driver");
    // create a connection
    conn = DriverManager.getConnection(
          "jdbc:mysql://localhost:3306/dummy_sales", "sys",
          "admin");
}
catch(SQLException e){
```

```
        // handle exception
    }
    finally{
        try{
            conn.close(); // this closes a connection
        }
        catch(SQLException e){
            // handle exception
        }
    }
```

Notice that both statements are wrapped in a `try-catch` block that catches an `SQLException` because both statements throw an `SQLException`. In fact, virtually every task that you perform associated with handling database interaction throws an `SQLException`. The `SQLException` class is located in the `java.sql` package.

Closing database connections

After you get a connection to a database, you're free to execute as many SQL statements as you need through that connection. As long as you continue to execute SQL statements or work with their results, you must keep the connection open.

When you're finished, however, you should close the connection at your earliest convenience. Many database vendors charge their licensing fees based on the number of concurrent connections that you keep open. Leaving connections open longer than necessary may cause you to incur a higher licensing fee than you need for your database.

In the previous example, you find the code for closing a database connection located in the finally block of the `try-catch-finally` statement. Closing a connection also throws an `SQLException`, so you have to place it inside a `try-catch` block.

Executing SQL Statements in Java

All SQL statements executed from Java are managed by objects called . . . you guessed it, statements. When you need to execute an SQL statement from Java, you first have to get a `Connection` object from the database. With the `Connection` object, you can create Java `Statement` objects by passing the SQL statement as a string to the appropriate `Connection` method.

I identify the methods for creating Statement objects in Table 10-2.

Table 10-2 Connection Methods for Creating Statements

Method	*Description*
createStatement()	This method returns a generic Statement object.
prepareStatement()	You must supply a SQL statement as a String to this method as an argument. It returns a Prepared Statement object.
prepareCall()	This method is used to create database-stored proce dure and function calls. It returns a Callable Statement object.

The Statement class

As Table 10-2 implies, three kinds of Statement objects are available in Java. The base Interface of all the Statement objects is java.sql.Statement. The Statement object is returned by the Connection.createStatement() method. The steps for using a Statement are

1. **Create the Statement object by executing the Connection.createStatement() method.**
2. **Execute the SQL statement.**

   If you need to execute a query, you call the Statement.executeQuery() method, passing in the SQL statement that you want to execute as a String. If you need to execute an insert, update, or delete statement, you use the Statement.executeUpdate() method, passing the SQL insert, update, or delete statement in as a String.
3. **The executeQuery() method returns an ResultSet object containing the results of the query.**

   The executeUpdate() method returns an int indicating the number of rows affected by the SQL statement. Depending on what kind of Statement you execute, you'll have to assign the return value to the appropriate type of variable.

The code in Listing 10-1 illustrates the execute of both a Select statement and an update statement using the Statement object.

Listing 10-1: Using Statement to Execute Selects and Updates

```
try{
    // register the driver
    Class.forName("org.gjt.mm.mysql.Driver");
    // get a connection
    Connection conn = DriverManager.getConnection(
            "jdbc:mysql://localhost:3306/dummy_sales", "sys",
            "admin");

    // Now I have a connection, so I am ready to execute a
            statement.
    Statement stmt = conn.createStatement();
    // The following statement creates an SQL statement as a
            string.
    String select = "SELECT * FROM orders WHERE customer_id =
            1";

    // Now I'll execute the select.
    ResultSet rs = stmt.executeQuery(select);


    // Let's try an update. Because I already have a
            statement object, I don't have to create another
            one.
    //First I store the update statement in a String.
    String update = "UPDATE customers SET credit = 4000";

   // Now I execute the update statement. Note the return
            value is the count of the number of rows affected
            by the statement.
   int changeCount = stmt.executeUpdate(update);
}
catch(SQLException e){
    // handle exception
}
```

The PreparedStatement class

`java.sql.PreparedStatement` is derived from the `Statement` interface. It extends the `Statement` class to support parameterized statements. With parameterized statements, you can write a generic SQL statement and then supply variables when the `Statement` is executed to adjust the results that you expect to receive.

The steps to creating and using a parameterized statement are

1. **Write the SQL statement you wish to execute as a `String`.**

In each position where you want to pass a value to the SQL statement, place a question mark (?). The question mark is a placeholder for the parameter that you wish to assign.

2. **Create the `PreparedStatement` object.**

   This is accomplished by executing the `Connection.prepareStatement()` method, passing the SQL statement that you wrote in Step 1 as a parameter.

3. **Assign values to all the parameters for the statement.**

   When created, the `PreparedStatement` object assigns placeholders for each parameter that it expects to receive for the SQL statement. Java identifies the parameters by their order, with the first parameter being in index position 1, the second in index position 2, and so on. To assign a value to a particular parameter, you can use the `PreparedStatement.setObject()` method, passing the index position and the value as parameters. Note that the value passed into the `setObject()` statement cannot be a primitive datatype.

4. **After all the parameters have been assigned, you're ready to execute the statement.**

   Executing the `PreparedStatement` is similar to executing a statement. For queries, use the `PreparedStatement.executeQuery()` method. That returns a `ResultSet` containing the results of the query. For inserts, updates, or deletes, use the `PreparedStatement.executeUpdate()` method. It returns an `int` containing the number of rows affected by the statement.

The only difference between `PreparedStatement` objects and `Statement` objects regarding use of the `executeQuery()` and `executeUpdate()` methods is in the `PreparedStatement` — the methods accept no parameters. The `PreparedStatement` object is assigned an SQL statement to execute when it is created. The distinction is important because although `PreparedStatement` objects inherit the `executeQuery()` and `executeUpdate()` methods from the `Statement` object, they cannot use those methods to execute `PreparedStatement` objects.

Remember that the `executeQuery()` and `executeUpdate()` methods of the `PreparedStatement` don't take parameters. They are the only methods that you should use to execute `PreparedStatement` objects.

The code in Listing 10-2 illustrates the use of a `PreparedStatement`.

Listing 10-2: Executing a PreparedStatement

```
try{
    // register the driver
    Class.forName("org.gjt.mm.mysql.Driver");
    // get a connection
    Connection conn = DriverManager.getConnection(
           "jdbc:mysql://localhost:3306/dummy_sales", "sys",
           "admin");

    // Now define an SQL statement.
    String select = "SELECT * FROM orders WHERE customer_id =
           ?";
    // I am ready to create a PreparedStatement.
    PreparedStatement stmt = conn.prepareStatement(select);

    // Before executing the statement, assign the values to
           it.
    stmt.setObject(1, "1"); //seting parameter 1 to value "1"

    // Now execute the statement.
    ResultSet rs = stmt.executeQuery();

    // Now I am going to do an update.
    String update = "UPDATE customer SET credit = ?";

    /* Note that if I want to execute a different SQL
           statement, I have
     * to create a new PreparedStatement object.
     */
    stmt = conn.PrepareStatement(update);

    // Again, assign the variables.
    stmt.setObject(1, "4000");

    // Now execute the statement.
    int changeCount = stmt.executeUpdate();
}
catch(SQLException e){
   // handle exception
}
```

The CallableStatement class

`java.sql.CallableStatement` is derived from the `PreparedStatement` interface. The `CallableStatement` class is available to support executing functions and stored procedures, which are small programs stored inside the database.

Although most major databases support the creation of stored procedures and functions, several do not. The consequence for those that do not is the lack of an implementation for the `CallableStatement` class. Consequently, you can only use this class for databases that support stored procedures and functions. The `CallableStatement` is not implemented for the JDBC driver provided on the CD that comes with this book.

The `CallableStatement` is very similar to the `PreparedStatement`, although a bit more complex. Nevertheless, it's relatively simple to use after you understand it. The practical distinction between a `CallableStatement` and a `PreparedStatement` is that a `CallableStatement` can handle SQL variables called *out parameters*. Out parameters are passed out of a procedure or function call through the parameter list. Normally, when you see a function call such as the one in the following example, all the values are assumed to be passed into the call, and at most, a single value is returned:

```
returnValue = myFunction( valueIn1, valueIn2, valueIn3);
```

Out parameters are variables that are assigned a value after they're passed into a function. This value is retained after the function is called, as implied by the following example.

```
myFunction( valueIn1, valueOut1, valueOut2);
```

The handling of out parameters requires some extra steps and a bit more complexity, but the initial steps of using a `CallableStatement` are familiar. Here's a review first to clear them out of the way.

1. **Write the stored procedure or function call that you wish to execute as a `String`.**

   Place a question mark (?) in the call for each parameter that the procedure or function call requires. This is very similar to writing parameterized SQL statements, with the exception that the statements being written are method calls.

2. **Create the `CallableStatement` object.**

   Execute the `Connection.prepareCall()` method, passing the procedure or function call that you write in Step 1 as a parameter.

3. **Assign the values for the parameters that you pass into the statement.**

   This is identical to assigning parameters in the `PreparedStatement` and uses the `CallableStatement.setObject()` method. The method accepts the parameter index that you want to assign your value to as well as the value that you wish to assign to that index.

Now the similarities end because out parameters are not handled the same way as in parameters. Instead of assigning a value to an out parameter, you must register a placeholder for the out parameter, indicating to the CallableStatement what type of data you expect. The type of data refers to its SQL datatype, as implemented in the database, and not to the Java datatype.

To aid you in registering the SQL datatype with the CallableStatement, the java.sql package includes an object called Types that has a static variable for each standard SQL datatype. Thus, if the SQL datatype of the out parameter is VARCHAR, for example, you can register the datatype by referencing the VARCHAR field of the java.sql.Types class.

If the database that you use has a field defined in a datatype other than one of those available in the java.sql.Types class, you can use the java.sql.Types.OTHERS field to register the type of the out parameter.

Registering out parameters is accomplished with the CallableStatement.registerOutParameter() function. The first argument of this function is the position of the out parameter in the parameter list. The second argument is the SQL type code corresponding to the SQL type of the out parameter. This is illustrated in the following example.

```
statement.registerOutParameter( 1, java.sql.Types.
        VARCHAR);
```

In most cases, ordered lists are numbered starting with the number zero (0). That is not the case with references to parameters in PreparedStatement objects and CallableStatement objects. These parameters are numbered starting with the number one (1).

4. **After you register all the values you are passing into the CallableStatement, register all the values that you need to receive out of the statement.**

5. **After all the parameters have been assigned, you're ready to execute the CallableStatement.**

   To execute the statement, use the executeUpdate() method. The CallableStament.executeUpdate() method accepts no parameters and returns an int value.

6. **After the statement has been executed, you can retrieve the values of the out parameters by calling the appropriate getter method associated with the SQL Type Code assigned for that out parameter.**

Table 10-3 identifies all the types of data handled by the java.sql.TYPES class, broken into categories by whether they represent text, numeric, time, or other types.

Table 10-3 SQL Type Codes of the java.sql.Types Class

Category	*SQL Type Codes*
text	Types.CHAR, Types.CLOB, Types.LONGVARCHAR, Types.VARCHAR
numeric	Types.BIGINT, Types.BINARY, Types.BIT, Types.DECIMAL, Types.DOUBLE, Types.FLOAT, Types.INTEGER, Types.LONGVARBINARY, Types.NUMERIC, Types.REAL, Types.SMALLINT, Types.TINYINT, Types.VARBINARY
time	Types.DATE, Types.TIME, Types.TIMESTAMP
other	Types.ARRAY, Types.BLOB, Types.DISTINCT, Types.JAVA_OBJECT, Types.NULL, Types.OTHER, Types.REF, Types.STRUCT

Several getter methods are in the `CallableStatement` interface, each corresponding with one or more SQL Type codes from the `java.sql.Types` class. To get the value of an `out` parameter, you must use the appropriate type of getter method and also identify the index position of the `out` parameter that you're retrieving. Table 10-4 identifies all the getter methods, their corresponding SQL Types codes, and their return types. (Get a byte, get a date, get a blob, get the time, get a life. . . .)

Table 10-4 CallableStatement Getters

Getter Method	*SQL Type Codes*	*Return Type*
getArray()	java.sql.Types.ARRAY	java.sql.Array
getBigDecimal()	java.sql.Types.NUMERIC	java.math.BigDecimal
getBlob()	java.sql.Types.BLOB	java.sql.Blob
getBoolean()	java.sql.Types.BIT	boolean
getByte()	java.sql.Types.TINYINT	byte
getBytes()	java.sql.Types.BINARY, java.sql.Types.VARBINARY	byte[ ]
getClob()	java.sql.Types.CLOB	java.sql.Clob
getDate()	java.sql.Types.DATE	java.util.Date
getDouble()	java.sql.Types.DOUBLE	double

(continued)

Table 10-4 *(continued)*

Getter Method	*SQL Type Codes*	*Return Type*
`getFloat()`	`java.sql.Types.FLOAT`	`float`
`getInt()`	`java.sql.Types.INTEGER`	`int`
`getLong()`	`java.sql.Types.BIGINT`	`long`
`getObject()`	`java.sql.Types.OTHER`	`java.lang.Object`
`getRef()`	`java.sql.Types.REF`	`java.sql.Ref`
`getShort()`	`java.sql.Types.SMALLINT`	`short`
`getString()`	`java.sql.Types.CHAR`, `java.sql.Types.VARCHAR`, `java.sql.Types.LONGVARCHAR`	`java.lang.String`
`getTime()`	`java.sql.Types.TIME`	`java.sql.Time`
`getTimeStamp()`	`java.sql.Types.TIMESTAMP`	`java.sql.Timestamp`

Although working with `CallableStatement` objects may seem a little daunting at first, after you use them a couple of times, they're just as easy as working with `PreparedStatement` objects. Listing 10-3 contains a code sample making use of a `CallableStatement`.

Listing 10-3: Using a CallableStatement

```
try{
    // Register the driver.
    Class.forName("org.gjt.mm.mysql.Driver");
    Connection conn = DriverManager.getConnection(
            "jdbc:mysql://localhost:3306/dummy_sales", "sys",
            "admin");

    /* Now define an stored procedure call. This is a
            hypothetical
     * example. I'll outline the values of the placeholders.
     * position 1 = customer Id
     * position 2 = credit limit
     * position 3 = OUT rows affected - SQL type INTEGER
     */
    String call = "setCredit(?, ?, ?)";
    CallableStatement stmt = conn.prepareCall(call);

    // Now register parameters passed in.
    stmt.setObject(1, "1"); // customer id 1
```

```
    stmt.setObject(2, "4000"); // credit limit 4000

    // Now register out parameters.
    stmt.registerOutParameter(3, java.sql.INTEGER); // rows
          effected

    // Now execute the statement. Use the executeUpdate()
          method.
    stmt.executeUpdate();

    // Now retrieve the result of the out parameter.
    int rowsChanged = stmt.getInt(3);
}
catch(SQLException e){
    // handle exception
}
```

Working with SQL Query Results

Every time that you execute an SQL Query, whether using the `Statement` or the `PreparedStatement` interface, you receive a return value of a `ResultSet`. The `ResultSet` is like an SQL cursor — it contains all the rows and columns of data returned by the database. You can scroll through the `ResultSet` a row at a time to read the values of those results.

As long as you're working with the `ResultSet` of a query, you must keep the connection you made to the database open. As soon as you close the `Connection` object, your `ResultSet` no longer contains any data and you get an `SQLException` when you try to get data out of the `ResultSet`.

In the upcoming release of the JDBC API version 1.3, an object called a *disconnected result set* enables you to work with the result of a query after the connection is closed.

Table 10-5 shows some valuable methods of the `ResultSet` object that you're likely to use in retrieving data from an SQL query.

Table 10-5 Important Methods of the ResultSet Object

Method	*Description*
`beforeFirst()`	Sets the cursor of this `ResultSet` before the first row.
`isAfterLast()`	Returns a Boolean `true` or `false` indicating whether the cursor for this `ResultSet` is after the last row.
`next()`	Moves the cursor to the next row.

(continued)

Table 10-5 *(continued)*

Method	*Description*
getMetaData()	Returns a ResultSetMetaData object containing infor mation about the number of columns, column names, and column types for this ResultSet.

Retrieving the values of a ResultSet is not overly complex but does require several steps. The required steps are enumerated below. You can see an example of this process in the upcoming Listing 10-4.

1. **Start by executing the** ResultSet.getMetaData() **method to return the metadata about this** ResultSet.

   The ResultSetMetaData object contains information on the number of columns in the ResultSet, the type of each column, and the name of each column.

2. **Set the** ResultSet **before the first row using the** ResultSet.beforeFirst() **method.**

3. **Increment through the** ResultSet **by using a** while **loop.**

   For each iteration of the loop, execute the ResultSet.next() method. This method retrieves the next row in the ResultSet. If gets a valid row, it returns true; otherwise, it returns false.

4. **For each iteration of the** while **loop, you need to retrieve the values out of that row in the** ResultSet.

   To do so, create a for loop to step through all the columns in the row. You can get the number of columns by executing the ResultSetMetaData.getColumnCount() method.

5. **While you increment through the** for **loop, you can retrieve the label for each column by executing the** ResultSetMetaData.getColumnLabel() **method, passing the column number as a parameter.**

   Likewise, you can get the value for that column by executing the appropriate getter method of the ResultSet object for the column type and passing the column number as a parameter.

Table 10-4 (earlier in this chapter) identifies getter methods for the CallableStatement. The good news is the ResultSet has an identical set of methods, so you can use the same table to find appropriate getter methods for the value you need to retrieve.

Although I cover here all the elements you need to perform routine database interaction in this chapter, I recommend investing in the JavaDoc documentation for the java.sql package. In addition to the methods that I identify in this chapter, you will find several other useful classes and methods in the `java.sql` package. You'll find this documentation in the standard edition Java SDK documentation. See Appendix A for more information on getting the documentation for the standard edition Java SDK.

Listing 10-4: Retrieving Values from a ResultSet Object

```
try{
  // The following statement creates an SQL statement as a
          String.
  String select = "SELECT * FROM orders WHERE customer_id =
          1";

  // Now I'll execute the select statement.
  ResultSet rs = stmt.executeQuery(select);

  // Get the ResultSetMetaData of the ResultSet.
  ResultSetMetaData data = rs.getMetaData();

  // Set the ResultSet before the first row.
  rs.beforeFirst();

  // Start a while loop to step through the resultset rows.
  while(rs.next()){
    rowCount++; // increment
    for(int index = 0; index < data.getColumnCount();
          index++){
      StringBuffer row = new StringBuffer(rowCount);
      row.append(": ");
      row.append(data.getColumnLabel(index));
      row.append(" = ");
      if(rs.getString(index) != null){
        row.append(rs.getString(index));
      }
      System.out.println(row.toString());
    }
  }
  // example of output:
  /* 1: customer_id = 1
   * 1: order_id = 3
   * 1: order_date = 2001-08-03 15:09:12
   */
}
catch(SQLException){
  // handle exception
}
```

To read about integrating JDBC and database functionality with JSP applications, see Chapter 11, where I address strategies that you can apply effectively integrate JDBC and JSP to make powerful database applications on the Internet.

Chapter 11

Manipulating Data with JavaBeans

In This Chapter

- Integrating JavaBeans and JDBC
- Executing queries from JavaBeans
- Executing updates from JavaBeans

Creating data-driven JavaServer Pages (JSP) applications is where the true power and flexibility of JSP applications becomes apparent. With *data-driven* JSP applications, you can create an entire Web site that's controlled by the information that you maintain in a database.

In Chapter 10, I present the fundamentals of interacting with a database using Java Database Connectivity (JDBC). Using these principles, I present some options for implementing database interaction in your JSP application. As this chapter details, the database interaction is actually implemented through the JavaBeans used by your JSP application. With those JavaBeans, you can write information into the database and retrieve information from the database, building powerful applications in the process.

Charting the Lifecycle of a Single User Request

A *lifecycle* describes all the events that occur to complete a process, from the start to the end. Just like the fruit fly you may remember studying in high school biology class, a user request has a lifecycle, as shown in Figure 11-1. As you proceed through this chapter, I cover some topics that may not be entirely intuitive until you see the lifecycle of a user request, including database interaction.

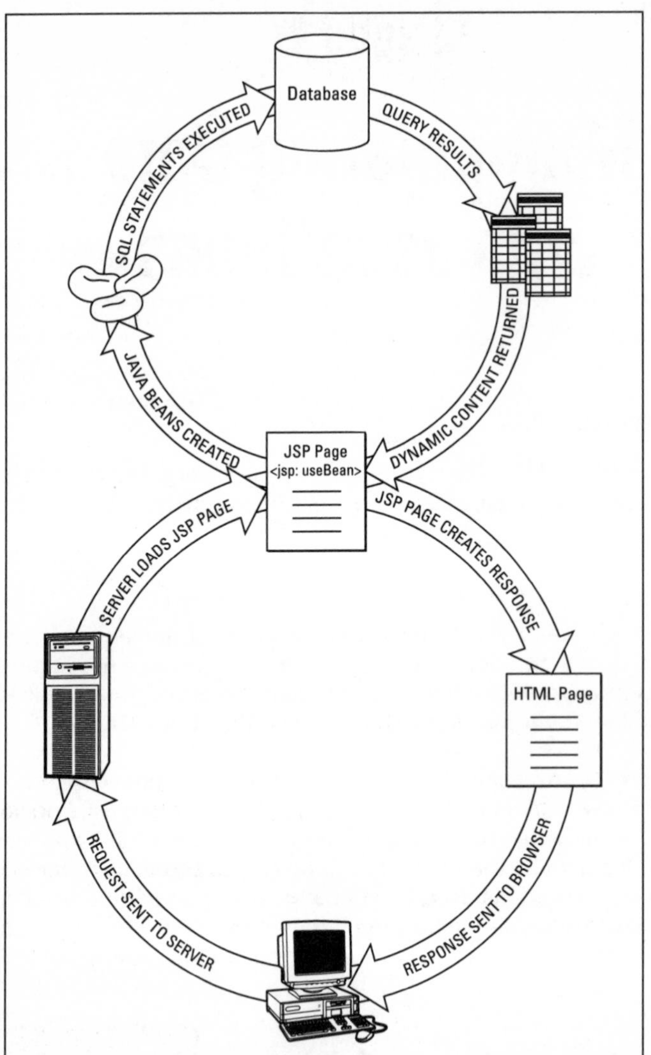

Figure 11-1: Lifecycle of a user request.

In earlier chapters of this book, I cover the process of responding to user requests from a pretty simple perspective that doesn't include databases. Now, with the new layer, the lifecycle of a user request gets a little bigger:

1. **The request lifecycle begins from users' browsers when they submit a request for some page.**

   The request typically contains some values that are submitted by the user on the HyperText Markup Language (HTML) form and a Uniform Resource Locator (URL) to the Web server.

2. **Your Web server receives the request.**

   At this point, it may perform some evaluation on the received values and then probably forwards the request to the next JSP page to be displayed to the user.

3. **The JSP page being prepared for the user has to get some information out of the database to present some dynamic information.**

   Perhaps the user wants to see the status of an order or his account information. The JSP uses a JavaBean and initializes it with parameters identifying the user as well as other attributes necessary to get the requested information.

4. **The JavaBean has a set of values; and when requested, the JavaBean executes a Structured Query Language (SQL) query against the database.**

   This query is most likely a parameterized query, and the values submitted by the user are used as the parameters for the query.

Integrating JavaBeans and JDBC

Most of the chapters in this book are specifically oriented to JSP pages, which have the primary concern of presenting information to a user. But JSP pages typically rely on JavaBeans for generating that information. Consequently, the interaction between an HTML page and a database should be coordinated by JavaBeans, and not by the JSP pages themselves.

The dual purpose of JavaBeans is to implement application services and to collect data for use by the user interface. After you write a JavaBean to perform this service, you can reuse the JavaBean in a variety of contexts.

Creating a reusable class to manage database interaction

Java is an object-oriented language, and one of the driving ideas behind object-oriented languages is to create reusable units of code. That's why I recommend creating a reusable Java class for managing your database interaction. You accomplish two tasks by doing this:

- **Reusable code:** When you create a class for managing SQL statements, you only have to write all the code to work with a database once. After that, you get to reuse the same code over and over.

- **The Big Picture:** With a reusable manager class for SQL statements, you can focus on writing SQL queries without having to worry about all the details behind how your application interacts with the database. In fact, after you write and test the SQL Manager, you don't have to worry about it anymore. Instead, you can focus your energy on writing SQL statements you need to retrieve data and update data for your application.

Although you may choose to create your own solution for managing SQL statements and database interaction, you should feel free to use the solution I present in this book. My class is called `SQLManager`. (I wanted to call it `ThingAMaJigger`, but my technical editor said the name wasn't meaningful enough. Go figure.) Here are some guidelines I use to create a class called `SQLManager` that handles all my SQL Statements.

- My class has to be able to open a connection and close a connection to the database. If I were working with connection pooling software, as I describe in Chapter 10, the `SQLManager` class should handle getting a connection from the pool and returning it to the pool.
- My class has to handle parameterized select, insert, update, and delete statements. By this, I mean that I want to provide an SQL statement to the `SQLManager` and the parameters for that statement. The `SQLManager` class should then handle the process of constructing the statement and execute it.
- After executing a select statement, I want my class to return columns of data from the `ResultSet` how I request them. This is important because I use those methods to initialize JavaBean properties, as you see in the next section "Executing select statements from JavaBeans." If I expect only a single row to be returned by a select statement, I want to have a way to get a single value instead of an index of values.
- My class needs to have appropriate exceptions to address error conditions I may encounter. I can envision four different error conditions.

  I may try to request a column from a `ResultSet` when I used my `SQLManager` to perform an update. Because updates don't generate `ResultSet` objects, I want to throw an exception in this case.

  I may request a column in a `ResultSet` that does not exist, because I used either the wrong name or the wrong column index.

  If I expect to receive a single row from a select statement and I get any other number of rows, I want to throw an exception.

  If the database generates an `SQLException`, I want to receive it.

In Table 11-1, I provide a summary of the classes I generate with these requirements. (See the upcoming Table 11-2 for the methods of the `SQLManager` class.)

Table 11-1 Classes for SQL Management

Class Name	*Description*
`InParameter`	This class stores parameters that I pass into a parameterized select statement.
`SQLManager`	This class coordinates all interaction with the database: creating connections, preparing statements, executing them, and returning the results.
`NoSuchLabelException`	This exception is thrown when I request the values for a column using a label that is not defined in the `ResultSet` of a query.
`NotASingleRowSelectException`	This exception is thrown when I try to execute a select statement that should return a single row, and instead returns a different number of rows.
`OutOfRangeException`	This exception is thrown when I request the values for a column using a number, and the number does not correspond to a column in the `ResultSet` returned by the query.
`ResultSetUndefinedException`	This exception is thrown when I try to request the values from a `ResultSet` but have not created a `ResultSet` by executing a query.

Of the classes identified in Table 11-1, the SQLManager class is the most important. It coordinates all of the database interaction classes and is the primary consumer of all the other classes. Even if you create your own solution for interacting with a database, you'll probably end up with a class very similar to the SQLManager class.

Table 11-2 identifies the methods I placed in the SQLManager class to coordinate database interaction. The SQLManager class has five methods for getting columns of data out of a `ResultSet`. Two take the column *label* as a parameter to determine which column to return. The other two take the column *number* as a parameter to determine which column to return. The last returns the `ResultSet` of the query, in the event that you need to present tabular data in your JSP page.

The *column label* is the label that you assign — if you assign a label — to the column in the select clause of the select statement. Otherwise, it's the entire expression of the column in the select clause. Column numbering starts with 1 in ResultSet objects, where *1* is the first column listed in the select clause, *2* is the second column, and so on.

The following code sample illustrates these points.

```
SELECT UPPER(TRIM(first_name)) AS first_name
     , UPPER(TRIM(last_name))
FROM customers
```

In the previous example, first_name is the column label for the first column because the first column uses the AS keyword to assign the label first_name. The second column does not have a label, so the entire expression of the second column is used as its label: UPPER(TRIM(last_name)). You can also refer to the first column using the column index of 1, and the second column with the column index of 2.

Some JDBC drivers I've worked with force the column label to all uppercase characters. I don't think it's mandatory for JDBC drivers to do so, but the column label is case-sensitive in a JDBC driver. Don't be surprised if you try to get a column with a mixed-case label and the column can't be found.

Table 11-2 lists the methods of the SQLManager class.

Table 11-2 Methods of the SQLManager Class

Method	*Description*
openConnection()	This private method opens a connection to the database.
releaseConnection()	This private method closes a connection to the database.
executeQuery()	This method is public and allows the user to execute a query without parameters.
executeParameterQuery()	This method is public and allows the user to execute a query with parameters.
executeUpdate()	This method is public and allows the user to execute an insert, update, or delete without parameters.
executeParameterUpdate()	This method is public and allows the user to execute an insert, update, or delete with parameters.

Method	*Description*
`release()`	This is a public method to be executed when you're finished using the `SQLManager`.
`getResultSet()`	This is a public method that returns the `ResultSet` of a query. When you need to present data in a tabular format, the other options for retrieving data from the `SQLManager` don't work. Instead, retrieve the ResultSet from the `SQLManager` and work with it directly.
`getSingleRowColumn()`	This public method accepts the label for a column as an argument, returns the value of that column as a `String`, and is only applied to statements that return a single row.
`getColumn()`	This is a public method that accepts the label for a column as an argument and returns an `Iterator` class of the values in that column.
`getSingleRowColumn()`	This public method accepts the column number for a column as an argument, returns the value of that column as a `String`, and is only applied to statements that return a single row.
`getColumn()`	This is a public method that accepts the column number for a column as an argument and returns an `Iterator` class of the values in that column.

As you digest the elements of the `SQLManager` class that I create, you may note a correlation between the values returned by the `SQLManager` and the way that JavaBeans manage properties. The way that I create this class is not haphazard, and here's why:

- JavaBeans can have indexed properties (properties that hold multiple values) or simple properties (which hold only a single value). The `SQLManager` has methods to support each type of property. Indexed properties are retrieved with the methods that return `Iterator` classes, and simple properties are returned by the methods that return a `String`.

- The reason for including the `NotASingleRowSelectException` class should be clearer. If I want to retrieve a single value from a query and instead I get multiple values, I can't store those multiple values in a simple property. The `NotASingleRowSelectException` class alerts me to this condition.

Executing select statements from JavaBeans

Executing SQL from a JavaBean can be handled in a couple of different ways. The most direct method is to create a connection inside the JavaBean, using the JDBC Application Program Interface (API) that I cover in Chapter 10. You can then prepare a statement inside the JavaBean, execute it, and handle the results. The alternative is to use a class like the `SQLManager` that I outline in the previous section.

Create a class to manage your SQL interaction with the database; after you write this, you get to reuse the functionality of the SQL manager class over and over, without making any changes. Furthermore, if you need to maintain the SQL connection functionality, you can do so once and have the change affect all the classes that use the manager.

When you write JDBC functionality directly into each one of your JavaBeans, you have to update each JavaBean that interacts with a database each time you have to make a change to the JDBC functionality. Further, duplicating the same functionality across multiple classes increases the risk of simple typographical errors.

Although I strongly recommend using an `SQLManager` type class to handle your SQL connections, I provide an overview of both approaches here so that you can choose for yourself. (Choices are what America is all about, right? Paper or plastic? Ketchup or mustard? Microsoft or . . . maybe that was a bad example.)

JavaBean database support with the SQLManager class

Creating database interaction with a JavaBean that uses the `SQLManager` class is about as simple as you can get. In fact, you can follow this simple formula to create JavaBeans with database support when using the `SQLManager`:

1. **When you code the JavaBean, create a `private static final String` variable containing the SQL statement that you want to execute.**

   If you need to execute more than one SQL statement, create one of these variables for each statement. Making the variable static and final limits the overhead of the statement and ensures that no one can change it later on.

2. **If your SQL statement is parameterized, create JavaBean properties for each parameter in the statement.**

3. **If you execute a select statement, create JavaBean properties for each column returned by the select statement. If the select statement can return more than one row, make sure that your JavaBean properties are indexed properties.**

   Indexed properties are properties that can hold multiple values. You'll find more on the subject in Chapter 8.

4. **Create a variable for the `SQLManager` class to handle all the database interaction.**

5. **For each SQL statement that your JavaBean contains, create a method called `executeXXX`, where `XXX` is the name of the statement that you give to the variable in Step 1.**

   This method should perform a couple of tasks. First, it should call on the `SQLManager` to execute the SQL statement. Second, if the SQL statement is a query, the method should use the `SQLManager` to retrieve the results of the query and initialize the corresponding properties that you create in Step 3 with those results.

Your JavaBean will be responsible for handling any exception thrown by the `SQLManager` class. You'll need to handle those exceptions in the `executeXXX` method of your JavaBean.

The code in Listing 11-1 illustrates a simple JavaBean that uses my `SQLManager` class to execute a query.

Listing 11-1: JavaBeans Using the SQLManager Class

```
package dummies.sqlbeans;

import java.sql.SQLException;
import dummies.sql.*;
import java.util.Iterator;

public class SimpleQuery {
    /**
     * This is my simple Customers query that returns the
     * first name, last name, and credit for a customer,
     * given the customer_id. I make it static and final
     * because it is the same for every instance of this
     * bean, and never changes. Static variables are only
     * created once when a class is loaded, and all classes
     * share them.
     */
```

(continued)

Listing 11-1 *(continued)*

```
private static final String GET_CUSTOMER =
    "SELECT first_name AS firstName " +
    "     , last_name AS lastName " +
    "     , credit " +
    "FROM customers " +
    "WHERE customer_id = ?";

// this property stores the customerId parameter
private int customerId = 0;
// these properties hold the results
private String firstName = new String();
private String lastName = new String();
private String credit = new String();
private SQLManager query = new SQLManager();

/**
 * All JavaBeans must have an empty constructor
 */
public SimpleQuery() { }

/**
 * Use this method to set the customerId value prior to
 * executing the query. The customerId is the parameter
 * for the query.
 */
public void setCustomerId( int customerId ) {
    this.customerId = customerId;
}

/**
 * Use this method to get the customerId value
 */
public int getCustomerId() { return this.customerId; }

/**
 * This method returns the first name, to be used by the
 * <jsp:getProperty> tag after the query has been
 * executed.
 */
public String getFirstName() { return firstName; }

/**
 * This method returns the last name, to be used by
 * <jsp:getProperty> tag after the query has been
 * executed.
 */
```

```
public String getLastName() { return lastName; }

/**
 * This method returns the customer's credit amount, to
 * be used by the <jsp:getProperty> tag after the query
 * has been executed.
 */
public String getCredit() { return credit; }

/**
 * This is the method of the JavaBean you use to execute
 * the query. It calls on the SQLManager class to execute
 * the query, given the parameter customerId. The method
 * also sets the values for firstName, lastName, and
 * credit, based on the results of the query.
 */
public void executeGetCustomer() {
    // This try block contains all the code necessary to
    // execute the query and retrieve the results using
       the
    // SQLManager.
    try{
         InParameter parameters[] = {new InParameter()};

        parameters[0].setValue(Integer.toString(customerId
        ));
         query.executeQuery(this.GET_CUSTOMER,
        parameters);
         firstName =
        query.getSingleRowColumn("FIRSTNAME");
         lastName = query.getSingleRowColumn("LASTNAME");
         credit = query.getSingleRowColumn("CREDIT");
    }
    // In the following catch blocks I catch all the
        exceptions.
    catch(SQLException e){
        // handle exception
    }
    catch(ResultSetUndefinedException e){
        // handle exception
    }
    catch(NotASingleRowSelectException e){
        // handle exception
    }
    catch(NoSuchLabelException e){
        // handle exception
    }
    // Because I always need to try and close the
        connection, I've
```

(continued)

Listing 11-1 *(continued)*

```
        // added this final block. It gets executed, whether
            or not
        // the try block throws an exception.
        finally{
            try{
                query.release();
            }
            catch(SQLException e){
                // handle exception
            }
        }
    }
}
```

This JavaBean is now ready to use in a JSP page. This bean requires one scriptlet block in the JSP page to call the `SimpleQuery.executeGetCustomer()` method. Other than that, you use this bean the same way you use any other, creating it with the `<jsp:useBean>` tag, initializing properties with the `<jsp:setProperty>` tag, and retrieving properties with the `<jsp:getProperty>` tag.

JavaBeans with database connectivity built-in

If you choose not to use an `SQLManager` class like I created, you can still execute queries from within a JavaBean. The process is a little more involved, but not much. Follow this formula to create database connections and execute SQL statements from within a JavaBean.

1. **When you code the JavaBean, create a `private static final String` variable containing the SQL statement that you want to execute.**

   If you need to execute more than one SQL statement, create one of these variables for each statement. Making the variable static and final limits the overhead of the statement and ensures no one can change it later on.

2. **If your SQL statement is parameterized, create JavaBean properties for each parameter in the statement.**

3. **If you're executing a select statement, create JavaBean properties for each column returned by the select statement. If the select statement can return more than one row, make sure that your JavaBean properties are indexed properties.**

   At this point, I diverge from the previous example using an `SQLManager` class. In your bean class, you have to have code to register the database driver because you have to use the `DriverManager` to get a connection to the database.

4. **For each SQL statement your JavaBean contains, create a method called `executeXXX`, where `XXX` is the name of the statement you give to the variable in Step 1.**

   Inside this method, you have to perform several steps:

   1. Create a connection.
   2. Prepare an SQL statement.
   3. Initialize all the parameters for the statement.
   4. Execute the statement. If it is a query, you have to store the `ResultSet` in a variable.
   5. Work through the `ResultSet`, get the result of the query for each column, and store it in the parameters identified in Step 3.

That last step is a lot of work, and it yields a JavaBean that looks very different than the JavaBean using the `SQLManager` class. For an example of the implementation and a comparison of the differences between using the `SQLManager` and connecting from a JavaBean directly, take a look at the sample code in Listing 11-2. The code in Listing 11-2 creates a JavaBean that does exactly the same tasks as the code in Listing 11-1.

Listing 11-2: JavaBeans without an SQLManager Class

```
package dummies.sqlbeans;

import java.sql.*;
import java.util.Iterator;

public class ComplexQuery {

    /*
     * This block is called a static initializer. It gets
     * executed once when the class is loaded, causing the
     * SQL Driver to be loaded.
     */
    static {
        try{
            Class.forName( "org.gjt.mm.mysql.Driver" );
        }
        catch(ClassNotFoundException e){
        }
    }

    /**
     * This is my Customers query, that returns the first
           name,
```

(continued)

Listing 11-2 *(continued)*

```
     * last name, and credit for a customer, given the
     * customer_id. I make it static and final because it is
     * the same for every instance of this bean, and never
     * changes. Static variables are only created once when a
     * class is loaded, and all classes share them.
     */
    private static final String GET_CUSTOMER =
        "SELECT first_name AS firstName " +
        "     , last_name AS lastName " +
        "     , credit " +
        "FROM customers " +
        "WHERE customer_id = ?";

    private int customerId    = 0;
    private String firstName = new String();
    private String lastName  = new String();
    private String credit    = new String();

    /** All JavaBeans must have an empty constructor */
    public ComplexQuery() { }

    /**
     * Use this method to set the customerId value prior to
     * executing the query. The customerId is the parameter
     * for the query.
     */
    public void setCustomerId( int customerId ) {
        this.customerId = customerId;
    }

    /**
     * Use this method to get the customerId value
     */
    public int getCustomerId() { return this.customerId; }

    /**
     * This method returns the first name, to be used by the
     * <jsp:getProperty> tag after the query has been
           executed.
     */
    public String getFirstName() { return firstName; }

    /**
     * This method returns the last name, to be used by
     * <jsp:getProperty> tag after the query has been
           executed.
     */
```

```
public String getLastName() { return lastName; }

/**
 * This method returns the customer's credit amount to be
 * used by the <jsp:getProperty> tag after the query has
 * been executed.
 */
public String getCredit() { return credit; }

/**
 * This is the new method for managing the query process.
 * This example is a little more complex than the
 * previous solution, but not much. Nevertheless, this
 * still costs more in effort, and makes the code more
 * difficult to maintain than the solution with the SQL
 * manager is.
 */
public void executeGetCustomer() {
    ResultSet rs;
    PreparedStatement ps;
    Connection conn;

    try{
    // get the connection
    conn = DriverManager.getConnection(
        "jdbc:mysql://localhost:3306/dummy_sales",
        "sys", "admin" );
        try {
            /* This prepareStatement call is only
        supported in JDBC
             * 2.0 it allows you to move forward and
               backward
             * through results in a result set. If the
               second two
             * parameters are left off, you can only go
               forward
             * through the result set.
             */
            ps = conn.prepareStatement( this.GET_CUSTOMER
                , ResultSet.TYPE_SCROLL_INSENSITIVE
                , ResultSet.CONCUR_READ_ONLY);

            // Now I have to set the parameter.
            ps.setInt(1, customerId);

            /* Here I execute the query, storing it in
               the
```

(continued)

Listing 11-2 *(continued)*

```
                 * ResultSet.
                 */
                rs = ps.executeQuery();

                // Now I verify the query returned only a
            single row.
                if(rs.first() && !rs.next()){
                    /* Then I set the cursor in the ResultSet
                       to the
                     * first row.
                     */
                    rs.first();
                    /* Finally I retrieve the results from
                       the row,
                     * storing them into the JavaBean
                       properties.
                     */
                    firstName = rs.getString( "FIRSTNAME" );
                    lastName = rs.getString( "LASTNAME" );
                    credit = rs.getString( "CREDIT" );
                }
                else{
                    /* If the statement returns the wrong
                       number of
                     * rows, I'll handle it here.
                     */
                }
            }
            catch ( SQLException e ) {
                // handle exception
            }
            rs = null;
            ps = null;
            conn.close();
        }
        catch ( SQLException e ) {
            // handle exception
        }
    }
}
```

Note the 25 extra lines of code for the class in Listing 11-2 compared with the class in Listing 11-1. As you multiply that extra effort out across all the JavaBeans that you write requiring database access, you see that the number adds up rapidly and the cost of maintaining that code adds up quickly as well.

Determining the best way to store ResultSet data

If you're retrieving information from a database to display in an HTML form, the way you need to present that information may have some influence on how you choose to store the data retrieved from the database in your JavaBean. When I retrieve data for display in an HTML form, I generally categorize that task into three broad categories:

- Most of the data I retrieve is stored in single value fields, such as text `<INPUT>` elements or check box `<INPUT>` elements. This data is typically held in a simple JavaBean property, since there is only one value associated with each element on a form. The `SQLManager.getSingleRowColumn()` methods are typically the ideal solution for retrieving values of this kind, since you should only receive a single value from the database.
- Some data I retrieve is stored in list-oriented elements, such as `<SELECT>` elements or radio button `<INPUT>` elements. The data for these elements is best held in indexed JavaBean properties. Each list on the JSP page has only a single column of values. The `SQLManager.getColumn()` methods are ideal for this solution because you want to store the entire column of data in the JavaBean.
- The most complex way to represent data in an HTML form is using the HTML `<TABLE>` element. If you have to build an HTML page containing invoice line items, you'll probably be organizing those line items in tabular format. When you build a `<TABLE>` dynamically based on data from a database, you have to build the table one row at a time. Because you may have more than one row, you cannot use the `SQLManager.getSingleRowColumn()` statement. And because the table has to be built row-by-row, not column-by-column, you cannot use the `SQLManager.getColumn()`.

When you need to present data in tabular format using the HTML `<TABLE>` element, the best solution is to store the `ResultSet` object from the query in your JavaBean and retrieve results from that object row-by-row, as you need them.

Several excellent examples of retrieving tabular data and displaying that data in an HTML `<TABLE>` element appear in Bonus Chapter 1 on the companion CD.

Executing Updates from JavaBeans

Compared with managing queries from JavaBeans, handling updates is a lot simpler. In fact, the process for managing inserts, updates, and deletes is the same. Here's an overview of the steps required to perform an update from a JavaBean:

1. **When you code the JavaBean, create a `private static final String` variable containing the insert, update, or delete statement that you need to execute.**

2. **If your SQL statement is parameterized, create JavaBean properties for each parameter in the statement.**
3. **If you need to report how many rows the statement affects, create a JavaBean property that holds the change count.**
4. **Create a variable for the `SQLManager` class. You use this variable to handle all the database interaction.**
5. **For each SQL statement that your JavaBean contains, create a method called `executeXXX`, where `XXX` is the name of the statement you give to the variable in Step 1.**

   With insert, update, and delete statements, the execute method only needs to pass the statement and parameters to the `SQLManager` class and to store the change count. It's a single statement.

The code in Listing 11-3 is an example of a JavaBeans performing an update based on data received from a JSP.

Listing 11-3: A JavaBean Performing an Update

```
package dummies.sqlbeans;

import java.sql.SQLException;
import dummies.sql.*;
import java.util.Iterator;

public class UpdateBean {
    /**
     * This update statement can change the first name, last
     * name and credit for a given customer_id.
     */
    private static final String UPDATE_CUSTOMER =
        "UPDATE customers " +
        "SET first_name = ? " +
        "    , last_name = ? " +
        "    , credit = ? " +
        "WHERE customer_id = ?";

    // This property stores the customerId parameter.
    private int customerId = 0;
    // These properties store the new column values.
    private String firstName = new String();
    private String lastName = new String();
    private String credit = new String();
    private SQLManager update = new SQLManager();

    // This property holds the change count.
    private int changeCount = 0;

    /**
```

```
 * All JavaBeans must have an empty constructor.
 */
public SimpleQuery() { }

/**
 * Use this method to set the customerId value prior to
 * executing the query. The customerId is the parameter
 * for the query.
 */
public void setCustomerId( int customerId ) {
     this.customerId = customerId;
}

/**
 * Use this method to set the new first name.
 */
public void setFirstName(String firstName) {
    this.firstName = firstName;
}

/**
 * Use this method to set the new last name.
 */
public void setLastName(String lastName) {
    this.lastName = lastName;
}

/**
 * Use this method to set the new credit.
 */
public void setCredit(String credit) {
    this.credit = credit;
}

/**
 * Use this method to get the change count after the
 * update is executed.
 */
public int getChangeCount(){ return changeCount; }

/**
 * This is the method of the JavaBean you use to execute
 * the query. It calls on the SQLManager class to execute
 * the update, given the parameters customerId,
 * firstName, lastName, and credit.
 */
public void executeUpdateCustomer() {
```

(continued)

Listing 11-3 ***(continued)***

```
        /* This try block contains the code necessary to
         * initialize the statement parameters and execute
         * the update. The change count is stored to the
         * changeCount property of the JavaBean.
         */
        try{
            // initializing the parameter array
            InParameter parameters[] = {new InParameter(),
                new InParameter(),new InParameter(),new
           InParameter()};

            // setting the parameters
            parameters[0].setValue(firstName);
            parameters[1].setValue(lastName);
            parameters[2].setValue(credit);

           parameters[3].setValue(Integer.toString(customerId
           ));

            // executing the update
            changeCount =
           update.executeUpdate(this.UPDATE_CUSTOMER,
                parameters);
        }
        // In the following catch block, I catch the
           SQLException.
        catch(SQLException e){
            // handle exception
        }

        // Because I always need to try and close the
        // connection, I've added this final block. It gets
        // executed whether or not the try block throws an
        // exception.
        finally{
            try{
                update.release();
            }
            catch(SQLException e){
                // handle exception
            }
        }
    }
}
```

After you create the SQL code to interact with a database from inside a JavaBean, the tasks of setting SQL statement parameters in a JavaBean and of displaying the results of an SQL statement on a JSP are simply a matter of getting and setting JavaBean properties.

The only special thing about executing SQL in a JavaBean is remembering that the JSP has to have a brief scriptlet that executes the method you create to execute the SQL statement. That method needs to be executed after the parameters are set but before the results are retrieved.

With SQL statements that return a single row of data, you can use `<jsp:getProperty>` tags to retrieve the result of the statement. But if you have an SQL statement that returns multiple rows of data, they have to be stored as indexed properties in the JavaBean. Chapter 8 provides information on working with indexed properties. In addition, take a look at Chapter 12 to see an example of retrieving indexed properties using a custom tag.

Part V

Breaking the Envelope: JSP Advanced Features

"Sometimes I feel behind the times. I asked my 11-year old to build a database for my business's Web site, and he said he would, only after he finishes the one he's building for his baseball card collection."

In this part . . .

If you want to be a "best of class" programmer with JavaServer Pages (JSP) technology and you don't want to spend a lot of time getting there, Part 5 is for you. This part covers a variety of topics of interest to both Web designers and Java developers.

Chapter 12 kicks off with an exploration of JSP custom tags, perhaps the most exciting feature of JSP development for both Web designers and Java developers. Chapter 13 introduces the use of cookies in JSP applications. Chapter 14 provides a complete reference on the process of deploying JSP applications, a must-have skill for serious JSP programmers. Finally, Chapter 15 gives an introduction to JSP application architectures, which are formulas that you can use to ensure that you create a great JSP application.

Don't delay: Be the envy of your peers, and the master of your domain! Master the topics covered in Part 5 and nothing can stop you!

Chapter 12

Introducing Custom Tag Libraries

In This Chapter

- Overview of JSP tag extensions
- Comparing custom tags with actions
- Using custom tag libraries to extend JSP functionality
- Including custom tag libraries in your JSP project

The JavaServer Pages (JSP) specification provides a lot of great features for dynamic server-side development. But the creators of this specification rightfully recognized that JSP couldn't do everything. That's why the JSP specification addresses the need for *custom tag libraries*, which are libraries of special tags that extend the function of standard JSP actions. By providing an Application Programming Interface (API) for the creation of new action tags, the JSP model is more durable and extensible to the ever-changing needs of software developers.

The JSP specification specifically envisioned third-party application vendors extending the JSP framework through custom tags specialized to address needs beyond the scope of the specification. Several third-party vendors now offer tag libraries through open-source licensing or for purchase. This chapter addresses how make use of existing custom tag libraries and how to create your own custom tags.

Before writing your own custom tags, take a look at libraries available for sale or for free. Writing your own custom tags can get pretty complex, and existing libraries do a lot of routine tasks well.

The Role of Custom Tag Libraries

Custom tag libraries are used to extend the standard action tags provided by the JSP specification (such as the `<jsp:useBean>` and `<jsp:forward>` tags). One of the major advantages of using custom tags is that they can virtually eliminate the need to embed Java code in your JSP while supporting just about any task that you can support with JSP scriptlets or expressions. Using custom tags is good for the following reasons:

- **Reusability:** Custom tags can encapsulate the behavior associated with repetitive tasks that you might normally have to implement over and over if you perform those tasks with scriptlets or expressions. You can write the behavior associated with a custom tag once and then reuse it as often as necessary.
- **Maintenance:** Custom tags make your JSPs easier to maintain by reducing or eliminating Java code in the JSP. I find that JSPs with a lot of Java code written in scriptlets end up more verbose (wordy), more complex, and prone to errors when developers hand the pages off to Web designers.
- **Simplicity:** If you use custom tags to perform all the complex tasks that aren't handled by JSP standard actions, you don't need Java developers to get involved with the development of the presentation of a Web page. When dividing the responsibilities of JSP development between Web designers and Java programmers, keeping a clean separation between the user interface (the JSP itself) and the application code (the JavaBeans and other Java programs) makes managing the software development effort easier.

JSP custom tags can perform just about any task that you can perform with a scriptlet or expression. Whenever you perform a kind of task with a scriptlet that has the possibility of being reused elsewhere in your JSP application, consider using an existing custom tag to perform the task or creating your own custom tag.

The Components of Tag Libraries

Custom tag libraries are bundles of Java classes developed using the tag extension API. To use a custom tag, you need to

- Develop the custom tag.
- Package the tag in a Java ARchive File (JAR).
- Include an eXtensible Markup Language (XML) document, called the tag library descriptor (`.tld`) file, that describes the structure of the custom tag.

Tag support classes

Tag support classes are the Java classes used to create JSP actions; they implement the software code necessary to make the action tags work. (Read through Chapter 3 for coverage of the standard JSP action tags, such as the `<jsp:useBean>` and `<jsp:forward>` actions.) Each tag support class can have methods to support the behavior of the action that you need to create as well as properties (with getter and setter methods) for supplying data necessary to perform the action. The properties of a tag support class correspond with the attributes of the JSP tag. As an example, for the tag `<jsp:useBean id="foo" class="Foo" scope="request"/>:`, the properties of the tag support class supporting this action tag are `id`, `class`, and `scope`.

In Bonus Chapter 4, located on the CD-ROM that accompanies this book, I provide a detailed review of the API for the tag support classes.

The tag library descriptor file

The tag library descriptor (`.tld`) file is an XML-based file describing the contents of a tag library and each tag support class in a library. Each tag library comes with one `.tld` file. The JSP container uses the `.tld` file to find the tag support classes for each custom tag and to map the attributes of a custom tag in a JSP to its corresponding property in the custom tag support class. For example, when you write `<jsp:useBean id="foo" class="Foo" scope="request"/>` on a JSP, the `.tld` file makes it possible for the JSP container to know you want to create or reference an object called `foo` of the class `Foo` in the request object.

Using Tag Libraries in Your JSP Applications

Use custom tags to perform just about any task imaginable. To get your imagination revving, read this overview of the Struts tag libraries created by the Jakarta Project of the Apache Software Foundation. For a real-life example, I show you how to create a JSP by using custom tags and then review deploying custom tags in a JSP application.

The source code for Version 1.0 of the Struts tag libraries is located on the CD included with this book. You can find additional resources on Struts at its official home page `http://jakarta.apache.org/struts/`.

The four struts tag libraries are

- **The struts-html library:** Provides a set of custom tags that you can use to create HyperText Markup Language (HTML) elements such as tables, object elements, and basic HTML-form elements. Although not complete, the struts-html library suggests the possibility of creating of JSPs without any HTML code. You can use the struts-html library to add HTML elements to your JSP dynamically.

- **The struts-logic library:** Provides a set of custom tags to use in place of software logic implemented with scriptlets. Use struts-logic tags to implement property readers that read indexed properties and that perform actions based on comparative expressions (such as equal, not-equal, greater-than, less-than, and other comparative operations). The struts-logic library illustrates the true power of JSP custom tags by performing complex logical operations in a concise style consistent with the tag-based structure of HTML and JSP action tags. This is my favorite library because its use virtually eliminates the need for JSP scripting elements to perform logical operations in JSPs.
- **The struts-template library:** Provides a set of custom tags used to generate template-based HTML pages. Use template tags to generate JSPs that serve as templates for dynamic Web pages. Creating template-based Web pages with the struts-template library makes it easier to modify the appearance of an entire Web site by changing the content of a particular template. Changes to the template automatically get updated in all the JSPs that use the template.
- **The struts-bean library:** Provides a set of custom tags that extend the capability of the JSP standard bean tags to a bean-referencing framework that integrates with the rest of the struts-library tags.

Even if you decide to implement your own custom tag libraries, don't overlook the Struts tag library documentation, either on the Struts Web site or the Struts deployment file on this book's CD. For installation instructions of the struts deployment files, skip down to the upcoming section "Deploying custom tag libraries."

Including tag libraries in your JSP

The first step to using a custom tag library is to reference the `.tld` file associated with the tag library in your JSP by using the `taglib` directive. The `taglib` directive tells the JSP engine to load the tag library associated with the `.tld` document so that your JSP can use the tags included in the document. Read through Chapter 4 for comprehensive coverage of the `taglib` directive syntax.

Given a custom tag library called `foo-tags`, the following code snippet illustrates the use of the `taglib` directive to include `foo-tags` in your JSP.

```
<%@ taglib uri="http://localhost:8080/webapps/login/
          web-inf/foo-tags.tld" prefix="foo"/>
```

After a tag is introduced with a given prefix (such as the prefix `foo` in the above snippet), no other tag library should use that prefix for the given page. Do not incur the wrath of the Prefix Police.

Although you have broad discretion in your choice of terms to use for prefixes in the taglib directive, there are several prefixes reserved by Sun Microsystems and not available to you. The prefix `jsp` is reserved for JSP standard action tags, and you cannot use that for custom tags. In addition, the prefixes `jspx`, `java`, `javax`, `servlet`, `sun`, and `sunw` are reserved by Sun Microsystems. Using these prefixes gets you in trouble with the Prefix FBI.

Referencing tag actions in JSPs

After you reference the `.tld` file for the tag library that you want to use, you're free to use any custom tag in that library. To do so, just create an action tag with the prefix specified in the `taglib` directive, followed by a colon and the name of the custom tag custom tag you want to use. For example: If the `foo` tag library contains a tag called `fooGetter`, the corresponding tag action is

```
<foo:fooGetter>
</foo:fooGetter>
```

Like standard tags, custom tags can have additional attributes, defined by the `.tld` document and identified in the documentation for any tag library. Attributes can be optional or required, depending upon the constraints specified in the `.tld` document. If a given tag has required attributes, the values of those must be specified in the action element for the tag.

Custom tag body content

Custom tags can have three different kinds of body content: none, JSP, or tag-dependent. The tag `.tld` file specifies the type of body content that a tag accepts. The way that you compose a custom tag on a JSP is determined by the kind of body content that it accepts.

When a custom tag has no body content, the tag is expressed with a single tag and doesn't have a closing tag. Examples of tags with no body content include `<jsp:getProperty>` and `<jsp:setProperty>` tags. The following code snippet illustrates a tag with no body content. (For all you Marty Feldman fans: I . . . ain't got no bahhhh-deee . . . and no-bah-dee cares for meeeee.)

```
<foo:IAintGotNoBodyTag/>
```

Tags with JSP body content can accept any kind of content that can be placed in a JSP. That includes other tags and HTML. Tags with JSP content are not aware of the tags within their body. (Sounds painful.) The following code snippet illustrates a tag with JSP body content.

```
<foo:bodyTag>
  <P>I can put anything I want in the body of this tag.
  <P>Including another tag such as: <foo:IAintGotNoBodyTag/>
</foo:bodyTag>
```

Tags with tag-dependent body content can contain nested custom tags that interact with the outer tag. These tags typically form a hierarchical relationship with each other, as in the following snippet. See whether you can identify the bottom of the food chain.

```
<org:corpTag>
  <org:president>
    <org:director>
      <org:deskJockey>
      </org:deskJockey>
    </org:director>
  </org:president>
</org:corpTag>
```

A custom tag example

In Chapter 4, I create a JSP error page using JSP scriptlets to dynamically display the content of a Java exception and to display the attributes stored in implicit JSP `page`, `request`, `session`, and `application` objects. The code for implementing this behavior is rather complex, making for a lengthy, difficult-to-read JSP. To illustrate how powerful and easy JSP custom tags are to use, I recreate the same JSP error page using tags from the Struts tag libraries.

Review the final state of the JSP error page from Chapter 4 (see Listing 12-1). The error page includes a couple of JSP expression tags to retrieve the exception message and stack trace for this error. Additionally, note the several scriptlets that extract the contents of the JSP `application`, `session`, and `request` objects. My goal is to completely eliminate all the scriptlets and expression tags, replacing them with custom tags from the Struts tag libraries.

Listing 12-1: A JSP Error Page with Scriptlets

```
<%@ page isErrorPage="true"%>
<%@ page import="java.util.*"%>
<html>
<head>
<title>Error Page</title>
<meta http-equiv="Content-Type" content="text/html;
            charset=iso-8859-1">
</head>

<body bgcolor="#FFFFFF" text="#000000">
<%-- The exception.getMessage() statement returns the name of
            the error --%>
```

```
The error is: <%=exception.getMessage()%>
<P>
<%-- The exception.printStackTrace() statement returns the
     stack, which is all the classes in the execution
     path. --%>
The stack trace is:
<P>
<%
  PrintWriter myOut = new PrintWriter(out);
  exception.printStackTrace(myOut);
%>
<hr>
<P>
Here are the attributes of the application:
<%-- The following for loop presents all the attributes
     stored in the implicit application object. --%>
<%
  Enumeration loop = application.getAttributeNames();
  while (loop.hasMoreElements()){
    String name =  (String) loop.nextElement();
%>
              <BR><%=name%>:
              <%=application.getAttribute( name).toString()%>
<%
  }
%>
<hr>
<P>
Here are the attributes of the session:
<%-- The following for loop presents all the attributes
     stored in the implicit session object. --%>
<%
  loop = session.getAttributeNames();
  while (loop.hasMoreElements()){
    String name =  (String) loop.nextElement();
%>
              <BR><%=name%>:
              <%=session.getAttribute( name).toString()%>
<%
  }
%>
<hr>
<P>
Here are the attributes of the request:
<%-- The following for loop presents all the attributes
     stored in the implicit request object. --%>
<%

  loop = request.getAttributeNames();
```

(continued)

Listing 12-1 ***(continued)***

```
  while (loop.hasMoreElements()){
    String name =  (String) loop.nextElement();
%>
            <BR><%=name%>:
            <%=request.getAttribute( name).toString()%>
<%
  }
%>
<P>
Here are the parameters of the request:
<%-- This block shows all the request parameters sent by the
     user. There are two loops because request attributes can
     have more than one value per name. The out loop steps
     through all the parameters and the inner loop steps
     through all the values for each parameter. --%>
<%
  loop = request.getParameterNames();
  while (loop.hasMoreElements()){
    String name = (String) loop.nextElement();
    for(int index = 0; index <
           request.getParameterValues(name).length; index++){
%>
            <BR><%=name%>:
            <%=request.getParameterValues( name)[index]%>
<%
    }
  }
%>
<%-- the implicit page attributes cannot be displayed because
     as soon as the page that throws an error is out of
     scope, the attributes are no longer available --%>

</body>
</html>
```

Note that this JSP presents the contents of indexed properties; each of the implicit objects in the page can have multiple attributes, which means that you can't access them with a standard `<jsp:getProperty>` tag. By converting this JSP to a page that uses custom tags, you can eliminate virtually all the Java code embedded in the JSP, making the solution easier to use, understand, and maintain. To convert this page:

1. **Create a JavaBean that contains all the Java code in this JSP.**

   The JavaBean (`ExceptionStateBean`) provides properties that return the attributes of the `request`, `session`, and `application` implicit objects. The `ExceptionStateBean` also reports the exception message and the stack trace.

2. **Include the Struts tag libraries in your JSP application deployment.**

   Read about this in the upcoming section "Deploying custom tag libraries."

3. **Include two Struts tag libraries: struts-bean and struts-logic.**

   The struts-bean library provides methods to access the `ExceptionStateBean`, and the struts-logic library includes an tag called `iterate` used to present each of the values in the indexed properties that hold the `application`, `session`, and `request` data.

After you complete these three conversion steps, you should have a revised JSP, as shown in Listing 12-2. Note that the new JSP is limited to two very short scriptlets: one that initializes the JavaBean and one that prints the stack trace. The resulting JSP is more concise, easier to read, and easier to maintain. Thoreau said it best: "Our life is frittered away by detail. Simplify, simplify."

Find this JSP, `tagErrorPage.jsp`, on the CD that comes with this book. You'll also find to the source code for all the Java classes there.

Listing 12-2: Revised JSP Error Page Using Struts Custom Tags

```
<%@ page isErrorPage="true"%>
<%@ taglib uri="/WEB-INF/struts-bean.tld" prefix="bean" %>
<%@ taglib uri="/WEB-INF/struts-logic.tld" prefix="logic" %>

<%@ page import="utils.*"%>
<html>
<head>
<title>Error Page</title>
<meta http-equiv="Content-Type" content="text/html;
           charset=iso-8859-1">
</head>
<jsp:useBean id="exceptionData"
           class="utils.ExceptionStateBean" scope="page">
  <%exceptionData.initialize(pageContext);%>
</jsp:useBean>
<body bgcolor="#FFFFFF" text="#000000">
The error is:
<jsp:getProperty name="exceptionData"
           property="exceptionMessage"/>
<P>
<%-- The exceptionData.getStackTrace(out) statement returns
     the stack, which is all the classes in the execution
     path. --%>
The stack trace is: <%exceptionData.getStackTrace(out);%>
```

(continued)

Listing 12-2 ***(continued)***

```
<hr>
<P>
Here are the attributes of the application:
<%-- The following for loop presents all the attributes
            stored in the implicit application object. --%>
<logic:iterate name="exceptionData"
            type="utils.ApplicationData" id="appData"
            property="applicationData">
   <BR><bean:write name="appData" property="attributeName"/>:
       <bean:write name="appData" property="attributeValue"/>
</logic:iterate>
<hr>
<P>
Here are the attributes of the session:
<%-- The following for loop presents all the attributes
            stored in the implicit session object. --%>
<logic:iterate name="exceptionData" type="utils.SessionData"
            id="sessionData" property="sessionData">
   <BR><bean:write name="sessionData"
            property="attributeName"/>:
       <bean:write name="sessionData"
            property="attributeValue"/>
</logic:iterate>
<hr>
<P>
Here are the attributes of the request:
<%-- The following for loop presents all the attributes
            stored in the implicit request object. --%>
<logic:iterate name="exceptionData"
            type="utils.RequestAttribData" id="reqAttribdata"
            property="requestAttribData">
   <BR><bean:write name="reqAttribdata"
            property="attributeName"/>
       <bean:write name="reqAttribdata"
            property="attributeValue"/>
</logic:iterate>
<hr>
<P>
Here are the parameters of the request:
<%-- This block shows all the request parameters sent by the
     user. There are two loops because request attributes can
     have more than one value per name. The out loop steps
     through all the parameters and the inner loop steps
     through all the values for each parameter. --%>
<logic:iterate name="exceptionData"
            type="utils.RequestParamData" id="reqParamData"
            property="requestParamData">
```

```
  <logic:iterate name="reqParamData" type="java.lang.String"
          id="value" property="parameterValues">
  <BR><bean:write name="reqParamData"
          property="parameterName"/>:
     <bean:write name="value"/>
  </logic:iterate>
</logic:iterate>
<%-- the implicit page attributes cannot be displayed because
     as soon as the page that throws an error is out of
     scope, the attributes are no longer available --%>

</body>
</html>
```

Deploying custom tag libraries

To include a custom tag library in your JSP application, you must include the support classes for the tag library and the `.tld` file in your JSP. You also have to include a reference to the tag library in the `web.xml` file deployed with your JSP application.

How you deploy custom tag libraries differs depending on the kind of JSP container to which you deploy. The instructions I provide in this chapter cover deploying JSP applications to a stand-alone Tomcat JSP container. If you deploy to any other JSP container, or use Apache and Tomcat together, see the deployment documentation located at the Struts home page for more information (`http://jakarta.apache.org/struts/`).

In this section, I assume that you understand the basics of deploying JSP applications. If not, I recommend that you first read through Appendix A.

Deploying tag library descriptor files

The TLD file (identified by a `.tld` extension) of a custom tag library tells your JSP application where to find the tag support class for each custom tag. This file also tells the JSP container how to map the attributes of your custom tag in the JSP to the properties of the corresponding tag support class. Because TLD files are part of the set of XML-based files that describe the content of your JSP application, it's customary to place them in the `WEB-INF` directory of your JSP.

Updating the web.xml file

Because your JSP application does not implicitly know about custom tag libraries, you need to provide information about each custom tag library that you use in the `web.xml` file. When a Web application is loaded for the first time, your JSP container reads the contents of the `web.xml` file to discover all the information it needs about each custom tag library that you use in your JSP application.

Check out this very simple `web.xml` file (from Chapter 2), which is displayed in the following code snippet:

```
<?xml version="1.0" encoding="ISO-8859-1"?>

<!DOCTYPE web-app
  PUBLIC "-//Sun Microsystems, Inc.//DTD Web Application
          2.2//EN"
  "http://java.sun.com/j2ee/dtds/web-app_2_2.dtd">

<web-app>
</web-app>
```

For each custom `.tld` file that you deploy, you have to add a `<taglib>` element inside the `<web-app>` element of your `web.xml` file. The following code snippet illustrates the syntax of a `<taglib>` element.

```
<?xml version="1.0" encoding="ISO-8859-1"?>

<!DOCTYPE web-app
  PUBLIC "-//Sun Microsystems, Inc.//DTD Web Application
          2.2//EN"
  "http://java.sun.com/j2ee/dtds/web-app_2_2.dtd">

<web-app>
  <taglib>
    <taglib-uri>/WEB-INF/struts-template.tld</taglib-uri>
    <taglib-location>/WEB-INF/struts-template.tld</taglib-
          location>
  </taglib>
</web-app>
```

The `<taglib>` element contains two sub-tags: a `<taglib-uri>` element and a `<taglib-location>` element. Both are required. The first element specifies that the Uniform Resource Identifier (URI) you use in a `taglib` directive of your JSP refers to a tag library. In Listing 12-2, the second and third lines contain `taglib` directives. The `uri` attribute of each `taglib` directive is identical to the `<taglib-uri>` element corresponding to that tag library in the `web.xml` file.

The second element is the `<taglib-location>`, which specifies the location of the `.tld` document for your JSP application relative to the root directory of your JSP application.

Deploying the tag Java ARchive file (JAR)

Each tag library is deployed using a *Java ARchive* (JAR) file, which is a specialized form of archive file used for deploying Java applications. An *archive file* is a file that contains multiple files (like a ZIP file) and may be compressed. By convention, any Java libraries used in a JSP application are deployed to a `lib` directory, which should be a subdirectory of the `WEB-INF` directory in your JSP application. You can discover more about how JSP applications are organized in Chapter 14.

Chapter 13

Working with Cookies

In This Chapter

- Explaining all about cookies
- Figuring out the rules for cookies
- Creating and storing cookies
- Retrieving data from cookies

If you have some experience developing Web sites or even if you're an accomplished Web surfer, you've probably heard of cookies. I'm not talking about your grandma's cookies, mind you, but cookies for the digital age.

Cookies are small files that store a single property per cookie. Each cookie has a name, a value, and some additional information that the user's browser and your Web server use to manage the cookie. Cookies can be used in a variety of applications, including JSP applications.

Here are some ideas on the types of information that you could store:

- Some Web sites write the user login and password or an access code in a cookie that's stored on the user's browser. This is typically done to make it more convenient for the user to login to the Web site later.
- Some Web sites will store a little bit of personal information about the user in a cookie, such as the user's name. If you travel to a Web site and it immediately presents you with a greeting such as, "Welcome, Mac Rinehart . . . if you're not Mac Rinehart, click here," it's a pretty safe bet that the Web site has stored some personal information about you in a cookie.
- You can store a database key that gives you access to information about a user's preferences in your Web site.
- You can store a computer ID in a cookie so that you can recognize what workstation is logging in to the Web server and then present information targeted to the user of that workstation.

Regardless of the type of information that you store in a cookie, remember to keep it small and don't be dependent on the cookie for your application to function. Users can prevent cookies from being saved in their browser. Because cookies are typically used to store a reference to some information on the server that indicates the identity and preferences of a user, some users disable them for privacy concerns.

Think of cookies as nice to have for implementing noncritical features. That way, you won't put control over the stability of your application in the hands of a user.

Rules for Cookies

The two current versions of the cookie specification are Version 0 and Version 1. Version 0 cookies have the broadest level of support in browsers, but the type of data that they contain is much more constrained than Version 1 cookies. Before you undertake the task of storing information in a cookie, be sure that you review and understand the following rules.

- The data that you store in a cookie can occupy 4K of disk space at most. Thus, you have to keep your cookies bite-sized (pretty small).
- Although you can create multiple cookies and store them on a user's computer, a browser is only required to maintain the last 20 cookies from each Web domain. A *domain* is the base Internet address for a Web server (for example, `www.myWebSite.com` is a domain). If you create a lot of cookies, a browser will start deleting older cookies after 20 of them are stored from your domain. If your Web site is hosted on someone else's domain, a user's browser may delete your cookies after a user exceeds 20 cookies from that domain, even if you've only stored 1 or 2 cookies on the computer.
- A browser is only required to store up to 300 cookies overall. So, if your user exceeds 300 cookies, the host computer will start deleting cookies to keep the count below 300. Call it caloric-intake maintenance.
- You cannot store executable programs in a cookie. Cookies are only for storing data, and a browser will not run any program in a cookie. Cookies are a treat — not the main course.
- Cookies can only store a single value. With Version 0 cookies, the value cannot contain white space, brackets, parentheses, equal signs, commas, double quotes, slashes, question marks, at signs (@), colons, or semicolons.

As you can see from the rules above, the things you can do with a cookie are limited. In addition, you are somewhat at the whim of a user in terms of how reliable cookies are.

For example, if a user gets more cookies than his computer can handle, your cookie might be deleted. Also, security-conscious users can choose to disable cookies in their browsers, in which case no cookies are stored. Finally, when a user deletes the Internet temporary files stored on their computer (which some choose to do periodically), all cookies are deleted.

With Version 1 cookies, you can create a list of key-value pairs as the value stored by the cookie. Key-value pairs are usually expressed as a key (a variable) followed by an equal sign and then a value. An ampersand (&) sign separates each key value pair. For example, you might have a cookie with the value:

```
ingredients?flour=2cups&milk=2cups&eggs=2&sugar=1cup&vanilla=
        1tsp
```

In this example, the cookie identifies ingredients. Each ingredient is a parameter, and they are all separated by question marks.

If you need to store multiple values in a cookie and have to use Version 1 cookies, consider delimiting keys and values by an underscore character: `key1_value1_key2_value2`. When you extract this string in your JSP application, you can use the `java.util.StringTokenizer` class to extract the keys and values out of the string.

Creating and Storing Cookies

In JSP applications, cookies are represented by the Java class `javax.servlet.http.Cookie`. To create a cookie, you must create an instance of the `Cookie` class, initialize a variety of cookie attributes, and store the cookie in the `response` object. First read through Table 13-1 for a variety of methods you use to create and initialize cookies.

Table 13-1 Methods to Prepare a Cookie

Method	*Description*
`setComment ( comment)`	Use this comment to describe the purpose of the cookie. Netscape Version 0 cookies do not support comments.
`setDomain ( domain)`	This identifies the domain that can read the content of a cookie. The domain must contain two dots (`.foo.com` or `www.foo.com`, but not `foo.com`). If no domain is specified, the cookie is only visible to the Web server it originates from.

(continued)

Table 13-1 ***(continued)***

Method	*Description*
`setMaxAge` `( seconds)`	This identifies the maximum amount of time that a Web browser should try to maintain a cookie. A cookie is created with a time stamp. When the timestamp plus the maximum age is exceeded, a Web browser will delete a cookie. If no maximum age is specified, the cookie is deleted when the Web browser is shut down.
`setPath` `( relativePath)`	This specifies the relative path under which a cookie is visible. If the path `/example` is specified, only JSPs in the directory `/example` and its subdirectories will have access to the cookie.
`setSecurity` `( booleanValue)`	This indicates to the browser that the cookie should only be sent with a secure communication protocol, such as Secure HyperText Transfer Protocol (HTTPS), instead of HyperText Transfer Protocol (HTTP). The default value is `false`.
`setValue` `( text)`	This indicates a new value for the cookie. Version 0 cookies cannot contain white space, brackets, parentheses, equal signs, commas, double quotes, slashes, question marks, at signs (@), colons, or semicolons.
`setVersion` `( versionNumber)`	This indicates the version number of cookie protocol that this cookie complies with. Currently the cookie protocol has Versions 0 and 1. The default value is `version 0`.

Cookies can be created in a JSP by using scriptlet code. You can also create a JavaBean wrapper around a cookie so that most of the effort of creating cookies and initializing their attributes is performed with standard JSP action tags. You can use the following steps to create a cookie with a scriptlet.

1. **Create a new instance of the cookie object.**

   The constructor for the cookie object accepts the name of the cookie as its first parameter and the value of the cookie as its second parameter. Both parameters are string values.

2. **Initialize the properties of the cookie using the setter methods identified in Table 13-1.**

   Unless you want the browser to delete your cookie when a user shuts down his browser, be sure to set the expiration date of the cookie.

3. **After you create it, the cookie needs to be attached to the implicit** `response` **object.**

   The method for attaching the cookie is `response.addCookie()`, with the cookie passed as a parameter.

Any cookies that you create must be added to the implicit `response` object before any of the content from a JSP is sent to the user's Web browser. To be safe, place the scriptlet code before any body content in your JSP. Remember that body content is any content of a JSP that gets sent to the browser. Also remember that the JSP container sends any body content preceding a `<jsp:include>` tag to the browser as soon as the `<jsp:include>` tag is encountered. Thus, you should place any cookies above `<jsp:include>` tags in your JSP.

Listing 13-1 contains a code sample that illustrates the process of creating a cookie with a scriptlet. (Yes, according to food groups by Buckwheat, a cookie is considered a foo' stuff.)

Listing 13-1: Scriptlet Code for Creating a Cookie

```
<%
  /* first construct the cookie. The first parameter is the
   * name, the second is the value.
   */
  Cookie cookie = new Cookie( "foo", "foo' stuff");

  //now initialize the properties of the cookie
  // none of these initialization methods are required.
  cookie.setComment("this sample cookie does nothing.");
  cookie.setDomain(".myDomain.com"); // remember...two dots
         required
  cookie.setMaxAge(60 * 60 * 24 * 7); // one week worth of
         seconds
  cookie.setPath("/foo"); // only visible under the /foo
         directory
  cookie.setSecurity(false); // not secure, defaults to false
  cookie.setVersion(0); // cookie spec version, defaults to 0

  // finally, add the cookie to the response
  response.addCookie(cookie);
%>
```

Retrieving Data from Cookies

When you receive a request from a user, the implicit object will contain all the cookies that originate from the Web server receiving the request as well as the domain of the Web server. The user's Web browser handles this task, so you don't have to write any special code in a JSP to have the cookies sent to you.

By default, a cookie is only visible to the Web server where it was created. If you specify the domain of a cookie using the `Cookie.setDomain()` method, the cookie will be visible to all Web servers on that domain. If you specify a path for the cookie using the `Cookie.setPath()` method, the cookie is only visible in that directory and its subdirectories on the specified domain.

Table 13-2 contains several methods of the `Cookie` object that you can use to retrieve values of the cookie's properties.

Table 13-2 Methods to Get Information About a Cookie

Method	*Description*
`getComment()`	Returns the value of the comment as a string. Netscape Version 0 cookies do not support comments.
`getDomain()`	Returns the domain assigned to the cookie as a string.
`getMaxAge()`	Returns the maximum number of seconds that this cookie will persist on a browser before it is deleted. The return value `-1` indicates that the cookie is deleted as soon as the browser is shut down.
`getPath()`	Returns the path under which this cookie is visible.
`getSecurity()`	Indicates whether this cookie is secure or not.
`getValue()`	Returns the value stored in this cookie.
`getVersion()`	Indicates the version number of cookie protocol that this cookie complies with.

Cookies sent from a browser to your Web server will be held in the implicit `request` object. To get cookies out of the `request` object, follow these steps:

1. **Create a variable to hold the cookie that you want to retrieve.**
2. **The `request` object returns an array of cookie objects with the method `request.getCookies()`.**

   Execute this method, storing the cookie objects in a `cookies` array. If there are no cookies in the request, this method returns a `null` value.

3. **Verify that the `cookies` array is not `null`.**

   If it isn't, loop through the `cookies` array, looking for the cookie that you want to retrieve with the `Cookies.getName()` method. When you find the right cookie, assign it to the variable that you create in Step 1.

4. **You can now use the access methods displayed in Table 13-2 to retrieve information about the cookie or its value.**

The code in Listing 13-2 illustrates the preceding steps.

Listing 13-2: Retrieving a Cookie with a Scriptlet

```
<%
  Cookie foo = null; // create a variable to hold your cookie
  Cookie requestCookies[] = request.getCookies(); // get the
           cookies
  // verify cookies were returned
  if( requestCookies != null){
    // loop through cookies looking for the desired cookie
    for( int index = 0; index < requestCookies.length;
           index++){
      if(requestCookies[index].getName().equals("foo")){
        foo = requestCookies[index]; // save the cookie
      }
    }
  }
%>
```

Destroying Cookies

Good Internet etiquette dictates destroying cookies as soon as you no longer need them: A browser can only hold a predefined number of cookies. If you leave discarded cookies on a user's browser, the browser may be forced to delete other cookies that are still of value.

Although not complex, destroying a cookie is a little more involved than you might expect. Because cookies are stored on a Web browser, you can't get rid of them by pretending that they're not there. The Web browser continues to send the cookie to you until it expires; and every time that you send it back to the browser, the expiration date is renewed.

The only way to get a browser to permanently destroy a cookie is to force the cookie to expire. You can accomplish that task by with one of two strategies:

- Setting the maximum age of the cookie to `0` with the statement `Cookie.setMaxAge(0)` and sending the cookie back to the browser causes a cookie to be destroyed by the browser immediately.

- Setting the maximum age of the cookie to -1 with the statement Cookie.setMaxAge(-1) and sending it to the browser causes the cookie to be destroyed the next time that the browser is shut down.

Listing 13-3 illustrates the process of destroying a cookie.

Listing 13-3: Destroying a Cookie with a Scriptlet

```
<%
  // the first part is identical to retrieving a cookie
  Cookie foo = null; // create a variable to hold your cookie
  Cookie requestCookies[] = request.getCookies(); // get the
          cookies
  // verify cookies were returned
  if( requestCookies != null){
    // loop through cookies looking for the desired cookie
    for( int index = 0; index < requestCookies.length;
          index++){
      if(requestCookies[index].getName().equals("foo")){
        foo = requestCookies[index]; // save the cookie
      }
    }
  }
  // now we destroy the cookie
  if( foo != null){
    foo.setMaxAge(0); // set expiration to 0 seconds
    response.addCookie(foo); // return the cookie to the
          browser
  }
%>
```

Chapter 14

Deploying JSP Applications

In This Chapter

- Defining the Web ARchive file format (WAR)
- Building a WAR file
- Creating the `WEB.XML` deployment descriptor file

One of the main challenges of creating Internet applications, whether static Web pages or dynamic applications, is deploying the application successfully: Internet applications are typically a loose collections of files with references to each other.

If a file gets moved from its folder by accident, all the links to that file are broken because the links depend on knowing where the file is located. If you've ever tried to navigate to a Web site only to find that the Web page can't be found, you've experienced a similar problem.

If you're selling your Internet application, this issue becomes more complex because the application typically has to be deployed to an environment over which you have no control. Don't underestimate the challenge of moving an application from the server where it was developed and tested to a client Web site with an unknown server configuration.

To facilitate the deployment of JavaServer Page (JSP) applications, the JSP specification defines a special deployment file called a Web ARchive (WAR) file. Using WAR files makes deployment of JSP applications very easy. In this chapter, you discover the requirements for creating a WAR file and how to deploy a WAR file to the Tomcat servlet container.

Not all JSP containers support deployment in the WAR file format. If a container doesn't support this format, it's not fully compliant with the JSP specification. As you make the decision of which JSP container to use, be sure that you can deploy JSP applications in the WAR format. Your best resource for gaining this information is the vendor's documentation and/or sales reps.

The WAR Format

The *WAR file format* is a deployment file created to be the Internet answer to the custom install programs available for most desktop applications. A WAR is basically a JAR (Java ARchive) file with a special structure and some additional configuration files for JSP applications. See the basic structure of the contents of a WAR file in Figure 14-1.

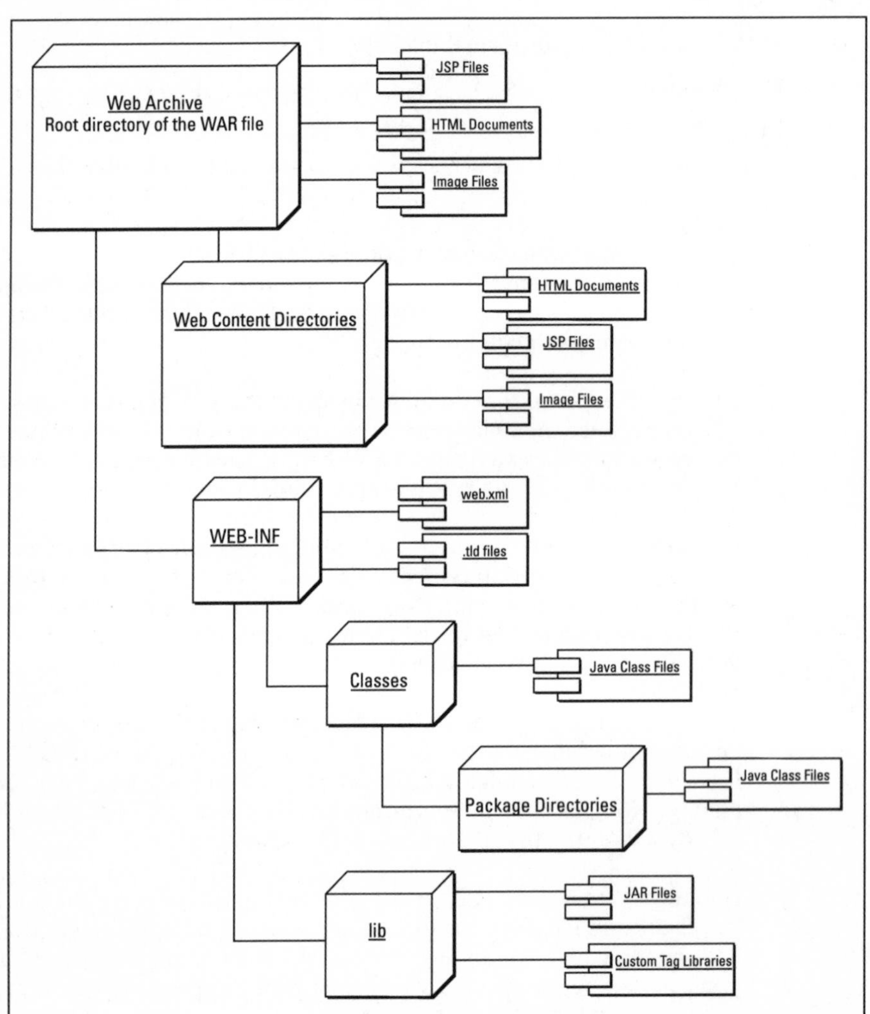

Figure 14-1: Structure of a WAR file.

In Figure 14-1, each cube represents a folder. The folders contain components, which are labeled by the type of files they represent. Here's an overview of the structure:

- **The top-level folder and all its subfolders except the `WEB-INF` folder are Web-content directories.**

  These contain the content displayed on a user's Web browser. Web content files include straight HyperText Markup Language (HTML) files, JSP files, images, and plug-in content such as Flash files, and `.mpeg` and `.wav` files. Typically the top-level folder is given the name of the entire Web application.

- **The `WEB-INF` folder is the configuration folder for the entire JSP application.**

  The `WEB-INF` folder contains a special file called the `web.xml` file. This file contains the configuration of the JSP application in an eXensible Markup Language (XML) format. If you use custom tag libraries in your JSP application, you also place the tag library descriptor file (TLD file) for each custom tag library used in the `WEB-INF` folder. The TLD file contains information about the content of the tag library. You can discover more on this topic in Chapter 12.

- **The WEB-INF folder contains two subfolders.**

  Those folders are the `classes` folder and the `lib` folder. The `classes` folder is where you put all the Java classes that you create for your JSP application. The `lib` folder contains any Java libraries that you use in your JSP application. *Java libraries* are Java classes contained in a JAR file. Custom tag libraries are stored in a JAR file and deployed to this folder of your JSP application.

When you create a WAR file for your JSP application, the standard deployment folder structure for JSP applications is the same as the structure in Figure 14-1.

Building a WAR File

A WAR file is pretty easy to build if you organize your JSP projects according to the WAR structure from the beginning. Follow the format that I specify in Appendix A for organizing your project, and you're already almost home.

Listing 14-1 contains the contents of a sample WAR file called `dummies.war`. The top-level folder of the `dummies.war` file is the `dummies` folder. Notice that it has the same name as the WAR file itself. Look at the listing and note that you don't see the `dummies` folder listed anywhere: The `dummies` folder is implicit.

Listing 14-1: Sample WAR File: dummies.war

```
/main.jsp
/login/password.jsp
/login/accessDenied.jsp
/errors/errorPage.jsp
/forum/miscChat.jsp
/forum/jspChat.jsp
/forum/servletChat.jsp
/forum/newThread.jsp
/forum/treadResponse.jsp
/images/miscIcon.gif
/images/jspIcon.gif
/images/servletIcon.gif
/WEB-INF/web.xml
/WEB-INF/forumTags_1_0.tld
/WEB-INF/classes/dummies/Controller.class
/WEB-INF/classes/dummies/sql/GetForum.class
/WEB-INF/classes/dummies/sql/GetThread.class
/WEB-INF/classes/dummies/sql/GetMessage.class
/WEB-INF/classes/dummies/sql/SaveMessage.class
/WEB-INF/lib/forumTags_1_0.jar
```

Organizing Web content

All the Web content files in a JSP application should be stored in the top-level folder of the WAR file and its subfolders. In Listing 14-1, the first 12 lines of the listing comprise the Web content. Web content should not be placed in the `WEB-INF` folder or its subfolders because these folders are reserved for Java classes and libraries.

About the context path

One of the main reasons for using WAR files is to help you move Web content files to different Web servers without having to change the paths of all the HREF (Hypertext Reference) and Uniform Resource Locator (URL) references in the Web content files. This is possible because the JSP container provides a context path that shows the path up to the top-level folder of the WAR file.

A *context path* defines the context of the JSP application. For example, if you create the JSP application displayed in Listing 14-1 on your development computer, the context might be `http://localhost:8080/dummies`. When you move that application to a Web server, however, the context might change to something like `http://myWebServer.com/dummies`.

URL references in JSP elements

In order to move JSP applications across different Web servers, the JSP container supplies the base URL for each URL reference contained in a JSP element.

JSP elements specify the URL from the base to the file that is the target of the URL. The portion of the URL specified by the JSP element is the *relative URL*.

Two kinds of relative URLs are supported by JSP elements: context-relative URLs and page-relative URLs. A context-relative URL starts with a forward slash character (/), and continues with the path relative to the top-level folder of the WAR file. All the paths identified in Listing 14-1 are legal context-relative URLs for the `dummies.war` file.

Although the context-relative URL is relative to the top-level folder of a JSP application, the page-relative URL is relative to the page in which it is specified. The page-relative URL does not begin with a slash character and it specifies the path from the current file to the file that's the target of the URL. When you use a page-relative URL, the JSP container specifies the context path plus the path to the base of the page relative URL.

URL references in HTML elements

Although JSP containers fill in the context path for a URL in a JSP element automatically, they can't do the same for URLs in HTML content. Thus, if you need to specify the path to an image in an `<IMAGE>` element or perhaps the URL to another JSP or Web page in an HTML `<FORM>` element, you need to provide the complete path to that element. This complete path is often called the absolute path. The *absolute path* is the combination of the context path and the relative path from the top-level folder of the WAR file.

You can get the context path of a JSP application from the `request` object, as illustrated in the following code snippet:

```
<HEAD>
  <BASE HREF="<%= request.getContextPath()%>/">
</HEAD>
<BODY>
  <FORM>
    <A HREF="login/password.jsp">login</A>
  </FORM>
</BODY>
```

In this example, the `<BASE>` HTML element is used to store the context path to a JSP application by getting the context path from the `request` object. When you store the context in the `<BASE>` element, every relative URL in an HREF throughout the HTML page from that point on automatically includes the context path.

Thus, in the previous example, the context path from the `<BASE>` element automatically gets attached to the beginning of the relative path in the `<A>` element.

The context path includes the top-level folder of a WAR file and doesn't end with a slash. All context-relative URLs must start with a forward slash and should not include the top-level folder of the WAR file.

Most of the modern browsers, including the latest versions of Internet Explorer and Netscape Navigator, automatically supply the base URL for attributes that contain URLs in the elements on an HTML page. Thus, you don't have to provide the `<BASE>` element. You can also use relative URLs in the HREF, SRC (source), and action attributes across a Web page, and the browser will supply the base URL for you. Even so, you may want to supply this information in the event the user's browser cannot handle the task on its own.

Organizing class files

Java class files are stored in the `WEB-INF\classes` folder of the WAR file and its subfolders. Java classes can be located in the default Java package or in an explicitly named package statement.

If you have a package statement at the top of a Java source file followed by the name of a package, the file is located in a named package. With no package statement in the Java source file, the class is located in the default Java package.

Java classes located in the default Java package should be placed directly in the `WEB-INF\classes` folder. Java classes located in a named package should be stored in a subfolder that corresponds to the package containing the Java class. For example, the `Controller.class` file in Listing 14-1 is located in the `dummies` package, whereas the rest of the class files in Listing 14-1 are located in the `dummies.sql` package.

Java classes stored in the `WEB-INF\classes` folder are automatically added to the class path of the JSP container whenever the JSP application containing the classes is used.

Organizing Java libraries

Java libraries are sets of related Java classes deployed in a JAR file. If you use third-party components in your JSP application, they're probably provided to you as a JAR file. Custom tag libraries are also distributed as JAR files. See Chapter 12 for more on JAR files and their creation.

To include JAR files in a WAR file, merely place the JAR file in the `WEB-INF\lib` folder of the JSP application. In Listing 14-1, the `forumTags_1_0.jar` file is placed in the `WEB-INF\lib` folder, illustrating the deployment of a JAR file.

When you place a JAR file in the WEB-INF\lib folder, the contents of the JAR file are added to the class path of the JSP container when that JSP application is accessed.

Custom tag libraries are deployed as JAR files but they also create a special configuration file called a TLD file. This file describes the structure of the tag library to the JSP application that uses it. If you deploy a tag library to your JSP application, be sure to place the corresponding .folders file in the WEB-INF folder of the JSP application.

Creating the web.xml file

One of the most important features of the WAR file is the web.xml file. JSP containers use the web.xml file to gather important configuration and environment information about the JSP application housed in the WAR file.

Every WAR file must have a web.xml file. Think of the web.xml file as the central nervous system of the WAR file. Fortunately, the web.xml file is pretty easy to create. Unfortunately, creating the web.xml file rapidly becomes tedious for large Web applications. The most basic form is illustrated in the following code snippet.

```
<?xml version="1.0" encoding="ISO-8859-1" ?>

<!DOCTYPE web-app PUBLIC "-//Sun Microsystems, Inc.//DTD Web
  Application 2.3//EN" "http://java.sun.com/dtd/web-
          app_2_3.dtd">
<web-app>
</web-app>
```

The first line in the previous example tells the JSP container what XML version is used for this document. It must appear on the first line of the web.xml document, prior to any white space characters.

The <!DOCTYPE> tag tells the JSP container how to find the Document Type Descriptor (DTD) file for web.xml files. The DTD file describes the structure of the web.xml file to the JSP container.

With each version change to the WAR file format, the <!DOCTYPE> tag is changed. For JSP 1.1 applications, the <!DOCTYPE> tag is>:

```
<!DOCTYPE web-app
  PUBLIC "-//Sun Microsystems, Inc.//DTD Web Application
          2.2//EN"
  "http://java.sun.com/j2ee/dtds/web-app_2_2.dtd">
```

Finally, note the <web-app> tag. All the details about the JSP application go inside the body of this tag. It must be present in every web.xml file. However, very simple JSP applications, such as the example in Listing 2-3 of Chapter 2, may not have any body content.

Specifying JSP application attributes in a WAR file

The web.xml file has five subelements of the <web-app> tag available for specifying properties of the JSP application over all. Each of these optional elements is identified and described in Table 14-1.

Table 14-1 Properties of JSP Applications

Property	*Description*
<description>	Use this to document the purpose of the Web application.
<display-name>	If graphical configuration tools are available for JSP containers, the value specified here is used as the name for the application held in the WAR file.
<icon>	This element contains URLs to icons that can be used by graphical configuration tools. The URL is relative to the top-level folder of the WAR file.
<welcome-file-list>	This list identifies the file to be used when a user submits a request to the server and the request URL doesn't contain a file. This tag can have several subelements, each which identifies a file. The JSP container will search for these files in the order they appear, and return the first one found.
<distributable/>	This is an empty tag indicating the JSP application that's simultaneously run in multiple JSP containers. This feature is intended to support large-scale JSP applications.

Listing 14-2 illustrates a web.xml file with each of the items in Table 14-1. Because the <web-app> tag can potentially have numerous subelements, I recommend listing these elements at the top so that they're easily accessible. The URLs specified in the <icon> elements and in the <welcome-file> elements are relative to the top-level folder of the WAR file.

Listing 14-2: A web.xml file Defining Properties of a JSP Application

```
<?xml version="1.0" encoding="ISO-8859-1" ?>

<!DOCTYPE web-app PUBLIC "-//Sun Microsystems, Inc.//DTD Web
  Application 2.3//EN" "http://java.sun.com/dtd/web-
           app_2_3.dtd">
<web-app>
  <distributable/>

  <description>
    This is a sample description of a JSP application.
  </description>
  <display-name>
    Sample Application
  </display-name>
  <icon>
    <large-icon>/images/sample32x32Icon.gif</large-icon>
    <small-icon>/images/sample16x16Icon.gif</small-icon>
  </icon>
  <welcome-file-list>
     <welcome-file>/welcome.jsp</welcome-file>
     <welcome-file>/home.html</welcome-file>
  </welcome-file-list>
</web-app>
```

Controlling the JSP container from a WAR file

In the `web.xml` file, you can take advantage of a few subelements of the `<web-app>` tag to manipulate configuration parameters of the JSP container. These configuration subelements are extremely useful for defining global attributes and for influencing the behavior of the JSP application. Table 14-2 identifies the subelements of the `web.xml` file that you can use to configure the JSP container.

Table 14-2 JSP Container Configuration Elements

Element	*Description*
`<session-config>`	This element give you control over the session management of the JSP container. The element currently allows you specify the *session timeout,* which is the duration of inactivity allowed by the session before the JSP container can destroy it.
`<context-param>`	This element allows you to create parameters that are loaded into the application when the application is accessed by the first user on your site.

Context parameters are accessed by the JSP application through the implicit application object by using the method `application.getInitParameter( name)`, where `name` is the name of the context parameter. Listing 14-3 contains a `web.xml` file fragment that illustrates the use of the elements in Table 14-2.

Keep in mind these important rules when working with the elements in Listing 14-3.

- **You can have only one `<session-config>` element per `web.xml` file.**

  The `<session-timeout>` subelement of the `<session-config>` element specifies the session-timeout duration in number of minutes.

- **You can specify as many `<context-param>` elements as you need in a JSP application, but no two `<context-param>` elements can have the same value for the `<param-name>`.**

  The `<param-name>` and `<param-value>` subelements are required when specifying a `<context-param>` element. The `<description>` subelement is optional.

Listing 14-3: Elements of the web.xml file for JSP Container Configuration

```
<?xml version="1.0" encoding="ISO-8859-1" ?>

<!DOCTYPE web-app PUBLIC "-//Sun Microsystems, Inc.//DTD Web
  Application 2.3//EN" "http://java.sun.com/dtd/web-
            app_2_3.dtd">
<web-app>
  <sesion-config>
    <session-timeout>30</session-timeout>
  </session-config>

  <context-param>
    <param-name>userName</param-name>
    <param-value>webUser</param-value>
    <description>
      Identifies the username for the database
    </description>
  </context-param>

  <context-param>
    <param-name>password</param-name>
    <param-value>changeOnInstall</param-value>
    <description>
      The password to the database.
    </description>
  </context-param>
  ...
</web-app>
```

As you can see from the example in Listing 14-3, `<context-param>` elements are a nice place for storing configuration parameters such as the database `username`.

Including servlet classes in a WAR file

Mixing the use of JSPs and servlet classes in the same application is a common practice and a natural union of two closely related technologies. If you include servlet classes in your JSP application, you need to identify them in the `web.xml` file. Servlet classes are identified in the `web.xml` file by the inclusion of a `<servlet>` tag for each servlet used by the JSP application.

The JSP container uses the information in the `web.xml` file to locate servlet classes. In addition, you can tell the JSP container to preload servlet classes, and you can specify initialization parameters for servlet classes. Table 14-3 contains a listing of the subelements of the `<servlet>` tag.

Table 14-3 Subelements of the <servlet> Tag in a web.xml File

Element	*Description*
`<servlet-name>`	This element identifies a name that can be used in the body of a URL to request this servlet. It is mandatory.
`<servlet-class>`	This element identifies the fully qualified name of the class for this servlet. It is mandatory.
`<description>`	This provides a description of the purpose for the servlet.
`<display-name>`	The display name is used by visual JSP container configuration tools if they are available.
`<icon>`	This is used to identify the icon used to display the servlet in a visual JSP container configuration tool.
`<init-param>`	This element specifies an initialization parameter for the servlet, which is loaded when the servlet is initialized before its first use.
`<load-on-startup>`	The presence of this element indicates that the servlet is to be loaded when the JSP container is started. It can be empty or can contain a number identifying the order in which the servlet should be loaded.

As indicated in Table 14-3, the only two required attributes of the `<servlet>` element are the `<servlet-name>` element and the `<servlet-class>` attribute. The function of the `<display-name>`, `<icon>`, and `<description>` elements is identical to the equivalent elements in the `<web-app>` element.

The <init-param> element in the <servlet> element is very similar to the <context-param> element. The <init-param> identifies an initialization parameter to load for the servlet itself. The <init-param> has three subelements: <param-name>, <param-value>, and <description>. You can create as many <init-param> elements as you need to handle the initialization parameters for the servlet.

These parameters are loaded when the servlet is loaded and are available for the lifespan of the servlet. The <init-param> is passed into the servlet as a string. If the String value represents some other type of object, such as a date or a number, it's the responsibility of the servlet to parse the parameter and convert it to its intended type. Because Servlet classes don't have access to implicit objects, you have to call the ServletConfig.getInitParameter() method to access initialization parameters specified in the <init-param> element.

The final subelement of the <servlet> element is the <load-on-startup> element. The <load-on-startup> element can be either an empty tag (ends with /> and does not have a body) or contain a number indicating the order in which the servlet should be loaded during the start-up process.

The <load-on-startup> element allows you to specify the order in which servlet classes are loaded by the JSP container to maintain dependencies between servlet classes. That way, if one servlet has to be loaded before another can be loaded, the JSP container will load them in the order that you specify. If the order of the loading of the servlet objects is not important but you still want the servlet loaded on startup, indicate that by using the empty tag <load-on-startup/>.

For servlet objects that you frequently use in your JSP application, include the <load-on-startup> tag. This will save you the trouble of loading the servlet on the first request, which cuts down on response time. If you have servlet classes that don't get used very often, you may choose not to include the <load-on-startup> option just to cut down on the memory utilization of your Web server.

Listing 14-4 contains an example of a <servlet> element with all the possible subelements.

Listing 14-4: The <servlet> Tag of a web.xml File

```
<?xml version="1.0" encoding="ISO-8859-1" ?>

<!DOCTYPE web-app PUBLIC "-//Sun Microsystems, Inc.//DTD Web
  Application 2.3//EN" "http://java.sun.com/dtd/
           web-app_2_3.dtd">

<web-app>
  <servlet>
```

```
    <servlet-name>foo</servlet-name>
    <servlet-class>dummies.Foo.class</servlet-class>
    <description>
       This is an example servlet.
    </description>
    <display-name>Foo Servlet</display-name>
    <icon>
      <small-icon>
         /images/foo16x16Icon.gif
      </small-icon>
    </icon>
    <init-param>
      <param-name>question</param-name>
      <param-value>Why?</param-value>
      <description>
        why not?
      </description>
    </init-param>
    <load-on-startup>1</load-on-startup>
  </servlet>
  ...
</web-app>
```

Mapping alternate servlet URLs in WAR files

Sometimes the folder hierarchy that you define for your Web application isn't the same as the structure that you want to present to the outside world. For example:

- **Container versus consumer:** The folder hierarchy that you use in your JSP application should be meaningful to the JSP container and provide a coherent organizational structure for your application. But the URLs y'all use should be short, easy to type, and easy to remember. That makes it easier for the users of your site to remember. Thus, the way that you present the application and the way that you organize it are guided by different and conflicting objectives.
- **Hacker insurance:** When you use the same URL paths as the physical paths on your Web server, you give hackers a road map to the folder structure of your Web server, making it easier for them to try to hack your Web site.

A bonus is that you can specify an alternate URL for each servlet in your Web application by using the `<servlet-mapping>` element. The `<servlet-mapping>` element has two subelements: `<servlet-name>` and `<url-pattern>`. The `<servlet-name>` element identifies the name of the servlet that you provide an alternate mapping for. The name should correspond to a name provided in an already defined `<servlet>` element. The `<url-pattern>` element identifies the URL path that you want users to use, relative to the top-level folder of the WAR file.

The following code snippet illustrates the use of the <servlet-mapping> element.

```
<web-app>
  <servlet>
    <servlet-name>Foo</servlet-name>
    <servlet-class>dummies.Foo.class</servlet-class>
  </servlet>
  <servlet-mapping>
    <servlet-name>Foo</servlet-name>
    <url-pattern>/Products</url-pattern>
  </servlet-mapping>
</web-app>
```

In this example, I create an alternate URL mapping for the Foo class. Without the <servlet-mapping> element, assuming that the name of this WAR file is dummies, the URL is

```
http://www.your-domain.com/dummies/Foo
```

With the <servlet-mapping> element, the URL becomes

```
http://www.your-domain.com/dummies/Products
```

You can use the * wild card to create special <servlet-mapping> elements that apply to all URL requests matching the pattern. For example, if you want to have all URL requests with a *.stuff pattern mapped to the Foo servlet, use the following <servlet-mapping> element:

```
  <servlet-mapping>
    <servlet-name>Foo</servlet-name>
    <url-pattern>*.stuff</url-pattern>
  </servlet-mapping>
```

Referencing JSPs in a WAR file

By default, you don't have to make references to JSPs in the web.xml file. However, you may choose to do so, particularly if you want to precompile and preload JSPs when the JSP container is started. Further, you can pass initialization parameters to a JSP in the same manner that you pass initialization parameters to servlet classes.

JSPs are converted into servlet classes by the JSP container in a process called *translation.* When users access your JSPs , they're actually working through a servlet class that was created by the JSP container from your JSP. Consequently, the <servlet> element used to refer to servlet classes in a Web application is also used to refer to the JSPs.

Note one minor difference between referring to a servlet and referring to a JSP. When referring to a JSP page, you substitute the `<jsp-file>` subelement for the `<servlet-class>` element. The `<jsp-file>` subelement contains the relative URL from the top-level folder of the WAR file to the JSP file itself.

The code in Listing 14-5 illustrates an example of a `<servlet>` element referring to a JSP file.

Listing 14-5: Referring to a JSP file with a <servlet> Element

```
<?xml version="1.0" encoding="ISO-8859-1" ?>

<!DOCTYPE webapp
  SYSTEM "http://java.sun.com/j2ee/dtds/web-app_1_2.dtd">
<web-app>
  <servlet>
    <servlet-name>NewThread</servlet-name>
    <jsp-file>/forum/newThread.jsp</jsp-file>
    <description>
       Use this JSP to start a new topic thread.
    </description>
    <display-name>New Thread</display-name>
    <icon>
      <small-icon>
         /images/NewIcon.gif
      </small-icon>
    </icon>
    <init-param>
      <param-name>topic</param-name>
      <param-value>please specify your topic</param-value>
      <description>
        default topic field value
      </description>
    </init-param>
    <load-on-startup/>
  </servlet>
  ...
</web-app>
```

Including custom tags in a WAR file

To make use of custom tags in a JSP application, you must include a `<taglib>` element in the `web.xml` file. This element tells the JSP container how to locate the TLD file for the custom tag library. Each tag library that you use in a JSP application must have its own `<taglib>` element.

The `<taglib>` element has two required subelements: `<taglib-uri>` and `<taglib-location>`. The `<taglib-uri>` tag contains the value of the Uniform Resource Indicator (URI) attribute for the `taglib` directive of your JSPs. The `<taglib-location>` subelement contains the path to the TLD file, relative to the top-level folder of the JSP application.

In order to use a custom tag in a JSP, you have to place a `taglib` directive at the top of the page. This directive has an `URI` attribute, which tells the JSP container where to find the TLD file.

The JSP container takes the URI that you provide in the `taglib` directive and searches for a `<taglib-uri>` element with a corresponding value. When it finds the URI, it takes the corresponding `<taglib-location>` and uses that to find the TLD file.

The following sample code illustrates a use of the `<taglib>` element in the `web.xml` file.

```
<web-app>
  ...
  <taglib>
    <taglib-uri>/forumTags</taglib-uri>
    <taglib-location>/WEB-INF/forumTags_1_0.tld</taglib-
          location>
  </taglib>
  ...
</web-app>
```

Supporting additional document types for JSP applications

Although most of the content that you find on the Internet is HTML content, many other different types of documents get sent across the Web, including images, movies, and portable document files (PDFs). Many of these file transfers are handled by a Web server and are not directed to the JSP container.

However, if you include additional file types in your JSP application and the requests for those documents are routed through the JSP container, you must register the document types in the `web.xml` file. Doing so tells the JSP container how to interpret the type of content being handled.

To support this registration process, all types of documents are identified by a unique type specification called a Multipurpose Internet Mail Extensions (MIME) type. The Internet Assigned Numbers Authority (IANA) manages the MIME type registry for all document types. You can find a complete listing of document types at

```
www.isi.edu/in-notes/iana/assignments/mediatypes/
```

To register a special document type with your JSP container, you must include the `<mime-mapping>` element in your `web.xml` file. The `<mime-mapping>` element has two required subelements: `<extension>` and `<mime-type>`. The `<extension>` subelement identifies the file extension of the documents that you want mapped to this MIME type. The `<mime-type>` identifies the MIME type associated with the given document extension.

The following example illustrates the use of the <mime-mapping> element.

```
<web-app>
  ...
  <mime-mapping>
    <extension>pdf</extension>
    <mime-type>application/pdf</mime-type>
  </mime-mapping>
  ...
</web-app>
```

Table 14-4 contains a listing of common documents and their corresponding MIME types. Note that JSP containers can handle HTML and plain text documents by default; no <mime-mapping> element is required for documents of those types.

Table 14-4 Mapping Documents to MIME Types

Document Extension	*MIME type*
html	text/html
jpeg	image/gif
pdf	application/pdf
mpeg	audio/mpeg or video/mpeg
gif	image/gif

Packaging the WAR file

After you have all the files organized in your JSP application and you're finished defining the web.xml file, you're ready to build the WAR file. Building the WAR file is identical to creating a JAR file (which I describe in detail in Chapter12). Here's a review of the steps:

1. **From the Start Menu, choose Run, type** command, **and press Enter.**

   This should launch a DOS command window. If your command window pops up and disappears, try the same step but type **cmd.exe** in place of **command**.

2. **Change folders on your computer so that you're in the folder that contains your entire JSP application.**

   This should be one folder above the top-level folder of the JSP application.

3. **At the command prompt, type the `jar` command, specifying at least the options `cf` to create a JAR and direct output to a file, the file name of the JAR file, and the top-level folder of the JSP application.**

   On my computer the solution looks like the following example:

   ```
   jar cf dummies.war c:\jsp-apps\out\dummies
   ```

4. **Press Enter.**

   The output of this command is a WAR file called `dummies.war`.

The Next Step: Deployment

After you master creating WAR files for JSP applications, you're ready to undertake the final phase of application development . . . deploying your JSP application.

Although all JSP-compliant containers must be able to handle WAR files, each can have its own deployment methodology. Therefore, you need to check the documentation of your JSP container to determine how to deploy the WAR file after you finish creating it.

Here are the steps for deploying to the Tomcat JSP container:

1. **Place a copy of the `dummies.war` file you just created into the `webapps` folder located directly under the top-level folder of your Tomcat installation.**
2. **Open the `server.xml` file, which is located in the `conf` folder, directly under the top-level folder of your Tomcat installation.**
3. **Search for the term `context path=` in the `server.xml` file.**

   You should find an XML style tag that starts with that phrase. You need to create a similar entry for the `dummies.war` file.

4. **Create a copy of the example solution provided in the `server.xml` file.**
5. **Update your copy so that it looks like the highlighted text in Figure 14-2.**
6. **Save the file by choosing File⇨Save, and then exit by choosing File⇨Exit.**
7. **After you have this information saved in the `server.xml` file, restart Tomcat by running `shutdown.bat` and then `startup.bat` in the `bin` folder under the Tomcat root folder.**

After you complete these tasks, Tomcat automatically loads the `dummies.war` file, and it's ready to use. Congratulations!

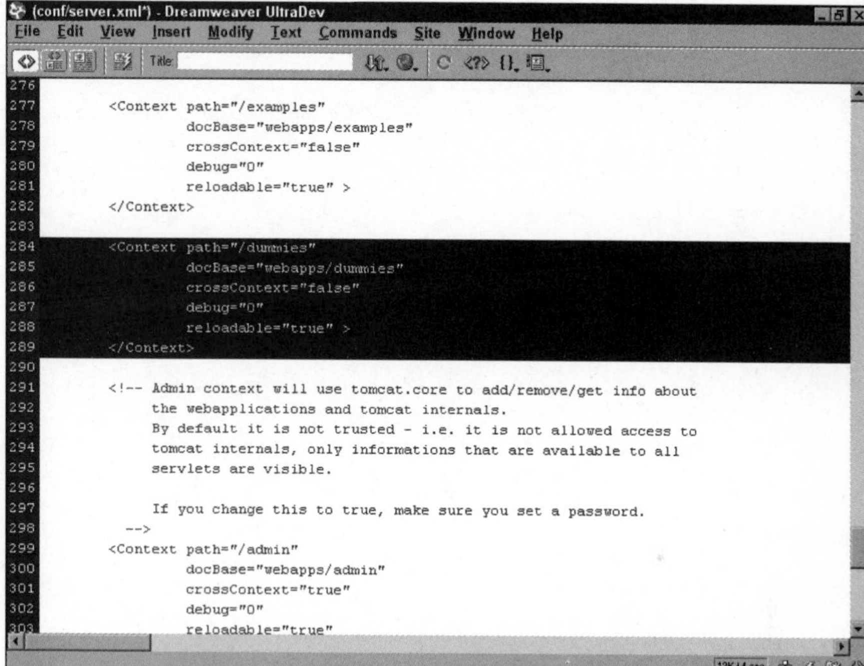
(conf/server.xml*) - Dreamweaver UltraDev
File Edit View Insert Modify Text Commands Site Window Help
Title:
<Context path="/examples"
docBase="webapps/examples"
crossContext="false"
debug="0"
reloadable="true" >
</Context>
<Context path="/dummies"
docBase="webapps/dummies"
crossContext="false"
debug="0"
reloadable="true" >
</Context>
<!-- Admin context will use tomcat.core to add/remove/get info about
the webapplications and tomcat internals.
By default it is not trusted - i.e. it is not allowed access to
tomcat internals, only informations that are available to all
servlets are visible.
If you change this to true, make sure you set a password.
-->
<Context path="/admin"
docBase="webapps/admin"
crossContext="true"
debug="0"
reloadable="true"

Figure 14-2: Creating a <context> tag in the server.xml file.

I confess: This deployment strategy works, but it's not necessarily the ideal solution. The truth is that Tomcat and other JSP containers are usually highly configurable. To take advantage of the configuration options, you should look into the administration documentation for the JSP container that you're using. You can find documentation on administering Tomcat at `jakarta.apache.org/tomcat/index.html`. Choose the link to the documentation for your version of Tomcat from the Documentation links on the left margin of the page.

Chapter 15

Two Architectures for JSP Applications

In This Chapter

- Understanding application architectures
- Checking out the JSP Model 1 architecture
- Looking at the JSP Model 2 architecture
- Deciding which architecture to use

Whether you're familiar with the topic of application architectures or not, this chapter provides you with some good information to help you design great JSP applications. An *application architecture* is kind of like the blueprint for an application. It tells you about the basic design, how different parts of the application work together and the software "materials" that you need to build a JSP application.

This chapter identifies two standard architectures used with JSP applications, identifies their pros and cons, and gives you a little guidance in deciding which architecture is right for you. And, for no extra charge, I give you my official opinion on which of these two architectures is best.

When developing the architecture of any application, you must define a framework for how the application works. The process of creating an application architecture should accomplish the following goals:

- **Test, test, test:** Test your ideas about how to develop the application, making sure that those ideas are sound and will accomplish your goals before you invest a lot of energy in writing code.
- **Standardize:** Define a standard formula for developing application components. After developing the application architecture, you should have a standardized method for creating application components. Standardizing ensures that your application is consistent, easier to learn, and easier to maintain.

- **See the big picture:** Define the big picture for the application development process. When you're defining an architecture for your application, you shouldn't be as concerned with the internal mechanics of Java classes and how features are implemented. Instead, focus on the relationship between Java classes and how they interact with each other.
- **Start with building blocks:** Produce the building materials for your application. Create a library of Java classes and utilities to use over and over to develop multiple features of your application.

To provide some uniformity and guidance in developing JSP applications, the writers of the JSP specification identified two possible application architectures that writers of JSP applications should attempt to implement. These architectures are not mandatory but they will help you to develop JSP applications. These architectures help out because they promote reuse of code, simplify maintenance of your software, and make your applications more flexible to change.

These two JSP application architectures are the Model 1 and the Model 2 architecture. They serve to normalize the method for creating JSP applications so that software developers who move from one application to another can rapidly understand and become productive in the new environment. Adhering to the guidelines of these architectures reduces your amount of effort when designing your application; and, as a bonus, you have the confidence of knowing that you're using a proven methodology to create your JSP application.

Logical Responsibilities of JSP Applications

Before diving into the details of the JSP Model 1 and Model 2 architectures, I want to take a minute to identify the tasks that JSP application architectures strive to normalize. Take a look at the responsibilities of a JSP application, which can be divided into three logical responsibilities: the model, the view, and the controller. These are often repeated components in applications of all kinds, and so are referred to as the *model-view-controller pattern*. The JSP Model 1 and Model 2 architectures are two different architectures used to ensure that the responsibilities of model-view-controller pattern are handled in a JSP application.

The model

The *model* of any application refers to the structure of the data handled by the application and the relationship between different data elements. A JavaBean is a perfect example of a component that handles the model of a set of related pieces of data. Each piece of data is stored in a JavaBean property. The properties of a single JavaBean define the scope of a related set of data. Whether the JavaBean has indexed properties or simple properties is another model element.

The key concept to retain about a model is that it defines the structure between logically related pieces of data, but it doesn't define the way they are presented. In other words, if a JavaBean is a pure model component, it can't contain any visual properties — it can only be a non-visual representation of data.

In Chapter 8 of this book, I state that a JavaBean can contain data and that the same JavaBean can be used in JSP applications, Java Swing applications, and other types of applications. You make a JavaBean reusable by making sure that it doesn't contain any information that determines the type of application it has to be included in. Consequently, if you place HyperText Markup Language (HTML) attributes inside a JavaBean, it's no longer simply a model of data and is not reusable in other types of applications.

The view

The *view* of any application refers to its visual organization. Components of an application that handle the view are responsible for taking data from the model and providing a visual organization for that data. This is the most characteristic feature of a JSP itself.

The *template data* of each JSP is the view of that part of the application. Remember that the template data refers to any part of a JSP that isn't JSP-specific. Thus, JSP standard actions, directives, and scripting elements are not template data, but everything else in a JSP (including all HTML content) is template data.

When you wrap HTML elements around the JSP standard actions, thus creating a presentation for the content of those properties, you are creating the view of your application. If the view and the model of an application are kept separate, different views can be created for the same model. But if the two are intertwined, the flexibility of your JSP application is severely limited.

The controller

The *controller* of an application is the portion of the application that controls the flow of the application. If you have several steps that need to be performed to move a user through a process, the controller is the portion of the application that makes sure that the user moves through all the steps — and in the proper order, if that factor is important.

When you think of the controller, think of an air traffic controller. The air traffic controller directs the traffic of airplanes, telling them which routes to fly, which runways to land on, and when they can land and take off. They are the coordinators of all air traffic.

Likewise, the controller of a JSP application is responsible for determining where the user goes next and the route of a user through your application. The `<jsp:forward>` action is a controller; it directs the flow of a JSP application from one page to another.

The JSP Model 1 Architecture

The JSP Model 1 architecture, the simpler of the two architectures, is structured in a way that's very similar to the model for a Web site with static Web pages. With the Model 1 architecture, the JSP fills the roles of controller and view while delegating model role to JavaBeans. In the Model 1 architecture:

- **JavaBeans are used to create the model for a JSP application.**

  Each JSP gathers the data that it needs by accessing JavaBeans by using the `<jsp:useBean>` tag, setting properties via `<jsp:setProperty>` tags, and executing methods of JavaBeans with scriptlets. JSPs, through standard actions and scriptlets, are responsible for coordinating the use and actions of JavaBeans.

- **JSPs directly fill the role of the controller responsibility.**

  The controller behavior of the JSP is the portion that directs the flow of the JSP application. This behavior can be implemented with the `<jsp:forward>` action if the JSP needs to direct the flow of the application on another JSP. In addition, the Uniform Resource Locator (URL) for the JSP can be placed in the action attribute of the HTML `<FORM>` element. Thus, when a user submits an HTML page, the content of the form is sent directly to the next JSP.

- **JSPs also fill the role of the view.**

  The view behavior determines the appearance of the Web page sent to a user. The output of a JSP is an HTML page that gets sent to the browser. The JSP creates this HTML page by laying out the content of the JavaBeans. Thus, the JSP's prime function is to serve this task of view. JSPs can use a combination of actions such as the `<jsp:getProperty>` tag, scriptlets, and custom tag libraries to extract data from JavaBeans and lay that content out. Check out these chapters for more information:

  - Chapter 3 covers all the standard JSP action tags, such as the `<jsp:useBean>` tag and `<jsp:getProperty>` tag.

  - Chapter 4 covers JSP directives and scripting elements, including scriptlets.

- Chapter 12 introduces the powerful features of custom tag libraries, providing background on their use in JSP applications.
- Bonus Chapter 4 provides you with the background that you need to create your own custom tag libraries.

Because the JSP Model 1 architecture blurs the control and view roles of an application, you lose some of the benefits of the model-view-controller pattern. I explore this issue further in the upcoming section "Pros and cons of the Model 1 architecture."

Figure 15-1 illustrates the typical flow of a JSP application using the Model 1 architecture. The number associated with each arrow indicates the order in which to read the diagram.

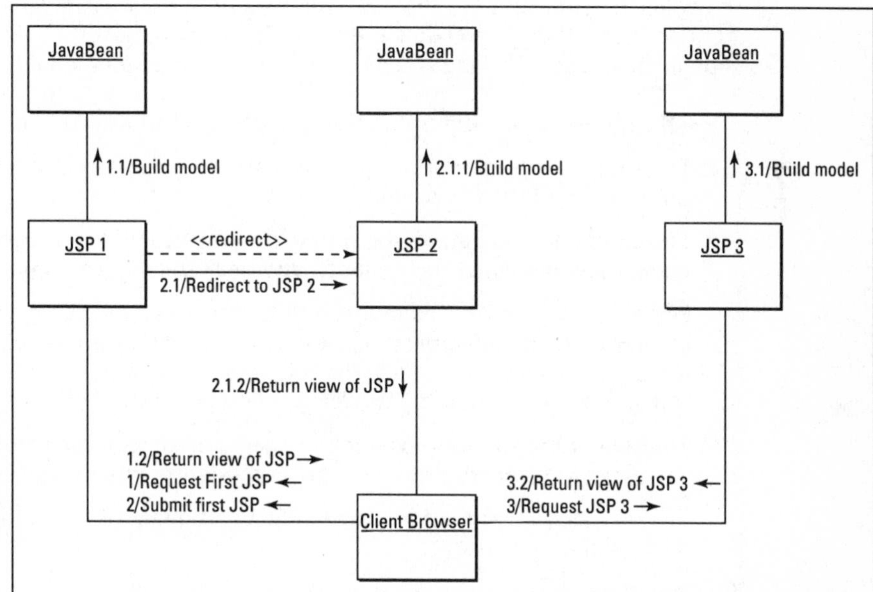

Figure 15-1: A diagram of the Model 1 architecture.

The distinguishing characteristic of the Model 1 architecture is that the responsibilities of controller and view are both housed in the JSP itself. Figure 15-1 indicates this by showing JSPs as the central point of control for creating JavaBeans, directing flow, and generating the view of the application.

The JSP Model 2 Architecture

The JSP Model 2 architecture is more complex than the Model 1 architecture but is also more adaptable. The key distinction between the two is that the Model 2 architecture separates the controller and view responsibilities, leaving the JSP responsible only for generating the view.

The separation between these two responsibilities is made possible by the introduction of a Java class called the `Servlet`. JSPs are actually compiled into `Servlet` classes the first time that a JSP container loads them. Creating the JSP Model 2 architecture means writing a servlet that performs the controller responsibility of the JSP.

Because the JSP Model 2 architecture cleanly separates the model, view, and controller responsibilities, it is often referred to as the *model-view-controller* architecture. Although you do have some flexibility in how the architecture is implemented, the following steps describe the fundamental concepts:

1. **All requests to a JSP application are directed to the controller servlet.**
2. **The servlet analyzes the request, creating an appropriate model builder class for the request.**
3. **The controller executes a method telling the model builder to create the model, passing along the `request` and `session` objects as parameters.**

   Many people refer to this model builder class as a factory because the builder class manufactures classes, just as a factory in the real world manufactures products. I use the term *model builder* because this class is responsible for building the JSP applications model objects.

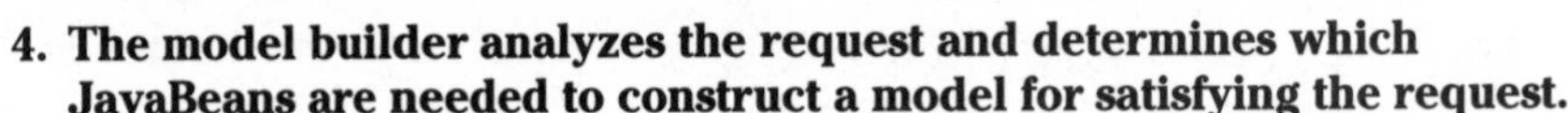

4. **The model builder analyzes the request and determines which JavaBeans are needed to construct a model for satisfying the request.**

   The resulting JavaBeans are the model component of the model-view-controller architecture.

   Model builders may be responsible for building the model for one JSP, or multiple JSPs. The following code snippet illustrates one way that the model builder can determine which model to create:

```
public String buildModel(HttpRequest request){
  String nextJSPPage = "/default.jsp";
  if(request.getParameter("nextModel") != null){
    if(request.getParameter("nextModel").
    equals("login")){
      nextJSPPage = buildLoginModel(); // to build login
         model
    }
    else
if(request.getParamter("nextModel").equals("orders")){
```

```
        nextJSPPage = buildOrdersModel(); // to build
          orders model
     }
   }
   return nextJSPPage;
}
```

In the previous example, the method buildModel() (a method of the model builder class) gets instruction from the request object as to which model to build, and then delegates the responsibility for building the model to another method. In this example, the delegate method is responsible for creating all the JavaBeans necessary to create the next JSP. The delegate method accomplishes the task by creating the JavaBeans, setting their properties, and executing any Structured Query Language (SQL) statements that are necessary. After the model is built, the model builder class attaches the JavaBean containing the model to the request object as an attribute, and control is returned to the controller servlet. The model builder class may also attach the name of the next JSP to the request, as the previous example illustrates by means of a nextJSPPage attribute.

5. **The controller servlet analyzes the request to determine which JSP should receive the model. Two possibilities as to how the next page can be determined are**

   - The controller servlet can hold an index of JSPs, and based on some parameter in the request, can look up the next page in the index.
   - The model builder can be smart enough to direct the controller servlet to the appropriate page.

   Either way, the controller servlet redirects the flow of the application to the new JSP, which is very similar to a <jsp:forward> action.

6. **After the JSP receives the redirect, it builds the view of the JSP based on the model contained in the JavaBeans attached to the request in Step 2.**

   When complete, the view is sent back to the user as the next HTML page.

Figure 15-2 illustrates this process and the order of the flow through the JSP application.

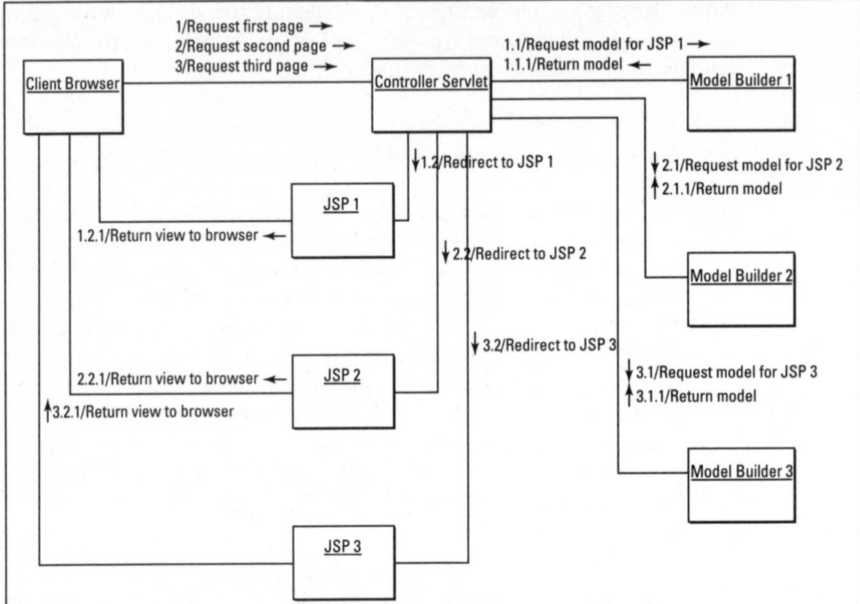

Figure 15-2: A diagram of the JSP Model 2 architecture.

The JSP Model 2 architecture places a servlet class in the driver's seat of your JSP application. This `Servlet` class — the controller servlet — determines which model builder to create as well as which JSP will respond to a request. This is fundamentally different from the Model 1 architecture, in which each JSP is a controller. The bottom line is that all JSP applications built with the Model 2 architecture provide a clear division of the model, view, and controller responsibilities, allocating those duties to different classes.

The JSP Model 2 architecture requires a much deeper understanding of the core Java Application Programming Interface (API) and of the servlet API. Unfortunately, those topics are beyond the scope of this book. *JavaWorld* has an excellent article on creating a JSP application using the JSP Model 2 architecture. The article is "Understanding JavaServer Pages Model 2 Architecture: Exploring the MVC Design Pattern," by Govind Seshardi. You can find it on the Internet at `www.javaworld.com`.

Mixing Filtering into The Architecture

Filtering is a new feature of servlet and JSP applications introduced with the Servlet 2.3 specification, which was released parallel with the JSP 1.2 specification. *Filters* are programs that intercept user requests before a JSP gets them, performing operations that can modify a request. Filters can also modify the output of a JSP before it's sent back to a user. These capabilities make filtering an excellent tool for handling previously awkward operations such as user authentication, encryption, decryption, compression of responses, and a variety of other solutions.

Be sure to check out Bonus Chapter 5 on this book's companion CD for background on creating filters and finding some additional resources for this new feature. I'm very excited about this new capability and its implications for JSP application design. As with all new technologies, if you're considering using filters in a production system, you should carefully analyze your choice to ensure that it represents an acceptable risk for your project.

Choosing an Architecture to Use

Deciding which application architecture to use for creating JSP applications is probably one of the first things you should do when building a JSP application. For those who are not skilled Java programmers and don't have access to assistance from a Java programmer, the only realistic option may be the Model 1 architecture because it's far easier to implement.

However, if you have the background to build an application using the Model 2 architecture or you have access to Java programmers who can help you, you'll benefit from some added flexibility in your JSP application and you'll have more options to grow and enhance your application in the future.

Pros and cons of the Model 1 architecture

The main benefit of the Model 1 architecture is its simplicity. Because it only depends on JSPs and JavaBeans, anyone with a little experience in Java and a copy of this book can create a JSP application using the Model 1 architecture.

In addition, it's easier to deploy changes to the flow of your JSP application because the JSP container can automatically reload JSPs that are updated without being restarted. Unfortunately, using the Model 1 architecture also requires some sacrifices.

The main drawback of the Model 1 architecture is that it collapses the controller and view responsibilities in the JSP itself. Because of this, the JSP application is less adaptable to change. When changing the layout of a JSP, you have to be careful not to break the links between pages.

Perhaps the most difficult task of maintaining JSP Model 1applications is changing the flow of the application. Imagine that you have one JSP that calls another and you want to insert a new JSP in between the two. Doing this is like inserting a new link in a chain. First you must break the chain. Then you must join one end of the chain to the new link. Finally you must join the new link to the other end of the chain.

As soon as any complexity is introduced into the links between JSPs, this task of breaking and reordering the flow of JSPs becomes very tedious with JSP Model 1 applications.

The bottom line: If you have a simple JSP application and you aren't going to change it very often, the Model 1 architecture is adequate. But if you're developing a sophisticated application and the application needs to be easy to modify and extend, the Model 1 architecture is not a good choice.

Pros and Cons of the Model 2 architecture

The JSP Model 2 architecture is the preferred approach of Java professionals when developing JSP applications simply because it's a more elegant design.

But although any Yahoo can tell you that the Model 2 architecture is better, not everyone can tell you why (not even the Brobdingnagians, Houyhnhnms, and Lilliputians). For the Swift ones in the crowd, here are this Yahoo's reasons for preferring Model 2 architecture:

- **A cleaner design:** The Model 2 provides a cleaner division of responsibility between the Java classes used to create the application. That's important because when you can clearly and succinctly state the responsibility of each Java class that you create, the entire structure of your application becomes easier to understand.
- **More flexible and adaptable:** Model 1 architecture is "tightly coupled" whereas the Model 2 architecture is "loosely coupled." *Coupling* refers the tightness of the bond between Java classes. The Model 1 architecture is tightly coupled because the bond between one JSP and the next is encoded directly into the JSP itself. Conversely, the Model 2 solution is loosely coupled because the command that directs the application to the next JSP is typically parameterized, allowing you to easily modify the sequence of pages by changing the parameter. This makes the Model 2 solution more adaptable to change.
- **Extensibility:** The extensibility of an application refers to the ability of the application to grow to support greater numbers of users while minimizing change to the application. To be fair, both Model 1 and Model 2 architectures are ultimately servlet applications because JSPs are compiled into servlet classes. Servlet applications are very extensible. However, when moving into enterprise scale applications — applications that run on several server computers at once — many businesses

choose to introduce the added technology of Enterprise JavaBeans into their JSP application. Making the transition to Enterprise JavaBeans is not necessary for small-scale Web sites, but if you really start dealing with a lot of Internet traffic, the migration is easier if you start out with a JSP Model 2 architecture.

Unfortunately, with the good comes the bad, and the downside of the Model 2 architecture is its complexity. If you feel that you're not prepared to deal with the added complexity of the Model 2 architecture, then it may not be the right choice.

When I built my first Model 2 architecture JSP application, I was required to learn several advanced concepts in Java programming. I accomplished that task successfully, even though I didn't have a great deal of experience with Java at the time. I believe that taking the time to review those concepts not only made me a better programmer: They made the program that I developed better. Although this effort cost me a couple of weeks, the flexibility of the application that I created and the additional experience that I gained was well worth it.

My advice: Even if you don't feel like you're a guru (just a Yahoo), you should make the choice of which architecture to use based on the requirements of the application that you're creating and not so much on the skills that you possess. If you feel that you need the Model 2 architecture, read the article I referred in the section "The JSP Model 2 Architecture" earlier in this chapter. Then try it. It will be worth the effort.

Part VI
The Part of Tens

"Give him air! Give him air! He'll be okay. He's just been exposed to some raw HTML code. It must have accidently flashed across his screen from the server."

In this part . . .

Where do you go if you need help developing a JavaServer Pages (JSP) application? What about adding some really cool features to your JSP application, or mastering some techniques for creating truly excellent JSP applications?

Look no further — you'll find the answers in the Part of Tens.

Chapter 16

Ten (Or So) Places to Look When You Have a Question

In This Chapter

- Local support groups
- Cool online sites for all things JSP
- Great resources for answering your JSP application questions

In this book, I strive to provide you with a solid foundation and excellent reference information for the creation of JavaServer Pages (JSPs). But I'll be the first to admit that I'm not perfect, and although I hope that you find this book useful, inevitably you'll have questions that aren't addressed in these pages. When you do encounter those questions, you're sure to get the answer at one of these locations.

Although you're probably looking for answers if you're reading this chapter, remember that most resources for posting questions on the Internet depend on average people like you and me to respond to the questions of others. If you see an inquiry and you think you can help, please respond. That's what makes community forums work.

Your Local Java User Group

I'm a big fan of local Java user's groups. The number one reason is because you can easily to get holed up in your work and lose touch with the community of Java developers who share your experiences. Local user's groups are a great way to meet fellow Java and JSP programmers and to learn more about what's going on in your area.

The second big reason to join a local Java user's group is that it's easier to ask questions of people you know, and the people who respond are usually more respectful, courteous, and willing to help than strangers. A personal connection tends to make people who might not make the time to respond to questions from across the globe more willing to respond to the same questions from their local community.

Finally, local Java user's groups are a great place to network with your peers and potential employers. Don't pass the opportunity by: Be sure to join the local Java user's group today.

You can find listings for Java User's Groups (or JUGs) on the home page `java.sun.com`. Look for the scrolling menu that contains listings for states and international JUG listings, find your state or country, and then click that name. You'll get listings for all the JUGs in the area. In addition, if you don't have a local JUG, you'll see information on how to form one there.

JavaRanch

Partner, if you're ready to hitch yer horse and take a load off, visit the Big Moose Saloon at the JavaRanch, otherwise known as `www.javaranch.com`. They don't serve no whisky, though, just pure Java! The JavaRanch is a great place to visit, particularly if you're looking for some well-written tutorials that make difficult topics seem easy.

If saloon life isn't your style, perhaps you'd rather talk to Gramps about the world over some steaming hot Java, or get some advice and cookies from Granny. Of course, there's also the Campfire, Code Barn, Round Up, Cattle Drive, Chicken Coop, and Bunkhouse. Bottom line is, there's something here for everyone, and the Ranch is a friendly place for Java greenhorns. (So says the Web site.)

Who says JSP wranglers aren't up to speed with New Age psychology? If you're looking for a little personal help, check out the article, "Getting in Touch with your Inner Class." It's a hoot!

java.sun.com Technology Forums

Although a little slower to respond to questions than the local Java user's group, you'll find a lot of useful information in the Java Technology Forums at `forum.java.sun.com`. Actually, as far as global communities go, these forums are about the best that I've encountered. Here are a few useful guidelines for getting a response to your question:

- Obviously if you're asking a question, you can't be expected to know the answer, but try to get a clear sense of the problem before you post the question. That means doing your research and pinpointing a precise location where you think the trouble is coming from.

- Be sure to post questions in the correct forum. There are a lot of different technology forums at JavaSoft, and if you post a question in the incorrect forum, you probably won't get an answer. In addition to posting in the correct forum, don't post your question in more than one forum.
- Before you post a question, look through the technology forum for similar questions to see whether you can find the answer you're looking for. If you ask the same question that someone else did and the answer is already there, you can be sure that most people will ignore your inquiry.
- Include a code sample, or the actual snippet of code, that's generating your problem when you ask the question. That helps people help you.
- Try to be concise and to the point with questions you ask, but make sure not to leave out important details. Vague questions result in vague answers, if they get any answers at all.
- If you discover the answer to your own question, be sure to post the solution and how you discovered it as a response to your question. That's a courtesy to your fellow programmers for a couple of reasons. First, you save time for people who consider responding because you update them that you already have the solution. Second, you help others who have similar questions by sharing how you found the solution.

Macromedia's UltraDev Newsgroup

Macromedia provides several on-line forums for those needing support and development assistance with projects. I've found the forums to be very heavily traveled, and the community of users is pretty supportive to those in need. You can access the forums at `www.macromedia.com/support/forums`.

This site is a great place to visit if you're looking for product support for any of Macromedia's products, or if you're looking for help with Dynamic HyperText Markup Language (DHTML), HTML, JavaScript, or other front-end technologies.

MySQL Mailing Lists

If you're looking for help with MySQL, you have a couple of options. If you want paid support, you can subscribe to a support service from MySQL. Alternatively, the free solution is to subscribe to the MySQL mailing list at `www.mysql.com/documentation/lists.html`.

The MySQL product is a publicly developed product, which means developers from around the world voluntarily contribute to the development effort. When you post messages to the MySQL mailing list, the MySQL development community at large and the contributors to MySQL software development are likely to receive the call for help.

Tomcat Users Mailing List

Tomcat can sometimes be a tricky product to work with. The difficultly is compounded by scant documentation. The good news is that the documentation base is expanding, and you can post questions on a mailing list.

Here's my advice. First, check the documentation to see whether you can find the answer to your question there. The Tomcat documentation provides a complete overview of installing Tomcat for all kinds for platforms and configurations. If you have installation questions, this should be your first resource. To find the documentation for Tomcat, navigate to the following URL and locate the documentation links on the left margin of the page:

```
http://jakarta.apache.org/tomcat/index.html
```

If you can't find the answer you're looking for in the documentation, give the Tomcat User's mailing list a try. This list is incredibly busy. I've received upwards of 30 messages a day from this list on a regular basis. So, if you're not prepared to deal with that much e-mail, this is not the right resource for you.

Before signing up for the Tomcat mailing lists, be absolutely sure to read the List guidelines, which are posted at the first Web page at the beginning of this section. My experience is that the level of traffic through Tomcat mailing lists makes people irritable, and if you break the rules, you can expect to be flamed. The URL for the Tomcat user's mailing list is:

```
jakarta.apache.org/site/mail.html
```

jGuru

When you come to a site that uses JSPs to implement the technology, you know you're visiting the right place to ask JSP questions. The jGuru site, at `www.jguru.com/forums/index.jsp`, has numerous discussion forums devoted to a variety of Java technologies. You can also find tutorials and articles about Java technology available at the jGuru site. Be sure to make a stop here as you proceed on your quest for help; prepare to be enlightened.

JSP Insider

JSP Insider (www.jspinsider.com/index.view) is a site created by JSP developers, using JSP technology, for the JSP community. At this site, you find articles, tutorials, and sample code. The staff at JSP Insider also publishes the JSP Buzz, an e-mail newsletter. In its pages, you find breaking news, musings about whatever, and links to JSP and Web development resources and articles.

This site is definitely a gem.

JS World

There comes a time when you have to admit that Java isn't everything. And then it's time to pay serious attention to related topics that contribute to the creation of great JSP applications. JavaScript is definitely an important topic, and you can discover more at the JavaScript (JS) World site (www.jsworld.com).

The cool thing about JavaScript is how many powerful creations you can accomplish with it. When I first started using JavaScript, I thought it was a nice tool for form validation. But it seems that every few months, I step into some task with JavaScript that was theoretically "not possible" when I started, and truly amazing when I finished.

At JS World, you can discover more on the basics of JavaScript, and you can also see the breaking edge of the JavaScript technology.

Chapter 17

Ten (Or So) Strategies for Developing Better JSP Applications

In This Chapter

- Planning your design
- Keeping it simple, Stupid
- Implementing Joint Application development
- Making use of a prototype
- Testing with JUnit
- Implementing an iterative development cycle
- Refactoring
- Knowing when to document

Deadlines . . . we all have them. Whoever said death and taxes were the only things you could count on in life forgot to include deadlines. Have you ever encountered a realistic deadline? I haven't, and I don't think they're very common. That's why we have to work smarter and not harder. The techniques that I list in this chapter are nothing new, but it helps to review some principles of quality software development every now and then. When it's crunch time for me, these are the strategies I fall back on to get out of the tight spots — and they (usually) work.

Plan Your Work; Work Your Plan

Sometimes I get this feeling that I don't need a plan: I can start writing code because I know exactly what needs to happen and how to do it. But nine times out of ten, that strategy ends up with me stuck in some complex problem wondering what to do next. When I'm wondering how to solve those complex problems, it's invariably because I didn't work according to a plan.

That's why my number one strategy for quality, and rapid, software development is quality planning. For me, quality planning means the following:

- **Understand the requirements of your project.** Implementing software that doesn't do what it was supposed to creates more rework than any other reason. One critical element to look for in order to ensure that you have well-defined requirements is a set of acceptance criteria for each requirement. *Acceptance criteria* are specific and detailed results that the software must produce under normal operating conditions for the requirement to be satisfied. If you don't have acceptance criteria, go back to the customer and get them.
- **Develop a quality design.** When I design, I like to start with a *logical model* of the system, which is a "big picture" view of the software system, showing the relationships between different classes in a software system but not all the details of each class. I then move into each of those classes to implement the internal structure that makes the logical mode possible. I find that using the Unified Modeling Language (UML) to generate software designs helps me come up with software solutions that I know will work before I start writing code.

Several design methodologies can help you to plan the software development process and ultimately to write better software. I find UML particularly useful because it defines a set of software diagrams that illustrate system requirements, develop logical software models, and implement the software you need.

Another excellent way to get better designs is to study *software design patterns,* which are principles of software design that are distilled from experienced software developers' experiences of solving the same problem over and over. No need to reinvent the wheel, as it were. Software design patterns can help you identify typical software design problems and guide you in implementing a solution that addresses those problems appropriately.

Several books on software design patterns are on the market right now, including a forthcoming book on design patterns used in the J2EE API. Here are a couple of recommendations:

- *Patterns in Java Volume 1: A Catalog of Reusable Design Patterns Illustrated with UML* by Mark Grand (Wiley Computer Publishing). I find this book useful because it has Java examples whereas most design pattern books provide samples in C++. Check the book's Web site for software updates that correct defects with the code examples.
- *Core J2EE Patterns* by Dan Malks, Deepak Alur, and John Crupi (Sun Microsystems Press). This soon-to-be-published book promises to be an excellent window into the best of the best patterns for use with J2EE software applications (which includes JavaServer Page applications). I'll add this book to my own collection as soon as it's available.

TogetherSoft makes an excellent Integrated Development Environment (IDE) that's based on the UML development process. An IDE is a software development tool that provides several features, typically including a text editor, compiler, debugging features, and wizards that help you create classes faster. The standard edition of TogetherSoft's IDE can actually generate Java and C++ code from diagrams that you create to model your software design. This tool also comes preloaded with several software design pattern templates that you can use to generate the basic framework of an application. Check out the TogetherSoft Web site at `www.togethersoft.com` to learn more about this product: It's excellent!

Practice KISSing (Or, Keep It Simple, Stupid)

When you face a complex, problematic software development and you're really racking your brain to find a solution to the problem, try breaking the problem into smaller, simpler pieces. Breaking a large problem into smaller, more manageable pieces is called *decomposition*. Decomposition makes software easier to understand, more adaptable, and easier to maintain. It's also great for your garden and flowerbeds, but not so wonderful for mummies.

Software development is one of the most complex endeavors that humankind has ever undertaken. It's mind-boggling and can lead to cranial decomposition itself if you're not careful. Not pretty. That's why I recommend simplifying the software all that you can. Develop software that's clearly outlined and performs a narrowly defined and well-understood set of tasks.

Implement Joint Application Development

If I cut off a finger every time I witnessed miscommunication between software developers and business customers result in poorly designed software, I wouldn't have any digits left. Face it: Software engineers do not talk the same language as the rest of the world. I used to talk the language of business, but after a year of software development work, I saw the eyes glaze over when I talked to business people.

The only way to deal with this lingo barrier is to allow your customers to have high visibility on the software development process. Allow customers to observe and participate in the software development process throughout the development lifecycle. Joint Application development is a development methodology that deliberately includes business customers in the software development process. The following principles are simple, prevent arthritis, and keep your fingers where they belong (on your hands).

- Plan the software with business leaders.
- Identify key customers who can observe and verify that the software satisfies their requirements.
- Include those customers in the definition of functional requirements and the design.

Work from a Prototype

Once I had the task of developing a client module for a software product I was working on. I understood the business well, and I had the requirements document right in front of me. I couldn't go wrong, right? I designed the software; I developed all the user interfaces; I wrote all the classes; and I did the database work. Everything was excellent and worked great — but when I presented it to my customers, it flopped! I had to redo the whole thing. D'oh! If only I had developed a prototype. . . .

Software prototypes may be nothing more than a mock-up of the user interface of the software that you write. For a JSP application, a prototype might be the HTML output that you expect a user to see on the page. If you're using JavaScript validation rules, you might implement a couple of prototypes to illustrate how the user interacts with the page, and what happens when incorrect data is entered. Prototypes shouldn't take a lot of work, but they should clearly give the user an idea of what to expect.

Although I have never developed the perfect prototype (ahem), that's how I know that prototypes do work. Think of it this way: Nine times out of ten, you won't get it right the first time. That's the purpose of the prototype — to ensure that you don't invest a lot of energy into a project, only to discover that the excellent software you write is not what your customer wants.

Write Unit Tests with JUnit

A *unit test* is a test applied to a single software unit. In Java, that unit is typically a single class. The task of the unit is simple. First, verify that when correct data is provided to the methods in a class, the class behaves as expected. Second, verify that when incorrect data is provided to the methods in a class, the class performs appropriate validations and rejects the invalid data.

JUnit is a set of free (gotta like the price) Java classes that you can use to write the software tests that exercise the methods in your programs, ensuring that each class you write behaves as expected. Unit tests are typically concerned with the public methods of a class and not the internal mechanics of the class. Unit tests are valuable because they verify that a single program unit (such as a class in Java) interacts with the rest of the software in a predictable way.

After you write a unit test for a class, keep that unit test and maintain it. If you ever maintain that piece of software, you can run it through the unit test again to verify that any changes you make don't introduce defects into the software.

Use an Iterative Development Cycle

A *software development cycle* (or lifecycle) consists of all the major tasks to be performed in order to complete development of one software release. Typically, software development lifecycles consist of the following tasks:

- **Defining requirements for the release.** In this stage, the goal is to get a complete definition of what the software must do and the outcomes of those actions. The things that the software must do are the *requirements*, and the outcomes of those actions are the *acceptance criteria*.
- **Develop a logical design.** In this stage, technical people work with customers to develop a high-level design of the system that satisfies the requirements and then implement the user interface desired by the customers.
- **Develop a detailed system design.** In this stage, the internal mechanics of the software are completely specified. The outcome of this stage is basically the complete blueprint for the software to be developed.
- **Code the software.** Working from the detailed design, coders turn the design into a usable program that satisfies all the acceptance criteria. Coders should perform their own unit testing and system testing to ensure that they have developed a product that satisfies the design constraints and system requirements. The outcome of this phase should be the software and the unit tests for the software.
- **Test the software.** In this stage, Quality Assurance engineers typically perform an acceptance test to ensure that the software meets the system requirements. After the acceptance test is passed, the software engineers may perform a variety of tests to verify the software is robust, to identify software defects, and to ensure that the software achieves performance benchmarks. This phase usually terminates with alpha and beta tests. In alpha tests, key users try out the software in a test environment. In beta tests, key customers receive a release of the software to use in a production environment.

- **Deploy the software.** In this phase, the software is deployed from the test environment to the production environment. For JSP applications, this phase may be as short as deploying a single Web ARchive (WAR) file to a Web server and restarting the Web server. See Chapter 14 to discover more about building and deploying WAR files
- **Support the software.** Unless you're using highly evolved and very expensive methodologies to develop your software, you're bound to have software defects released into production. Even the most meticulous software engineers make mistakes. (They're the ones with missing fingers.)

When software development shops follow the steps above in the order identified, they're engaged in a development methodology called the *waterfall methodology,* which is the most traditional of software development methodologies. In the waterfall methodology, each part of the software development cycle is called a *phase*, the completion of each phase is a milestone in the project, and each phase must be completed before the next phase is started.

Iterative development lifecycles improve on the waterfall methodology because although performing all the same tasks, they break a large software project into a set of small development lifecycles, each of which releases a small piece of software that can be used on its own. Iterative development improves on the waterfall methodology in the following ways:

- **Shorter development cycles:** Because each development cycle is shorter, customers have greater visibility on the progress and outcomes of a software development project. Iterative development cycles are typically scoped to a task that two or three people can complete in two weeks to a month. Increasing customer visibility on a development project lowers the risk that you make a wrong turn and develop something that doesn't satisfy customer requirements.
- **Shorter completion times:** Waterfall methodologies typically take a long time to complete (anywhere from six months to over two years). Conversely, iterative development cycles lead to small, predictable releases on a biweekly to monthly basis. Thus, iterative development cycles are more responsive to business needs. I've been on waterfall projects where the entire user interface of the product had to be redeveloped multiple times because of requirements changes in the middle of the project. Making changes part way through a development cycle substantially increases the risk, but iterative development mitigates that risk by keeping the development cycle short.
- **More fun, less grind:** The iterative development cycle keeps software development interesting. Instead of getting stuck in a rut, working on the same software for month after month, you get to do a lot of different software development projects, each over a very short period.

Refining the Art of Refactoring

Refactoring is the process of adapting your software design while you add new features to the software product. When you develop a large product, inevitably the original design of the product doesn't envision some problem that you encounter while coding. You're forced to develop a workaround because you're on a deadline and you have to get the product out the door. And after doing this for several features, the original design is no longer sufficient or consistent with the actual software you've developed. That's when it's time to refactor.

When you refactor software, you change the internal structure of the software without changing the function. Whereas software systems are traditionally derived from some design, refactoring is the method of distilling a new design from the existing software system. Engaging in periodic refactoring increases the longevity of your software product and eliminates the need to have the perfect design before you start developing.

Document Your Code

Documentation is one of those too-often neglected tasks. Although some may recommend that you document every line of code, I think that's a bit excessive. The JavaDoc standard provides an excellent basis for determining the appropriate level of documentation. *JavaDoc* is the standard documentation methodology specified by Sun Microsystems for Java classes. Describe every class, method, and attribute using the JavaDoc standard. From there, my recommendation is to write an in-line document whenever you are developing code that has to be done a certain way for a reason.

Describing the purpose of classes and functions, as well as the reasons why they're developed they way they are, is critical to maintaining a repository of technical knowledge about how a program works. Comments pay off when you have to share code with others and are invaluable when you have to return to code that you've written in the past.

I find that when software projects are finished, the documents that describe their design are often filed away and never referenced again. Although old design documents can become obsolete, it may also be that your design is not referenced because no one knows about the design document's existence or where to find it. To prevent this from happening, put a reference to the design document that a class is based on, as well as information about where that document can be found. I can't guarantee someone will look at it in the future, but at least folks can't grouse that they didn't know where to find it.

Chapter 18

(Almost) Ten Tricks for Cool JSP Features

In This Chapter

- Mover controls
- Master detail lists
- HTML e-mail forms
- JavaMail API
- XML and JSP

Okay, I confess, I've always had trouble with counting. So, there aren't exactly ten tricks in the following pages, but they definitely are cool. Quality wins over quantity, right?

Creating a Mover Control with JavaScript

Mover controls are a powerful user interface component that you often find on client/server applications but you don't often find them on the Internet. Although there are facilities for easily creating such controls in many programming languages, doing so with HyperText Markup Language (HTML) is a tricky task.

A mover control consists of two lists, with controls that allow people to move items from one list into another list. Typically the *source list* presents a variety of options, and the *target list* represents the items chosen by a user from the options of the source list.

To get a clearer picture of what a mover control looks like, check out the sample displayed in Figure 18-1.

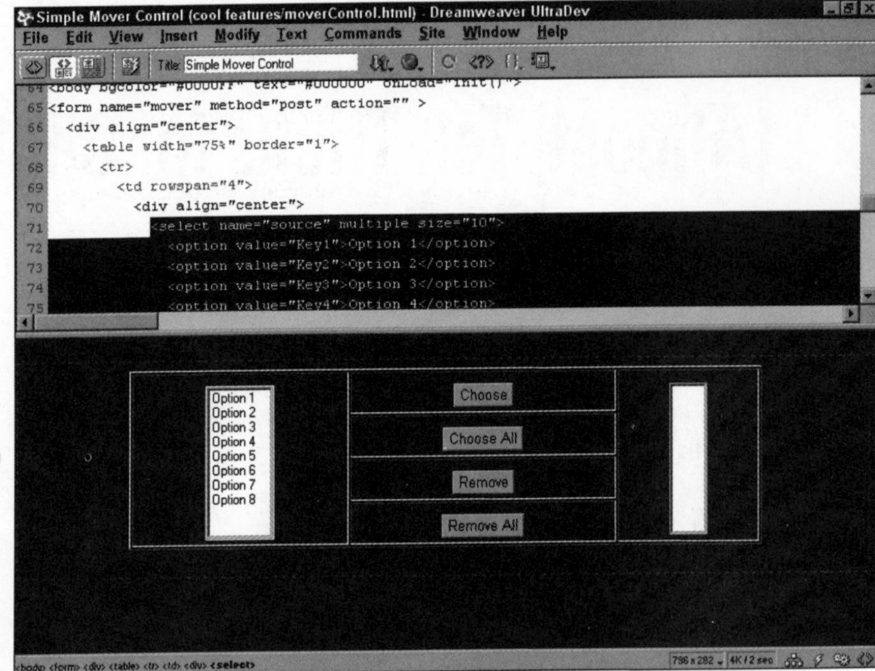

Figure 18-1: A mover control under development.

You can implement this same functionality with a `<SELECT>` HTML element that contains the attribute `multiple`. `<SELECT>` elements with the `multiple` attribute allow users to select multiple elements from a list but don't move those elements to another list. My advice is not to implement a mover control just because it's cool. If you can do the job with a `<SELECT>` list, you'll save yourself the extra effort associated with creating a mover control.

If you do stubbornly insist on creating your own mover control, here's a formula to help:

1. **Start by creating a table with three columns and four rows.**
2. **Place a `<BUTTON>` element in each cell down the center column, as illustrated in Figure 18-1, and then merge all the cells of the first and last column.**

   To merge the cells, use the attribute `rowspan=4` in the first `<TD>` element of each column.
3. **Place a `<SELECT>` list in the first and last columns of the table to create the basic layout of a mover control.**
4. **Configure some attributes of the elements in the mover control, starting with the `<SELECT>` elements.**

You want to allow multiple rows to be displayed at once, which is controlled with the size attribute of the <SELECT> element. You also want to give each <SELECT> element a meaningful name.

5. **Insert the `multiple` attribute to allow users to choose multiple elements at once.**

   With all these attributes specified, your <SELECT> elements should look something like this:

```
<SELECT name="source" size="10" multiple></SELECT>
```

6. **Give each button element a meaningful name and label.**

   I call mine `Choose`, `Choose All`, `Remove`, and `Remove All`. These labels correspond to the actions that the buttons will perform. Make sure that the button is a standard button and not a submit button.

7. **Add an `onClick` event handler to each button.**

   When you get done, each button should be similar to the following example:

```
<INPUT type="button" name="choose" value="Choose"
        onClick="">
```

With the HTML elements in place for the mover control, shift your attention to the JavaScript. JavaScript is the language that makes the mover control possible. You need four different JavaScript functions to implement the mover control. I've created examples for you, which are displayed in Listing 18-1. My functions are called `chooseSelected()`, `removeSelected()`, `chooseAll()` and `removeAll()`. The first function moves selected <OPTION> elements from the source list to the selected list. The second moves selected <OPTION> elements from the selected list to the source list. The third moves all <OPTION> elements from the source list to the selected list. The last moves all <OPTION> elements from the selected list to the source list.

I've created an `init()` method that stores references to my two select lists in JavaScript variables. This `init` method is executed by the `onLoad` event handler of the HTML <BODY> element. You can see the example in Listing 18-1.

In order to make the whole thing work, you have to add a function calls for all the functions listed in Step 7 into the `onClick` events of the respective buttons from Step 6. Thus, the `Choose` button should call the `chooseSeleted()` function in its `onClick` event handler, the `Remove` button should call the `removeSelected()` function in its `onClick` event handler, and so on.

A working mover controller example is supplied on the CD that comes with this book. Check it out!

Listing 18-1: JavaScript Methods for the Mover Control

```
. . .
<SCRIPT LANGUAGE="JavaScript">
  var sourceElement;
  var selectedElement;

  function init(){
    sourceElement = document.mover.source; // reference to
           source
    selectedElement = document.mover.chosen; // reference to
           chosen
  }

  function chooseSelected(){
    var selectedOptions = new Array();
    for(var index = 0; index < sourceElement.options.length;
           index++){
      if(sourceElement.options[index].selected == true){
        selectedOptions[selectedOptions.length] =
           sourceElement.options[index];
      }
    }
    for(var index = 0; index < selectedOptions.length;
           index++){
      sourceElement.options[selectedOptions[index].index] =
           null;
      selectedElement.options[selectedElement.length] =
           selectedOptions[index];
    }
  }

  function removeSelected(){
    var removeOptions = new Array();
    for(var index = 0; index <
           selectedElement.options.length; index++){
      if(selectedElement.options[index].selected == true){
        removeOptions[removeOptions.length] =
           selectedElement.options[index];
      }
    }
    for(var index = 0; index < removeOptions.length;
           index++){
      selectedElement.options[removeOptions[index].index] =
           null;
      sourceElement.options[sourceElement.length] =
           removeOptions[index];
    }
  }

  function chooseAll(){
    var selectedOptions = new Array();
    for(var index = 0; index < sourceElement.options.length;
           index++){
```

```
      selectedOptions[selectedOptions.length] =
           sourceElement.options[index];
    }
    for(var index = 0; index < selectedOptions.length;
           index++){
      sourceElement.options[selectedOptions[index].index] =
           null;
      selectedElement.options[selectedElement.length] =
           selectedOptions[index];
    }
  }

  function removeAll(){
    var removeOptions = new Array();
    for(var index = 0; index <
           selectedElement.options.length;
        index++){
      removeOptions[removeOptions.length] =
           selectedElement.options[index];
    }
    for(var index = 0; index < removeOptions.length;
           index++){
      selectedElement.options[removeOptions[index].index] =
           null;
      sourceElement.options[sourceElement.length] =
           removeOptions[index];
    }
  }
</SCRIPT>
<body bgcolor="#0000FF" text="#000000" onLoad="init()">
. . .
```

Creating Master Detail Lists with JavaScript

Sometimes form validation requires special interactions between different HTML controls on the same page. One of the earliest problems I had to face was a tool that allowed users to specify the species and breed of a pet using HTML controls. Obviously, you don't want a user choosing one species to be able to choose breeds from another species like, say, specifying that their cat is an English bulldog or a border collie. In this example, the items in the breed list should be dependent upon what element is selected in the species list.

This kind of master-detail relationship between two lists is easily implemented using JavaScript object arrays. To illustrate the creation of this type of control, I use a problem of choosing foods from the four food groups. The master control is a food group, and the detail is the food item that belongs to the food group.

Here's a step-by-step plan for making a master-detail control, using the four food groups as an example.

1. **Add two `<SELECT>` elements to your HTML form: One will be the master control and the other will be the detail control.**

   For this example, I'm naming the master control `foodGroups` and the detail control `foods`.

2. **In the master control, add an `onChange()` event handler.**

   This event calls the JavaScript function that you create to update the contents of the detail control. The `onChange()` event handler gets called every time that you change the value of the control containing it. For my example, I call a function called `populateFoods()` in this `onChange()` event handler. The HTML code for the handler is

   ```
   <SELECT name="foodGroups"
           onChange="populateFoods(this.value)">
   </SELECT>
   ```

3. **In the `<BODY>` tag, add an `onLoad()` event handler.**

   This event is run when the `<BODY>` element is finished loading in a browser. In the event handler, call a function called `init()` that will be created to initialize the contents of the `foodGroups` element. The code for the `foodGroups` example is

   ```
   <BODY onLoad="init()">
   ```

Now you're ready to start writing the JavaScript code that manages the master-detail control. I provide the code for my example solution in Listing 18-2. Take a few moments to look over this code.

Listing 18-2: JavaScript Functions for the Master-Detail Control

```
<SCRIPT LANGUAGE="JavaScript">
// this is a list of foodGroups
var groupsArray = Array();
// this is a list of foods
var foodsArray = Array();

var foodElement; // the foods <SELECT> element
var foodGroupElement; // the foodGroups <SELECT> element

function init(){
  // initialize foodElement
  foodElement = document.foodSelector.foods;
  // initialize foodGroupElement
  foodGroupElement = document.foodSelector.foodGroups;
  // create the array elements
```

```
  groupsArray[groupsArray.length] = new foodGroupObject("0",
          "Choose One");
  groupsArray[groupsArray.length] = new foodGroupObject("1",
          "Dairy");
  groupsArray[groupsArray.length] = new foodGroupObject("2",
          "Meats");
  groupsArray[groupsArray.length] = new foodGroupObject("3",
          "Vegetables");
  groupsArray[groupsArray.length] = new foodGroupObject("4",
          "Grains");

  foodsArray[foodsArray.length] = new foodObject("1",
          "Milk");
  foodsArray[foodsArray.length] = new foodObject("1",
          "Cheese");
  foodsArray[foodsArray.length] = new foodObject("2", "T-Bone
          Steak");
  foodsArray[foodsArray.length] = new foodObject("2",
          "Turkey");
  foodsArray[foodsArray.length] = new foodObject("2",
          "Salmon");
  foodsArray[foodsArray.length] = new foodObject("3",
          "Beets");
  foodsArray[foodsArray.length] = new foodObject("3",
          "Carrots");
  foodsArray[foodsArray.length] = new foodObject("3",
          "Spinach");
  foodsArray[foodsArray.length] = new foodObject("4",
          "Cereal");
  foodsArray[foodsArray.length] = new foodObject("4",
          "Bread");

  // initialize the values in the foodGroups <SELECT> element
  populateFoodGroups()
}

// This is a foodGroupObject, used as a groupsArray element
function foodGroupObject(id, value){
  this.id = id
  this.value = value
}

// This is a foodObject, used as a foodsArray element
function foodObject(parentId, value){
  this.parentId = parentId
  this.value = value
}

function populateFoodGroups(){
  for(var index = 0; index < groupsArray.length; index++){
    //create option element
```

(continued)

Listing 18-2 *(continued)*

```
      var newGroup = document.createElement("OPTION");
      newGroup.text = groupsArray[index].value;
      newGroup.value = groupsArray[index].id;
      foodGroupElement.options[foodGroupElement.options.length]
             = newGroup;
   }
}

// this function gets called to update the foods <SELECT>
          element
function populateFoods(selectedGroup){
  foodElement.options.length = 0; // removes foods <OPTION>
          elements
  for(var index = 0; index < foodsArray.length; index++){
    if( foodsArray[index].parentId == selectedGroup ){
      // these are foods belonging to the group selected by
          the user
      //the following lines of code create an <OPTION>
          element
      var newFood = document.createElement("OPTION");
      newFood.text = foodsArray[index].value;
      newFood.value = foodsArray[index].id;
      foodElement.options[foodElement.options.length] =
          newFood;
    }
  }
}
</SCRIPT>
```

The code in Listing 18-2 provides a complete solution of creating the master-detail control. Rather than give the blow-by-blow details of how I wrote it, I'm just going to give an overview of what it does. When creating a master-detail control of your own, you can follow the formula illustrated in this code.

- This code has two arrays: `groupsArray` and `foodsArray`. These arrays are called object arrays because the contain objects instead of simple values. The objects contained by the arrays are `foodGroupObject` and `foodObject`, respectively. I use an object array because each object that contains information that relates to the food is related to an associated food group.
- The `init()` function performs three tasks. First, I initialize the JavaScript variables providing references to my `<SELECT>` elements. Next, I initialize the values of the object arrays and also initialize the content of the `foodGroups` `<SELECT>` element, which is accomplished by calling the `populateFoodGroups()` function in the last line of the `init()` function. Remember, the `init()` function gets called from the body `onLoad()` event, causing the JavaScript environment to be initialized and the `foodGroups` `<SELECT>` element to be initialized as soon the body is loaded into a browser.

- Finally, the populateFoods() function is available to load the contents of the foods <SELECT> element. This function gets called when the value is changed in the foodGroups <SELECT> element. The value of the selected food group is passed in and used as a reference to find associated foods. See the populateFoods() function in Listing 18-2 to discover how the task is performed. When each food is identified, an <OPTION> element is created for that kind of food, and the element is inserted into the foods <SELECT> list.

An example of the master-detail control is provided on the CD that comes with this book. Just look for masterdetail.html, under the folder for this chapter. You can run it in your Web browser to see what a nifty device this can be.

Creating an HTML E-Mail Form

Creating an e-mail form for your Web application offers some nice feature enhancements. One great place to build an e-mail form is in your JSP error page. There you can capture user comments on an error page and have them mailed to your support e-mail address.

You can create e-mail forms using basic HTML, but the results are different depending upon the type of browser that the user employs. Nevertheless, this is perhaps the simplest solution for sending an e-mail. Every e-mail message is composed of four parts:

- **From:** The From address field identifies the sender.
- **To:** The To address field identifies the recipient.
- **Subject:** The Subject field identifies the subject.
- **Message:** The Message field contains the content of the e-mail message.

It naturally follows that an e-mail form contains all these components in the Web page. In HTML, <FORM> elements, the To address, and the Subject are identified in the <FORM> elements action attribute. This is illustrated in the following example:

```
<FORM METHOD="POST" ENCTYPE="text/plain"
        ACTION="mailto:support@mydomain.com?subject=Defect
        ">
```

The fact that this form contains an e-mail message is identified by the mailto: prefix on the beginning of the URL in the action attribute. This is followed by the e-mail address you want to send the message to. The subject is identified as a parameter of the URL.

If you use the HTML <FORM> to send an e-mail, you must have the method attribute set to POST. Setting ENCTYPE to "text/plain" causes the form data of the HTML <FORM> element to be sent as the message field.

When specifying the ENCTYPE of the <FORM> element as "text/plain", all form data will be sent to you in the message field of the HTML form. The final task is capturing the user's return e-mail address. The browser does this for you.

The following example illustrates the finished e-mail form:

```
<FORM METHOD="POST" ENCTYPE="text/plain"
          ACTION="mailto:support@mydomain.com?subject=Defect
          ">
  This defect is your fault. Please tell us what you did
          wrong:
  <INPUT TYPE="textarea" NAME="comments">
  </INPUT>
  <INPUT TYPE="hidden" NAME="stack trace"
          VALUE="<%exception.printStackTrace();%>">
  <INPUT TYPE="submit" name="submit" value="Send Email">
<FORM>
```

When submitted, the resulting e-mail will look something like this:

```
TO: support@mydomain.com
FROM: john.doe@middleville.com
SUBJECT: Defect
MESSAGE:
comments=I followed the directions. I promise, it won't
          happen again.
stack trace = exception stack trace here
```

Of course, you should probably not blame the user for defects in your Web site.

If you use e-mail forms in your JSP error pages, try using a scriptlet to customize the subject to the exception message text. You can also include the stack trace and other error information in hidden fields of the HTML form. Just remember when you do so that you're giving the user access to that information. If you don't want the user to see it, don't send it in the e-mail.

Sending E-Mail with the JavaMail API

The JavaMail Application Program Interface (API) is a set of classes specified by Sun Microsystems for interacting with mail servers to send and receive e-mail. By using this API, you can actually write a complete e-mail program that receives and manages e-mail messages. That's a little beyond the scope of this book, but sending simple text messages is not.

The JavaMail API is part of the Enterprise Edition SDK. To use it, you have to install the Enterprise Edition SDK on your computer.

Before diving into the task of creating an e-mail message with JavaMail API, first consider why you want to use it. If you want to send e-mail message from a user to someone, consider using HTML forms to send e-mail, as I describe in the previous section, "Creating an HTML E-Mail Form." That's a lot easier, and it works just as well. If, however, you want to notify someone of a defect from the server, the JavaMail API is a great way to do it.

In order to send a message with JavaMail API, you need to provide five basic pieces of information. Well, actually, you don't need to provide them all — some are required and some are not.

- **Mail server name:** The API needs to know the name of your mail server. This name is provided as a `String` in the format of `mail.server.com`, where `mail` is the name of the server, `server` is the domain name, and `.com` is the domain extension. This piece of information is required to send an e-mail message.
- **Recipient address:** The API needs to know the e-mail address of each recipient. You must specify at least one recipient but you can specify more if you wish. For that reason, the recipient is supplied as an array of `String` objects, each `String` containing an e-mail address.
- **Subject:** If you want the mail message to have a subject, you must supply the `subject` attribute. The subject is also a `String`.
- **Sender identification:** Although not required, it's customary to supply an e-mail address identifying the sender of the e-mail. In this case, the sender is the JSP container itself, which probably doesn't have a valid e-mail address. You can, however, identify the JSP container as an alias and use the Webmaster's e-mail address as the sender. To do so, you would specify the sender in the format: `JSP Container <webmaster@domain.com>`.
- **Text:** The e-mail message should contain some text. Again, this is not required, but it's convenient if you want the recipients to do something in response to receiving the message. The content of the message is also supplied as a `String`.

To construct the e-mail and send it, you can create and define a method directly in the JSP itself (by using a declaration scripting element), or you can build a JavaBean that performs the task for you. In either case, the method to send the message should look something like the code in Listing 18-3.

Listing 18-3: Sending E-Mail with JavaMail API

```
<%@ page import="javax.mail.*, javax.internet.mail.*,
        java.util.*"%>
<%!
  public void sendMessage(String mailServer
    , String[] recipient
    , String sender
    , String subject
    , Sting messageBody) throws AddressException,
          MessagingException {

    // initialize message properties
    Properties props = new Properties();
    props.put("mail.smtp.host", mailServer);
    // Session refers to javax.mail.Session, not the session
          object
    Session mailSession = Session.getDefaultInstance(
          mailProps, null);
    int length = recipient.length;
    InternetAddress[] recipients = new
          InternetAddress[length];
    for(int count = 0; i < length; i++){
      // create recipient addresses
      recipients[count] = new
          InternetAddres(recipient[count]);
    }
    // create sender address
    InternetAddress sender = new InternetAddress(from);

    // create email message
    Message email = new MimeMessage(mailSession);
    email.setFrom(sender);
    email.setRecipients(Message.RecipientType.To,
          recipients);
    email.setSubject(subject);
    email.setContent( messageBody, "text/plain");

    // send Message
    Transport.send(email);
  }
%>
```

The method in Listing 18-3 performs all the tasks to create a plain text message with no attachments. The steps performed by the method are

1. First, the method creates a properties file and stores the properties to be used in creating the mail session therein. The only relevant property in this case is the name of the mail server. As you can see from the code, the `mailServer` information is associated to the tag `"mail.smtp.host"`, which is a standard property name identified by the JavaMail API. The value should be the identity of your mail server.

2. Next, a default mail session is created. The mail session holds properties used by classes of the JavaMail API for transporting e-mail messages. The session ultimately is placed in the e-mail message, where other classes of the JavaMail API can access it as needed.
3. The third task is the creation of `InternetAddresses` for the recipients and the sender of the e-mail. The `InternetAddress` class is just a special class that stores and verifies the format of an e-mail address.
4. After all the previous tasks are completed, the function creates a `MimeMessage`, which is stored in a `Message` variable. The `MimeMessage` is a subclass of `Message`, so it can be stored in the `Message` type variable without casting. The sender, recipient, subject, and body of the message are initialized. Note the argument `"text/plain"` supplied in the `email.setContent()` function. That tells the e-mail message that the content type of the message is plain text.
5. Finally, the message is sent, using the `Transport.send()` function, which is a static method of the `Transport` class.
6. The method throws two exceptions: `AddressException` and `MessagingException`. The first exception indicates that one or more of the e-mail addresses supplied is not a valid address. The `MessageException` is a generic exception indicating that the e-mail message could not be delivered. Both of these exceptions must be handled.

After you finish defining this method, sending an e-mail should be pretty straightforward. Listing 18-4 contains a sample JSP that sends an e-mail to the author of this book (ahem, me). In fact, you can use this message to give me feedback and constructive criticism. Just try to keep it nice . . . I'm a sensitive guy.

Although I'm happy to receive your feedback directly, the publishers would also like it, and they have a special venue for feedback. If you want to send feedback to the publishers, visit them on the Internet at `www.dummies.com/register.html`.

Listing 18-4: Sample E-Mail Form

```
<html>
<head>
<%@ page import="java.util.*, javax.mail.*,
            javax.mail.internet.*"%>
<title>Feedback Sender</title>
<meta http-equiv="Content-Type" content="text/html;
            charset=iso-8859-1">
</head>
<%!
  public void sendMessage(String mailServer
    , String[] recipient
```

(continued)

Listing 18-4 *(continued)*

```
    , String sender
    , String subject
    , Sting messageBody) throws AddressException,
           MessagingException {

    // initialize message properties
    Properties props = new Properties();
    props.put("mail.smtp.host", mailServer);
    // Session refers to javax.mail.Session, not the session
           object
    Session mailSession = Session.getDefaultInstance(
           mailProps, null);
    int length = recipient.length;
    InternetAddress[] recipients = new
           InternetAddress[length];
    for(int count = 0; i < length; i++){
      // create recipient addresses
      recipients[count] = new
           InternetAddres(recipient[count]);
    }
    // create sender address
    InternetAddress sender = new InternetAddress(from);

    // create email message
    Message email = new MimeMessage(mailSession);
    email.setFrom(sender);
    email.setRecipients(Message.RecipientType.To,
           recipients);
    email.setSubject(subject);
    email.setContent( messageBody, "text/plain");

    // send Message
    Transport.send(email);
  }
%>

<body bgcolor="#FFFFFF" text="#000000">
<H1> YOUR FEEDBACK WAS SENT. THANKS!</H1>
<%
  try{
    String server = "your.server.com";
    String subject = "Love the book";
    String[] recipient = "feedback@sextanttech.com";
    String sender = "JSP dummy/guru
           <your.email.address@domain.com>";
    String message = "Your message here";
    sendMessage(server, recipient, sender, subject, message);
  }
  catch(AddressException e){
%>
    <br>One of the email addresses supplied is invalid.
           Please correct and try again.
```

```
<%
  }
  catch(MessagingException e){
%>
    <br>This message could not be sent for the following
           reason:
    <br><%=e.getMessage()%>
<%
  }
%>
</body>
</html>
```

Building XML Documents with JSP pages

XML, or eXtensible Markup Language, is the latest rage of the Internet and is as significant an innovation today as HTML was in the beginning of the Internet. XML was created in response to a need for a markup language that describes content. To clarify, it's best to compare XML with HTML.

With HTML, you have a series of elements that organize content. But these elements are dumb, which is to say they don't know descriptive information about the content — they just know how to organize and display the content on a Web browser.

XML, on the other hand, has elements that are used to label the content and to identify what type of content each element contains. Because XML is descriptive, it can be used to organize data in meaningful ways. XML is important because it allows Internet computers send content that is meaningful, rather than just sending pretty pictures.

XML is extensible because, as the document author, you get to decide what the each XML element is called. For example, if I want to create an XML document describing cars, I would create elements that are meaningful for that task. Here's what it would look like:

```
<cars>
  <car>
    <make>Ford</make>
    <model>Escort</model>
    <year>1995</year>
    <color>white</color>
  </car>
</cars>
```

There are many books available about XML technology. If you're interested in understanding XML in detail, try *XML For Dummies,* 2nd Edition, by Ed Tittel and Frank Boumphrey (published by Hungry Minds, Inc.).

Although I don't intend to go into great detail about how to use XML, I do want to illustrate the use of JSP technology to create dynamic XML documents. You can easily build dynamic XML files applying the same principles that you apply to creating HTML files.

The only difference between generating XML content and generating HTML content is that you must include a JSP directive identifying the content type as `"text/xml"` at the beginning of the JSP. Listing 18-5 contains an example JSP that creates XML output. The page directive is displayed on the first line.

Listing 18-5: Building an XML Document with a JSP

```
<%@ page contentType="text/xml"%>
<?xml version="1.0" encoding="ISO-8859-1"?>
<jsp:useBean id="cars" class="dummies.CarInfo" scope="page"/>

<cars>
<%
  if(cars.isValid()){
    while(cars.hasNext()){
%>
      <car>
        <make><jsp:getProperty name="cars"
           property="make"/></make>
        <model><jsp:getProperty name="cars"
           property="model"/></model>
        <year><jsp:getProperty name="cars"
           property="year"/></year>
        <color><jsp:getProperty name="cars"
           property="color"/></color>
      </car>
<%
    }
  }
%>
</cars>
```

In the Listing 18-5, the `cars.isValid()` function causes the JavaBean to execute a Structured Query Language (SQL) query returning car information. The `cars.hasNext()` function causes the JavaBean properties to be updated for each row returned by the query. Standard `<jsp:getProperty>` tags are then used to retrieve the values of the JavaBean properties and place them in the XML document.

As you can probably determine from Listing 18-5, building an XML document is not that difficult; in fact, it's pretty much exactly like building a Web page, with the exception that the output is XML and not HTML. The bottom line is that JSPs don't care what kind of output you want to generate — they only care about the JSP specific tags in your JSP. So output what you like, say what you like, and have fun.

Part VII
Appendixes

"What I'm looking for are dynamic Web applications and content, not Web innuendoes and intent."

In this part . . .

Before you can do anything with JavaServer Pages (JSPs), you have to configure the correct environment. Read though Appendix A for everything you need to know about how to set up your computer using the software on the CD-ROM that accompanies this book. Appendix B gives you a quick rundown on the contents of the CD-ROM that accompanies this book: bonus content, code samples, and trial versions of software.

Appendix A

Configuring the JSP Environment

In This Appendix

- Discovering how to install the Java software development kits
- Installing and configuring the Tomcat JSP container
- Installing the MySQL Database
- Ensuring configuration success
- Picking tools for developing JSPs and Java code

I remember when I first started developing Web applications. Getting all the software installed and configured was a major hassle. I recall wishing for one resource that I could go to for reference information on how to configure all the tools that I needed. "If only there were a book with everything I needed to know about configuring my computer for Web development," I wished to myself. Who would have guessed I'd be writing that book!

I devote this Appendix to getting you off on the right foot configuring your computer for JSP development. I provide the information that you need to know about what software to install and how to install it. All the software that I cover in this Appendix is also provided on the CD at the back of this book. The software I cover in this Appendix comprises the basic software that you need to run JSPs and is also the software that I assume you have while you read this book. The programs that you need are

- **The Java 2 Software Development Kit (SDK), Standard Edition**

  This product provides you with all the basic Java functionality for developing single-user applications.

- **The Java 2 SDK, Enterprise Edition**

  This product provides you with several Web-based Java technologies, including the functionality to develop JSPs. Many of the examples in this book make use of Java classes in the Enterprise Edition, which is why you need it.

- **The Tomcat JSP container, version 4.0**

  This product enables your computer to run JSPs and deliver JSP-based content to the Internet.

The Java 2 SDK, Enterprise Edition software available on the CD with this book is intended for Windows NT computers — it's not supported on Windows 95, 98, Me, or other Windows desktop versions. I have, however, installed this SDK edition on Windows Me and tested all the software provided with this book on Windows Me: It seems to work fine. If you plan to do anything more strenuous than the topics I cover in this book, you may run into troubles if you're running your program on desktop editions of the Windows operating system.

The Tomcat JSP container is licensed under a public license agreement, which basically means that you can use it at no charge but also at your own risk. Several related products are developed for commercial purposes, which you may prefer if you plan to develop a commercial product. If you plan to use another product, you need to follow the installation and deployment instructions provided with that product.

Tomcat and the Java SDKs are rapidly evolving products. The directions that I provide here apply to installation of the Java SDKs and the Tomcat JSP container that ship with this book. You may discover newer version of these products available from their respective vendors, so remember to always check for updates online. If you use an online update, be sure to refer to those installation directions and release notes to check for differences in the installation procedures compared with what I provide here. Check out the following URLs for more information:

- Navigate to `http://jakarta.apache.org/tomcat/index.html` for the latest information on the Tomcat JSP container.
- Point your browser to `http://java.sun.com/j2se/1.3/` for the latest information on the Java Standard edition SDK.
- For Java Enterprise Edition updates and news, visit `http://java.sun.com/j2ee/`.

Installing the Java 2 Software Development Kit (SDK)

Sun Microsystems has defined several editions of Java targeted for different computing needs. Each edition has a Java Runtime Environment (JRE) for running Java programs and an SDK for developing Java programs. The three editions are

- The **Standard Edition,** which defines the core Java classes. These core classes are used in virtually all Java programs. Even when working with the other editions, this edition needs to be installed to have access to fundamental Java classes.

- The **Enterprise Edition,** which defines Java classes for use with Internet and enterprise computing environments, such as wide area networks (WANS). The Enterprise Edition includes the classes for developing JSPs.
- The **Micro Edition,** which defines Java classes for use with consumer electronics devices, PDAs, and small wireless devices such as hand-held computers and cellular phones.

The solutions in this book require the Standard Edition and Enterprise Edition of the Java 2 SDK.

Back to the basics: Installing the standard SDK

The Standard Edition SDK is the Java software development kit with all the core Java classes for developing Java applications. These Java classes make up a powerful, reusable framework of programs that developers can use to build Java applications for personal computing. When developing software with the Enterprise Edition, which includes JSP development, you also want to install the Standard Edition on your computer.

If you're using a Linux or Unix computer, you need to get the Java 2 SDK from Sun Microsystems directly. This product is available for download on a variety of different operating system environments at Java's official Web site: `java.sun.com`.

Installing the Standard Edition in Windows is very easy. Just follow these simple steps:

1. **Insert the CD included with this book into your computer's CD-ROM drive.**
2. **Double-click the My Computer icon on your desktop and choose your CD-ROM drive.**
3. **Find the file `j2sdk-1_3_1-win.exe` and double-click this file to run the install program.**
4. **If you're installing to the C: drive on your computer, click the Next button to accept all the defaults.**

   Otherwise, pick the drive that you want when prompted and leave all other attributes at their default settings.
5. **Click the Finish button when you reach the last screen to finish the install process.**

Note: Write down the path to the folder where you install the Standard SDK. You need this information in a moment when you configure your computer to run the SDK.

When the install program finishes, the fun begins. Several tools come with the Java SDK that Tomcat and other products need to use. In order to use those tools, you need to know how to find them. To assist with that task, define environment variables in the Windows operating system that tell programs where to look for particular tools.

Setting up environmental variables is different depending on which version of the Windows operating system that you use. To set your environment up, follow one of the sets of instructions that apply to your computer. In this Appendix, I break down the set-up for each software development kit by Windows version: 95, 98, or Me; Windows NT; and Windows 2000.

If you're using an alternate operating system, such as Linux or Unix, be sure to get the installation and setup recommendations from Sun Microsystems when you download the software. On the Web page where you start the download for the Java Standard SDK, look for the INSTALLATION link. Follow this link to get installation instructions for your platform.

Configuring environmental variables for Java Standard SDK on Windows 95, 98, and Me

Setting up environmental variables in Microsoft's personal computing operating systems is a slightly more manual process than it is in Windows NT and 2000, but it's not too difficult. Just follow the steps below and you're home free.

1. **To launch Windows Explorer, choose Start➪Run, type** explorer **in the Open textbox of the Run window, and then click OK.**
2. **Navigate to your C drive (`C:\`), find the `autoexec.bat` file, right-click this file, and choose Edit from the pop-up menu.**

   Windows executes the `autoexec.bat` file automatically when it starts up. Some of the settings in this file are critical for programs to run properly. Before you make changes, make a back-up copy of the `autoexec.bat` file.

   - Select the `autoexec.bat` file, right-click the file, and choose Copy from the pop-up menu.
   - Right-click the background and choose Paste from the pop-up menu.

     This creates a copy of the `autoexec.bat` file on your computer (probably named `Copy of Autoexec.bat`). This copy is your backup.
   - You can rename that file to `autoexec.bat` to restore the original settings.

3. **After you open the `autoexec.bat` file, you find several system variables, which are created using the `SET` DOS command. The syntax is**

```
SET <variable_name>=<value>[;<value2>. . . ]
```

4. **Add a value to the `PATH` variable, which should already be created.**

   Find the line with the `PATH` variable, go to the end of the line, and add the path to the `bin` directory under the top-level directory for the standard SDK that you just installed.

   (On my computer, the path is `C:\jdk1.3.1\bin;`.)

5. **Next you need to add the `CLASSPATH` variable, which may not be created yet.**

   In the time that I've worked with Java, the best practices for use of the `CLASSPATH` variable have changed a lot. Traditionally, the `CLASSPATH` variable was used to identify the location of Java classes and libraries. When you develop JSP applications, you don't really need this feature anymore. Nevertheless, it's customary to define the `CLASSPATH` variable and point it to the current directory. To achieve that, type the following statement in the `autoexec.bat` file:

```
SET CLASSPATH=.
```

6. **Save your changes and exit by choosing File⇨Save and then File⇨Exit.**

For an example of the `autoexec.bat` file with these changes from my computer, see Figure A-1. Note that some variations may exist between this and the `autoexec.bat` file on your computer, but the part relating to the standard SDK should be the same.

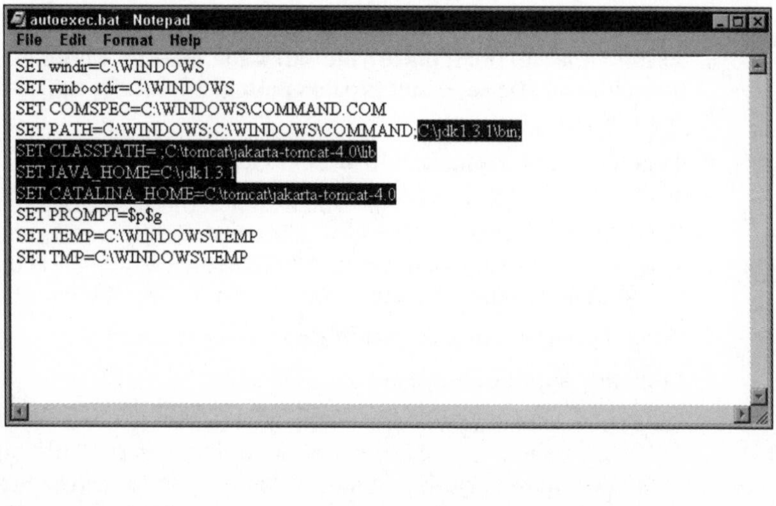

autoexec.bat - Notepad

File Edit Format Help

```
SET windir=C:\WINDOWS
SET winbootdir=C:\WINDOWS
SET COMSPEC=C:\WINDOWS\COMMAND.COM
SET PATH=C:\WINDOWS;C:\WINDOWS\COMMAND;C:\jdk1.3.1\bin;
SET CLASSPATH=.;C:\tomcat\jakarta-tomcat-4.0\lib
SET JAVA_HOME=C:\jdk1.3.1
SET CATALINA_HOME=C:\tomcat\jakarta-tomcat-4.0
SET PROMPT=$p$g
SET TEMP=C:\WINDOWS\TEMP
SET TMP=C:\WINDOWS\TEMP
```

Figure A-1: The autoexec.bat file after you complete SDK configuration.

Configuring environment variables for Java Standard SDK on Windows NT

With Windows NT, setting up environmental variables is made easier. In addition, you don't have to restart your computer for the changes to take effect. Just follow these directions and you'll be in business.

1. **From the Start menu, choose Settings⇨Control Panel.**
2. **Double-click the System icon and choose the Environment tab of the System Properties window that appears.**

   On the Environment tab, you see a pane with a list of System Variables at the top and a pane with User Variables at the bottom. You'll modify the settings in the System Variables pane.
3. **Scroll through the System Variables list to find the** `CLASSPATH` **variable, and then highlight it by clicking the variable name.**

   If the `CLASSPATH` variable doesn't appear in the System Variables list, click the blank line at the bottom of the list of variables and type **CLASSPATH** in the Variable textbox at the bottom of the window.
4. **Place your cursor at the end of any content in the Value textbox, ensuring that the last item in the box has a semicolon (;) typed after it.**
5. **In the Value textbox, type a period (.).**

   If you install the Java 2 Standard SDK in a directory other than the default directory, you have to replace this information with the paths to the corresponding files on your own computer. Be sure to click the Set button when you're finished.
6. **Scroll through the System Variables list, find the** `PATH` **variable, and highlight this variable so that it displays in the Variable textbox at the bottom of the screen.**
7. **In the Value textbox, place your cursor at the end of the existing content, making sure that the last path in the box is followed by a semicolon (;).**
8. **Type** C:\jdk1.3.1\bin; **in the Value textbox.**

   This instruction assumes that you installed the Java 2 Standard SDK to the default installation directory. If you installed to a different directory, you have to type the path to the `bin` directory under the top-level installation directory for your Java Standard SDK installation.
9. **When finished, click the Set button.**
10. **Click the Apply button, and then click OK.**

    See Figure A-2 for an example of the setting for my `CLASSPATH` variable. The value of your `CLASSPATH` variable will be different, but otherwise the dialog box should be similar to what you see in Figure A-2.

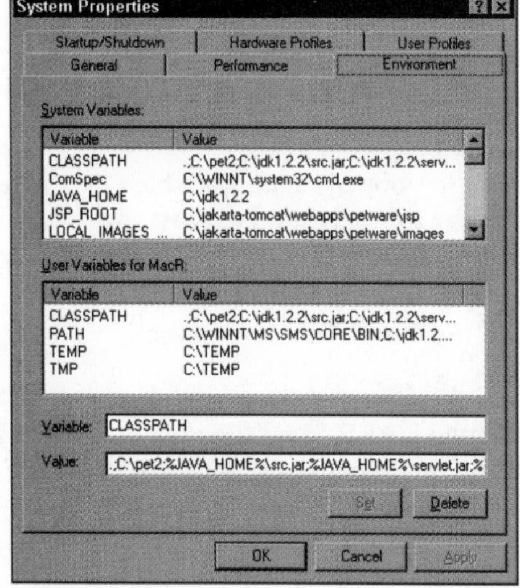

Figure A-2: Setting the CLASSPATH variable in Windows NT 4.0.

Configuring environmental variables for Windows 2000

In a perfect world, you'd have only one way to set up things for all Windows operating systems. Unfortunately, this isn't a perfect world. Thankfully, configuring environmental variables for Windows 2000 computers isn't too much different from Windows NT computers. To configure the environment on your Windows 2000 computer, follow these simple steps:

1. **From the Start menu, choose Settings⇨Control Panel.**
2. **In the Control Panel frame, double-click the System icon and choose the Advanced tab.**
3. **In the Advanced tab, click the Environment Variables button.**

   A small window (`Environment Variables`) opens. Look for two scroll boxes in this window: `User Variables for [your userId here]` and `System Variables`. Make your changes in the System Variables box.
4. **Scroll through the System Variables list and find the variable labeled `CLASSPATH`. When you find it, highlight the variable with your mouse and click the Edit button.**

   If you don't find this `CLASSPATH` variable, click the New button to add the variable.

   In either case, a small window pops up with two text fields: `Variable Name` and `Variable Value`.
5. **If the variable name is empty (because you're creating a new variable), type the value** CLASSPATH **in the field.**

6. **In the Variable Value field, type a period (.).**
7. **Click OK to accept the changes.**

   Figure A-3 shows an example of the CLASSPATH setting on my Windows 2000 computer.

8. **Locate the** `PATH` **variable in your Systems Variables list. When you find it, highlight it and click the Edit button. Position your cursor at the end of the Variable Value textbox and make sure the last character in the field is a semicolon (;).**
9. **Type** C:\jdk1.3.1\bin; **in the Variable Value textbox.**
10. **Click OK to save your changes.**

    Note that the value I supplied is based on the default installation directory. Be sure to use the correct installation directory for your SDK installation.

    After you finish setting the PATH variable, you're finished with the environment configuration for the Java SDK.

11. **Click OK in the Environment Variables window and then click OK in the System Variables window.**

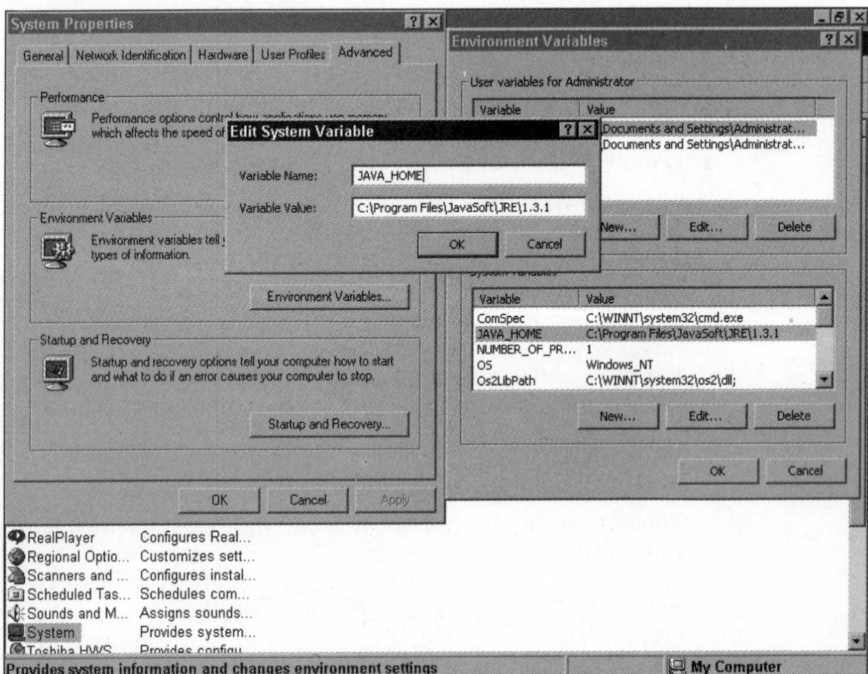

Figure A-3: Setting the CLASSPATH variable on Windows 2000.

The final frontier: Installing the Enterprise Edition SDK

Installing the Enterprise Edition of the Java 2 (J2EE) SDK is very similar to installing the Standard Edition. The Java code that supports creating JSPs is part of the Enterprise Edition of the Java SDK. You can download the latest version of Java 2 Enterprise Edition from the Sun Microsystems Web site at `http://java.sun.com/j2ee`.

The Java 2 Enterprise Edition is not certified as compatible with Windows 95, 98, Me, or other personal editions of the Windows desktop operating system. Regardless, the solutions in this book are all tested using the Windows Me operating system, and they work fine. For real-world solutions, however, I do not recommend using a Windows desktop computer.

At the time of this writing, the Windows XP operating system had not been released. For the latest compatibility information on the Java SDKs and Windows XP, visit the JavaSoft Web site (`java.sun.com`). Also, you can find versions of the J2EE software for different operating systems including Unix and Linux at `http://java.sun.com/j2ee/`.

To install the Java 2 Enterprise Edition SDK on your computer, follow these steps:

1. **Connect to the Internet using your Internet modem software, and start Internet Explorer or Netscape Navigator on your computer.**
2. **After you're on the Web, type the Internet address** java.sun.com/j2ee **in your Web browser's Address box, and press Enter.**

   This takes you to the home page for the Java 2 Enterprise Edition Software. From this home page, you'll see a link to the current Enterprise Edition SDK. Follow this link to bring up the download page for the J2EE download page.

   The download Web page presents different download options, depending on what kind of operating system that you use.
3. **Choose appropriate options for your computer and click the Continue button to move to the next step.**

   The download page presents several options to you. You can decide whether to download the J2EE SDK as one large file or as multiple files appropriate for saving on 3.5-inch floppy disks. You can also choose which computer operating system that you intend to install the J2EE SDK on. The page provides directions to help you decide which options are best for your computer. If your target platform is a Windows 98 or Me computer, choose the Windows NT, 2000 option.

4. **To download the Java 2 Enterprise Edition software, you have to review and accept a license agreement online. To accept the license agreement, click the Accept button.**

   Be sure that you read every word, twice or three times if necessary. Then call your legal team, discuss your options, pay them, offer a prayer to the deity of your choice, and accept the terms to continue. Or you could just accept the agreement in the first place if you want to be hasty.

5. **After accepting the terms of the license agreement, you are offered several download locations to choose from. Pick one and start to download the file.**

   Your browser may query whether you want to run the program or save it to your computer. Choose the Save option and save the file to your desktop. This is a large file, so it may take a while to finish depending on how fast your Internet connection is.

   For Windows computers only: After the download is finished, you see a file called `j2sdkee-1_3_1-win.exe`. (Note: Because Sun periodically provides updates to its software, the file name may vary slightly for updates.)

6. **Double-click this file to start the installation program.**

   For all other operating systems, follow the installation directions provided on the `java.sun.com` Web site.

   I recommend accepting all the defaults in the installation program because it makes it easier to follow the subsequent directions for configuring your computer. If you need to choose an alternative drive, pick the target drive when prompted by the install program. Be sure to write down the installation directory because you need this information later.

After the Java 2 Enterprise Edition (J2EE) finishes installing, you need to configure some system environmental variables, just like you did when installing the Standard Edition.

Configuring environmental variables for Java Enterprise SDK on Windows 95, 98, and Me

After you finish installing the J2EE software, you need to wrap things up by setting up some environmental variables on you computer. This section guides you through the process for Windows 95, 98, and Me computers. If you're using Windows NT or 2000, refer to the next section.

1. **To launch Windows Explorer, choose Start⇨Run, type** explorer **in the Open textbox of the Run window, and then click OK.**
2. **Navigate to `C:\` and find the `autoexec.bat` file.**

3. **Right-click this file and choose Edit from the pop-up menu.**

   You find several system variables in the `autoexec.bat` file, which are created using the `SET` DOS command. The syntax is

   ```
   SET <variable_name>=<value>[;<value2>. . . ]
   ```

   You need to add a value to the `PATH` variable, which should already be created.

4. **Find the line with the `PATH` variable, go to the end of the line, and add the path to the `bin` folder under the top-level folder for the J2EE SDK that you just installed.**

   On my computer, the path is

   ```
   SET PATH=%PATH%C:\ C:\j2sdkee1.3\bin;
   ```

5. **Create the `J2EE_HOME` variable, if it's not already created.**

   In my autoexec.bat file, the `J2EE_HOME` variable looks like this:

   ```
   SET J2EE_HOME=C:\j2sdkee1.3
   ```

   You may note a minor variation with your `autoexec.bat` file depending upon the installation path of your J2EE SDK software.

6. **Create a `JAVA_HOME` variable that points to the top-level installation folder for your J2SE SDK.**

   In my `autoexec.bat` file, the value looks like the following statement:

   ```
   SET JAVA_HOME=C:\jdk1.3.1
   ```

7. **Save your changes and exit by choosing File➪Save and then choosing File➪Exit.**

Configuring environmental variables for Java Enterprise SDK on Windows NT and 2000

Setting up environmental variables for Windows NT and 2000 is much easier than it is for Windows 95, 98, and Me. The following steps guide you through the process.

1. **From the Start menu, choose Settings➪Control Panel.**

2. **Double-click the System icon and choose the Environment Tab from the System Properties window that appears.**

   You see a pane with a list of System Variables at the top and a pane with User Variables at the bottom. You want to modify the settings in the System Variables pane.

3. **Scroll through the System Variables and find the `PATH` variable.**

   When you find this variable, highlight it so that it displays in the Variable textbox at the bottom of the screen.

4. **In the Value textbox, place your cursor at the end of the existing content, ensure the last path in the box is followed by a semicolon (;), and then type** C:\j2sdkee1.3\bin;.

   This instruction assumes that you installed the J2EE SDK to the default installation directory. If you installed to a different directory, you have to type the path to the `bin` directory under the top-level installation directory for your J2EE SDK installation.

5. **When finished, click the Set button.**
6. **Create the** `J2EE_HOME` **variable by scrolling to the bottom of the System Variables list and choosing the blank line.**
7. **In the Variable textbox, type** J2EE_HOME; **in the Value textbox, type** C:\j2sdkee1.3.
8. **Click the Set button to apply the change.**
9. **Set the** `JAVA_HOME` **variable by scrolling to the bottom of the System Variables list and choosing the blank line.**
10. **In the Variable textbox, type** JAVA_HOME; **in the Value textbox, type** C:\jdk1.3.1.
11. **Click the Apply button, and then click OK.**

Refer to Figure A-2 for an example of the setting for my `CLASSPATH` variable. The value of your `CLASSPATH` variable will be different but similar to what you see in that figure.

Installing Java SDK documentation

You install the documentation for the Java 2 Standard separately from the SDK. If you plan to write Java code, this documentation is a very useful source of information about how to make use of the classes in the Standard Application Programming Interface (API) and the Enterprise API for JSP development. To install the Java 2 Standard Edition documentation:

1. **Start your Web browser software and type** http://java.sun.com/j2se/1.3/docs.html **in the Address text box on your browser; then press Enter.**

   This takes you to the page containing the Java 2 Standard Edition documentation.

2. **Scroll down the page until you see the heading** `Download Java 2 SDK 1.3.1 Docs - HTML Format:`**, and then click the Continue button.**

   The HTML page that appears contains the terms and conditions of using Java 2 SDK, Standard Edition, Documentation 1.3.1.

3. **Be sure to read all the fine print, and then click the Accept button at the bottom of the page to continue.**

   You are presented with several sites from which you can download the documentation. Choose an option and press the corresponding button.

4. **From the File Download dialog box that appears with these two options:** `Run this program from its current location` **or** `Save this program to disk`**, choose the second option and click OK.**

   A Save As dialog box appears in which you can select the directory on your computer where you want to save the file.

5. **Choose to save the file on your desktop by clicking the View Desktop button to the right of the Save In drop-down list; then click the Save button to continue.**

6. **Find the file** `j2sdk-1_3_1-doc.zip` **and double-click it to launch the archive file viewer.**

   The contents of this `.zip` file should be unpacked in the top-level directory of your Java 2 Standard Edition directory. Unpacking this file creates a directory called `DOC`.

7. **Inside the** `DOC` **directory, find the** `API` **directory. Double-click the** `API` **directory and then double-click the** `index.html` **file.**

   This is the main page for the Standard SDK documentation, which is all based in HTML.

Installing a Tomcat JSP Container

The Tomcat JSP Container is an open source development project of the Apache Software Foundation, and the official reference implementation of JavaServer Page container technology. A *JSP container* is a program that runs JSPs and serves the JSP content to the Internet. As the official reference implementation, Tomcat implements all the features required to make a JSP container conform to the JSP specification. In consequence, Tomcat often leads other commercially developed JSP containers in implementing JSP features.

Install Tomcat version 4.0, the latest production release at the time of this writing, from the CD in the back of this book. Tomcat installation files are also available over the Internet from the Apache Software Foundation at `jakarta.apache.org/tomcat/index.html`. If you're installing Tomcat on a non-Windows computer, you need to get an installation file from the Tomcat Web site.

Tomcat can be installed as a stand-alone program (referred to as a *Type 1 container*), or it can be integrated with the Apache Web Server. The installation directions that I provide in this book are sufficient to install Tomcat as a stand-alone program.

The stand-alone solution is sufficient for personal use, but if you want to implement a production system using Tomcat, I recommend installing Apache Web Server and Tomcat together. You can get instructions for installing both programs and configuring them to work together at

```
jakarta.apache.org/
```

The user guide documentation at this site is a valuable resource that provides information on all kinds of Tomcat configuration issues. Be sure to take a look.

Back in the good old days, installing Tomcat required a lot of complicated steps. This book includes a simple install program that handles all those steps for you.

To install Tomcat as a stand-alone JSP container:

1. **Insert the CD included with this book into your CD-ROM drive.**
2. **Double-click the My Computer icon on your desktop and choose your CD-ROM drive.**
3. **Find the file `jakarta-tomcat-4.0.exe` and double-click it to launch the installation wizard for Tomcat.**
4. **Follow the directions in the installation wizard to complete the installation.**

Before you install Tomcat, be sure you have the Java 2 SDK version 1.3 installed on your computer.

Verifying Successful Configuration

After you have all the Java SDKs and Tomcat installed, verify that everything works properly. Testing these products is pretty easy. To get started, I explain how to start and stop Tomcat, which you'll need to do a lot when developing JSP programs. Then I tell you how to use the sample JSP programs provided with Tomcat to verify that your program is set up properly.

Starting and stopping Tomcat

The Tomcat JSP container comes with a set of command line utilities used to start and stop the Tomcat service. *Command line utilities* are programs that are run in a command window, such as DOS. With Windows, you can run these programs either by double-clicking them or by executing them from an MS-DOS window. The utilities for starting and stopping Tomcat are `startup.bat` and `shutdown.bat`.

Double-clicking to start `startup.bat` and `shutdown.bat` is acceptable for normal use, but when you're troubleshooting, I recommend that you run them from an MS-DOS window. If you run them from the MS-DOS window and encounter a problem, you can see what the error message is. If you start them by double-clicking and encounter a problem, the service flashes on and off, and you won't be able to get the error message.

To run `startup.bat` and `shutdown.bat` from an MS-DOS window:

1. **From the Start menu, choose Run, and type** command **in the Open textbox.**
2. **Click OK.**
3. **Change directories to the `bin` directory under your Tomcat top-level directory.**

   In my computer, I type **CD C:\tomcat\jakarta-tomcat-4.0\bin** to get to the right directory. The path you type may be different depending on where you installed Tomcat.
4. **From the `bin` directory, type** startup.bat **and press Enter.**

   The batch file should print some text in the command window and then launch a new DOS window, similar to what you see in Figure A-4. This window should remain open until you shut down Tomcat.
5. **To shut down Tomcat, switch to the original DOS window, and type** shutdown.bat.

   The second DOS window should close after the `shutdown.bat` program executes. If these steps worked okay, you're ready to proceed to the next section. If not, skip down to the upcoming section "Troubleshooting your installation."

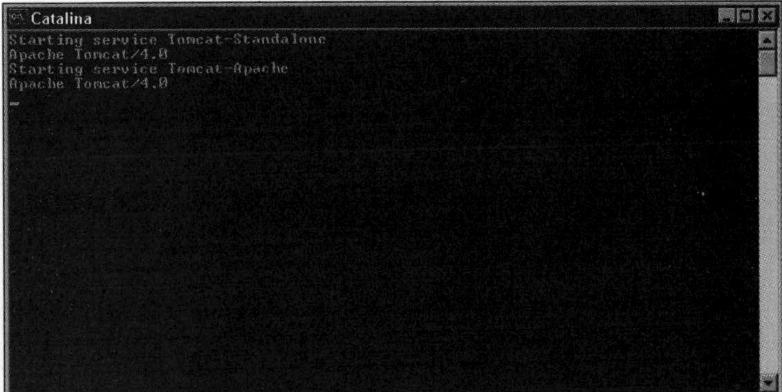

Figure A-4: Tomcat running in an MS-DOS command window.

Although I show you how to start these programs from MS-DOS, that's not necessary all the time. Because you will execute these programs often, I recommend making shortcuts to them on your desktop or taskbar. In fact, with the new install program, it is possible to start Tomcat as a Windows service, and to create a program group for Tomcat in the Start menu. These options are presented in the installation wizard.

Running the sample JSP applications

To support the troubleshooting process, and to help you learn about JSP development, Tomcat ships with several sample JSP applications. If you can run these JSP applications, you know that Tomcat is working properly. To run the sample applications, you'll need to know the name of your computer. To find this name, perform the following steps:

1. **From the Start menu, choose Settings⇨Control Panel.**
2. **Double-click the Network Icon and choose the Identification tab from the Network window that appears.**
3. **Write down the text that you see in the** `Computer Name` **text field.**

Now, start Tomcat, following the first three steps in the earlier section "Starting and stopping Tomcat." To run the sample programs:

1. **Launch your browser.**
2. **In your browser's Address textbox, type** http://<computer_name>:8080 **where** `<computer_name>` **is the name of your computer.**

   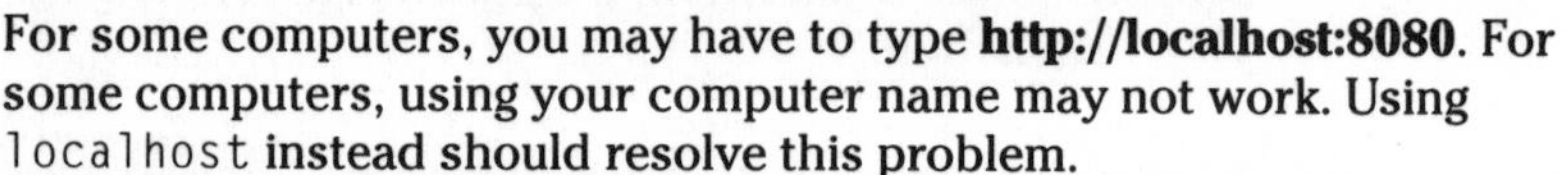

   For some computers, you may have to type **http://localhost:8080**. For some computers, using your computer name may not work. Using `localhost` instead should resolve this problem.

3. **Press Enter.**

   You should see a page that reads `Tomcat Version 4.0` at the top. Scanning down this page, you should see two hyperlinks: one to JSP Examples and one to Servlet Examples.
4. **Follow the link to JSP Examples.**

   This link takes you to an index page with several JSP programs.
5. **Choose any program and follow the Execute link.**

   If the program runs, Tomcat works! (Unfortunately, that means I'm the only one left to blame if the JSP programs you write don't work.) Note that the first time when you run a JSP, it may take a while to load, but that speed should improve after your initial run.

Troubleshooting your installation

In a perfect world, all these steps will work flawlessly, and you won't have any problems. But we all know how that goes . . . sigh. In anticipation of when you might encounter a problem, here are a few tips on how to troubleshoot your installation.

Problem: When I try to start Tomcat, I get a message stating `Out of environment space`, and Tomcat doesn't start.

Solution: This message means that you need more memory allocated to your MS-DOS session. Changing the memory settings can be kind of tricky, but if you follow these steps, you should be okay.

1. **From the taskbar, choose Start⇨Run and type** explorer **in the Open textbox of the Run dialog box.**
2. **Click OK.**

   This should launch Windows Explorer.
3. **Navigate to the** `C:\Windows` **directory and scroll through the file list until you see the file** `command.com`**.**
4. **Right-click the file and choose Properties from the pop-up menu.**
5. **In the Properties dialog box that appears, click the Memory tab.**
   - In the Conventional Memory section, choose 640 from the Total drop-down list. In that same area, choose 1024 from the drop-down list for Initial Environment.
   - In the Extended (XMS) Memory section, choose 1024 from the Total drop-down list.
   - Finally, choose 1024 from the Total drop-down menu of the MS-DOS Protected-Mode (DPMI) Memory section.
6. **Click the Apply button and then click OK to close the Properties dialog box.**

Problem: When I try to start Tomcat, I get an error message reading `You must set JAVA_HOME to point at your Java Development Kit installation.`

Solution: The `JAVA_HOME` environmental variable is not defined or is misspelled. Review the instructions for setting up the Tomcat environment in the earlier section "Installing a Tomcat JSP Container." Ensure that you have created the `JAVA_HOME` variable and that the variable and contents are not misspelled. Verify that the content of the `JAVA_HOME` directory is the path to the top-level directory of your Java Standard SDK installation. After you're satisfied that all these values are correct, save your settings. If you're using a desktop version of Windows (such as Windows 95, 98, or Me), restart your computer to make sure that the settings take effect.

Installing the MySQL Database

In Chapters 10 and 11 of this book, I address the mechanics of using a database with JSP applications. The chapters use a database created in the MySQL database, which is a publicly licensed database engine. You can use any database that you like to perform these examples, but I include a copy of the MySQL database on the CD at the back of this book for your convenience. (Swell guy that I am. . . .)

If you choose to use a different database engine, you can use the `database.sql` script file to create the database that I use in the examples in the back of this book. The script file includes all the ANSI-standard SQL statements to create and populate the data of the database used for Chapters 10 and 11. Note that some minor modifications may be necessary to run this script file in a database other than MySQL. For further information, see the upcoming section, "Creating and populating the database."

Running the MySQL install program

The MySQL database can be used with virtually all the major operating systems. The installation file that I include with this book's companion CD works with all Windows operating systems. The following instructions are for installations on Windows operating systems. For installation files and instructions for installing MySQL on other operating systems, visit the MySQL Web site at `www.mysql.com`.

Because MySQL is a relatively young database, it hasn't fully implemented all the features that you might expect from a mature database engine. In addition, the creators of MySQL have some different notions on transaction management theory than those dictated in the SQL specification. Thus, although it's adequate for the examples in this book, you may not want to use this database if you need the advanced capabilities of more mature database products. For more information on forthcoming features of MySQL, see the MySQL Reference manual, which is included in the installation of the MySQL database in the `docs` directory.

To install MySQL on your computer, follow these steps:

1. **Insert the CD that comes with this book into your CD-ROM drive.**
2. **Launch Windows Explorer by choosing Run from the Start menu, type** explorer **in the Open text field, and then press Enter.**
3. **From the Exploring window that opens, choose your CD-ROM drive, and locate the file** `mysql-3_23_38-win.zip` **on the CD.**

4. **Copy this file to the desktop of your computer by highlighting it with your mouse and dragging it to the desktop icon while holding your left mouse button down.**

   When the file is finished copying, close Windows Explorer by clicking the X button in the upper-right corner of the screen.

5. **Close all the open programs on your computer and take a look at the desktop.**

   You should see an icon for the `mysql-3_23_38-win.zip` file.

6. **Double-click this file to launch the ZIP file viewer and see the contents.**

   In the ZIP file viewer, you should see a file called `setup.exe`.

7. **Double-click the `setup.exe` file to start the installation process.**

   Follow the instructions on the installation program until you reach the screen titled `Setup Type`.

8. **Choose the Typical set-up option and click the Next button.**

   The installer installs MySQL on your computer.

Configuring MySQL for use

Before you use MySQL for the first time, you need to perform some basic configuration steps. These steps identify you as the administrator of the MySQL database, giving you full control of the database engine so that you can create and maintain database files. Configuring MySQL for the first use is very simple.

1. **Launch Windows Explorer by choosing Run from the Start menu, typing** explorer **in the Open text field, and then pressing Enter.**

2. **In the Exploring window that opens, navigate to the directory** `C:\mysql\bin`.

3. **Double-click the `winmysqladmin.exe` file.**

   This launches the administration program for Windows computers. If this is the first time that you've used MySQL on this computer, the program starts a program called WinAdminMySQL Quick Setup.

4. **Type in the username and password that you want to use to administer your MySQL database with and then click OK.**

   Don't forget your username and password; you need them to maintain the MySQL database.

That's all you need to do to get started with MySQL. To work with the database administration tool in the future, look for the traffic light located on the Taskbar in the lower-right corner of your screen. Click this traffic light and choose the Show Me option to display the MySQL administration console.

When you install MySQL, it places an icon in the `Startup` folder of your computer. Every time that you restart your computer, the MySQL database automatically starts. When the database starts, the MySQL administration console displays briefly on your computer desktop before disappearing.

Creating and populating the database

The MySQL ships with a character-based client tool called `mysql.exe`. You use the client tool to write SQL statements that are executed in the MySQL database. You can also run batch files that contain a number of SQL statements using the `mysql.exe` client tool.

On this book's CD, I include a batch file called `database.sql` that contains all the statements necessary to create the database that I use in Chapters 10 and 11 of this book. To build that database, follow these steps. To use this batch file, you have to perform a couple of minor changes as I outline below.

1. **Insert the CD included with this book into your computer's CD-ROM drive.**
2. **Launch Windows Explorer by choosing Run from the Start menu, typing** explorer **in the Open text field, and then pressing Enter.**
3. **From the Explorer window that opens, view the contents of the CD and find the file labeled** `database.sql`**.**
4. **Right-click this file and choose the Open With option from the pop-up menu.**

   A window opens displaying a number of different programs on your computer.
5. **Choose the Notepad icon and click OK.**

   The contents of the `database.sql` file are displayed in the Notepad text editor.

   The first line of this program contains the statement `DROP DATABASE dummy_orders;`.
6. **If this is the first time that you're running this program, you need to make this statement into a comment by placing a # character in front of it.**

   Note: If you're creating the `dummy_orders` database in another database engine such as SQL*Server or Oracle, you have to change all the # characters to a double dash character (`--`). ANSI standard comments in SQL begin with two dashes, but MySQL comments begin with a pound sign (#).

   The third statement in the `database.sql` file reads `GRANT ALL ON dummy_orders TO macr`. This statement gives full control of the `dummy_orders` database to the user with the username `macr` (that's me).

7. **For your database, replace** `macr` **with your own username.**
8. **When finished with these changes, choose Save As from the file menu, navigate to the folder** `c:\mysql\bin`**, and click the Save button.**

If you're using a database other than the MySQL database, you can still use the statements in this script file to create the database. Because of some possible differences between the ways that your database and the MySQL database works, review the SQL statements in the file and make sure that they're valid for your database. In particular, note that the `CREATE TABLE` statements include an `AUTO_INCREMENT` keyword that's specific to the MySQL database. You must remove this keyword from all the statements before you can execute them.

For the MySQL database, after you perform the modifications that I identify in the previous set of steps, follow these instructions to build the database in your MySQL installation.

1. **Choose Run from the Start menu, type** command **in the Open text field, and press Enter.**

   This should launch an MS-DOS window on your computer.
2. **Navigate to the root of the C: drive.**
3. **Change directories to the** `c:\mysql\bin directory`**, type the command** mysql < database.sql **at the command prompt, and press Enter.**

   If everything works perfectly (and there's no reason that it shouldn't) your computer will run the `database.sql` script and create the `dummy_orders` database in your MySQL installation. If there are any problems, the `mysql.exe` program displays an error message. Otherwise, the command executes with no messages.

To verify that everything went as planned, start the MySQL admin tool by clicking the traffic light icon on your task bar and choosing the Show Me option from the pop-up menu. In the Admin tool, choose the Databases tab. You should see a field in the upper-right corner of the databases tab labeled `Databases`. In this tab, you see a database icon labeled `dummy_orders`. If it's there, everything worked and you're off to the races!

Picking an Editor

Editors can make your life a lot easier when it comes to authoring JSPs. Of course, you can write a JSP in Notepad. But who wants to author Web pages in Notepad when you have so many more cool options at your disposal with Web page editors? Web page editors offer several features that are important to you as a Web page author, including:

- **Color-coded errors:** Most editors use syntax color-coding that helps you read the Web code you write, giving you a clear visual cue if you misspell a keyword.
- **Layout assistance:** A lot of editors have code beautification features that help lay out the content that you write to make it easier to read.
- **Parallel code/creation viewing:** Some editors give you the ability to look at the code that you write and then view the Web page in a separate window.
- **HTML configuration help:** Some editors give you access to property dialog boxes that allow you to configure HTML elements without having to know all the keywords of the HTML syntax.
- **HTML insertion help:** Several editors include menus or wizards that allow you to insert HTML elements from a list.

These features have one simple purpose: to make your life easier. Take advantage of them! On the CD that comes with this book, I include an evaluation copy of Dreamweaver UltraDev 4, which is a Web page and JSP authoring tool distributed by Macromedia (`www.macromedia.com`). Feel free to install this editor, or you can browse the Internet for other Web page editors that suit your needs. If you choose to use a different editor, be sure that it supports JSP authoring.

When it comes to Java editors, look for the features that I mention earlier in this section. If you're already writing Java code, you probably already have a Java editor. None of the programs in this book require a Java editor, and I show you how to create your programs using the simple tools of Notepad and a DOS window. Nevertheless, if you don't have an editor, I highly recommend getting one.

My preferred Java editor is JBuilder 5.0, developed by Borland Inprise Corp (`www.borland.com/jbuilder/`). Unfortunately, I wasn't able to include a copy of this software on the CD. But you can download it from the Internet, by navigating to the aforementioned Web site.

Appendix B

About the CD

With the price of technical references what they are these days, my goal is to give you as much bang for your buck as possible. That's why I load the CD that comes with this book with great software and several working JavaServer Pages (JSPs), JavaScript, and Java examples. Here's a preview of the great titles that you'll find on this CD:

- A trial version of Dreamweaver UltraDev Version 4 by Macromedia. This application is a full-featured Web page authoring tool, and you can use it to create JSPs, too!
- An evaluation version of HomeSite Version 4.5.2 from Macromedia. This is another great Web page authoring tool. Compare this with UltraDev and pick the one you like best.
- A freeware version of Sun's Java 2 Software Development Kit (SDK) Standard Edition, Version 1.3 for Windows.
- The Tomcat JSP container. You need a JSP container to run JSPs. This one, from the Apache Software Foundation, is open source.
- The open-sourced version of Struts custom tag library, also from the Apache Software Foundation. This custom tag library enables you to implement a lot of cool features with JSPs.
- The GNU-licensed MySQL Database version 3.23. This open-source database is attracting a lot of attention.
- A freeware version of Adobe Acrobat Reader Version 5.0.
- Forte for Java, release 2.0, Community edition.
- Java 2 SDK Standard Edition, version 1.3, for Windows.
- Extra, extra, bonus chapters on the CD. Included on the CD is a complete example of a JSP application, including JSPs, JavaBeans, and database interaction with Java Database Connectivity (JDBC). You'll also find a brief guide to the SQL language and an overview of the Java language. Last but not least, you'll find coverage on filters and how to create custom tag libraries.
- Tons of sample JSPs and Java source code. Source files are located in folders according to the chapter in which they appear in the book.

System Requirements

Make sure that your computer meets the minimum system requirements listed below. If your computer doesn't match up to most of these requirements, you may have problems using the contents of the CD.

- A PC with a Pentium II or faster processor, or a Mac OS computer with a G3 or faster processor.
- Microsoft Windows 98, 2000, Me, or XP is required for most of the software on this CD. The source code can be read with all Windows versions, or Mac OS system software 7.6.6 or later.
- At least 128MB of total RAM installed on your computer. Many of the software titles on this CD are RAM intensive. For best performance, we recommend that PCs have 256MB of total RAM.
- A CD-ROM drive.
- A sound card for PCs. (Mac OS computers have built-in sound support.)
- A monitor capable of displaying at least 256 colors or grayscale.
- A modem with a speed of at least 14.4 Kbps.

If you need more information on the basics, check out these books published by Hungry Minds, Inc.: *PCs For Dummies,* by Dan Gookin; *Macs For Dummies* and *iMacs For Dummies,* both by David Pogue; and *Windows 95 For Dummies, Windows 98 For Dummies, Windows 2000 Professional For Dummies, Microsoft Windows Me Millennium Edition For Dummies,* and *Windows XP For Dummies,* all by Andy Rathbone.

Using the CD with Microsoft Windows

To install the items from the CD to your hard drive, follow these steps.

1. **Insert the CD into your computer's CD-ROM drive.**
2. **Choose Start⇨Run.**
3. **In the dialog box that appears, type** D:\HMI.EXE.

   Replace *D* with the proper drive letter if your CD-ROM drive uses a different letter. (If you don't know the letter, see how your CD-ROM drive is listed under My Computer.)
4. **Click OK.**

   A license agreement window appears.

5. **Read through the license agreement, nod your head, and then click the Accept button if you want to use the CD — after you click Accept, you'll never be bothered by the License Agreement window again.**

   The CD interface Welcome screen appears. The interface is a little program that shows you what's on the CD and coordinates installing the programs and running the demos. The interface basically enables you to click a button or two to make things happen.

6. **Click anywhere on the Welcome screen to enter the interface.**

   Now you are getting to the action. This next screen lists categories for the software on the CD.

7. **To view the items within a category, just click the category's name.**

   A list of programs in the category appears.

8. **For more information about a program, click the program's name.**

   Be sure to read the information that appears. Sometimes a program has it's own system requirements or requires you to do a few tricks on your computer before you can install or run the program, and this screen tells you what you might need to do, if necessary.

9. **If you don't want to install the program, click the Back button to return to the previous screen.**

   You can always return to the previous screen by clicking the Back button. This feature allows you to browse the different categories and products and decide what you want to install.

10. **To install a program, click the appropriate Install button.**

    The CD interface drops to the background while the CD installs the program you chose.

11. **To install other items, repeat Steps 7–10.**

12. **When you've finished installing programs, click the Quit button to close the interface.**

You can eject the CD now. Carefully place it back in the plastic jacket of the book for safekeeping.

Using the CD with Mac OS

To install the items from the CD to your hard drive, follow these steps.

1. **Insert the CD into your computer's CD-ROM drive.**

   In a moment, an icon representing the CD that you just inserted appears on your Mac desktop. Chances are that the icon looks like a CD-ROM.

2. **Double-click the CD icon to show the CD's contents.**
3. **Double-click the License Agreement icon.**

   This is the license that you are agreeing to by using the CD. You can close this window once you've looked over the agreement.
4. **Double-click the Read Me First icon.**

   The Read Me First text file contains information about the CD's programs and any last-minute instructions you may need in order to correctly install them.
5. **To install most programs, open the program folder and double-click the icon called Install or Installer.**

   Sometimes the installers are actually self-extracting archives (which just means that the program files have been bundled up into an archive), and this self-extractor unbundles the files and places them on your hard drive. This kind of program is often called a `.sea`. Double click anything with `.sea` in the title, and it will run just like an installer.
6. **Some programs don't come with installers. For those, just drag the program's folder from the CD window and drop it on your hard drive icon.**

What You'll Find

Here's a summary of the software on this CD arranged by category. If you use Windows, the CD interface helps you install software easily. If you use a Mac OS computer, you can use the Mac interface to quickly install the programs.

Shareware programs are fully functional, free, trial versions of copyrighted programs. If you like particular programs, register with their authors for a nominal fee and receive licenses, enhanced versions, and technical support. *Freeware programs* are free, copyrighted games, applications, and utilities. You can copy them to as many PCs as you like — for free — but they offer no technical support. *GNU software* is governed by its own license, which is included inside the folder of the GNU software. There are no restrictions on distribution of GNU software. See the GNU license at the root of the CD for more details. *Trial, demo,* or *evaluation* versions of software are usually limited either by time or functionality (such as not letting you save a project after you create it).

System requirements vary drastically, depending on the intended use of the software. If you intent to serve JSPs on a high-volume Web site, congratulations! JSP technology is an excellent choice. But don't consider these system requirements to be appropriate for your Web server. The recommendations below are appropriate for desktop computers and small-scale personal Web sites only.

JSP and Web page authoring tools

Dreamweaver UltraDev, version 4.0 from Macromedia

For Windows98/2000/Me/XP and Mac. Trial version. Dreamweaver UltraDev is a full-featured Web page authoring tool that helps you create great HyperText Markup Language (HTML) pages. You can use this tool to author standard HTML pages, JavaScript, and JSPs. The tool allows you to preview your work while you edit and it identifies syntax problems automatically. This is my JSP editor of choice. The trial license is good for 30 days.

System requirements:

- Intel Pentium processor or equivalent 166+ MHz
- 170MB of available disk space
- 64MB of memory
- 256-color monitor capable of 800 x 600 resolution

HomeSite, version 4.5 from Allaire

For Windows 98/2000/Me/XP. Evaluation version. HomeSite is a leading HTML authoring tool and supports the development of JSPs and JavaScript as well. This tool is known for its excellent code editor.

System requirements:

- Pentium-compatible processor
- 64MB of memory (128MB is suggested)
- 25MB of available disk space (for installation)
- 256-color monitor capable of 800 x 600 resolution

Document reader software

Acrobat Reader 5.0 from Adobe

For Windows 98/2000/Me/XP and Mac. Freeware. Acrobat Reader is the de facto standard for cross-platform, secure documents. You can use this software to read some of the source files that I provide.

System requirements:

- 64MB of memory
- 24MB available disk space

- 70MB of disk space for Asian fonts (optional)
- Intel Pentium processor or equivalent

Database products

MySQL version 3.23 from MySQL AB

For Windows 98/2000/Me/XP. GNU Public License. MySQL has rapidly become a popular database for those seeking a low-cost, high-performance system for small- to mid-sized databases. This book uses MySQL for illustrating database interaction in JSP programs. A sample database is provided with the book.

System requirements:

- Pentium-compatible processor
- 30MB of disk space (for installation)

I could not find specific memory requirements for the MySQL database; however, I recommend that your computer has at least 128MB of memory. It will probably run on less, but with this type of software, more memory is generally better. I use 256MB in my configuration and I'm satisfied with the performance.

I provide installation and configuration instructions for MySQL in Appendix A.

JDBC Driver for MySQL by Mark Mathews

For all platforms. GNU Software. This JDBC driver is developed under the GNU-GPL licensing agreement, which means that it's a publicly licensed extension to the SQL platform. You can use this JDBC driver to connect to your SQL database from JSP applications to execute SQL statements. Because it's publicly licensed, you can contribute your own extensions to the driver. If you're interested, Mark Mathews has provided this driver to the world at no charge — but he does accept donations. If you're interested in helping out a starving programmer, find more information on how to send him your contribution by visiting his product page on the Internet at SourceForge (`mmmysql.sourceforge.net`).

Java and JSP products

Java Software Development Kit (SDK), Standard Edition 1.3 for Windows from Sun Microsystems

For Windows98/2000/Me/XP. Freeware. The Standard Edition provides you with the basic classes that make up the standard Java Application Programming Interface (API). If you're developing Java classes to run with your JSP pages, you need this software.

System requirements:

- Intel Pentium II or equivalent processor 166+ MHz
- 48MB RAM
- 70MB of disk space

Installation and configuration instructions for the Standard Edition Java SDK are provided in Appendix A.

Tomcat JSP container, Version 4.0 by the Apache Software Foundation

For Windows 98/2000/Me/XP. Open source. The Tomcat JSP container is a special program that runs JSPs and Java servlet programs. This reference product represents the standard implementation of JSP containers, including all required features for JSP containers fully compliant to the JSP specification.

Although I couldn't find any published system requirements for this software, my recommendation is a Pentium II processor, 166 MHz or better. I also recommend at least 128MB of memory, preferably 256MB or better if you can swing it. Ultimately, the requirements for this software are dependent upon how you need to use it. If you intend to use Tomcat for an Internet Web server on a high-traffic site, you'll need to do a lot better than the recommendations here. But if you're just using it to practice on your personal computer, 128MB is fine.

Installation and configuration instructions for Tomcat are available in Appendix A.

Struts custom tag library, Version 1.0 from the Apache Software Foundation

For all platforms that support Java. Open source. Struts is a special library of JSP custom tags that extends the standard functionality available to JSP programs. This increases the flexibility of JSPs and makes creating JSPs easier for Web developers who have limited Java experience. That doesn't mean that Struts is for weenies; it's an excellent way to improve the maintainability of your JSP code.

To run the Struts custom tag library, you must have a JSP container that supports custom tag libraries (Tomcat, for example).

Forte for Java, Version 2.0 Community Edition from Sun MicroSystems

For Windows 98/Me, and Windows 2000 with Service Pack 2 or greater. Commercial version. This Java IDE from Sun MicroSystems was a late arrival to the Java IDE market, but it's rapidly catching up with its competitors. The good news is it includes basic support for building JSPs, as well as support for all the standard edition Java classes that you need to create. If you want to build more full-featured enterprise applications such as applications that include Enterprise JavaBeans, you'll need to upgrade to the Forte for Java Enterprise Edition.

System requirements for Windows operating systems:

- Intel Pentium II or equivalent processor 350+ MHz (Pentium III 450 MHz processor recommended)
- 128MB RAM minimum (256MB recommended)
- 128MB swap file size (256MB recommended)

  A *swap file* is space reserved on your computer's hard driver that a program can use as extra memory, kind of like RAM.

- 110MB of disk space (for installation)
- Java 2 Standard Edition (J2SE), Version 1.3.1, which is supplied on the CD

Author's sample code

All the examples in the book are included on the CD. I've done my best to give a lot of examples illustrating all aspects of JSP technology and associated technologies that you'll use when you develop JSPs. Included are JSPs, JavaScript samples, and Java code samples. You'll also find the Acme Sales Web site, which is a complete, fully functional JSP application — including database interaction — used to illustrate JSPs in action. My examples are sorted by chapter, with the source code from each chapter located in a corresponding folder on the CD.

If You've Got Problems (Of the CD Kind)

I tried my best to compile programs that work on most computers with the minimum system requirements. Alas, your computer may differ, and some programs may not work properly for some reason.

The two likeliest problems are that you don't have enough memory (RAM) for the programs you want to use, or you have other programs running that are affecting installation or running of a program. If you get error messages such as `Not enough memory` or `Setup cannot continue`, try one or more of these methods and then try using the software again:

- **Turn off any anti-virus software that you have on your computer.** Installers sometimes mimic virus activity and may make your computer incorrectly believe that it's being infected by a virus.
- **Close all running programs.** The more programs you're running, the less memory is available to other programs. Installers also typically update files and programs; if you keep other programs running, installation may not work properly.
- **In Windows, close the CD interface and run demos or installations directly from Windows Explorer.** The interface itself can tie up system memory, or even conflict with certain kinds of interactive demos. Use Windows Explorer to browse the files on the CD and launch installers or demos.
- **Have your local computer store add more RAM to your computer.** This is, admittedly, a drastic and somewhat expensive step. However, if you have a Windows 95 PC or a Mac OS computer with a PowerPC chip, adding more memory can really help the speed of your computer and enable more programs to run at the same time.

If you still have trouble installing the items from the CD, please call the Hungry Minds Customer Service phone number: 800-762-2974 (outside the U.S.: 317-572-3994).

Index

• Symbols •

• A •

• B •

• D •

• E •

• J-K •

• L •

• M •

• N •

• P •

• Q-R •

• S •

• T •

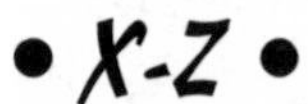
• X-Z •

Notes

Notes

Notes

Installation Instructions

Using the CD with Microsoft Windows

To install the items from the CD to your hard drive, follow these steps.

1. **Insert the CD into your computer's CD-ROM drive.**
2. **Choose Start⇨Run.**
3. **In the dialog box that appears, type** D:\HMI.EXE.

   Replace *D* with the proper drive letter if your CD-ROM drive uses a different letter. (If you don't know the letter, see how your CD-ROM drive is listed under My Computer in Windows 98/NT.)
4. **Click OK.**

   A license agreement window appears.
5. **Read through the license agreement, nod your head, and then click the Accept button if you want to use the CD — after you click Accept, you'll never be bothered by the License Agreement window again.**
6. **Click anywhere on the Welcome screen to enter the interface.**
7. **To view the items within a category, just click the category's name.**
8. **For more information about a program, click the program's name.**
9. **If you don't want to install the program, click the Go Back button to return to the previous screen.**
10. **To install a program, click the appropriate Install button.**
11. **To install other items, repeat Steps 7–10.**
12. **When you've finished installing programs, click the Quit button to close the interface.**

For installation instructions for Mac users, please see the "About the CD" appendix.

Hungry Minds, Inc. End-User License Agreement

READ THIS. You should carefully read these terms and conditions before opening the software packet(s) included with this book ("Book"). This is a license agreement ("Agreement") between you and Hungry Minds, Inc. ("HMI"). By opening the accompanying software packet(s), you acknowledge that you have read and accept the following terms and conditions. If you do not agree and do not want to be bound by such terms and conditions, promptly return the Book and the unopened software packet(s) to the place you obtained them for a full refund.

1. **License Grant.** HMI grants to you (either an individual or entity) a nonexclusive license to use one copy of the enclosed software program(s) (collectively, the "Software") solely for your own personal or business purposes on a single computer (whether a standard computer or a workstation component of a multi-user network). The Software is in use on a computer when it is loaded into temporary memory (RAM) or installed into permanent memory (hard disk, CD-ROM, or other storage device). HMI reserves all rights not expressly granted herein.

2. **Ownership.** HMI is the owner of all right, title, and interest, including copyright, in and to the compilation of the Software recorded on the disk(s) or CD-ROM ("Software Media"). Copyright to the individual programs recorded on the Software Media is owned by the author or other authorized copyright owner of each program. Ownership of the Software and all proprietary rights relating thereto remain with HMI and its licensers.

3. **Restrictions On Use and Transfer.**

   (a) You may only (i) make one copy of the Software for backup or archival purposes, or (ii) transfer the Software to a single hard disk, provided that you keep the original for backup or archival purposes. You may not (i) rent or lease the Software, (ii) copy or reproduce the Software through a LAN or other network system or through any computer subscriber system or bulletin-board system, or (iii) modify, adapt, or create derivative works based on the Software.

   (b) You may not reverse engineer, decompile, or disassemble the Software. You may transfer the Software and user documentation on a permanent basis, provided that the transferee agrees to accept the terms and conditions of this Agreement and you retain no copies. If the Software is an update or has been updated, any transfer must include the most recent update and all prior versions.

4. **Restrictions on Use of Individual Programs.** You must follow the individual requirements and restrictions detailed for each individual program in Appendix C of this Book. These limitations are also contained in the individual license agreements recorded on the Software Media. These limitations may include a requirement that after using the program for a specified period of time, the user must pay a registration fee or discontinue use. By opening the Software packet(s), you will be agreeing to abide by the licenses and restrictions for these individual programs that are detailed in Appendix C and on the Software Media. None of the material on this Software Media or listed in this Book may ever be redistributed, in original or modified form, for commercial purposes.

5. **Limited Warranty.**

   (a) HMI warrants that the Software and Software Media are free from defects in materials and workmanship under normal use for a period of sixty (60) days from the date of purchase of this Book. If HMI receives notification within the warranty period of defects in materials or workmanship, HMI will replace the defective Software Media.

   (b) **HMI AND THE AUTHOR OF THE BOOK DISCLAIM ALL OTHER WARRANTIES, EXPRESS OR IMPLIED, INCLUDING WITHOUT LIMITATION IMPLIED WARRANTIES OF MERCHANTABILITY AND FITNESS FOR A PARTICULAR PURPOSE, WITH RESPECT TO THE SOFTWARE, THE PROGRAMS, THE SOURCE CODE CONTAINED THEREIN, AND/OR THE TECHNIQUES DESCRIBED IN THIS BOOK. HMI DOES NOT WARRANT THAT THE FUNCTIONS CONTAINED IN THE SOFTWARE WILL MEET YOUR REQUIREMENTS OR THAT THE OPERATION OF THE SOFTWARE WILL BE ERROR FREE.**

   (c) This limited warranty gives you specific legal rights, and you may have other rights that vary from jurisdiction to jurisdiction.

6. **Remedies.**

   (a) HMI's entire liability and your exclusive remedy for defects in materials and workmanship shall be limited to replacement of the Software Media, which may be returned to HMI with a copy of your receipt at the following address: Software Media Fulfillment Department, Attn.: *JavaServer Pages For Dummies*, Hungry Minds, Inc., 10475 Crosspoint Blvd., Indianapolis, IN 46256, or call 1-800-762-2974. Please allow four to six weeks for delivery. This Limited Warranty is void if failure of the Software Media has resulted from accident, abuse, or misapplication. Any replacement Software Media will be warranted for the remainder of the original warranty period or thirty (30) days, whichever is longer.

   (b) In no event shall HMI or the author be liable for any damages whatsoever (including without limitation damages for loss of business profits, business interruption, loss of business information, or any other pecuniary loss) arising from the use of or inability to use the Book or the Software, even if HMI has been advised of the possibility of such damages.

   (c) Because some jurisdictions do not allow the exclusion or limitation of liability for consequential or incidental damages, the above limitation or exclusion may not apply to you.

7. **U.S. Government Restricted Rights.** Use, duplication, or disclosure of the Software for or on behalf of the United States of America, its agencies and/or instrumentalities (the "U.S. Government") is subject to restrictions as stated in paragraph (c)(1)(ii) of the Rights in Technical Data and Computer Software clause of DFARS 252.227-7013, or subparagraphs (c) (1) and (2) of the Commercial Computer Software - Restricted Rights clause at FAR 52.227-19, and in similar clauses in the NASA FAR supplement, as applicable.

8. **General.** This Agreement constitutes the entire understanding of the parties and revokes and supersedes all prior agreements, oral or written, between them and may not be modified or amended except in a writing signed by both parties hereto that specifically refers to this Agreement. This Agreement shall take precedence over any other documents that may be in conflict herewith. If any one or more provisions contained in this Agreement are held by any court or tribunal to be invalid, illegal, or otherwise unenforceable, each and every other provision shall remain in full force and effect.

Sun Microsystems, Inc.

Binary Code License Agreement

READ THE TERMS OF THIS AGREEMENT AND ANY PROVIDED SUPPLEMENTAL LICENSE TERMS (COLLECTIVELY "AGREEMENT") CAREFULLY BEFORE OPENING THE SOFTWARE MEDIA PACKAGE. BY OPENING THE SOFTWARE MEDIA PACKAGE, YOU AGREE TO THE TERMS OF THIS AGREEMENT. IF YOU ARE ACCESSING THE SOFTWARE ELECTRONICALLY, INDICATE YOUR ACCEPTANCE OF THESE TERMS BY SELECTING THE "ACCEPT" BUTTON AT THE END OF THIS AGREEMENT. IF YOU DO NOT AGREE TO ALL THESE TERMS, PROMPTLY RETURN THE UNUSED SOFTWARE TO YOUR PLACE OF PURCHASE FOR A REFUND OR, IF THE SOFTWARE IS ACCESSED ELECTRONICALLY, SELECT THE "DECLINE" BUTTON AT THE END OF THIS AGREEMENT.

1. LICENSE TO USE. Sun grants you a non-exclusive and non-transferable license for the internal use only of the accompanying software and documentation and any error corrections provided by Sun (collectively "Software"), by the number of users and the class of computer hardware for which the corresponding fee has been paid.

2. RESTRICTIONS. Software is confidential and copyrighted. Title to Software and all associated intellectual property rights is retained by Sun and/or its licensors. Except as specifically authorized in any Supplemental License Terms, you may not make copies of Software, other than a single copy of Software for archival purposes. Unless enforcement is prohibited by applicable law, you may not modify, decompile, or reverse engineer Software. You acknowledge that Software is not designed, licensed or intended for use in the design, construction, operation or maintenance of any nuclear facility. Sun disclaims any express or implied warranty of fitness for such uses. No right, title or interest in or to any trademark, service mark, logo or trade name of Sun or its licensors is granted under this Agreement.

3. LIMITED WARRANTY. Sun warrants to you that for a period of ninety (90) days from the date of purchase, as evidenced by a copy of the receipt, the media on which Software is furnished (if any) will be free of defects in materials and workmanship under normal use. Except for the foregoing, Software is provided "AS IS". Your exclusive remedy and Sun's entire liability under this limited warranty will be at Sun's option to replace Software media or refund the fee paid for Software.

4. DISCLAIMER OF WARRANTY. UNLESS SPECIFIED IN THIS AGREEMENT, ALL EXPRESS OR IMPLIED CONDITIONS, REPRESENTATIONS AND WARRANTIES, INCLUDING ANY IMPLIED WARRANTY OF MERCHANTABILITY, FITNESS FOR A PARTICULAR PURPOSE OR NON-INFRINGEMENT ARE DISCLAIMED, EXCEPT TO THE EXTENT THAT THESE DISCLAIMERS ARE HELD TO BE LEGALLY INVALID.

5. LIMITATION OF LIABILITY. TO THE EXTENT NOT PROHIBITED BY LAW, IN NO EVENT WILL SUN OR ITS LICENSORS BE LIABLE FOR ANY LOST REVENUE, PROFIT OR DATA, OR FOR SPECIAL, INDIRECT, CONSEQUENTIAL, INCIDENTAL OR PUNITIVE DAMAGES, HOWEVER CAUSED REGARDLESS OF THE THEORY OF LIABILITY, ARISING OUT OF OR RELATED TO THE USE OF OR INABILITY TO USE SOFTWARE, EVEN IF SUN HAS BEEN ADVISED OF THE POSSIBILITY OF SUCH DAMAGES. In no event will Sun's liability to you, whether in contract, tort (including negligence), or otherwise, exceed the amount paid by you for Software under this Agreement. The foregoing limitations will apply even if the above stated warranty fails of its essential purpose.

6. Termination. This Agreement is effective until terminated. You may terminate this Agreement at any time by destroying all copies of Software. This Agreement will terminate immediately without notice from Sun if you fail to comply with any provision of this Agreement. Upon Termination, you must destroy all copies of Software.

7. Export Regulations. All Software and technical data delivered under this Agreement are subject to US export control laws and may be subject to export or import regulations in other countries. You agree to comply strictly with all such laws and regulations and acknowledge that you have the responsibility to obtain such licenses to export, re-export, or import as may be required after delivery to you.

8. U.S. Government Restricted Rights. If Software is being acquired by or on behalf of the U.S. Government or by a U.S. Government prime contractor or subcontractor (at any tier), then the Government's rights in Software and accompanying documentation will be only as set forth in this Agreement; this is in accordance with 48 CFR 227.7201 through 227.7202-4 (for Department of Defense (DOD) acquisitions) and with 48 CFR 2.101 and 12.212 (for non-DOD acquisitions).

9. Governing Law. Any action related to this Agreement will be governed by California law and controlling U.S. federal law. No choice of law rules of any jurisdiction will apply.

10. Severability. If any provision of this Agreement is held to be unenforceable, this Agreement will remain in effect with the provision omitted, unless omission would frustrate the intent of the parties, in which case this Agreement will immediately terminate.

11. Integration. This Agreement is the entire agreement between you and Sun relating to its subject matter. It supersedes all prior or contemporaneous oral or written communications, proposals, representations and warranties and prevails over any conflicting or additional terms of any quote, order, acknowledgment, or other communication between the parties relating to its subject matter during the term of this Agreement. No modification of this Agreement will be binding, unless in writing and signed by an authorized representative of each party.

Java(TM) 2 Software Development Kit (J2SDK), Standard Edition, Version 1.3 For Windows
SUPPLEMENTAL LICENSE TERMS

These supplemental license terms ("Supplemental Terms") add to or modify the terms of the Binary Code License Agreement (collectively, the "Agreement"). Capitalized terms not defined in these Supplemental Terms shall have the same meanings ascribed to them in the Agreement. These Supplemental Terms shall supersede any inconsistent or conflicting terms in the Agreement, or in any license contained within the Software.

1. Software Internal Use and Development License Grant. Subject to the terms and conditions of this Agreement, including, but not limited to Section 4 (Java(TM) Technology Restrictions) of these Supplemental Terms, Sun grants you a non-exclusive, non-transferable, limited license to reproduce internally and use internally the binary form of the Software complete and unmodified for the sole purpose of designing, developing and testing your Java applets and applications intended to run on the Java platform ("Programs").

2. License to Distribute Software. Subject to the terms and conditions of this Agreement, including, but not limited to Section 4 (Java (TM) Technology Restrictions) of these Supplemental Terms, Sun grants you a non-exclusive, non-transferable, limited license to reproduce and distribute the Software in binary code form only, provided that (i) you distribute the Software complete and unmodified and only bundled as part of, and for the sole purpose of running, your Programs, (ii) the Programs add significant and primary functionality to the Software, (iii) you do not distribute additional software intended to replace any component(s) of the Software, (iv) you do not remove or alter any proprietary legends or notices contained in the Software, (v) you only distribute the Software subject to a license agreement that protects Sun's interests consistent with the terms

contained in this Agreement, and (vi) you agree to defend and indemnify Sun and its licensors from and against any damages, costs, liabilities, settlement amounts and/or expenses (including attorneys' fees) incurred in connection with any claim, lawsuit or action by any third party that arises or results from the use or distribution of any and all Programs and/or Software.

3. License to Distribute Redistributables. Subject to the terms and conditions of this Agreement, including but not limited to Section 4 (Java Technology Restrictions) of these Supplemental Terms, Sun grants you a non-exclusive, non-transferable, limited license to reproduce and distribute the binary form of those files specifically identified as redistributable in the Software "README" file ("Redistributables") provided that: (i) you distribute the Redistributables complete and unmodified (unless otherwise specified in the applicable README file), and only bundled as part of Programs, (ii) you do not distribute additional software intended to supersede any component(s) of the Redistributables, (iii) you do not remove or alter any proprietary legends or notices contained in or on the Redistributables, (iv) you only distribute the Redistributables pursuant to a license agreement that protects Sun's interests consistent with the terms contained in the Agreement, and (v) you agree to defend and indemnify Sun and its licensors from and against any damages, costs, liabilities, settlement amounts and/or expenses (including attorneys' fees) incurred in connection with any claim, lawsuit or action by any third party that arises or results from the use or distribution of any and all Programs and/or Software.

4. Java Technology Restrictions. You may not modify the Java Platform Interface ("JPI", identified as classes contained within the "java" package or any subpackages of the "java" package), by creating additional classes within the JPI or otherwise causing the addition to or modification of the classes in the JPI. In the event that you create an additional class and associated API(s) which (i) extends the functionality of the Java platform, and (ii) is exposed to third party software developers for the purpose of developing additional software which invokes such additional API, you must promptly publish broadly an accurate specification for such API for free use by all developers. You may not create, or authorize your licensees to create, additional classes, interfaces, or subpackages that are in any way identified as "java", "javax", "sun" or similar convention as specified by Sun in any naming convention designation.

5. Trademarks and Logos. You acknowledge and agree as between you and Sun that Sun owns the SUN, SOLARIS, JAVA, JINI, FORTE, and iPLANET trademarks and all SUN, SOLARIS, JAVA, JINI, FORTE, and iPLANET-related trademarks, service marks, logos and other brand designations ("Sun Marks"), and you agree to comply with the Sun Trademark and Logo Usage Requirements currently located at http://www.sun.com/policies/trademarks. Any use you make of the Sun Marks inures to Sun's benefit.

6. Source Code. Software may contain source code that is provided solely for reference purposes pursuant to the terms of this Agreement. Source code may not be redistributed unless expressly provided for in this Agreement.

7. Termination for Infringement. Either party may terminate this Agreement immediately should any Software become, or in either party's opinion be likely to become, the subject of a claim of infringement of any intellectual property right.

For inquiries please contact: Sun Microsystems, Inc. 901 San Antonio Road, Palo Alto, California 94303

(LFI#90955/Form ID#011801)

To obtain Forte for Java, release 2.0, Community Edition, English, you must agree to the software license below. Sun Microsystems, Inc. Binary Code License Agreement

READ THE TERMS OF THIS AGREEMENT AND ANY PROVIDED SUPPLEMENTAL LICENSE TERMS (COLLECTIVELY "AGREEMENT") CAREFULLY BEFORE OPENING THE SOFTWARE MEDIA PACKAGE. BY OPENING THE SOFTWARE MEDIA PACKAGE, YOU AGREE TO THE TERMS OF THIS AGREEMENT. IF YOU ARE ACCESSING THE SOFTWARE ELECTRONICALLY, INDICATE YOUR ACCEPTANCE OF THESE TERMS BY SELECTING THE "ACCEPT" BUTTON AT THE END OF THIS AGREEMENT. IF YOU DO NOT AGREE TO ALL THESE TERMS, PROMPTLY RETURN THE UNUSED SOFTWARE TO YOUR PLACE OF PURCHASE FOR A REFUND OR, IF THE SOFTWARE IS ACCESSED ELECTRONICALLY, SELECT THE "DECLINE" BUTTON AT THE END OF THIS AGREEMENT.

1. LICENSE TO USE. Sun grants you a non-exclusive and non-transferable license for the internal use only of the accompanying software and documentation and any error corrections provided by Sun (collectively "Software"), by the number of users and the class of computer hardware for which the corresponding fee has been paid.

2. RESTRICTIONS. Software is confidential and copyrighted. Title to Software and all associated intellectual property rights is retained by Sun and/or its licensors. Except as specifically authorized in any Supplemental License Terms, you may not make copies of Software, other than a single copy of Software for archival purposes. Unless enforcement is prohibited by applicable law, you may not modify, decompile, or reverse engineer Software. You acknowledge that Software is not designed, licensed or intended for use in the design, construction, operation or maintenance of any nuclear facility. Sun disclaims any express or implied warranty of fitness for such uses. No right, title or interest in or to any trademark, service mark, logo or trade name of Sun or its licensors is granted under this Agreement.

3. LIMITED WARRANTY. Sun warrants to you that for a period of ninety (90) days from the date of purchase, as evidenced by a copy of the receipt, the media on which Software is furnished (if any) will be free of defects in materials and workmanship under normal use. Except for the foregoing, Software is provided "AS IS". Your exclusive remedy and Sun's entire liability under this limited warranty will be at Sun's option to replace Software media or refund the fee paid for Software.

4. DISCLAIMER OF WARRANTY. UNLESS SPECIFIED IN THIS AGREEMENT, ALL EXPRESS OR IMPLIED CONDITIONS, REPRESENTATIONS AND WARRANTIES, INCLUDING ANY IMPLIED WARRANTY OF MERCHANTABILITY, FITNESS FOR A PARTICULAR PURPOSE OR NON-INFRINGEMENT ARE DISCLAIMED, EXCEPT TO THE EXTENT THAT THESE DISCLAIMERS ARE HELD TO BE LEGALLY INVALID.

5. LIMITATION OF LIABILITY. TO THE EXTENT NOT PROHIBITED BY LAW, IN NO EVENT WILL SUN OR ITS LICENSORS BE LIABLE FOR ANY LOST REVENUE, PROFIT OR DATA, OR FOR SPECIAL, INDIRECT, CONSEQUENTIAL, INCIDENTAL OR PUNITIVE DAMAGES, HOWEVER CAUSED REGARDLESS OF THE THEORY OF LIABILITY, ARISING OUT OF OR RELATED TO THE USE OF OR INABILITY TO USE SOFTWARE, EVEN IF SUN HAS BEEN ADVISED OF THE POSSIBILITY OF SUCH DAMAGES. In no event will Sun's liability to you, whether in contract, tort (including negligence), or otherwise, exceed the amount paid by you for Software under this Agreement. The foregoing limitations will apply even if the above stated warranty fails of its essential purpose.

6. Termination. This Agreement is effective until terminated. You may terminate this Agreement at any time by destroying all copies of Software. This Agreement will terminate immediately without notice from Sun if you fail to comply with any provision of this Agreement. Upon Termination, you must destroy all copies of Software.

7. Export Regulations. All Software and technical data delivered under this Agreement are subject to US export control laws and may be subject to export or import regulations in other countries.

You agree to comply strictly with all such laws and regulations and acknowledge that you have the responsibility to obtain such licenses to export, re-export, or import as may be required after delivery to you.

8. U.S. Government Restricted Rights. If Software is being acquired by or on behalf of the U.S. Government or by a U.S. Government prime contractor or subcontractor (at any tier), then the Government's rights in Software and accompanying documentation will be only as set forth in this Agreement; this is in accordance with 48 CFR 227.7201 through 227.7202-4 (for Department of Defense (DOD) acquisitions) and with 48 CFR 2.101 and 12.212 (for non-DOD acquisitions).

9. Governing Law. Any action related to this Agreement will be governed by California law and controlling U.S. federal law. No choice of law rules of any jurisdiction will apply.

10. Severability. If any provision of this Agreement is held to be unenforceable, this Agreement will remain in effect with the provision omitted, unless omission would frustrate the intent of the parties, in which case this Agreement will immediately terminate.

11. Integration. This Agreement is the entire agreement between you and Sun relating to its subject matter. It supersedes all prior or contemporaneous oral or written communications, proposals, representations and warranties and prevails over any conflicting or additional terms of any quote, order, acknowledgment, or other communication between the parties relating to its subject matter during the term of this Agreement. No modification of this Agreement will be binding, unless in writing and signed by an authorized representative of each party.

FORTE(TM) FOR JAVA(TM), RELEASE 2.0, COMMUNITY EDITION, SUPPLEMENTAL LICENSE TERMS

These supplemental license terms ("Supplemental Terms") add to or modify the terms of the Binary Code License Agreement (collectively, the "Agreement"). Capitalized terms not defined in these Supplemental Terms shall have the same meanings ascribed to them in the Agreement. These Supplemental Terms shall supersede any inconsistent or conflicting terms in the Agreement, or in any license contained within the Software.

1. Software Internal Use and Development License Grant. Subject to the terms and conditions of this Agreement, including, but not limited to Section 4 (Java(TM) Technology Restrictions) of these Supplemental Terms, Sun grants you a non-exclusive, non-transferable, limited license to reproduce internally and use internally the binary form of the Software complete and unmodified for the sole purpose of designing, developing and testing your Java applets and applications intended to run on the Java platform ("Programs").

2. License to Distribute Software. Subject to the terms and conditions of this Agreement, including, but not limited to Section 4 (Java (TM) Technology Restrictions) of these Supplemental Terms, Sun grants you a non-exclusive, non-transferable, limited license to reproduce and distribute the Software in binary code form only, provided that (i) you distribute the Software complete and unmodified and only bundled as part of, and for the sole purpose of running, your Programs, (ii) the Programs add significant and primary functionality to the Software, (iii) you do not distribute additional software intended to replace any component(s) of the Software, (iv) for a particular version of the Java platform, any executable output generated by a compiler that is contained in the Software must (a) only be compiled from source code that conforms to the corresponding version of the OEM Java Language Specification; (b) be in the class file format defined by the corresponding version of the OEM Java Virtual Machine Specification; and (c) execute properly on a reference runtime, as specified by Sun, associated with such version of the Java platform, (v) you do not remove or alter any proprietary legends or notices contained in the Software, (vi) you only

distribute the Software subject to a license agreement that protects Sun's interests consistent with the terms contained in this Agreement, and (vii) you agree to defend and indemnify Sun and its licensors from and against any damages, costs, liabilities, settlement amounts and/or expenses (including attorneys' fees) incurred in connection with any claim, lawsuit or action by any third party that arises or results from the use or distribution of any and all Programs and/or Software.

3. License to Distribute Redistributables. Subject to the terms and conditions of this Agreement, including but not limited to Section 4 (Java Technology Restrictions) of these Supplemental Terms, Sun grants you a non-exclusive, non-transferable, limited license to reproduce and distribute the binary form of those files specifically identified as redistributable in the Software "RELEASE NOTES" file ("Redistributables") provided that: (i) you distribute the Redistributables complete and unmodified (unless otherwise specified in the applicable RELEASE NOTES file), and only bundled as part of Programs, (ii) you do not distribute additional software intended to supersede any component(s) of the Redistributables, (iii) you do not remove or alter any proprietary legends or notices contained in or on the Redistributables, (iv) for a particular version of the Java platform, any executable output generated by a compiler that is contained in the Software must (a) only be compiled from source code that conforms to the corresponding version of the OEM Java Language Specification; (b) be in the class file format defined by the corresponding version of the OEM Java Virtual Machine Specification; and (c) execute properly on a reference runtime, as specified by Sun, associated with such version of the Java platform, (v) you only distribute the Redistributables pursuant to a license agreement that protects Sun's interests consistent with the terms contained in the Agreement, and (vi) you agree to defend and indemnify Sun and its licensors from and against any damages, costs, liabilities, settlement amounts and/or expenses (including attorneys' fees) incurred in connection with any claim, lawsuit or action by any third party that arises or results from the use or distribution of any and all Programs and/or Software.

4. Java Technology Restrictions. You may not modify the Java Platform Interface ("JPI", identified as classes contained within the "java" package or any subpackages of the "java" package), by creating additional classes within the JPI or otherwise causing the addition to or modification of the classes in the JPI. In the event that you create an additional class and associated API(s) which (i) extends the functionality of the Java platform, and (ii) is exposed to third party software developers for the purpose of developing additional software which invokes such additional API, you must promptly publish broadly an accurate specification for such API for free use by all developers. You may not create, or authorize your licensees to create, additional classes, interfaces, or subpackages that are in any way identified as "java", "javax", "sun" or similar convention as specified by Sun in any naming convention designation.

5. Java Runtime Availability. Refer to the appropriate version of the Java Runtime Environment binary code license (currently located at http://www.java.sun.com/jdk/index.html) for the availability of runtime code which may be distributed with Java applets and applications.

6. Trademarks and Logos. You acknowledge and agree as between you and Sun that Sun owns the SUN, SOLARIS, JAVA, JINI, FORTE, and iPLANET trademarks and all SUN, SOLARIS, JAVA, JINI, FORTE, and iPLANET-related trademarks, service marks, logos and other brand designations ("Sun Marks"), and you agree to comply with the Sun Trademark and Logo Usage Requirements currently located at http://www.sun.com/policies/trademarks. Any use you make of the Sun Marks inures to Sun's benefit.

7. Source Code. Software may contain source code that is provided solely for reference purposes pursuant to the terms of this Agreement. Source code may not be redistributed unless expressly provided for in this Agreement.

8. Termination for Infringement. Either party may terminate this Agreement immediately should any Software become, or in either party's opinion be likely to become, the subject of a claim of infringement of any intellectual property right.

For inquiries please contact: Sun Microsystems, Inc. 901

San Antonio Road, Palo Alto, California 94303

FI#91205/Form ID#011801)

[more information available at http://www.gnu.org/copyleft/gpl.html]

GNU GENERAL PUBLIC LICENSE

Version 2, June 1991
Copyright © 1989, 1991 Free Software Foundation, Inc.
59 Temple Place - Suite 330, Boston, MA 02111-1307, USA

Everyone is permitted to copy and distribute verbatim copies of this license document, but changing it is not allowed.

Preamble

The licenses for most software are designed to take away your freedom to share and change it. By contrast, the GNU General Public License is intended to guarantee your freedom to share and change free software @md to make sure the software is free for all its users. This General Public License applies to most of the Free Software Foundation's software and to any other program whose authors commit to using it. (Some other Free Software Foundation software is covered by the GNU Library General Public License instead.) You can apply it to your programs, too.

When we speak of free software, we are referring to freedom, not price. Our General Public Licenses are designed to make sure that you have the freedom to distribute copies of free software (and charge for this service if you wish), that you receive source code or can get it if you want it, that you can change the software or use pieces of it in new free programs; and that you know you can do these things.

To protect your rights, we need to make restrictions that forbid anyone to deny you these rights or to ask you to surrender the rights. These restrictions translate to certain responsibilities for you if you distribute copies of the software, or if you modify it.

For example, if you distribute copies of such a program, whether gratis or for a fee, you must give the recipients all the rights that you have. You must make sure that they, too, receive or can get the source code. And you must show them these terms so they know their rights.

We protect your rights with two steps: (1) copyright the software, and (2) offer you this license which gives you legal permission to copy, distribute and/or modify the software.

Also, for each author's protection and ours, we want to make certain that everyone understands that there is no warranty for this free software. If the software is modified by someone else and passed on, we want its recipients to know that what they have is not the original, so that any problems introduced by others will not reflect on the original authors' reputations.

Finally, any free program is threatened constantly by software patents. We wish to avoid the danger that redistributors of a free program will individually obtain patent licenses, in effect making the program proprietary. To prevent this, we have made it clear that any patent must be licensed for everyone's free use or not licensed at all.

The precise terms and conditions for copying, distribution and modification follow.

TERMS AND CONDITIONS FOR COPYING, DISTRIBUTION AND MODIFICATION

0. This License applies to any program or other work which contains a notice placed by the copyright holder saying it may be distributed under the terms of this General Public License. The "Program", below, refers to any such program or work, and a "work based on the Program" means either the Program or any derivative work under copyright law: that is to say, a work containing the Program or a portion of it, either verbatim or with modifications and/or translated into another language. (Hereinafter, translation is included without limitation in the term "modification".) Each licensee is addressed as "you".

   Activities other than copying, distribution and modification are not covered by this License; they are outside its scope. The act of running the Program is not restricted, and the output from the Program is covered only if its contents constitute a work based on the Program (independent of having been made by running the Program). Whether that is true depends on what the Program does.

1. You may copy and distribute verbatim copies of the Program's source code as you receive it, in any medium, provided that you conspicuously and appropriately publish on each copy an appropriate copyright notice and disclaimer of warranty; keep intact all the notices that refer to this License and to the absence of any warranty; and give any other recipients of the Program a copy of this License along with the Program.

   You may charge a fee for the physical act of transferring a copy, and you may at your option offer warranty protection in exchange for a fee.

2. You may modify your copy or copies of the Program or any portion of it, thus forming a work based on the Program, and copy and distribute such modifications or work under the terms of Section 1 above, provided that you also meet all of these conditions:

   a) You must cause the modified files to carry prominent notices stating that you changed the files and the date of any change.

   b) You must cause any work that you distribute or publish, that in whole or in part contains or is derived from the Program or any part thereof, to be licensed as a whole at no charge to all third parties under the terms of this License.

   c) If the modified program normally reads commands interactively when run, you must cause it, when started running for such interactive use in the most ordinary way, to print or display an announcement including an appropriate copyright notice and a notice that there is no warranty (or else, saying that you provide a warranty) and that users may redistribute the program under these conditions, and telling the user how to view a copy of this License. (Exception: if the Program itself is interactive but does not normally print such an announcement, your work based on the Program is not required to print an announcement.)

   These requirements apply to the modified work as a whole. If identifiable sections of that work are not derived from the Program, and can be reasonably considered independent and separate works in themselves, then this License, and its terms, do not apply to those sections when you distribute them as separate works. But when you distribute the same sections as part of a whole which is a work based on the Program, the distribution of the whole must be on the terms of this License, whose permissions for other licensees extend to the entire whole, and thus to each and every part regardless of who wrote it.

Thus, it is not the intent of this section to claim rights or contest your rights to work written entirely by you; rather, the intent is to exercise the right to control the distribution of derivative or collective works based on the Program. In addition, mere aggregation of another work not based on the Program with the Program (or with a work based on the Program) on a volume of a storage or distribution medium does not bring the other work under the scope of this License.

3. You may copy and distribute the Program (or a work based on it, under Section 2) in object code or executable form under the terms of Sections 1 and 2 above provided that you also do one of the following:

   a) Accompany it with the complete corresponding machine-readable source code, which must be distributed under the terms of Sections 1 and 2 above on a medium customarily used for software interchange; or,

   b) Accompany it with a written offer, valid for at least three years, to give any third party, for a charge no more than your cost of physically performing source distribution, a complete machine-readable copy of the corresponding source code, to be distributed under the terms of Sections 1 and 2 above on a medium customarily used for software interchange; or,

   c) Accompany it with the information you received as to the offer to distribute corresponding source code. (This alternative is allowed only for noncommercial distribution and only if you received the program in object code or executable form with such an offer, in accord with Subsection b above.)

   The source code for a work means the preferred form of the work for making modifications to it. For an executable work, complete source code means all the source code for all modules it contains, plus any associated interface definition files, plus the scripts used to control compilation and installation of the executable. However, as a special exception, the source code distributed need not include anything that is normally distributed (in either source or binary form) with the major components (compiler, kernel, and so on) of the operating system on which the executable runs, unless that component itself accompanies the executable.

   If distribution of executable or object code is made by offering access to copy from a designated place, then offering equivalent access to copy the source code from the same place counts as distribution of the source code, even though third parties are not compelled to copy the source along with the object code.

4. You may not copy, modify, sublicense, or distribute the Program except as expressly provided under this License. Any attempt otherwise to copy, modify, sublicense or distribute the Program is void, and will automatically terminate your rights under this License. However, parties who have received copies, or rights, from you under this License will not have their licenses terminated so long as such parties remain in full compliance.

5. You are not required to accept this License, since you have not signed it. However, nothing else grants you permission to modify or distribute the Program or its derivative works. These actions are prohibited by law if you do not accept this License. Therefore, by modifying or distributing the Program (or any work based on the Program), you indicate your acceptance of this License to do so, and all its terms and conditions for copying, distributing or modifying the Program or works based on it.

6. Each time you redistribute the Program (or any work based on the Program), the recipient automatically receives a license from the original licensor to copy, distribute or modify the Program subject to these terms and conditions. You may not impose any further restrictions on the recipients' exercise of the rights granted herein. You are not responsible for enforcing compliance by third parties to this License.

7. If, as a consequence of a court judgment or allegation of patent infringement or for any other reason (not limited to patent issues), conditions are imposed on you (whether by court order, agreement or otherwise) that contradict the conditions of this License, they do not excuse you from the conditions of this License. If you cannot distribute so as to satisfy simultaneously your obligations under this License and any other pertinent obligations, then as a consequence you may not distribute the Program at all. For example, if a patent license would not permit royalty-free redistribution of the Program by all those who receive copies directly or indirectly through you, then the only way you could satisfy both it and this License would be to refrain entirely from distribution of the Program.

   If any portion of this section is held invalid or unenforceable under any particular circumstance, the balance of the section is intended to apply and the section as a whole is intended to apply in other circumstances.

   It is not the purpose of this section to induce you to infringe any patents or other property right claims or to contest validity of any such claims; this section has the sole purpose of protecting the integrity of the free software distribution system, which is implemented by public license practices. Many people have made generous contributions to the wide range of software distributed through that system in reliance on consistent application of that system; it is up to the author/donor to decide if he or she is willing to distribute software through any other system and a licensee cannot impose that choice.

   This section is intended to make thoroughly clear what is believed to be a consequence of the rest of this License.

8. If the distribution and/or use of the Program is restricted in certain countries either by patents or by copyrighted interfaces, the original copyright holder who places the Program under this License may add an explicit geographical distribution limitation excluding those countries, so that distribution is permitted only in or among countries not thus excluded. In such case, this License incorporates the limitation as if written in the body of this License.

9. The Free Software Foundation may publish revised and/or new versions of the General Public License from time to time. Such new versions will be similar in spirit to the present version, but may differ in detail to address new problems or concerns.

   Each version is given a distinguishing version number. If the Program specifies a version number of this License which applies to it and "any later version", you have the option of following the terms and conditions either of that version or of any later version published by the Free Software Foundation. If the Program does not specify a version number of this License, you may choose any version ever published by the Free Software Foundation.

10. If you wish to incorporate parts of the Program into other free programs whose distribution conditions are different, write to the author to ask for permission. For software which is copyrighted by the Free Software Foundation, write to the Free Software Foundation; we sometimes make exceptions for this. Our decision will be guided by the two goals of preserving the free status of all derivatives of our free software and of promoting the sharing and reuse of software generally.

NO WARRANTY

11. BECAUSE THE PROGRAM IS LICENSED FREE OF CHARGE, THERE IS NO WARRANTY FOR THE PROGRAM, TO THE EXTENT PERMITTED BY APPLICABLE LAW. EXCEPT WHEN OTHERWISE STATED IN WRITING THE COPYRIGHT HOLDERS AND/OR OTHER PARTIES PROVIDE THE PROGRAM "AS IS" WITHOUT WARRANTY OF ANY KIND, EITHER EXPRESSED OR IMPLIED, INCLUDING, BUT NOT LIMITED TO, THE IMPLIED WARRANTIES OF MERCHANTABILITY AND FITNESS FOR A PARTICULAR PURPOSE. THE ENTIRE RISK AS TO THE QUALITY AND PERFORMANCE OF THE PROGRAM IS WITH YOU. SHOULD THE PROGRAM PROVE DEFECTIVE, YOU ASSUME THE COST OF ALL NECESSARY SERVICING, REPAIR OR CORRECTION.

12. IN NO EVENT UNLESS REQUIRED BY APPLICABLE LAW OR AGREED TO IN WRITING WILL ANY COPYRIGHT HOLDER, OR ANY OTHER PARTY WHO MAY MODIFY AND/OR REDISTRIBUTE THE PROGRAM AS PERMITTED ABOVE, BE LIABLE TO YOU FOR DAMAGES, INCLUDING ANY GENERAL, SPECIAL, INCIDENTAL OR CONSEQUENTIAL DAMAGES ARISING OUT OF THE USE OR INABILITY TO USE THE PROGRAM (INCLUDING BUT NOT LIMITED TO LOSS OF DATA OR DATA BEING RENDERED INACCURATE OR LOSSES SUSTAINED BY YOU OR THIRD PARTIES OR A FAILURE OF THE PROGRAM TO OPERATE WITH ANY OTHER PROGRAMS), EVEN IF SUCH HOLDER OR OTHER PARTY HAS BEEN ADVISED OF THE POSSIBILITY OF SUCH DAMAGES.

END OF TERMS AND CONDITIONS